PATHWAYS
An Autobiography

OTHER BOOKS BY EDWARD REAUGH SMITH
FROM STEINERBOOKS

*The Burning Bush: Rudolf Steiner, Anthroposophy,
and the Holy Scriptures: Terms & Phrases* (1998)

The Incredible Births of Jesus (1998)

*The Disciple Whom Jesus Loved:
Unveiling the Author of John's Gospel* (2000)

*David's Question: What Is Man? (Psalm 8:4) —
Rudolf Steiner, Anthroposophy, and the Holy Scriptures:
An Anthroposophical Commentary on the Bible* (2001)

*The Soul's Long Journey:
How the Bible Reveals Reincarnation* (2003)

*The Temple Sleep of the Rich Young Ruler:
How Lazarus Became the Evangelist John* (2011)

PATHWAYS
An Autobiography

EDWARD REAUGH SMITH

SteinerBooks
2014

SteinerBooks | 2014

An imprint Anthroposophic Press, Inc.
610 Main St., Great Barrington, MA 01230
www.steinerbooks.org

Copyright © 2014 by Edward Reaugh Smith. All rights reserved. No part of this publication may be reproduced, stored in a retrieval system, or transmitted, in any form or by any means, electronic, mechanical, photocopying, recording, or otherwise, without the prior written permission of the publisher.
Design: William Jens Jensen

LIBRARY OF CONGRESS CONTROL NUMBER: 2014942210

ISBN: 978-1-62148-107-2 (paperback)
ISBN: 978-1-62148-103-4 (hardcover)
ISBN: 978-1-62148-104-1 (eBook)

Contents

Preface by Paul V. O'Leary	vii
Family and Early Years	1
High School	39
College 1950–1953	75
Law School till Marriage and Military	109
Marriage, Law School, and the Draft	123
Army	130
Wrapping up Law School	176
Looking Forward from 1957	181
Law Practice 1957–1984	187
My Solo Practice (March 1, 1961–August 15, 1962)	206
The Smith Firm Years	217
Section of Images	270
Investment and Business	284
Charity, Civic Work, Politics, and Travel	362
The Threefold Denouement	401
Running	402
Music	449
The Appearance of Destiny	486
Timeline of Significant Events in the Life of Edward Reaugh Smith	535
Bibliography	547

Dedication

This is the account of two youths who fell in love with each other on first sight in the summer of 1950, and have walked on in that love, devotion, and support for over six decades. It is called an autobiography, but from the time I met Jo Anne, in whatever I was doing, she was there by my side making that path passable, so it is an account of our journey together. An accomplished person in her own right, much loved by many, both within and beyond our extended families, a school teacher and more in our earliest years, a mother par excellence of our children, and cherished Mimi to all of theirs. Those who have known us well know, and have often observed, that whatever successes I have had were possible only because she was always there for me in those endeavors. The road has not always been smooth, but as we look back over the years, we do so recognizing that our walk together over the decades has been the most meaningful aspect of our lives. This autobiography can only be, and is, dedicated to Jo Anne.

Preface

This story of a human life is told by that human being himself; as such it is properly called an "autobiography." It seems self-evident that no one knows more about the life of Edward Reaugh Smith than Ed Smith himself. Yet it is my task, nay my privilege and honor, to tell you some things about Ed which he might not say about himself. Jo Anne, his wife of sixty years, says that Ed has been devoted and caring to her, their children, and to extended family. While an essential ingredient, this aspect of his life is not unique, but it adds quality to what lies beyond it.

Ed is quite the special person. Not in the clichéd way that "everyone is special." You will find few clichés in his character. His life has unfolded through stages and phases which themselves are "special" but which, in aggregate, can only be described as "unique." This is not to gainsay the idea of each individual's uniqueness. We confirm that verity. Yet, the very title of this autobiography, *Pathways*, implies that more than one route, more than one trajectory, was followed to create the Ed Smith we know today as friend, teacher, lecturer, businessman, and author of *The Burning Bush*.

Hopefully this autobiography will provide some insight into *the manner* in which Smith is unique, as well as *how and why* he carved out the life he lived. You will learn the circumstances of his birth—the raw material he was provided with, even blessed with—and how he molded it through an exceptionally broad spectrum of experiences and events, challenges and crises, into a life which by any measure can be described as a "life well lived." He thrived on challenges, sought out distant, seemingly unattainable goals for himself, then set out to achieve them at high levels of success. Yet, the sum total of his life is greater than its individual parts.

His roots lie in small-town America, in the rural Midwest of Flora, Illinois. Born in the early part of the Great Depression his family was not wealthy by any means; but few people were then, and he wanted for naught. He was raised in a milieu of loving parents, embraced by loving aunts, uncles, and grandparents on all sides. He did well in athletics (football, basketball, and tennis), academics, and music (piano) in high school and was the 1950 class Valedictorian at Flora High. In September that same year he met Jo Anne Myers. He majored in accounting at Midwestern University (Wichita Falls, TX) and graduated with high honors. He received a scholarship to Southern Methodist University's Dedman School of Law (Dallas), matriculating in September 1953. Shortly after he and Jo Anne were married on September 10, 1954, his legal education was interrupted after its first year and a half by Uncle Sam and the Army draft. Smith spent nearly two years in the Army, got his CPA license while in the Service, then resumed his legal studies. He graduated cum laude from SMU Law and passed the Texas bar in 1957. He joined the prestigious law firm of Vinson & Elkins (Houston) in September. By the time he turned twenty-five (September 23, 1957) he had earned a Bachelor of Science degree in accounting, a law degree, a CPA license, had completed his military service, and had been married three years. This was one ambitious and talented young man out to make his mark on the world. He was determined to live life thoroughly and intensely, and to make a "success" out of himself. He was on the way to becoming "a man in full."

Success did follow...indeed. By 1959 he and Jo Anne had left Houston for Lubbock, a small but growing city just south of the Texas Panhandle. Happily and successfully employed there for two years by a small law firm, he chose to open his own private law office early in 1961. Word of his success got around so that a year and a half later he brought in a younger partner, Norton Baker, and for the early years of a growing firm practiced as Smith & Baker. Norton became not only a law partner but also a life-long friend. Smith's law practice thrived, as did several ancillary business interests, and he participated actively in community and social affairs. Recruited by their church staff, Ed and Jo Anne organized a newly formed young married couples' Sunday School Class. It met first on Easter Sunday, 1963. Jo Anne served for ten years as its administrative guide before returning to their home class. Ed taught the class through Easter Sunday, 1988, primarily going through the Bible three times from Genesis to Revelation during that quarter century.

Always an avid mountain climber and hiker after moving to Lubbock, he began running three miles a day in 1963. In August 1963 (age 30) a severe illness brought him close to death, and he had a "near death experience."

Civic Activities

Civic activities occupied much of his time during the '60s and '70s. Ed served three years on the Lubbock Planning & Zoning Commission and was on the executive committee of Texas Tech University Foundation, first as secretary, then as chairman. He was a member and chairman of Texas Tech University Medical School Foundation. In the 1960s he served as Lubbock County Chairman for the Republican candidates for Governor, Lieutenant Governor, and Legislator; in 1970 he was Lubbock County chairman for George H. W. Bush in his U. S. Senate race. Later, as interest in humanity and spiritual interests grew, he left the Republican Party and became completely inactive in politics. For three years, during his sons' early teen years, he led their Boy Scout troop's "mountain man" on backpacking trips first to New Mexico and then Colorado.

Running

Ed always liked athletic involvement. With family, church, and civic duties, little free time was available for team sports. An avid hiker, he naturally turned to running. Starting modestly in 1961, he began more serious running in 1963, but only started recording his progress in 1967. By 1973 he had increased his daily run to six miles. He became active in the West Texas Running Club and ran in many distance races.

Characteristically, Ed set himself the lofty goal of running "The Big One," the Boston Marathon. He ran the Boston Marathon in 1979, an adventure that produced both great personal satisfaction and many amusing stories. He ran no marathons after that.

Music

In 1978, in the midst of a thriving law practice and simultaneously overseeing Resthaven (see below), his family's support amply provided for, Smith was drawn to renew his musical interest that had necessarily been largely curtailed since high school. He began taking music theory lessons from the head of Texas Tech's music department, with the long-term goal of playing one of the great piano concertos with a symphony orchestra. By the early 1980s he practiced the piano daily and intensely, squeezing time from other pursuits. After playing several private, living room recitals in late 1981, on March 23, 1982 Ed successfully accomplished his dream goal when he performed Beethoven's Third Piano Concerto before a packed house of several hundred in Texas Tech's Hemmle Recital Hall for the "Steinway Dedication Concert." The programmed event dedicated the Smith gift of a Steinway Concert Grand to the university's music department. He continued recital performances for two more seasons, recording his last recital program on April 24, 1984, therewith bringing his serious piano study and public performances to an end.

Philanthropic Activity

A vital part of the Smith family's active philosophy was the moral imperative of sharing one's wealth with worthy charitable causes.

Preface

they collectively asked themselves, "Who is this guy? And where the devil is Lubbock?" Gene Gollogly, then chairman of the board, made arrangements for himself and the then president to fly to Lubbock to meet this person who, "from out of nowhere," submitted such an exceptional piece of work.

Who but Ed Smith would have the chutzpah to *think* of writing even *one* book about anthroposophy and the Bible, never mind *a series of books*...after only six years of study? Then again, who but Ed Smith would have the brilliance, the practical capacity, and the confidence to *actually do it!* The very thought is breathtaking! The accomplishment—extraordinary.

Ed followed up *The Burning Bush* with two other major works designed to fulfill the promise of BB's Preface quoted above: *David's Question: What is Man* (2001) and *The Soul's Long Journey* (2003). Three shorter works were also authored, with parts of the first two derived from the major works: *The Incredible Births of Jesus* (1998); and *The Disciple Whom Jesus Loved* (2000). *The Temple Sleep of the Rich Young Ruler* appeared in 2011, although this latter publication, like "the big three," stands on its own as the fruit of exemplary biblical scholarship. The significance of his works will continue to grow. His penultimate book is this very book: *Pathways*. I say "penultimate" as we hope to have the manuscript on the *Book of Revelation* he is currently working on (Summer 2014) sometime next year.

Summing Up

I began this Preface with the statement that Ed Smith was "special," and that the phases of his life were so special that, when combined in one human being, his life can truly be said to be "unique." I am pleased to offer a few more examples of those "special" qualities.

Ed thrives on challenges and sets the bar high enough that he has to maximize his strength, and use his resources to the fullest extent, to reach the goals he sets for himself. He seems to enjoy the risk inherent in the challenge itself. This trait flows down into the minor events of daily life. For example, in 1970, after several days and nights of exhausting professional and personal activity, as he was driving home alone in mid-afternoon from a legal hearing in Colorado City, Texas, about 110 miles south of Lubbock, he fell asleep at the wheel of his new Buick LaSabre—at 75 mph. (The LaSabre was only insured for liability, not personal injury—another case of "assumption of risk.") He drove off the road into a culvert. When the Texas Highway Patrolman, who gave him personal assistance, wrote a ticket charging him with "driving an unsafe speed," Ed managed the quick and clever retort, "Officer, what speed do you consider safe when you are asleep?" Then there was the time in July 1964 when he and two friends had climbed to the top of Uncompahgre Peak near Lake City, Colorado. Enshrouded in clouds, at an elevation of 14,308 feet, all three of them were knocked down by lightning. He has encountered even more threatening conditions on another, even more challenging, "fourteener" nearby. The pleasure radiating from Ed when he tells tales of events like these betrays how much he has enjoyed them.

Then there was the event on April 17, 2010, not included in his autobiography, when he nearly made himself a eunuch. For years, on his regular walks for exercise, he carried plastic sacks and picked up flattened aluminum cans. It was ecologically beneficial and the long-time family maid sold them for gas money. On the occasion in question, walking among the fraternity houses, just north of the retirement community where he lived, a fruitful venue for empty aluminum cans, Ed spotted one lying a small distance inside a wrought-iron fence around the front yard of a "frat house." Eschewing the longer walk around to the open entrance, he estimated that he could put one foot over the fence and retrieve the can. He described the fence as "crotch-high" to himself. The can turned out to be slightly beyond his reach, but stretching for it he lost his balance and became impaled upside down upon the full six inches of one of the spear-shaped spikes on the top. It traversed its full length down to the crossbar entering near the crotch and

Preface

Resthaven

Its spiritual inspiration aside, Smith's near-death experience in late August 1963 initiated a chain of events that was to blossom into a major Pathway in his and his family's lives. The first step beyond the near-death experience was their purchase, as soon as he left the hospital, of burial spaces in the cemetery known as Resthaven of Lubbock. In closing the purchase through a Resthaven sales representative, it was made known to Smith that the owner's health and family considerations were prompting him to privately seek a responsible buyer for the property and business. The cemetery was only sixteen years old, well situated in the path of the city's growth, and with what to Smith were obvious business and investment enticements. In October of 1964 Smith closed that purchase, bringing in with him four other helpful minority shareholders. Of the ninety acres acquired, only a small portion had been dedicated and developed into burial spaces, and there were few other improvements. Within a year a start was made on adding a funeral home on the property. The story of the ownership and development of what was to become the dominant funeral and burial operation in a city of over 200,000 is a study in the growth, from simple beginning, of a very multi-faceted and successful business. It began as an investment, and over the course of the almost twenty-nine years of Smith's ownership interest, from 1964 to 1993, it increasingly grew into an instrument of conscious community service.

Rudolf Steiner and Anthroposophy

During his years of Bible study and teaching Sunday school, Ed had encountered a number of thorny questions about biblical issues the usual answers to which simply did not make sense to his logical, analytical mind. There was the question of repeated earth lives, or whether reincarnation was a reality or a fantasy. Through her father, Jo Anne had always ascribed to the cycle of birth, death, and rebirth as being complementary to, not contradictory of, genuine Christianity. Another set of issues concerned the divergent Nativity narratives set forth in the Matthew and Luke gospels, where contradictions abound. Problems remained unresolved in another area: the two perplexing Creation stories in Genesis. Ed's brilliant mind parsed the biblical texts, and his patient mind held itself open to the possibility of finding answers which might satisfy his requirements for factual accuracy, consistency and common sense. In a way, his background and wide variety of pursuits as an adult had prepared his personality for meeting the work of Rudolf Steiner in 1988, at age 56.

Like many people who first encounter Steiner, Ed dove in head first into Steiner's vast, encyclopedic oeuvre, buying all the Steiner books available in print and contacting anthroposophic libraries to secure copies of out-of-print or not-yet-published books and lectures. However, unlike most people who encounter Steiner, Ed determined early on that he was going to write a book about anthroposophy. And not just any book! He conceived of writing a *series of books* that would encompass Steiner's worldview (*Weltanschauung*) as revealed and supported by Steiner's biblical revelations. For Rudolf Steiner had answered Ed's long-simmering questions about reincarnation, the Creation, the Nativity, and the Passion, Crucifixion, Death and Resurrection of Jesus Christ.

In the summer of 1994, six years after reading an astonishing account about Rudolf Steiner, a name he had never encountered before, Ed started writing *The Burning Bush* (BB), first published in 1997, whose full title is *An Anthroposophical Commentary on the Bible. Terms and Phrases: Volume 1. THE BURNING BUSH.* We quote the opening line of its Preface: "This is the first volume of a series envisioned as a complete Bible commentary based upon the 'anthroposophical' understanding given to humanity by Rudolf Steiner during the first quarter of the twentieth century."

Many of us know, or are, anthroposophists who have studied Steiner's work for years—decades even—and who would never consider writing anything about anthroposophy, never mind a book. When the board at SteinerBooks received the newly published *BB*,

Family and Early Years

The Grand Entrance

I made my entry upon the earthly stage at 1:15 a.m., September 23, 1932, the autumnal equinox. That it was in the depths of the Great Depression did not concern me that day. I first became a teenager on September 23, 1945, one month after the announced surrender of Japan. World conflict entered my consciousness by 1938, and the ensuing war years weighed heavily upon all aspects of life. Depression and war thus encompassed my childhood, but my family was spared the greater heartbreak and suffering that was the lot of so many. Being poor was the normal lot in those days, but the commonality of it kept us from feeling poor. Dad always had a job that kept us from want and my Grandma Reaugh produced garden crops, raised chickens, and tended her own family flock. I was too young for military service during that monstrous war, and my dad was always just a tad older than the group then being drafted. Our hearts went out to neighbors and local families who lost family members in military service and none of our service relatives were wounded or killed.

Flora, a southern Illinois town of about 5,000 population, both then and to this day, was the setting for my youth. Life did not range far from home in those days. First the depression and then the war curtailed material goods. A child raised in those days, and in such an area as Flora, had much exposure to the simplicities of the countryside. It was farming country, but Flora was a B&O (Baltimore and Ohio) Railroad service area, and many locals were "railroaders" in some capacity or other. It was at the restaurant next to the depot where a young lawyer was having his lunch and announced that he was going to marry the lady who made his apple pie. When the girl, who was helping her mother run the place, was brought out, he noticed she was very young. He told her he was going to marry her when she grew up. Seven years later, and four days after her twentieth birthday, he did. They became my mother's parents.

Family

My dad was Frank Edward Smith, who went by Frank E. Smith and was called "Frank" or "Hank." Mother was Frances Elizabeth Reaugh Smith, called Frances. Dad's parents were Hiram Savage Smith, called Hiram, and Laura Etta Hosselton Smith, called Laura. Mother's parents were Richard Sprigg Canby Reaugh, known as R. S. C., but called "Sprigg," and Mary DeLong Reaugh.

Grandpa Smith had some college, enough to teach in a country school near where he farmed. Grandpa Reaugh was a lawyer, a judge, and then an abstractor. All of my grandparents had lived in Flora for many years before I was born. Some perspective of how much time I had with them can be seen from these birth and death dates:

Grandpa Smith, born in 1865, died September 4, 1936
Grandpa Reaugh, born November 23, 1870,
    died January 26, 1940
Grandma Smith, born April 6, 1872, died July 23, 1945
Grandma Reaugh, born February 19, 1877,
    died December 31, 1960

My memories of Grandpa Smith, who died nineteen days before my fourth birthday, are entirely vague. Memories of Grandpa Reaugh, who died when I was seven, are only slightly greater. My most vivid memory of each is of his corpse. We had just returned from a family car trip and Grandpa Smith's corpse was lying on a catafalque in his living room. When Grandpa Reaugh died, I remember dad coming into the kitchen where mother was working and saying, "It's your proceeding toward the knee. Unable to extricate himself alone, and apprehensive of its proximity to the femoral artery, he yelled for help. A nearby caretaker heard his cries and came to help lift him up and off in an internally tearing way. Ed walked a quarter of a mile to their apartment, holding his wound. Jo Anne threw away his bloody jeans and got him to the emergency room. Eventually, after his wound had been washed out and was being treated, lying on the surgical table he began to laugh, thinking what a hilarious tail-end tale this was going to provide. It did.

These instances of pushing himself into precarious situations are mentioned because confronting risk stimulates the "I." Consciously assuming risk is an Ego activity. Stepping out into the unknown is a decision of an Ego which has the courage and the confidence in its abilities to manage whatever may come its way. This surely is an apt description of Ed Smith.

Anyone who knows Ed knows he is not "predictable." In the same way one who sees a tulip grow from bulb to flower for the first time could never predict the glorious blossom after watching the green stem grow for the first few days, no one could have predicted that Resthaven's sculptured scenes of profound Christian events would spring from the mind of a CPA/lawyer from Lubbock, Texas.

Who would conceive of resuming a high school talent, piano performance, in their late 40s, with the goal of playing one of Beethoven's piano concertos with a full symphony orchestra in front of a packed recital hall crowd, and having the entire program recorded?

Which one of us would ramp up a running hobby into a mission to run the Boston Marathon?

How many are able to author works that readers often use as reference books on biblical and anthroposophical themes, and at the same time, have the ability to stand fully within the business world, being practical and gifted in earning money?

Who has ever encountered the difficult work of Rudolf Steiner and then within six years successfully commenced writing a book (and a profound book, at that) about Steiner's world view and its connections to the Bible? I know of no one. Not a single one—except Ed.

Of course, one individual could do any one of these things (except for the last one), or maybe two. That all of these talents, abilities and achievements are combined in a single personality—*that* is remarkable and *that* is what makes Edward Reaugh Smith "unique."

I have wanted to call Ed a "self-made man," but he considers the description to be a pompous moniker without favorable meaning. In any event, this one time manifestation of the Individuality who reincarnates from life to life is special and has unusual attributes. It is the Individuality standing behind Ed's personality that is unique. If we reflect on these qualities we can approach to the core of his being, to his eternal "I" or Ego. Anyone who is introduced to spiritual science at age 56 and then absorbs so much of it and to such great depth in a short period of time is someone who had learned it before, in a previous life or lives. Further, Ed did not just read Steiner and regurgitate derivative thoughts, parroting his teacher as in a mirror. He recreated the anthroposophical world conception within his own being, then poured it back out in a uniquely Ed Smith form. The essays in his major works make for difficult reading, it is true; his thoughts are woven together in an original fashion. Ed Smith gave birth to *original ideas*, ideas that weren't here before. He mentions three most important ones in the last chapter of *Pathways*:

- the connection between the "spiral of creation," the 144,000 mentioned in Revelation and the Fibonacci Series;
- the three references to the phenomenon of the Rainbow mentioned in the Bible and their meaning and significance;
- the idea that the "Law" which Christ came to fulfill is the Law of Karma.

Very few can contribute an authentically *new* idea about anything. Some can weave derivative thoughts into patterns which yield

Preface

fresh insights or perspectives about this or that. Such work is vital, and Ed Smith has contributed much in this manner. But bona fide new ideas? They don't come along very often.

Ed's own life is proof of the spiritual truths he has been writing about these past two decades. The course of his life was not merely determined from within by the genetically programmed consequences of his heredity, or determined from without by his environment. The "burning bush" of his own spiritual entelechy, his "I," reveals itself in being able to take up a career in law and business, an interest in running, and in the piano; to develop his abilities in each arena to the fullest extent, and then to drop each one in its turn, and begin some other enterprise. This pattern—the ability to initiate activity in one field, develop it to a high level of expertise, and then abandon it when fulfilled, displays an activity of his "I" par excellence. It reveals a maturity of Egohood capable of looking at life objectively, with the detachment required to be indifferent even to one's own abilities. He found the core of his true identity within himself, not just in his outer achievements, extensive though they be. To the friends, neighbors and colleagues he meets each day in Lubbock, Ed Smith is not what he appears to be. They do not know, and likely have no interest in knowing, the man described here. His life has manifested the truths: of reincarnation, of the eternal nature of the "I," of the Christian principle of "dying and becoming" in transforming the self, and of the objective nature of Intuition...by living them.

Ed Smith is that rare human being who can say to himself in all honesty that he has accomplished what he was born to do. He stayed true to himself and fulfilled his "primal karma." His written works have created what, in effect, constitute a Concordance between the biblical revelations of Spiritual Science and the Holy Bible. This achievement, extraordinary in itself, is and will continue to be important for the hundreds of millions of people who were raised on "The Good Book." Many who have studied the Bible will be able to find their way to the illuminating ideas of Spiritual Science through Ed's work, which makes anthroposophy more accessible to folks who might naturally shy away from anything "esoteric" or "occult." He has made a significant contribution to understanding the mysteries permeating the Bible and to the progressive revelation of the Christ Impulse in this New Age of the Second Coming, or in anthroposophical terms, when humanity may experience the Etheric Return of Christ. We are most grateful for his many achievements and for his deeply Christian life.

Paul V. O'Leary
East Sandwich, Massachusetts
July 27, 2014

dad." Mother's reaction is a vivid memory. She was standing at the side of the "ice box" just inside the back door. She said "Papa" and started crying. It must have been in the evening, for I then have a distinct image of seeing grandpa in his easy chair, as though sleeping with his mouth open and a Zane Grey western placed open face down on his lap as he had laid it. He had died peacefully in his sleep. Apparently, either grandma or Aunt Martha, who lived with them, or both, had come in from having been out, found grandpa, and called dad to go tell mother. I was seven years old, so had more memories of Grandpa Reaugh, though not a lot. I was permitted to attend his funeral, though I'm not sure I had yet enough awareness of the full significance of it all.

At the time of his birth, June 4, 1905, and until he was about five years old, dad's family lived on a small farm on the Little Wabash River to the northwest of, but very near, Clay City where he was born. The farm, much of which was bottomland that often flooded, was divided by the river. The house was on the side with the smaller acreage and was near a bluff with a beautiful oak tree on it and a steel-structured bridge just beyond, leading to the larger acreage. A significant part of the farm on both sides was in woods composed primarily of oak and hickory trees. As a farm, the land was probably seldom profitable, particularly as I was growing up, but there were non-farm benefits, and its river and woods played a major part in my upbringing. Clay City was only seven miles east of Flora, and the distance from our house to the farm was about that, but a good bit of it was over dirt roads, often muddy.

Grandpa lost the farm to foreclosure during the depression, but thanks to redemption rights that became law and the fact that dad was able to get the land leased for oil and gas, it was eventually redeemed from oil revenue. Dad had an older sister and a younger brother, the ownership of the farm being with them in common, but since neither of the others lived nearby, dad managed it for all. As I recall, the total acreage, including woods, was more than a quarter, but less than a half, section (thus between 160 and 320 acres).

The only house I ever lived in before the family moved briefly to Texas in 1950 was at 152 Meyer Street in Flora. Grandma Smith lived nearby, and Grandma Reaugh's house was an easy bike ride for me.

Grandma Reaugh

Grandma Reaugh was an active and colorful personality. She was something of an institution in Flora, having earlier been active in the women's suffrage movement. She survived well into my twenty-ninth year, whereas I was still twelve years old when Grandma Smith died, the last survivor of my other three grandparents. Grandma Reaugh was thus a major factor in my youth and young adulthood. References to "grandma" will be to her unless otherwise indicated.

As I have often said, if anyone in our family had wings (other than my mother), she would be the one, but she was an angel with a devilish gleam in her eye and a certain delightful feistiness that prevailed in spite of the several difficult, and even cruel, situations life threw in her path. A strong soul and spirit with practical bent, she was not the least bit sanctimonious. Joy abides in the remembering and telling of her.

Three accounts, two humorous and the last sad, portray something of grandma's ability to look on the bright side and to survive the difficult.

On the first occasion I was helping her clean out her garage when she fished out a toilet seat. Aha, she exclaimed, "A frame for the Pope's picture!" To appreciate the remark, it helps to know that she was raised in a Roman Catholic family, having left that church to marry Grandpa and then raised her children in the Protestant tradition.

The second anecdote involves her teenage son Richard and the chicken house. Grandma was a defacto truck farmer, cultivating and raising many vegetable crops, some of which (such as roasting ears) were sold, the rest providing healthy meals for her Flora clan.

But she raised chickens by the hundreds at a time. I've gone with her more than once to somewhere forty miles or so west of Flora to pick up baby chicks in large cardboard containers, probably a thousand at a time. She sold friers, and fried chicken was a rather regular Sunday fare for all of us. She could wring a chicken's neck or chop the head off and dress it down like a pro. But the main downside of this chicken operation was that the chicken house needed to be cleaned frequently, a task her offspring unhappily could not escape. It was dirty, dusty work, and hard on my hay fever, but it had to be done. The old straw had to be swept out and carried away, the floor and shelves cleaned, then lime put down on all of it followed by new straw.

My mother's younger brother Richard was always a strapping fellow, good-sized and very strong for those days. He had rigged up a backyard punching bag near the chopping block under a shade tree, just shy of the chicken yard. It was visible from the window over the kitchen sink. On the occasion in question he had his plans all made to join his friends for some common venture. There was only one problem. Grandma had in mind for him to clean the chicken house before he could join them. A considerable period of increasingly garrulous argumentation ensued. Richard was fit to be tied. Eventually realizing that his case was hopeless, he stomped out the backdoor. In a little while, as grandma tells the story, she looked out and he was in the backyard at his punching bag. He was pounding the bag with violent ferocity, each punch landing on a syllable of his statement, repeated over and over, "Clean *#@!! th-god *#@!! damn *#@!! chicken *#@!! house!! Clean *#@!! th-god *#@!! damn *#@!! chicken *#@!! house!!, etc., etc." But he cleaned the chicken house. Grandma would chuckle as she recounted this tale long after Richard had moved on in his life.

Earlier I spoke of cruel or difficult circumstances that Grandma overcame. One of those was infant daughter Cornelia's devastating death. Another was the burden of caring for her several siblings and their offspring living together when in or near Flora as an economically non-functional group. I have no memory or knowledge of Kate, Marie, or Roy except that I had heard all of their names at one time or another. Alice Jefferies Delong, the mother, died in 1928 four plus years before I was born. But I knew Sarah, Ed, Joe, and Bobbie who always lived together, and Bobbie's afflicted twin sons lived with them up to a point. Sarah had a sweet disposition but was always badly crippled, from an untreated broken leg as I understand. In walking, one of her feet would land at a ninety degree angle to the other one and she limped badly. Ed and Joe at least eventually developed an aptitude for alcohol, and Joe seems to me to have disappeared—I was never aware of his having passed away in Flora. Bobbie's was the sad situation. Though a letter of family information from mother does not say so, I had understood that Bobbie ran away with a circus fellow. At some point she came home with syphilis and gave birth to afflicted twin sons Roland and Robbie. Roland was not too badly afflicted, though one arm was deformed and twisted and may have been missing some fingers. Robbie was pathetically afflicted and was eventually institutionalized for care. I remember him eating fried eggs. He did not use his hands but simply put his face down to the plate and wrestled them into his mouth with his tongue. His speech was unintelligible, and he romped stumblingly around the yard, unable to walk normally.

In addition to her devotion to her own family and providing for their needs, grandma did so for her siblings. She and grandpa, doubtless before my birth, had bought a farm five miles west of Flora on the north side of Highway 50. I'm sure it was purchased with the care of the siblings in mind, for they all lived out there, and grandma would take things out to them and check on them.

The Vindication of Grandpa Reaugh

One cruel circumstance, however, stands out above all others in my mind. It had to do with the disbarment of Grandpa Reaugh by the Illinois State Bar Association in what turned out to be a complete and total injustice to him.

So far as I was aware, grandpa's only business during my years was as an abstractor. But he died when I was only seven, so my memories of all this is in mental images. He owned and operated the local title abstract office in Flora. It was on the west side of downtown, more or less north of the depot but on the north side of Highway 50 that went through town. The south part of his brick building was Uncle Ben's garage (he was an automobile mechanic and Chrysler-Plymouth dealer). Grandpa and grandma owned the building that the A & P Grocery Store was in just across the street to the east from grandpa's building. Later, during my years in Flora I was aware that grandpa had been a lawyer and a judge. People called him Judge Reaugh, and one of our neighbors told me once that Sprigg Reaugh was the smartest man he had ever known. Before I got out of grade school I already dreamed of being either a lawyer or a concert pianist. Perhaps it was because I stayed so busy with a lot of different involvements, as well as the war's domination of all minds, that I never sought out answers for why grandpa became an abstractor rather than continuing to practice law. In retrospect this seems particularly strange since being a lawyer myself was an increasingly attractive goal. My desire to become a lawyer was based upon my interest in things of the mind and my observation that the local lawyers seemed to me to be among the smartest people I knew.

It took many decades for the obvious injustice grandpa and grandma endured to come to my larger understanding. The first step on that path occurred while I was in law school at Southern Methodist University in Dallas. Flipping ahead one day in my course casebook on torts (civil actions for damages) during my first year there, I came across a case in which the style of the case—i.e., the case caption giving the names of the plaintiff and defendant, included the name Reaugh, the defendant. Naturally, I was highly curious, so I read it. It was immediately apparent that the Reaugh was grandpa. He was being sued for something like a breach of trust with regard to funds, or something along that line, and the judgement went for the plaintiff. Authors of casebooks for law student education are highly selective to illustrate the critical areas for study. Dad's death in Flora occurred right at the end of my first semester of law school. It must have been while back in Flora on that sad occasion that I asked grandma about the case. As best I can recall, and it is not the type of thing that would have easily escaped me, grandma's only response was to say that it was a very sad thing. Perhaps she might have added that she would tell me more someday, though I really do not remember anything to that effect. It was as though she was immediately crestfallen and did not want to talk about it, the occasion probably not being appropriate for it. I may have asked mother about it, but I have no recollection of receiving any more information from her or anyone else about it back then. Grandma was such a factor in my life that this weighed heavily on me for well over half a century—from early 1955 until around November 2011. A year or so before that my cousin Kay Eaton Lieder was in Flora and related to my sister the information that shed massive light on the whole tragic affair. Mary Anne then later related Kay's account to my wife Jo Anne and me.

Kay, Aunt Mary Eaton's second child, was a good many years younger than I. In the course of events she married one Larry Goldsby, who I believe had been a classmate of hers in Flora. Larry went on to college and became a lawyer, practicing in southern California. The marriage produced two children but ended in divorce.

The story goes like this. When it became apparent that Kay and Larry were going to marry, grandma called Kay over and said she needed to give her some background on the relationship between the Goldsby and Reaugh families. Grandma said that Grandpa Reaugh and a Mr. Goldsby, Larry Goldsby's grandfather, had been close friends and were business associates in the local savings and loan association in which one, probably grandpa, was chairman, and the other was president. An audit turned up a large amount, reportedly about $800,000 that had disappeared. Both of them were accused on the matter. I'm not aware of any criminal allegation, but I presume this was the basis of the case I came across in my law casebook in 1955. I've recently gone to some effort to find that case but have thus far not been successful. However, as a result of this apparent defalcation, the Illinois Bar Association peremptorily disbarred grandpa without a proceeding. As I understand it, and grandma may have said something to me about this at some point, the lawyers in town urged grandpa to fight that action but he declined. Doubtless this was the answer to why he became an abstractor.

But what grandma revealed to Kay before she married Mr. Goldsby's grandson was that soon thereafter Mr. Goldsby committed suicide but left a note in which he confessed full responsibility for the disappearance of all the funds for which grandpa had taken the fall. Cousin Kay also told me that all the money was recovered for the association, presumably primarily or entirely from Goldsby's estate. I have wondered since learning of this if grandpa was suspicious of the guilty party all along but would not make any assertion against his friend and associate. Whatever the truth is on that, when this "deathbed confession" came out, the State Bar proposed to reinstate grandpa. I presume this would have been after he had opened his abstract business. As I understand, grandpa's response to the Bar's proposal was, "You did not grant me a hearing before you revoked my license. I do not want your license now."

In working on this project I have recently gone back to the law library and tried without success to find that case I read in law school, and another lawyer friend in Massachusetts did a search for me on it, also unsuccessfully. Unfortunately, I had no name for the plaintiff, which might have made the search easier. Still it is a mystery why I could not find it. A staff member at the Texas Tech Law School found some Reaugh parties in case reports in her search, but none of them was the case I was searching for.

Later, in writing of my dad's remarkable 1922 Flora High School football team, I note that he played one end position and that the other end was played by a Raymond Goldsby. My cousin Kay confirmed that Raymond was the son of my grandpa's business associate in question. She also said that he moved to New York, had two daughters, and had not returned to Flora since his mother's funeral. His mother had been a good friend of grandma, and Kay indicated that grandma rather privately befriended her after the above-described tragic events.

In setting out this account I went back to read the eulogy given by Flora attorney Clarence T. Smith at grandpa's funeral. In my estimation, Clarence Smith, of no known relation to us, stood at the pinnacle of the legal profession in Flora. It was he, years later, who would effectively recommend dad for the job that was the happiest, and final, of his short life. It is inconceivable that the words of such a eulogy, spoken by one in a position to know, could have been said of one of whom there was an immoral fiber in his being.

My Parents

Dad, Frank E. Smith, was born on the family farm on the Little Wabash River on June 4, 1905. His family moved into town before dad started to school.

Mother, Frances Elizabeth Reaugh Smith, was born in Flora on October 14, 1906.

Both parents were, I think, good students, but neither ever attended college. Dad graduated from Flora High School in 1923 and mother in 1924. But as Jo Anne's 1995 "Family Ancestry" relates, doubtless from visiting with mother, the young students often gathered in each other's home for parties and after one such event, dad asked to walk mother home. Later, he would walk to her home on Sunday afternoons and they would sit on the porch together. Before long, she was "his" girl and they saw each other a couple of nights a week. They were married on Sunday, August 21, 1927, in the living room of the Reaugh home at 6:00 a.m. This was doubtless wise for dad was afraid that his friends would disrupt the wedding, so had only called the preacher late on the night before. He and mother honeymooned in the Missouri Ozarks.

After high school, dad worked as a bookkeeper for the Ford dealer and mother worked in the office of the International Shoe Company factory in Flora. Years later, after dad was in his next job, probably about 1937 or 1938, he took me with him out to the Ford dealership. An early version of television was being watched by several folks standing in the dealership office—I could not believe seeing it, but it was there. Perhaps our purpose in going was to see it. Televisions did not become common in homes until a few years after the end of the war.

Fortunately, dad was never without a job during the depression. Earnings were not great, and in retrospect most everyone was poor by later standards, but we did not feel poor because it was the common experience of the times. While dad never had any college, he did take the correspondence course in accounting from LaSalle Extension University in Chicago, which I presume was during his early days as a bookkeeper. Years later as I was finishing my accounting degree I took the LaSalle CPA Coaching Course in preparation for that exam.

Later dad went to work for F. H. Simpson, a fruit broker who operated out of Flora. Dad was the bookkeeper, but as time went on he became virtually the operation. Large shipments of fruit would come into Flora and be stored in the multi-level Ebner Ice & Cold Stage plant. Ever so many times I would go at night with dad into those refrigerated fruit warehouse floors where he would direct placement of incoming shipments or select produce for outgoing shipment. The fruit was always in bushel baskets. I always thought I would freeze before he got through.

The Simpson offices were above the Kroger Grocery Store in a building on the northwest corner of the main intersection in town, Main Street running north and south, and East North Avenue (U. S. Highway 50) running east and west. The other three corners, clockwise from the NW corner were occupied, respectively, by the bank, drugstore, and men's clothing store. The intersection was the place to loaf on Saturday night. The Simpson offices overlooked the intersection, but to get to those offices one had to enter near the north end of the building, climb two flights of stairs, and then go down a long, dark hall and turn left into dad's office.

During Dad's Simpson years one scenario occurred with great frequency. Flora was in the easternmost reaches of the central time zone, so in the fall and winter it got dark relatively early. Dad's working hours almost never ended before 6:00 p.m. While dad normally walked home most other times of the year, in those darker months I remember so well the countless times when mother would drive down and I would run upstairs to let dad know we were waiting for him in the car. He would never stop till he had gotten to a stopping place. I remember in particular the adding machine that was in his office. It stood near the door on legs of its own requiring the user to stand also. He used it a lot. It was a distinctly earlier vintage than the ten-key that would eventually send these monsters to museums and junkyards. If he headed to that machine while I waited for him, I knew I would be waiting a while longer.

Since dad pretty much ran the operation, the time came when he tried to buy it from Simpson. The latter did not want to sell. Dad resigned. This was around the time I entered high school, give or take a year, in the mid-1940s. I think his top salary while there had been about $150 per month. When dad resigned, for a period of time he had no regular job. However, while still working for Simpson he had been employed by the local school board and the city as bookkeeper for which I think each paid him $50.00/month. Times were a bit leaner, but we got by on that for a while. It was probably not until after he went to work again that he paid me a decent amount to get the monthly bank statement checks in numerical order to save him time in then reconciling those statement balances.

That lean interval soon ended and good fortune smiled on dad, and thus on the family as a whole. Dad had an excellent standing in Flora, as did the Reaugh family. The most successful lawyer in Flora was probably Clarence Smith (who had delivered Grandpa Reaugh's eulogy), of Smith, McCullum & Riggle. Clarence had a lawyer-client relationship with Pure Oil Company. The part of southern Illinois where Flora was had become fairly active in oil production. Through his involvement with that industry Clarence learned that the J. J. Lynn Oil Division out of Kansas City, which was active in the southern Illinois oil fields, was looking for a good land man. Dad was highly respected and, upon Clarence's unqualified recommendation, landed the job and performed most ideally. However, this transitional era in our family will be covered later.

Dad was a talented raconteur of humorous stories. Combine that with the homespun quality of the anecdotes he would tell, and one was in for true entertainment when he began an offering. Nor did it have to be the first time one heard the account. In fact, the evidence of his unusual abilities was reflected in the fact that the more he repeated it the funnier it got. His hearers, recognizing it, would begin laughing when he started and be howling by the time he had finished. He was only about five feet eight inches tall, broadly built, and would normally pantomime if the account permitted of it. An example was his demonstration of the time his group of fellows was fishing on the Little Wabash. Fishing lines would be set in the evening and run in the middle of the night and then early in the morning. One of the group did not like getting up in the night but did like to prepare meals around the campfire. On the occasion in question, as sometimes happened, a water mocassin took the fish bait and was hooked on the line, hauled into the boat and killed. Sleepyhead would remove his trousers before turning in for the night, so the others decided to have some fun with him. Upon returning to camp they hung the dead snake with care over the crotch of the pants so that it went an equal distance down each leg. This was a classic case for pantomime, and dad performed it with dramatic flair, mimicking Sleepyhead's jig, jumping from one leg to the other while shaking the raised leg with great urgency. Most of his stories were real-life accounts.

Mother was the flipside of dad's storytelling. No one loved a good story more than she. Particularly in later life, when she was of more matronly enhanced figure, it was doubly entertaining for a funny story to be told in her hearing. Everyone would laugh at the telling. But mother's laughter would begin, grow to the point of almost choking, then recovering, would burst out with a laughter so boisterous that she would shake all over, sometimes even going into repeated cycles. The result was that the whole group would begin another round of laughter, this round being sympathetic response to mother's display. Her love of a good story was reflected in our daughter Jillian's memorable impromptu sharing of memories at mother's funeral service. Jillian took note of the fact that a joke being a bit off-color would not in the least dampen mother's enthusiasm for its humor. Mother died at ninety-two and was ready to go. It was a funeral of rejoicing with great amounts of laughter, which I'm sure mother was enjoying from above. It must have been at least two or three years after her death before I ceased to have an instinctive reaction, upon hearing a good story, to pick up the phone and call her.

While I needed no one else to boost my estimation of mother, or of how lucky I was to have a mother such as she, more than one niece or nephew spoke to me about her being their favorite aunt. Saying that should not be taken as a put-down of any other, but simply that there was something about her that made others love her.

Dad had an intense and lifelong interest in football. He died long before football became the commercial monster it is today, and he played three decades before his death. The Flora High School team he played for in the fall of 1922 was not only undefeated but was also unscored on. The write-up in the 1923 annual reported the Southern Illinois Championship as being split between Flora and Murphysboro, both undefeated, but thirty-seven points were scored on Murphysboro. Flora tried to get a post-season game to resolve the title, but the powers did not permit this. Three Flora teammates made the Southern Illinois All-Star Team, two received Honorable Mention, and one other, my dad, received Mention. Another, described as being "without a doubt the best halfback in Southern

Illinois," was mysteriously not honored in any of these categories. Dad played one end position on the team. The other end was named Raymond Goldsby, son of Grandpa Reaugh's ill-fated business associate, though I do not know the year his defalcation either occurred or was confessed at his self-inflicted death.

Other Childhood Memories

During my earliest years, and until sometime in my grade school years when the railroad moved them from Flora to Washington, Indiana, the Spitlers, Bernard (pronounced BERN-erd) and Ruby, and their two children, Jack and Jane, lived just to the north of us. Jack was two years older; Jane my age. They were playmates, and I rode the railroad over and visited them in Washington the summer after they moved.

Ruby's father was called "Pop." He lived in a garage apartment in the northeast corner of their lot. He had a Model-T Ford, the early type that had a crank handle that was inserted in the crank slot at the bottom front of the vehicle. The car had to be cranked to get it started, and I remember seeing Pop many times cranking away trying to get it started. He might have been about as successful motivating an independent-minded jackass. When it would finally start, it sounded like a man waking up in a coughing fit.

Ruby used to come over when the summer had reached almost intolerably hot and humid levels and tell mother, "Well, summer is now officially here. Pop took off his 'long-handles' today."

Perhaps my biggest frustration as a child was wetting the bed—I was a bed wetter. It was awful to wake up in the middle of the night in a wet bed, but it was my experience many times. Just how long the awful experiences continued I do not recall, but I do recall that it extended into my early school days to some extent.

I remember having a fairly nice, curve-around basket-weave rocking chair. It was for the early years. I used it often, but most of all I remember sitting in front of the Christmas tree in front of our living room window and rocking back and forth while "visions of sugar plums danced in my head," so to speak. The colored ornaments were attractive, but the different colored electric lights absolutely enchanted me. I loved one particular set that eventually became but a single pink bulb through the normal attrition. It was in the shape of an elongated Christmas bell. Expectations of children were not as lavish then as now. Getting one or two things you wanted made it very special. And there was always a bowl of oranges and walnuts for they were still a special treat. We harvested hickory nuts from the woods and messy, stainy-hulled black walnuts, whose nutmeats were hard to pick out of the shell, from grandma's driveway, but English walnuts were a treat. I do not remember ever having pecans, but I remember some hazelnuts also. There was usually also some hard candy near the tree.

I must have been a challenge for my folks on Christmas morning. I would get so excited that I could not sleep the night before and would lie there straining to listen for Santa, even before I suspected the whole setup. But I did not give up on Santa till I was well into grade school. Why let go of a good thing till you had to? Eventually though, the talk among the school kids made me realize it was time to face the facts. Perhaps one of life's sadder moments. But to get back to my merciless practices, I can remember one year getting my folks up at 3:00 a.m. They never kept me though from coming to the tree when I wanted to, even if they came out shaking their heads and rubbing their eyes. I think it was special to them also. They were such loving parents.

My birthday was on September 23, but in 1938 a child reaching six before the end of December could start first grade. I do not remember my first day of school as such. But I remember hearing later what I had reported back to my folks after the first few days, when asked how I liked school. My opinion was, "We spend more time on the inside than the outside." In short, it had a major drawback.

Of knowledge about "the birds and the bees" I was oblivious, aside from realizing there was a difference between girls and boys. So when in January of 1939, my little sister Mary Anne, my only sibling, was brought home from the hospital, to the best of my recollection it was pretty much a news item to me. I have no memory of any impression of mother having taken on any different shape, as in pregnancy. Never did I call Mary Anne by her name until many years later. Dad came home calling her "Sister," and that name was all I ever called her until at a far more mature age, probably around her commencement of puberty when she requested that I use her name. It seemed unnatural at first, but those days are far behind now. Sister came home with a full head of virtually black hair, whereas I had been pretty much towheaded. The space of more than six years between our ages meant rather separated life interests through our youth. She was cute as a little one and pretty in her later years, but probably not until our dad's illness and our later adult lives did I mature enough to have adequate appreciation for her—another fact of which I'm not terribly proud. Her accomplishments in life have been considerable and I think we have shared an appropriate loving relationship since then. I must have had a devilish streak in me in my relationship to her while she was little. Her scream was her most potent protective device and it inevitably prompted my fleeing the scene. A little later, after I learned to handle the piano keyboard a bit, when we would be home in the evening, on occasion I would commence a moving sequence of scary chords from the base notes, accompanied by low-voiced narration of approaching horror, to terrorize her. I deserved a good flogging.

I do not remember anything with particularity that happened to me in second grade other than that I believe it was in the spring of that year, or early summer following, that my parents began to give me piano lessons. Grandma had an old upright piano that she gave to us that served until a few years later when we bought a Baldwin Acrosonic.

My first teacher was a man. But after a while I did not seem to be doing very well—to be truthful, at that point I did not like taking lessons or practicing. In any event, my parents arranged for me to change piano teachers. The lady selected, Miss Mary Ellis, was the grade school music teacher—she was not the band director. She would bring her mouth harp to class, give us the pitch, and launch us into each piece she taught us. She was also the volunteer choir director of the First Christian Church. Apparently I did not retrogress too much with her, and perhaps might even have made a little progress through the third grade, though no evidence of prodigy surfaced—the outdoors was still of great interest. But I was hanging on. It was in the fourth grade that she smoked me out.

When I think of everything that dad did for and with me, I realize in looking back that I did not do as much with my own children—for them, yes, but with them, no. It is a comparison unfavorable to me. That is not to say that I did not have some great times with them, particularly on vacations and in the mountains. But times and our circumstances were so different by then. I cannot recall precisely at what ages he began to take me fishing and then squirrel hunting, but doubtless at least some fishing had begun. I cannot think of anything that made me happier in those days than for dad to get home a little early in the afternoon and say, "Let's go fishing." I could dig worms in our backyard. There were a few different haunts we would go to. One of them was the slough on the farm. The river itself was more the scene of overnight fishing; from a boat, setting trot or throw lines or setting poles in the bank, and then running the lines in the middle of the night and early the next morning. Another was Coon Creek (short, I suppose, for raccoon, as in coon dog), and there were one or two others. I loved sitting on the bank holding a pole with a cork on the line and worm on the hook. Of course, all I did was watch the cork and pull the line out as soon as the cork began to go under or bob away. At first I did not have much finesse in landing the fish. My tendency was to "wabash" it out with such vigor it would sail over my head and slam down on the bank behind me. Dad both baited the hook and took the fish off. In time, I became good at both, but the idea of putting the worm on took a while for me to warm up to, and it took even more daring to get around the sharp fins and teeth of the fish, particularly the jaws of the catfish. Eventually I also learned that the results were better if, instead of wabashing, a gentler pull on the pole was better to set the hook, consider the size and pull of the fish, and decide how to bring it ashore. We did not have dip nets on these pole fishing trips. Aside from catfish, most of those from our day fishing were perch, sunfish, or crappie. A real prize, mostly from overnight fishing, was called white perch. We threw any carp back. What a disappointment to think there was a nice big fish on the line only to pull out a carp, which seemed always to have attained a good size. Aside from the carp, which we did not eat, all the family liked fried fish.

Dad had a .22 rifle. During those depression and war years I do not think he had a shotgun. I was a pretty good shot with the .22. While I was still fairly young, he started taking me squirrel hunting. The best time to go was before daybreak, having picked out the day before a hickory tree where they were "cutting," which one could tell by the cuttings on the ground. Then get situated where the tree could be observed as the sun began to light the woods. On occasion, one might even get a long string and tie it to a sapling on the other side of the tree from yourself. If the squirrel learned you were down there it would hide on the opposite side, but pulling the string would often bring it around exposing it for a shot. Otherwise, some loose object could be thrown to land on the other side. In any event, this was a highly enjoyable outing, and all the family liked fried squirrel.

But there was one trying episode in the woods. Dad had made it known to me how to handle the situation if one had a serious need of a bathroom, none being otherwise available. The technique was to grab a branch of a sapling or small bush close to the trunk and with one long swish remove all the leaves on that branch. The result was a handful of leaves. That was to serve the role served by toilet paper in more genteel venues. He had demonstrated the procedure to me on occasion. On the occasion in question, it was I who needed to "go," but I refused to use that gross procedure. Dad's persuasive powers were not up to the occasion, for my resistance was immovable. We had to leave the woods and drive the seven miles or so to town for me to "go." Mother later described it. Dad came in shaking his head saying, "I never thought I would raise a son who could not 'go' in the woods." In later years, I went to the woods better prepared. As bright as he was, I wondered why dad did not think of that. My guess is that he was raised with Sears & Roebuck or Montgomery Ward catalogues in the privies, compared to which green leaves were not too bad.

During the entirety of my eight grade school years, there were two buildings, the older gray stucco building to the south and the red brick building to the north. Together they, with their ample playgrounds occupied a full east-west block and two full north-south blocks between East North Avenue and Third Street. There were about three full, dirt basketball courts along the north boundary on Third Street.

Aside from a friendly round with boxing gloves on, I was never in a fistfight. All fighting was done by wrestling, but seldom, if ever, out of real anger. I was often in wrestling bouts, both on the school ground and otherwise in the early grades. My memory on the matter is not inerrant, but I do not remember ever losing one of these—not, that is, until I engaged a boy from "the other side of the tracks," so to speak. I'm afraid I had judged him, probably instinctively from overall appearance, to be of very low class. So much so, in fact, that I wonder if he was actually in school. Probably he was, because it was on the school playground, but I do not think he was in school long for I have no other memory of him there. If the building were still there, I'm sure I could walk to within a few feet of the exact location.

The only thing I remember about that wrestling match is how short its duration and how in the very shortness of time I became the first human launched into outer space. When I started to engage him, the next thing I knew was that in a flash I was hurtling through the air and then thudding down hard, flat on my back. I think when the war started that I saw pictures of marines, and perhaps other soldiers, being trained in the Japanese martial art of jujitsu engagement.

And I think that professional wrestlers were able to perform such amazing feats. That is what I think my opponent applied, almost professionally, on me. He was street smart. I do not think I ever wrestled again. That ego-deflating humiliation prompted me to write wrestling off as a career option. Just a few years later, another fellow in Flora saved me from a boxing career.

So far as I remember, I always had top grades through grade school, with one exception, which surfaced big-time in the third grade (1940–1941). I got unsatisfactory in deportment—i.e., "self-control." Bob McBride went with me pretty well all the way through school, including the third grade. We had a very sweet teacher, Miss Elsie Winters. She taught 3A and her sister, Miss Una Winters, taught 3B. They lived together in a house just across the street east of the grade school that I passed by every day walking to and from school. While America was not yet at war, and as youngsters we were not yet fully aware of the fullness of the dark events unfolding in both Europe and Asia at the hands of Germany and Japan, I do remember radio reports and movie news with Lowell Thomas starting as far back as 1938. Still, life was pretty much as it had always been, in our limited experience. Perhaps I had a capacity for laughter at a younger age, but certainly by my days in third grade it blossomed bounteously. Bob McBride sat in the row to my right and, as I remember it, one seat farther back. So, for us to communicate, it was necessary for me to be the one who turned the most. It seems to me we were always laughing about something and getting called down for it. But when once something tickled our funny bones it was not that easy to turn it off; not, that is, so long as the teacher did not really come down on us. Strangely, I do not remember that sweet teacher ever doing that. Perhaps I just blocked those occasions from my memory bank. But it just goes beyond reason to expect spontaneous merriment to be suppressed when some hapless student farted. Uncontrollable giggling, or outright laughter, was automatic for us two. Fortunate were we when those occasions were but shortly before recess, the only hope for bringing laughter under control. Until then, the funnies lying just below any false calm kept bursting through.

It had to be about this year in my schooling, perhaps even a year earlier, when word was passed around in all the lower grades that there would be a tricycle race twice around the gymnasium during halftime of the next varsity basketball game. The grade school varsity games (as well as "curtain raiser" game, if any) were played in the high school gym. Very soon thereafter, if not already, the "new gymnasium" was built to the north of the existing high school building, but grade school games continued being played in the old high school gym. That is where the race was to be held. The seats were all wooden benches, but there was a second floor of benches all the way around. The benches on the first floor came to within but very few feet of the playing floor itself, a space barely wide enough, if that, to accommodate the tricycle racing path. As it turned out, only two participants turned up, Jimmy Large and I. Jimmy and his younger sister were always friends. He was a year older and grade ahead of me, but probably less athletically competitive. But he had one other disadvantage. His tricycle was not as large as mine was and I could make mine fairly fly. The race got under way and I do not think it was ever terribly close, but on one of the corner turns he must have lost control and his trike turned over with him on it. I completed the race and claimed my prize.

Jimmy was quite a journalist and got his start in high school. Julianna Uphoff taught bookkeeping and journalism and was the adviser for the staff of the two school publications, the student newspaper called "The Locust Log" and "The Harstan," the annual, an acronym from the school name, Harter-Stanford Township High School" (later simply "Flora High"). Jimmy was a stellar member of "The Locust Log" staff, but confessed to me that he raised a few hackles on Julianna's neck when he decided to put out a publication of his own that he called "The Termite," the initial issue of which was headlined, "Termite Threatens Log." Its longevity I do not remember, but Jimmy's career certainly did not end there. He became a Wall Street Journal reporter headquartered in Washington, DC. He passed away several years ago, from lung cancer I believe.

I'm guessing that if the tricycle race occurred while I was in the third grade that it was probably in the summer prior to the fourth grade when I got my first bicycle. It was surely a beauty. The fake "tank" between the two top bars was painted with bright colors. Red and yellow stick in my mind. It was a full-size "bike," such that while I could reach the full scope of the pedaling cycle, it stretched me out pretty good to do so. Well, I think my parents were probably watching, and likely there were also some envious young eyes on me. I wheeled it out our driveway right into the middle of Meyer Street. I do not remember if I got on it by myself or if someone held it for me and gave me a push. What I do remember is the route I took. A well-known fact of physics is that a straight line is the shortest distance between two points. The line of my travel may not have been perfectly straight, but if not it did not miss it far. There was a telephone poll off the east side of the street probably fifteen or twenty feet inside the south boundary of the Spitler lot next door. It seemed to be the north magnetic pole, for I rode majestically straight into that telephone poll. At the very least, it knocked the front wheel out of alignment with the handlebars, but that alone could be straightened. If at first you do not succeed, try, try again, and so I did, and that bike took me many a mile before advancing adolescence and high school activity gradually made it passé.

Not long after I got my new bike I was down at Grandma Smith's house and dad's brother, Uncle Harold, was there, having driven up with his family from Anna, as they often did. Years later he told me of a brief discussion he and I had on that occasion regarding my bicycle tires. He said I asked him, "Do you think I could put fifty pounds of air pressure in these tires?" His response was, "No, you could not put that much pressure in them." I replied, "I just did!"

My fourth grade teacher (class 4A) was Miss Helen Douglas. I remember four events from that year. The first of them occurred during the approaching Christmas holiday. We were reading an account that related to the birth of Jesus. My recollection had it coming from one of the New Testament nativity accounts, but as I search for the text, which in those days would have been only from the King James Version, the word that I'm looking for is not in either such account. So, it had to be some non-canonical text related to the Christmas story from which I was called upon to stand and read out loud to the class. I do not remember if several students were called upon in turn or if I was the only one. The critical point is that what I was obliged to read had Joseph leading Mary on an *ass*. I read along fluently until my eyes fell upon that horrible word. My tongue went into paralysis. There was no way I could say that word out loud in front of all my classmates. I might have had a good laugh if someone else had read the word "ass" out loud, but for me to read that word that I would not even speak was out of the question. I stopped, choked, immovable like an ass on a precipice. Miss Douglas urged me to read on, but I could not say that word. I do not remember how that impasse was resolved. All I remember is that it was a moment of sheer horror, beyond which all memory on the incident is wiped clean.

A far happier occasion was the cleaning of the fire escape tubes. Each of the two buildings had two tubes—one on the east and one on the west—that descended diagonally from a spot on the second floor to ground level. As an upperclassman in the south building, which housed the first through fourth grades, I was the lucky student selected to sit on top of a large mop-like seat and slide down each slide two or three times to clean it out for an imminent fire drill. That was a fun day to remember, I being for the day the envy of every other boy and I'm sure of some girls also.

Other than the fourth and final event of my fourth grade year, which will follow several memories that generally preceded it, the most vivid memory of all was what became the turning point in my piano playing career. Till then, I had plodded dutifully along, practicing just enough to keep from falling completely by the wayside. During one of my piano lessons, Miss Ellis got her calendar and studied it. She marked a date in it not too far distant and said to me, "On this day I want you to play this piece in front of your class." The thought of it terrified me. Seeing no escape, I applied the only option available—I practiced, hard. The day came. A piano was rolled in for the event. Evidently I got through it pretty well, for my classmates seemed to be duly impressed. Enough was said to light the fires of encouragement and interest. That is what I consider the turning point from the drudgery of practice and just getting through my lessons to enjoying practice and looking forward to the next lesson. Somewhere about this time I was asked to play, perhaps more than once, in the sanctuary of the First Christian Church, where Miss Ellis was choir director, on Sunday morning. It was the practice in those days for all those attending Sunday School to assemble in the sanctuary before going to class. I do not remember much of what it was for other than, I suppose, announcements and that kind of thing. It was before breaking for class one Sunday morning that I played. I remember the piece was called "The Happy Farmer." I liked it and played it pretty well I think. Maybe I played another time, I do not recall.

It was not long after that time in our church life when a preacher by the name of Howard Yanaka succeeded the longtime, increasingly elderly but much loved, Brother Doty. My mother's entire family belonged to that church. But dad had always been a Methodist from childhood. Mother took Mary Anne and me to Sunday School at First Christian, while dad went to Sunday School at the First Methodist Church one block south on Third Street. Neither would stay for church. Pastor Yanaka was much younger, rode a motorcycle (and perhaps drove a car too), and preached the doctrines that came out of the Cincinnati Bible Seminary. One of those was that you were going to hell if you were not baptized by immersion. I was baptized that way in that church. And I think it was by Yonaka. However, mother was not enamored with the change of character of the preaching and theology from that of the beloved Brother Doty. The time came, shortly after my baptism, which had to have been no later than when I was about nine years old, possibly early-on ten, that mother made the decision to move our membership over to dad's Methodist Church, where it remained throughout their lives except for the short period the family lived in Texas. She alone, of her own family, made such a move, though grandma was in full sympathy with her as were, probably, her local siblings.

Related to all of this, I used to get my hair cut by a couple of different barbers. One was named Tipp Maddox. His religion, if any, was cloaked. The other was Gene Cusick, a member of First Christian Church. I remember him urging me, while he had me in the barber chair, to try to do something to save my dad, who was going to hell if he did not correct his Methodist baptism by sprinkling into a full immersion before it was too late. I did not appreciate it nor act upon his plea, even if in those years I may have been bothered a little by it, whatever concern I may have had at the time having faded rather quickly.

One happy memory I have from First Christian Church is the Sunday school teacher we young boys had. His name was Charlie Snyder, who had a son one or two years older than I, as well as an even older boy and maybe others. Charlie was a good man. He ran an insurance agency and was well liked in town. He died of a sudden heart attack too soon as far as all Flora was concerned. Flora did not have a swimming pool until about the time I got to high school. Salem, twenty-seven miles west on Route 50 had one, as did Olney twenty-four miles east on the same highway. Charlie would plan to drive a few boys, all he could reasonably pack into his car, probably five, maybe six, over to Olney one time during the summer to swim. The lucky boys were determined from a tally that stretched over several weeks ahead of time. It kept count of the number of chapters of the Bible the boy had read, and these were noted each week and a running total was kept. No chapter could be read more than once for credit. Every boy read Psalm 117, the shortest chapter in the Bible, no one read Psalm 119, the longest. Psalms was a favorable book though, for it had a lot of short chapters.

I was one of the lucky winners. While driving to Olney, someone suggested that we play "burn out." It consisted in closing all the windows and turning on the heat full blast. The object was not to be the one to yell "enough." Southern Illinois is hot and humid in the summertime. Poor Charlie was a good sport and let the game commence, but it became extremely hot very fast and he capitulated quickly. Needless to say, it was good preparation for the swim that could not come too soon.

Dad was always solicitous that I should have opportunity to play sports. Football and basketball were his greatest focus. I've previously indicated the unusual 1922 Flora High team he played on. But at a point during my early grade years, probably when I was about eight or nine, he built and installed a very stable basketball goal for me at the east end of our side yard. He built a solid, reinforced, rectangular wood backboard upon which he anchored a standard steel basketball rim assembly complete (at least originally) with net. Then he acquired from some source a solid telephone pole in good condition and found a way to bury it sufficiently in the ground to be completely stable, and as I recall he got another pole and made a diagonal brace of it on the backside. Whether either or both of these were anchored in concrete I do not recall, but the post was and remained immovable. The backboard was bolted securely onto the vertical pole. Surely that must have been done before the final erection of the pole, a detail not within my careful observation. It became a favorite place for shooting baskets and playing one-on-one or two-on-two for several years, and was still standing when we left Flora after I graduated from high school in 1950.

That goal doubtless figured into my being fairly good in basketball on class teams, and then on the interscholastic grade school team. I may even have been captain of the grade school team, as a picture of the team seems perhaps to suggest. I continued to be actively involved in basketball through high school, but by then other players contributed greater talent than I did. We had winning teams, and three of our players had basketball scholarships in college.

The fourth and most memorable event of my fourth grade year was the surprise Japanese attack on our navy at Pearl Harbor on December 7, 1941, and the frightful weeks and months that followed. A Flora boy, Leslie Etchison, the uncle of one of my classmates, was on the Battleship Arizona, lost with it at Pearl Harbor. A neighbor boy, August ("Gussie") Haak (pronounced "hawk"), with a smile and energizing spirit no one can forget, a brother of Frances, one of my classmates and her only sibling, was a tail gunner on a bomber (a B-24 I think) in Italy. He used to write home to his family signing his name "Gussie the gunner; gunner today, goner tomorrow." His mother hated that, and he indeed was killed in action, from which his mother never really recovered. Families with loved ones in the war zones lived in anxiety that the dreaded telegram from the War Department would come, "We regret to inform you..." Service flags, visible from the street, became customary in the front window of every family who had a family member in the military service. They were rectangular with a red border enclosing a white field upon which there was a star for each service member. The star was blue except for one killed in action, it was gold. Blue and gold were the only officially recognized colors, but a silver star was often used for a member wounded in action. Able-bodied young men of military age not in uniform, if not in some critical occupation, became essentially extinct, and few there were who did not try to get in the service because of the general feelings of the people in those years.

The war so filled my head in this difficult period that I began to engage in my own acted-out, backyard war games against the so-called Axis Powers (Germany, Japan, and later Italy). I was getting a bit old for toys in the normal sense, but war equipment, even if toy, was necessary to act out war games. It could not be purchased in those days, and even if it could have been, I would not have wanted to pay for it. So it was necessary to make the equipment, which I did out of wood. I built fighter planes (not model planes, which could be bought, but cut out of blocks of wood with wings and tails added), an M-1 rifle with attachable bayonet, a machine gun that swiveled on a tripod like a regular thirty- or fifty-caliber machine gun then in use, and probably a few others. I shot down a lot of German Messerschmitt and Japanese Zero fighter planes after fierce dogfights in the skies. I hate to count the number of enemy soldiers, both German and Japanese, that I killed in battle. Imagination typical of younger years was rekindled in me to meet the challenges of the times. It is a bit hard to tell these things now, but it was hard for a young person like I was to keep hatred from reaching a boiling point. Of course, our military effort was focused upon killing (or capturing) the enemy. I'm afraid that loving and praying for our enemies, as admonished in the Sermon on the Mount, was given a vacation during those horrible times. After the war, our hearts in many cases began to go out to the people in those countries ravaged by what they had gone through. For many, however, who had seen the brutality of the Japanese military, especially those who had suffered it directly, forgiveness was slow to come. It is to the credit of our leaders that our nation gave so much assistance in the rebuilding and restoring of those countries. The time for charity had come, but aside from charity, it was a wise course to pursue.

By this time in school I was forming some pretty clear ideas of what I dreamed of pursuing as a lifetime career. Two things stood out. One was the law and the other was piano performance. I was increasingly impressed by my observations of lawyers and the thought that it was a profession of learning. Doubtless that was a considerable stimulant to me in how seriously I took my studies through the rest of my public school education. I was hungry to learn and to make good grades.

But the other prong of ambition was to be a concert pianist. Little did I appreciate at that stage how limited was the advanced piano instruction in a town like Flora, and neither the times nor the circumstances pointed toward seeking far more advanced instruction. Nevertheless, for a town like Flora, Miss Ellis was a good teacher. Mr. Jacobs had the band give a concert each spring. It was held in the only place that had a stage in the grade school system, namely, the gym in the newer Washington School. It also had on that stage the only grand piano in the grade school system. Grand pianos at that time in Flora were a rather special thing to get to play on, for there were not that many. At about that time Aunt Mary got one, and there was one on the stage in the auditorium on the second floor of the Carnegie Library building where, among other activities, piano teachers held their student recitals. Later, I was aware of one or two more, whether or not they were available during the war years.

Apparently Mr. Jacobs and Miss Ellis had gotten their heads together and decided that I should play a solo on that Washington School grand piano during that year's band concert. The piece I was to play was Paderewski's Minuet, a delightful number that I think few audiences let Paderewski finish his encores without performing. It apparently went quite well, for the applause was notable. I did not make much of that, however, until our family got home that evening, just being relieved to have gotten through it okay. Mother came to me and said, "Do you know what the audience wanted you to do?" I had no clue. She said they wanted me to come back out and play something else. Good thing I had not known that because I did not have any other piece prepared to play anyhow. The next year, however, on the piece, March Grotesque, by Christian Sinding, that I had won a first superior rating on at the Illinois State competition held on the Illinois Normal campus in Bloomington, the applause again continued on and on. Again, I had no second piece to play. I solved that by marching back out and playing the whole piece for them again.

Piano was my instrument of choice. For about four years between grade school and high school I played the cornet, and in high school took pipe organ lessons at the church, occasionally playing for an evening service. I happily gave up study of these instruments.

I remember the practice sessions for our graduation, to be held in the new high school gymnasium. Fellow classmate Gale Bryan and I played the music for the graduation ceremony. If I'm not mistaken, part of it was with four hands on the keyboard. While it may not have happened for me at that graduation, I do not think I have ever been able to remain dry eyed through the playing of Elgar's irresistibly poignant march, *Pomp and Circumstance*, at graduation ceremonies.

To my complete surprise, the American Legion Award (certificate and medal), presented each year to the student selected by the faculty, was presented to me during the ceremony. It was a signal honor. I sensed that my folks were very gratified by that.

Some aspects of my public school years began in grade school and carried on into the high school years, in some cases phasing in and out, waxing and waning and interweaving with other involvements. Word War II that began and ended within the grade school years brought an end to the depression years, though not in a way that could in any sense be called prosperous times. Jobs became plentiful, but the demands of the war introduced many austerities and anxieties. The young men and their women folk were directly affected by the sacrificial demands of military service. Home folks faced shortages in virtually everything due to the total commitment of the nation to the war effort. So many, if not most, things, sugar and shoes for example, were rationed, with books of stamps being issued for family allowances. Factories converted from the production of civilian to military products. Gasoline was strictly limited. Tires were not only rationed but were synthetic and inferior. Any piece of scrap metal lying in a field, or tinfoil peeled off of chewing-gum wrappers lying in a ditch, were salvaged and turned in as scrap. The dealers paid for it. Any money people had over and above their basic necessities generally went into the purchase of war bonds or stamps. Stamps were sold in denominations, the smallest being ten cents. Books were available at the post office in which to affix the stamps, and when filled with $18.75 worth of stamps, they could be turned in for a "war bond" redeemable in ten years for the face amount of $25. Larger denomination stamps, stamp books, and bonds were available. During these years, from the earliest on, I earned what I could (over and above my weekly allowance of twenty-five cents) from various sources.

At an early age, I set up a stand on our street to sell Kool-Aid for a penny a glass. I may have grossed a nickel overall, thanks to some kind neighbors, but not enough to turn a profit. Then there was the digging, cutting, and bundling of sassafras roots for the making of tea, a considerable effort that did not produce much revenue. Still a bit later, I got a barrel that I sat on the alley side of our garage. Perhaps with the help of some friends I would bike out to a pond, doubtless trespassing (but who cared then), and seine crawfish for sale as fishing bait, particularly for overnight river fishing. All of these were good early business lessons from which I began to sense the difference between hopeful projections and actual results in business ventures. Continuing my "Midas Touch," I sold few, if any, crawfish. But well I remember the decidedly unappetizing aroma from a tank full of decomposing crawfish and the frightful chore of disposition. With all due respects to my Cajun friends, that memory gives me a hard time facing a pile of boiled crawfish dumped on a newspaper, with the meat in the tails to be dug out with the fingers and plopped in the mouth.

But for a kid conscientious about doing my part in the war effort, I did buy a lot of savings stamps to convert into war bonds. The jobs I had before high school athletics, music competitions, studies, and a few other activities crowded them out included several independent activities. The income-generating things progressed in a rather general and natural sequence with the years.

I picked a good many wild blackberries in nearby, overgrown Lowery's field, or along fencerows in the country. Sometimes I went with mother to a former fruit orchard where the berries were more abundant. She could always out pick me by a mile. How she could navigate through those thorny bushes for the berries amazed me. I normally came home with a good supply of scratches on the hands and arms, even having gone in a long-sleeved shirt. A big part of my production went into homemade jelly, cobbler, or pie, all of which I loved, blackberry being my favorite in all these categories, a preference that has remained to this day. All of mother's production went into family food, but my production, when not with her, generally was sold. I got fifty cents for a heaping gallon bucket full. A memory from those days has stuck with me. Blackberries ripen well into the hot summer, so it was a good idea to get out early and get through. On this occasion, Jack Staley, a friend and later football teammate, and I were picking in Lowery's field. Our gallon buckets were only about half full, if that, and the prospects were not too good. There was a fallen log. We sat on the ground leaning against it, eating what we had picked. As it got hotter we got lazier and lazier. We got home with very few berries and made no money berry picking that day.

Perhaps the most lucrative venture was mowing yards. By modern standards we did not get much. Typically I got fifty cents for mowing a normal yard, perhaps as much as a dollar if the yard was unusually large. While gasoline-powered mowers were in existence during those years, young boys like we were did not have them. Push mowers were what we used, and sometimes we used the one the homeowner had, but not always. I did not own one myself, but our family did. The thing that made mowing more productive was that it was essentially a weekly job throughout the growing season. During grade school there was not the after-school conflict with athletic practice. For me there was always study and piano practice, but these could be done in the evening.

During the winter I had about four homes for which I carried coal. Almost all heating in those days was by coal. Typically each family had a coal shed near the alley that coal trucks could deliver the chunked coal into. Each family had buckets specifically designed for coal. To my utter amazement I googled "coal bucket" and not only saw pictures of them but also found such buckets for sale. I had anticipated that in this day they would be strictly museum pieces, for certainly I had not seen one since leaving Illinois in 1950. I do not remember how much I earned, but it may have been as much as a dollar for each day I carried, more likely something like three dollars a week to keep the customer with a supply of coal in her buckets. Typically I would carry enough buckets to last the household for two or three days. I remember carrying for Grandma Smith (do not remember if I got paid as much for that—if so, dad may have indirectly paid it), Mrs. Lusk who lived across the street from us, the Tom Pattons, who lived across from Grandma Smith and were her dear friends, and the Gill sisters who lived on East North Avenue closer to town and operated a beauty parlor business out of their house. I may have had one or two others, but these were my regulars, going two or three times a week and carrying whatever amount was necessary to keep coal in their buckets.

Then at a certain point I landed the only regular "job" I had in Flora. Dorothy Malinsky operated, perhaps even owned or licensed, the Sears Roebuck Order Office on the north side of East North Avenue downtown in the block east of the bank. Dorothy was well respected in Flora. Her father was Dr. Bowman, a medical doctor whose routine prescription for whatever ailed the patient was "drink buttermilk," from which he became known as "Buttermilk Bowman." But in the eyes of most of us school boys, her greatest claim to fame was as being the mother of three fine athletes, Dave, Bill, and Bob, in that order age-wise. I did not know Dave or Bill, other than by reputation, but I remember Bob who was an all-state fullback on the Flora team of 1945 to 1946 and played at least one year for the University of Illinois. Apparently his father Arlo B. Malinsky had died or separated from Dorothy before the years I knew her. Whether I heard of the job and applied, or she knew of me and offered me the job, I do not remember. In any event, I worked for her for a period. As I recall, it would have been before the athletic and other activities in high school began to consume large amounts of my time, so I assume that I probably only worked for her for a number of months or perhaps a year or a little more, probably within the eighth grade or high school freshman years. I did her janitorial work, inside and out (front walk and windows included) and was her stock-room boy. Incoming shipments from Sears had to be checked off and put in the alphabetically labeled bins for pick-up by the customers, and as I recall I was to retrieve packages when customers called if I happened to be there during that time. The hours were not long, but the work was regular and she paid regularly. I do not remember what the hourly pay was, but I was very happy to get it.

One summer, generally in the mid-1940s as I recall, my friend and classmate Jack Staley heard that O. C. Forsman, who had a silver-seed hay crop on his farm a bit south of Flora's Elmwood Cemetery, would hire us at a decent hourly wage to pitch hay lying cut in the field onto the horse-drawn harvest wagons and then unload it into the threshing machine. Each of us carried a pitchfork walking near the wagon and forking the hay onto it. It was a hot job, especially since we had to wear a long-sleeved shirt buttoned at the neck in a not entirely successful attempt to keep the chaff from the threshing machine from getting on our sweaty bodies. We worked for a week or two until the job was completed and we went in for our pay. Forsman seemed not to be willing to pay us, or perhaps the amount had not been sufficiently nailed down. But we left without being paid. We went to my mother, who apparently did not have the highest regard for Forsman to start with, and she got us in the car and went back in to "talk" to Forsman and we ended up being paid the amount we thought we should have. We were physically growing boys, but a mother could still come in mighty handy on such an occasion. She could be kind and gentle, but when the situation called for something more appropriate she could rise to the occasion.

Some things do not belong to any one school year, either because they transcend two or more years or because I am unable to reliably place an event in a specific year, or because they are actually threads that run on through life, as with the next item.

The first of these is headaches. Both of my parents suffered with them. From early ages my sister and I have each suffered headaches most of our lives. My earliest memory of a disruptive headache was at about the age of eight. It was at a young friend's birthday party. All of us boys were playing outside. My head ached such that I went inside and lay down. As time went on, the headaches became more severe, "migrainous." I could feel them coming on, but could seldom get rid of them without a terrible throbbing pain and eventually a retched vomiting. During my freshman year of football at Midwestern University, in Wichita Falls, a severe headache developed on the bus to the game. I suited up but excused myself with the coach soon after the game started, going out back of our bus and vomiting before returning to the game. Thankfully, the coach did not ask me to play that night. These headaches continued into my adult years. There were three occasions (in addition to the one when a drug-addicted anesthetist punctured my spinal column during an epidural) in midlife when I begged for, and was given, a shot of Demerol. Happily, one of the benefits of aging has been the disappearance, during the last several years, of these severe headaches.

Two memories relate to the cow we had. During my later grade school years, dad purchased a cow. We had it for at least two calvings. Those calvings stick in my mind because dad was always disgusted that they were bull rather than heifer, thus disposed of quickly—but not quickly enough for me. Those little bulls loved to butt me.

The first of these two cow memories is the delicious strawberry shortcake to which it contributed. Aunt Mary, who lived just south of grandma's house, had a strawberry patch. Grandma baked the best shortcake I ever ate (not too sweet), and we provided the rich cream to pour generously over it. No strawberry shortcake since has ever compared with this.

The second memory is my cigar-behind-the-cow story. To appreciate the opportunity I sensed upon this occasion, consideration needs to be given to the years of frustration I had experienced trying to get a satisfying smoke out of the corn silk-filled, corncob pipes I made in the middle of grandma's corn patch. That said, fortune certainly seemed to smile on me the day I found in a ditch a small box of tightly rolled petite cigars, containing several in good condition. I found and sold a coke bottle at the neighborhood gas station/grocery for two cents and bought a small box of matches for a penny. Dad milked our cow in the morning and I did it after school before supper. We kept the cow in the fenced lot just north of Grandma Smith's house. The barn with the feeding stall lay on the east end of the lot and opened to the south. The feeding stall was on the west side of the barn so that the cow fed facing the west and I sat on the north side of the cow, the cow's right side, to milk. In this way, I could not be seen by anyone looking into the barn. It was this happy arrangement that presented my opportunity to light up, which I did. As I began, the milk appeared white but it got greener as I continued puffing and milking. In the end, I was hard pressed to stagger home with the bucket of milk. I threw the remaining cigars away.

As I related earlier, grandma raised "roastineer" corn on the cob. This she did for many years. As I grew, my capacity to consume large quantities of food did too. A glob of butter slapped onto a slice of bread was then applied over the entire ear of corn. Salt then stuck well to the generously buttered corn. The ears were sizable, but I could plow through the entire ear coming up for air no more than once in the process. According to my memory, possibly enhanced by years of telling, I would typically consume about six such ears along with the rest of a meal. When this was topped off with one or two bowls of that fabulous strawberry shortcake and cream, one could rightly say, "It doesn't get any better than that."

During my early youth I buddied with a few boys who went all the way through the twelve years of public school with me. The four who come to mind are Don Walker, Bob McBride, Jack Staley, and Dwight ("Dude") Dulaney. While friendly with many others, each of these was a sort of special friend for a period, meaning that we would chum around and regularly be in each other's home. Don Walker was the only one who lived in the east end, several blocks east of our home. The other three all lived west of the grade school.

About halfway between Don Walker's house and mine, there was a grove of trees where we often met. We called it "Tarzan woods." Its trees were young enough that we could climb up a short way and then ride them to the ground doing the yell Tarzan made as he swung from tree to tree in the African jungle going to rescue Jane. Our imaginations were fairly active.

As inevitably happens, my childhood years came to a close. The move into high school launched my next significant life setting.

High School

During my high school years, and for many decades before that, the name of Flora's school was Harter-Stanford Township High School, generally called simply H. S. T. H. S. My diploma and all four annuals carry that designation. The name lasted only one more year after our graduation. It was changed in 1952 to Flora Township High School (F. T. H. S.) and at some point after that to the current Flora High School (F. H. S.).

High school was a distinctly different phase of life. Not only was the school physically situated in a part of Flora considerably farther from home, almost always traversed on foot, but those years involved increasingly greater focus upon a few channels of activity that seem to have been formative of a pattern for the rest of my life. Whereas the grade school years lent themselves to a year-by-year progression horizontally, so to speak, from first through eighth grade, the four high school years are better related vertically by individual activity type.

Those clearly distinct activities are four in number, namely, church, athletics, music, and academics. Each day seemed a blend of these four. Little time or energy was left for much else. What was left was largely spent with family activity or my older friend Charlie Rankin. Time with him was either church related or was spent hunting or just imbibing nature at the farm.

One benign circumstance, however, hovered over our family throughout these years. Earlier I related dad's employment with, and eventual resignation from, the Simpson fruit distribution business, followed by a period of looking for work while earning only modest income from the city and school district. It was in the summer of

1946 that he was employed by the J. J. Lynn Oil Company. It was the most rewarding and fulfilling work experience of his life. His felicitous work situation fed through to all of us. So, my high school years were happy insofar as they were influenced by the wonderfully warm and productive relationships within that company. The Lynn management displayed deep appreciation for dad's superior work and demonstrated a sincere interest in and generous attitude toward our entire family. Only in time, eventually decades, did I come to a much greater appreciation for the immense depth of J. J. Lynn's spiritual character.

Church

No part of my life was so fully consumed with church activities as my years in high school. Flora was in one of those mainly rural regions that could be described, and often was, as "Bible Belt." It seems I was there whenever the church doors were opened. That included Sunday school and church on Sunday morning, MYF (Methodist Youth Fellowship) followed by church on Sunday evening, prayer meeting on Wednesday evening, and choir practice on some other evening. And, of course, attendance at every session of every revival during those years. This was all without parental involvement except for Sunday school on Sunday morning. In retrospect, I think my parents, especially my dad, had arrived at a judgment about church activities and preaching in small Bible Belt communities that I came to myself later on even with respect to the larger churches and communities. Dad liked the teacher of the men's class and attended it regularly. He obviously did not care for the preaching that followed in church services. I was bothered a bit by that then. In retrospect, I have developed a high degree of admiration for his approach. In the last years of his life, when he already had the brain tumor that would kill him, we were living at first in Wichita Falls, Texas. He really liked both the men's class and the preaching at First Methodist Church there, and was quite regular in attendance at both. Unfortunately, that was for such a short time before his tumor took over his life and little time was left for him to enjoy that church relationship. But what little of it there was, was on a more meaningful level to him than what had prevailed in the much smaller community of Flora.

The prayer meetings in Flora lasted at least an hour and involved singing hymns, spontaneous prayer, and personal testimony from anyone who would speak forth. Young and inexperienced as I was, I participated, as did my girlfriend, who professed to be "saved and sanctified." Charlie Rankin would normally have been there, but was less involved in speaking out. I never claimed to have been "saved and sanctified," which incidentally also required abstinence from dancing, card playing, or movies. Happily I could dispense with dancing and playing cards, but no way was I giving up movies.

Some preaching, especially in the revivals, included a healthy dose of hell fire, and a lot of invitation to repent and come down to the front, and the invitational hymns were always extended with much emotional, soul-saving pleading. One revival sticks out in my mind more clearly than any other does. The evangelist was named Comer—Brother Comer. He drove into town in a Cadillac. As he got warmed up he would raise his right foot, shaking it in the air in sync with the urgency of the words pouring profusely from his mouth in high decibel. And always there was the collection, giving to the Lord, without detailing how it got to the Lord.

It was all part of my exposure to religion in southern Illinois in those days. Somehow I survived it, though in looking back I sometimes wonder how.

Sometimes I played the piano for the hymns at MYF or the prayer meetings, though playing hymns was never my cup of tea, and others were better at it. I took pipe organ lessons during part of my high school years and occasionally would play for the evening church service. I never adapted well to the organ. I particularly disliked having to play the pedals, which I was not much good at. The seat was a flat wood bench and it seemed like my butt did not have enough padding to keep my bones off of it as I wiggled around to trying to get my clumsy feet to hit the right pedal. My pipe organ career was short and undistinguished.

One thing stands out that is most meaningful to me. I was asked to give the message at the Easter Sunrise Service my senior year. The local paper reported, "One of the most interesting services reported to this office was the sunrise service at the First Methodist Church which featured Eddie Smith as the speaker..." I had prepared my speech and memorized it, and as I recall delivered it without hesitation and with good reception. Evidently it was also meaningful to my parents, for at my graduation from high school, the elegant corrugated leather scrapbook with "Eddie" engraved in gold on the front that my parents, dad in particular, had spent some effort and expense on, included a copy of that speech.

Athletics

Aside from physical education classes, organized sports for boys included football, basketball, track, and tennis. These team sports were interscholastic, with football and basketball conducted in conference competition. The conference as it existed during my years in Flora was called the "Little Egypt Conference," taking its name from the time when drought in the corn belt to our north necessitated farmers from that rich area coming to our southern region to get grain for their livestock—all reminiscent of the days of Joseph in Egypt. The conference comprised seven schools: Flora, Salem, Mt. Carmel, Lawrenceville, Fairfield, Bridgeport, and Olney. Baseball was not one of the school-organized sports, but virtually all of those who participated in school programs were involved in summer softball leagues, and routinely a more limited group of the better players got together and played baseball teams from other towns. I've carried for life the troublesome effects of a bad left ankle sprain at Carlisle, Illinois from such a summer game.

Back then there were no interscholastic sports for girls in Illinois, or at least any that our school participated in. There was a statewide Girls Athletic Association, the G. A. A., but all its activities, so far as I know, and certainly in Flora, were strictly intramural. Equity for girls was still almost a generation in the future when my class graduated. Title IX became law in 1972.

For all four years I participated in the football, basketball, and tennis programs, lettering my junior and senior years in each of them. Spring was a particularly busy time for me every year for as soon as the basketball season was over spring football practice and tennis competition began, and I also participated my first three years in the statewide piano solo competition.

Flora was, in those days, as it had been for years, a top contender in conference competition in both football and basketball.

Football practice began each year on August 25. It was muggy and hot. A ditty that seemed to help went, "Off your ass and on your feet; out of the shade and into the heat." Our varsity coach was Bert Dancey. He had played for the University of Illinois, and it was generally known that he was the substitute for the legendary Red Grange, widely known as the "Galloping Ghost." For perspective, "In 2008, he was named the best college football player of all time by ESPN, and in 2011, he was named the Greatest Big Ten Icon by the Big Ten Network."[1]

But though I suited up for some varsity games as a sophomore, and seem to recall getting into one or two games for a few plays, I did not get to Bert's (Coach Dancey's) practices till my last two years. Only three boys from my class were on the varsity second team our sophomore year though none of them were "starters," that is, on the first team. These three practiced with the varsity and not with the freshman-sophomore team that was coached by Dick Conley. One of these three did not play beyond his sophomore year, but the other two, Don Hall (fullback) and Harold

---

1 See http://en.wikipedia.org/wiki/Red Grange.

Davis (pulling guard) not only did but in later years were all conference selections.

I simply do not remember much about my freshman year, except that I was on the freshman-sophomore team, but I was not on the first team and do not remember how much I got to play. It was dramatically different my sophomore year. I was captain of the team, played fullback and linebacker and the team won every game. I recall that by halftime of our first game, playing Salem, our stiffest competition, my eyes were swollen nearly shut from the effect of tackling from the linebacker position—but worn proudly as a badge of honor. There were, of course, no face masks in those days, and the tackles were largely head down into the mid-level as runners came through the line.

Salem was usually Flora's toughest conference challenge, and this year it was the first game of our freshman-sophomore season. I was uptight about the situation, feeling a lot of responsibility on me for the first time. Adding to my anxiety was the boy who played fullback for Salem, my counterpart on the other team. His name was Stonecipher. Well I remembered, from the years 1943 to 1946, one Keith Stonecipher who played both basketball and football for teams that gave Flora fits.[1] They doubtless were related some way.

As I recall, on the first play Salem ran Stonecipher carried the ball, coming right through the line. I lowered my head and hit him waist high, taking him down for only a short gain. That was all I needed to jack up my confidence and fire up my spirits for the rest of the night. I recall feeling from that point a fierce determination to win and using some pretty strong language going up and down the line shouting encouragement to our linemen. I got enough hits to batter my face and eyes. And I'm sure I carried the ball many times

---

1 Salem Community High School established a Sports Hall of Fame in 1985, inducting only a few athletes from its entire past each year. Keith Stonecipher was so inducted in 1990 (http://salemwildcathalloffame.com/1990/keith-stonecipher/).

for gains and perhaps a touchdown or two. The main thing is, we won! We beat Salem, our toughest foe!

In all my days in Flora the football team ran from what is known as the "single-wing" formation. The line was unbalanced to the right or left, meaning that the two tackles played side by side on the heavy side of the line, there being a guard and end on one side of the center and a guard, two tackles, and an end on the other, the heavy, side. The quarterback, while occasionally taking a snap from center, lined up close to the line off slightly to the heavy side and served primarily as a blocking back. The other three backs were the wing back, close behind the heavy-side end, fullback a bit further back and slightly to the heavy side from the center, and the tailback still further back directly behind the center. Virtually all snaps from center came to either the fullback or tailback. Passes were not frequent and were generally thrown by either the fullback or tailback. The single-wing formation was primarily a running, not passing, formation. Flora's playbook did not seem to change much from year to year. Coach Dancey said he did not care if the other team knew our plays because if we ran them right they could not stop us. The bulk of our plays went to the heavy side. Those to that side bore a number indicating whether the line was heavy to the left or right, 51 being heavy to the left, and 52 heavy to the right. The letter A through D designated which two line positions the blocker and ball carrier were to go through, and wide was to be an end run. Most of our game was running the 51 and 52 series. Not as exciting as the passing teams of later years, but very effective if correctly and vigorously executed.

My junior year was a good one. We were conference champs, losing only the second game of the season to Centralia, a non-conference school at least three times larger than ours. We won all our other eight games. For all nine games we outscored our opponents 236 to 58. Only four boys from my class were starters that year, Don Hall at fullback, Harold Davis at light-side (pulling) guard, Jack Staley at left tackle, and myself at quarterback (blocking back).

Only when Don Hall went to the bench did I rotate to fullback, which I always liked because carrying the ball was more glamorous than blocking. Some of our players made all conference that junior year, but I'm unable to give the number or names with confidence. I was never named to the all-conference team.

The one play from that junior year that sticks out in my mind was in the Salem game. It was the pass play from fullback Don Hall to tailback Owen Bender. This was not in the playbook, but we were behind 6 to 0 in the second half. Owen Bender called signals. He told Duck Rice, the center, to snap the ball to Don Hall in a play that would move a bit to the right and Owen would light out down the field and Don was to throw it as far as he could because Owen said he would get under it. I remember looking up when the ball was in the air to see Owen and the Salem safety going neck and neck, both scrambling for the ball. Owen emerged with it. The safety was out of the play and Owen hightailed it for the end zone. We won every other game that year (except the one to Centralia) by at least two touchdowns. The final score against Salem was 12-6 in favor of Flora. Here is the short write-up in the annual about that game:

> The Salem Wildcats received a hard jolt at Salem. The Flora Wolves fought their way to a second half win after being behind 6 to 0 at the half. Flora turned on the heat in the third quarter to score on a long pass and tie up the game. Again in the early part of the fourth, a Salem pass was intercepted on the 30-yard line and Ed Smith plunged over to make the score 12 to 6.

Oddly enough, I have no memory of having made that touchdown, only of that fabulous pass play. Could the touchdown have come from that one play the quarterback ran, or was there some reason Don was out of the game and I was running as fullback?

Sadly, of the four classmates of mine who were starters our junior year, Jack Staley and Harold Davis died of heart attacks very early in their adult lives, and Don Hall died only a few years later from cancer.

One of the proudest aspects of that season is that the November 5, 1948, issue of the Chicago Daily News featured our team on the front page of its sports section. At the top of the page was a picture of the eleven starters in offensive formation (we lined up in T-formation before shifting to the single wing). The picture was subscribed by a summary of the season and the name of each player. Below that was the large, bold headline—"'STARLESS' FLORA STARS." The full-length column of text was captioned "Close '48 Grid Year at Olney." Flora is shown to be 243.8 miles south of Chicago, so this was quite a thing. Naturally, when dad put my elegant leather "scrapbook" together, a copy of that section of that paper was included. The picture itself, shown below, is also in the 1949 annual.

Seven of the eleven starters on the 1948 to 1949 football squad were seniors. They were an outstanding group of scrappers. On paper, our line was heavier the next year, but one has to conclude that it was not quite as competitive. From being conference champions my junior year, we slipped to a much less lustrous season as seniors. All starters were seniors. We ended the eight-game season with five wins and three losses. For several years the opening game was with Mt. Vernon, a town considerably larger than Flora, and we beat it so consistently that they dropped us, hence one less game that year. We opened the year with a 6–0 win over Centralia, the only team that had beaten our championship team the year before. Then, however, Salem beat us 14 to 7 scoring just before the end of the game, followed by losses of 14 to 0 at Mt. Carmel and 19 to 7 at Lawrenceville. We won the rest of our games, but losing the first three conference games made these victories a bit less meaningful. For the year we outscored our opponents 161 to 66, but that did not do much for the win–loss column. The one game that I felt we really got beat was at Lawrenceville. They had a fullback and a halfback that kept ripping us to shreds. Flora scored only once, and that was in the last quarter. The low spot for the season, however, was the game at Mt. Carmel. Their field was on the bank of the Wabash River, the boundary between Illinois and Indiana, and it was so muddy from overflow or rain that we could not keep our feet. Time after time, in running the ball, our backs slipped and fell. We failed to score at all. Mt. Carmel had not beaten Flora in fifteen years, and our game was one of only three they won that year.

Looking back it is obvious to me that in football in particular, though really in all my activities, dad took an intense interest and developed an inner, unspoken pride. I believe I could feel it even then though he seldom gave me any verbal praise that I can recall, nor did he often criticize. He was just always there and seemingly involved with me in the event. But there are two statements regarding my football talents, one critical and one complimentary, that have stuck in my mind. They have been deferred till this point because I do not remember at what point in my high school football days he made them, and perhaps they are recalled because I heard them more than once. Critically, I could never tackle hard enough to satisfy him fully. His comment on the subject was, "I want to hear their bones rattle." Had he survived till today, he could have seen plenty of that in the fierce collisions in college and professional football today, the subject of much medical concern in recent times, particularly on the effect of concussions or any knocks to the head. I've wondered in more recent times if his early midlife brain tumor might not have come from his having delivered or absorbed many of those impacts on that fabulous 1922 team.

On the other side of that coin, he remarked favorably about my ability, running low and hard through the line, to pick up additional yardage carrying tacklers along after they hit me. Memories of having done that so often have stuck with me. It was a great feeling, and as I watch football games today, normally only if Texas Tech is playing, I understand how strong ball carriers must feel when they are able to do that. Of course, it seems to me that I heard more of the tackling than the ball carrying comments. I do not remember making too many real long ground-gaining runs, but two have stuck with me from my sophomore year in the seventy-to-ninety-yard category for what would have been touchdowns except that they were both called back for penalty. The longer ninety-yard run was called back for one of our linemen having lined up offside. The other run would have stood up except my good friend, our pulling guard, the late Gerald French, clipped the nearest of my pursuers who was so far behind me at that point as to constitute no threat. But both of these were in games that we won by multiple touchdowns. Typically, dad did not comment on those plays at all.

Over the years I've observed some mothers becoming rabidly involved in their young children's games. Such was far removed from my mother. Except in one aspect, I have no memory of her showing any particular reaction to my athletic activity, good or bad. Probably she knew dad's commitment and involvement was plenty for me. She did show concern that I might be injured, but probably knew better than to just express the concern. It was my piano teacher, Miss Ellis who would say she hoped I did not injure my hands. Nothing happened along that line to seriously impede my piano playing. One injury to my hands has, however, had a lifelong, and increasingly severe, result. It was in football. Well do I remember the immediate event, though I do not remember whether it was in a game or a scrimmage in practice, or maybe just in tackling practice where opposite facing lines would be formed, basically equal in length; the coach would toss the ball to the next player in the ball-carrying line who was expected to give his best effort, within a reasonable range of running width, to evade the tackler coming from the front of the opposite line. Upon completion of each such instance, the players would run to the back of the opposite line from which they had just come. What I do remember is that I was carrying the ball and applying a stiff arm to the incoming tackler. At the conclusion of the play in question I looked in shock at the thumb on my left hand. It was sprung back from its base joint so that it looked like the cocked hammer on a pistol ready to be fired. I immediately and successfully jerked it back in place with my right hand, and do not remember any severe impediment from it either in that game or practice or in my piano playing back then. Nor do I remember it affecting my midlife return to the serious study of piano performance. However, in recent decades that injury has significantly manifested itself in that I have no grip whatsoever in my left hand. One cannot grip anything, such as trying to unscrew the lid on a container, without the thumb being a big part of the effort. No pressure at all can be applied by my left thumb. It flops back on the slightest application of the barest minimal force. I rationalize that I was able, in that midlife period, to play the piano without severe effect because the thumb motion in striking the piano key was essentially at a ninety-degree angle to that applied in unscrewing the lid of a jar.

Basketball practice always started on Saturday morning after our last football game on Friday night. As with football, I was active as a freshman and sophomore in both basketball and tennis, but it was in football that my memories are the clearest for those years, especially the sophomore year, and the annuals were not much help on the freshman-sophomore games in the major sports of football and basketball or of the results in the less emphasized competitions in track or tennis, for they contained only a group picture of the squad in all of these.

The starting five of one of Flora's best basketball teams, at least of the late forties and early fifties, was composed entirely of members of my 1950 graduating class during our final year (1949–1950) and part of our junior year, and at least eighty percent of the starters the rest of our junior year. My relative, Dale Smith (his great grandfather was the older brother of my grandfather) and Jack Theriot (he pronounced it THIR-i-et; a major league baseball player of later decades was pronounced, I believe, TERR-i-oh), were the most skilled and productive. Dale played forward and Jack point guard. Each attended college on basketball scholarship, Dale at Indiana State in Terre Haute, Indiana, and Jack at Southern Illinois University (SIU) in Carbondale, Illinois. I understand Jack became captain of that team.

High School

Unlike in football, I was a starter for only part of those two seasons. I started for probably the majority of games our junior year, but fewer times my senior year and then only in the earlier part of the season, which was the better year of the two in outcome. I played guard, but my ball handling skills were appreciably less than those of our regular point guard. I did win the trophy one of these years for highest percentage of free throws made, the winner's name each year being engraved and maintained for a period in the school's trophy display window. What my status might have been otherwise is speculative at best, but it is my belief that a particular vulnerability hindered my being more effective as these seasons progressed. I speak of a seemingly unique tenderness in the soles of my feet under the constant rigors of fast offense and man-to-man defense. We did not, of course, have shoes of the quality now generally available. The team had a liquid applicant called Tough Skin for the soles of our feet that was supposed to toughen them to the rigorous starting, running, stopping, and other demands of impact of foot on the hardwood floor. My feet were, I think, by far the most tender and vulnerable on the squad. The Tough Skin would produce what seemed to be a thick callous on the impacted parts of the sole (I have short, wide feet with a very high instep). But in my case, perhaps only in my case, would these slabs of apparent callous tear off along with the outer surface of the skin exposing a tender substratum of the epidermis, particularly on the ball and front pads of the foot. I well remember coming in after at least one game with blood coming through two pairs of sox. On the court, this condition became increasingly painful and doubtless limiting. It was increasingly hard to apply maximum effort in hard games as this phenomenon progressed. Increasingly I came off the bench for portions of games, while continuing to do my best to compete. I did not like not being out on the court in games, but probably suffered less with reduced playing time.

As juniors, our overall win–loss record was 12 to 8, while in conference games it was 7 to 5, losing twice each to Salem and

Lawrenceville and once to Olney. Our victory against Olney that year was at Olney. As time was about to expire we were down by two points and I was fouled in the act of shooting. Unless I could hit both free throws, we would lose the game. I made them both and we went on to win in overtime. We ended the season in fourth place in the conference, behind Salem, Lawrenceville, and Olney.

But we did not lose any starters from the 1948 to 1949 season as we moved into our senior year (1949–1950), and the outcome was very different. Apparently our annual had to go to press between the end of the regular season and statewide season-ending elimination tournaments leading to the final state champion (the same situation existed the previous year also). At the end of the regular season our won loss record was 21 to 3. We lost the opener to Centralia and then the next to last game against Paris, in overtime. In between, perhaps because of injuries, we lost to conference team Bridgeport 43–41 after having beaten them earlier 52 to 38. Our conference record was 11 to 1.

Two things stand out about that year. One of the prestigious early season tournaments was the Paris Holiday Tournament. We had played eight games before that with a 7-to-1 record. Immediately before that tournament we had attained a ranking of sixth statewide. During our years, there were no classes or divisions based upon school size. Every school in the state was ranked as against every other school in the state. The big prize that year was that we won the Paris tournament in a thriller, beating Paris in the championship game, on its own floor, by a score of 44 to 43. Our center Fred Forth (who stood 6 feet 4 inches) was captain of the all-tournament team. Dale and Jack were also on that team. Our statewide rank rose to number two, behind only Mt. Vernon which went on to win the state championship at the end of the season (for the second year in a row as I recall) and whose center, Max Hooper, set an all-time tournament high scoring record up to that point at 34 (Belcher of Anna-Jonesboro, where my Uncle Harold lived, had set it much earlier at 33, and it has been broken again, probably several times, in later years). Hooper was also quarterback on Mt. Vernon's football team, which we beat our junior year 33 to 12, after which Mt. Vernon bowed out of football competition with Flora, as previously stated.

All eyes were upon Flora as the season-ending elimination tournament play began. The District Tournament was in Flora. We won both games there to advance to the Regional Tournament held at Lawrenceville. Our first District game was against nearby Clay City which we blew out. Dale Smith put on a shooting clinic the likes of which, aside from Cheryl Swoopes in 1993 to win the NCAA championship for the Texas Tech women's team and some of the games Michael Jordan played for the Chicago Bulls, I have never seen. Dale scored 44 points in the normal 32-minute game. I do not know if he missed a shot all night long, from the floor or the free throw line, and an incredible number of his shots were long bombs, such that it came to the point that when he set and released his beautiful arching shot, an awed hush gripped the arena before it swished the net. Those shots only counted two points then, not three as they have now for many years. He would have scored well into the fifties otherwise. Statewide eyes were upon him. Unfortunately, though we won the next game, he only scored two that night as we advanced to the Regional Tournament at Lawrenceville.

We won the first game, against whom I do not recall. The championship game, from which the winner would go to the Sweet Sixteen at the University of Illinois in Champaign/Urbana, was against Lawrenceville on its home court. We had beaten Lawrenceville on both teams' home courts during the year, by scores of 53 to 48 and 53 to 45. One problem; Lawrenceville had a player named Wright. He was a slithering type of athlete; thin, quick and extremely agile. I remember seeing him run a kickoff back for a touchdown in football. He was giving us fits on the court that night. The coach thought I was good on defense. I was on the bench during a good part of the game, but someone had to stop Wright. Coach Hooker told me, "Get in there and watch him!" That is precisely what I did. I watched him make me look flatfooted. Repeatedly I resolved to keep him from getting to the goal for one of his countless lay-ups only to find myself fouling him as he again went around me for a lay-up. I fouled out in no time, and of course he hit all his free throws too. He ended up scoring 33 points and leading Lawrenceville to a one-point victory and a trip to the Sweet Sixteen—a bitter defeat for our squad after a brilliant season. Wright went on to play basketball for the University of Illinois.

Tennis competitions were generally played team-against-team, with individual players matched against counterparts in singles matches, followed by doubles teams similarly matched. Counterparts were determined basically by team ranking, pitting one team's players against those of the other school based upon each school's ranking of its players, both individually and in doubles pairs. Flora had the premier tennis player of the entire region in John ("Johnny") Powless. No one could beat him, and he played only singles. Don Walker and I were doubles partners, there being two other doubles teams. Only a limited number of interscholastic competitions were held each year, and I do not recall Flora playing in elimination tournaments at the season's end. Since tennis competition came so late in the school year, it was never included in that year's annual, which generally commented on the prior year's results.

John Powless always beat whomever he played against, although a good player from Mattoon may have given him trouble in one of our years. John started public school in the same class as our 1950 class, but was held back one year so that he was a year behind my class. Other than in tennis he was not a starter on either the football or the basketball varsity team during our junior and senior years. He was simply out of everyone else's class though in tennis. His father, Cecil ("Kayo") Powless had been the Southern Illinois amateur champion more than once. They had a tennis court in their backyard, the only private court and one of only a few courts in town (two others on East North Avenue [then U. S. 50] near my home and two at the high school).

John Powless went on not only to become a good basketball player for Flora in the 1951 class but also at Murray State University, but his career in both basketball and tennis ended up going beyond anything we might have imagined when we were playing with him in high school. His reputation is literally worldwide, especially in tennis.[1] I suppose I should brag about once winning a set from him on the court at his house. He was probably not feeling well that day.

At the end of our senior tennis season, an intra-squad elimination tournament was held to determine the two top players. All of us agreed to give one of the two trophies to John Powless and to compete for the other one. It is my recollection that the championship match for the second trophy was between my long and dear childhood friend, Don Walker and me. All through high school Don and I, being not only good friends but also fairly evenly matched in tennis skills, had played practice sets or matches against each other. One of us would win on a given occasion and the other on another occasion. It is probably fair to say that we were next in team rank below Powless. It is my memory that I won that year-end match, though I would not be surprised if Don might remember it otherwise. But who is going to pay much attention to the memory of either of us octogenarians? Nor does either of us really care at this point.

Such was the athletic portion of my high school activities.

Music

Two of the three musical instruments I played were more chores than fun. They were experience in different musical activity, but in the final analysis were happily dropped during my high school years. The cornet, which I had started in seventh grade under the band direction of E. C. Jacobs, continued through my sophomore year. The change of directors at the end of that year was my opportunity

---

1 See http://en.wikipedia.org/wiki/John_Powless.

to terminate that activity, which I did. It was probably in either my freshman or sophomore year that I began taking pipe organ lessons from Mrs. Harriet Sailor, the organist at First Methodist Church. That less-than-distinguished career and its termination have already been described.

It was the piano that held me captive. My involvement with it through grade school has been given. As there stated, while still in grade school, I wanted to be either a lawyer or a concert pianist. One would have to have been something of a prodigy, coming out of Flora, to have had a leg up on the latter. But several things gave wings to my dreams about it. Their sequence, or just what year each occurred, is not important, just that each event was such an inspiration at that stage of my life to perform great piano music. I expect these things all occurred over a very short time span of one or two, perhaps three, years. Two popular orchestras came to Flora to play in the new high school gymnasium. One was Sigmund Romberg's orchestra, the other Phil Spitalny's All-Girl Orchestra. Each had a pianist that inspired me. I remember especially the girl pianist playing Gershwin's Rhapsody in Blue. José Iturbi appeared in movies, where his seemingly short fingers flying over the keys excited me. Maybe nothing moved me so much as the 1945 movie "A Song To Remember," featuring Cornel Wilde playing the part of Chopin, whose nostalgic passion for the fate of his native Poland stirs one's blood in the performance of his "Heroic" Polonaise in A-Flat major, the melody of which became the popular song by the same title as the movie, the lyrics starting "Till the end of time..."

Having done well in the district and state piano solo competition while in the eighth grade, it was natural that I should enter into these annual competitions at the high school level. Doing so meant a great deal of intensive practice, all of which came to the attention of the local folks and I was invited to play solos at various events on many occasions. Only one do I remember most preciously, at the Flora Women's Club, or perhaps it was called the Business and Professional Women's Club. Whatever, it was meeting in the upstairs auditorium over the Carnegie Library, the place where the local piano teachers held all their student recital programs, one of which I played in every year from the third or fourth grade through my senior year. Grandma Reaugh was a member of the group and was in attendance on the day in question. At the conclusion of my playing, Grandma came up to me and said, "Eddie, you make me so proud." I would not take a million dollars for that memory, which brings tears to my eyes on each recollection.

Never did my rating in any of the high school competitions rise to the level attained in the eighth grade. Students at all high school classifications, freshman through senior level, were performing without designation insofar as the judges were concerned. I participated only my freshman, sophomore, and junior years, realizing by my senior year that I would not be continuing my music education but would focus upon the goal of becoming a lawyer. The performance rating was either a first, second, or third. These were based upon one's own performance, not how it compared with that of any other performer. If one played very well, a first rating was normally given, even though some of the others might also have been so rated. Only those who won a first could advance from the district competition to the state level. I got second ratings my freshman and sophomore years, with a first at the district level my junior year. I did not play well at the state meet and received a third. As I have said, particularly at the state meet, students coming from the larger cities or from families that launched their children with specially privileged musical training were thrown together. Miss Ellis had told me in my senior year that she could not carry me further and that I would have to go somewhere like St. Louis to get the type of training needed to advance.

The compositions that I played at these three contests were: as a freshman, Chopin's *Polonaise* in A, Op. 40, No. 1, known as his "Military" *Polonaise*; as a sophomore, Rachmaninoff's Prelude in G minor, Op. 23, No. 5; as a junior, Chopin's Etude Op. 10, No. 12, in C minor, known as his "Revolutionary" Etude, written by him in contemplation of the bombardment of Warsaw.

My feeling is that I played the "Revolutionary" very well at the district meet, and was thus not surprised by my "First" rating there. Equally was I aware of not playing it well at the state meet, so was not surprised at the "Third" there. That state performance was a disappointing and most worthily forgettable experience, rather like losing a very important ball game.

Perhaps the most significant musical experience of my high school years took place in the spring of my junior year on the evening of April 5, 1949, which in thinking back I believe would have fallen between the district and state competitions mentioned above, while I was still feeling good about the "first" rating at the District competition. Grand pianos in Flora were scarce. Aside from a used one Aunt Mary had acquired, the only ones I was aware of in those years were the one in the Carnegie Library building and the one on stage in the Washington School gym, where grade school band concerts were held. I've subsequently learned of two others in private homes, but I was not aware of them then, or at least I never had the opportunity to play on either of them. Playing on a grand, including just practicing, was something special for me in those days.

Thus was I pleased when the First Methodist Church board authorized the acquisition of a new grand piano. Further, I was honored when called upon to serve with Harriet Sailor and Esther Gatewood by going with the Baldwin dealer in Olney to the Baldwin factory, which was then in Cincinnati, to select a piano. The dealer in Olney was Orville Crackel, husband of one of my mother's dear friends from earlier years in Flora.

With this new Baldwin grand piano in town, a recital was planned, featuring vocalist Robert Brentlinger and me as the pianist, both students of Miss Ellis, in concert. It took place on the evening of April 5, 1949. Robert sang eight songs in three stage appearances, with Miss Ellis accompanying, and I played nine pieces in four appearances. His three were interspersed in my nine. I opened and closed the program. The pieces I played were:

> First appearance:
>   Prelude in G Minor, Rachmaninoff
>   *Turkish March,* Mozart
> Second appearance:
>   *Revolutionary Etude,* Chopin
>   Sonata *Pathetique,* Beethoven
> Third appearance:
>   *Liebestraum,* Lizst
>   Polonaise in C-Sharp Minor, Chopin
>   *Polish Dance,* Scharwenka
> Fourth appearance:
>   Polonaise in A-Flat Major, Chopin
>   *Rhapsody in Blue,* Gershwin

I played only the first of its three movements of the Beethoven *Pathetique* sonata. The Liebestraum (*Dream of Love*) is the last of Liszt's three compositions by that name, and the most famous. *Rhapsody in Blue* was the piano solo version. Miss Ellis had edited out for me a good bit of the middle part of the portion that preceded the beginning of the main theme, as it would have been too long otherwise. While the program does not include any encore, it seems to me that I did play a substantial piece as an encore, which, by my recollection, was Percy Grainger's arrangement of the first movement of Tchaikovsky's B♭ Minor Piano Concerto, from which was derived the music for the romantically enchanting song *Tonight We Love.*

This event, which came off well within the local community, was the pinnacle of my musical performance career prior to the period of serious classical piano studies and concert performance during my late forties and early fifties as will be more fully described as that part of my life story unfolds.

It would have also been in this time period when Orville Crackel invited me, as both a favor to him and an opportunity for me, to play in Olney on his local radio program, which I did. As I recall, it was the Tchaikovsky concerto version that I played there.

There was a terribly somber event that occurred on the memorable day of Tuesday, April 5, 1949. Saint Anthony's Hospital in Effingham, thirty-three miles north of Flora and widely used by patients from our area, was destroyed in the night by fire in which seventy-seven people perished.[1] The excellent new high school band director that school year was Herb Lee. His wife and their newborn infant were there. Both perished. The fire is dated April 4, because it started just before midnight on that date, but its destruction through the night was news all over Flora by the dawn on April 5. It was a bit of a burden to carry into the evening's recital.

As mentioned, I did not enter the interscholastic piano solo competition in my senior year. However, I did play in Miss Ellis's annual recital program in the spring of 1950. The composition performed was Malaguena, by Ernesto Lecuona (1894–1963). Clarence Smith, the locally prominent and successful lawyer who delivered the eulogy at Grandpa Reaugh's funeral, was in the audience that evening. His impressive presence was occasioned by his younger daughter Maureen being on the program. I think it was probably Charlie Rankin who overheard Clarence make a remark about me to the general effect of "remarkable" or "amazing." Frankly, I did not think my performance was anything out of the ordinary, but such words coming from him were a treasure to me in those days, and even now as I return in memory.

The piano in the upstairs auditorium over the Carnegie Library, upon which all of us piano students in Flora would have played in our various teachers' annual recitals, was a Knabe. The centrally located library, etched firmly in memory from those years, is no longer there, having been replaced by a beautiful one-story modern structure. Nor is the Knabe there. But, community heirloom as it had become, it is now on non-touchable display in the museum

---

1 See http://en.wikipedia.org/wiki/St._Anthonyh%27s_Hospital_Fire and http://effinghamdailynews.com/features/x519461560/60-Years-Later.

portion of the historical railroad depot, into the restoration of which my younger sister and husband, Mary Anne and Ron Ayers, have poured incredible energy and personal resources as well as leadership. Many contributed not only financially, but also by donating artifacts. The museum is itself a worthy and intriguing testament to the historical life of Flora and its surroundings.

Looking back into that priceless scrapbook dad handed to me at graduation, I find a handwritten note from Miss Ellis written at Christmas, 1969 in the later part of her life. The last portion of it reads:

> Have a happy Christmas & when you come to Flora come see me. I am usually at home. Thank you for being my best pupil.
> Very sincerely
> Mary L. Ellis
> I often think of the concert you & Bob Brentlinger gave.

Unless I'm overlooking something, the spring of 1950, my senior year, must have been a bit less hectic than spring in any of my prior three high school years. While I was involved on the tennis team and in its competitions, there would have been, for me, no spring football and no piano competitions.

Academic Scholarship

Reflecting back now with the perspective of an octogenarian, and in particular this octogenarian, my conviction is that the seeds for my academic success in high school were planted long before I was born. Three notable souls in Judeo-Christian tradition, namely, David, Jeremiah, and St. Paul, each claimed some form of an individuality before his earthly birth.[2] Each of them, though exceptional, was human. I'm confident that my own essential being, like theirs, existed long before birth in this life, like every other human being.

---

2 Ps. 139:13–16 (David); Jer. 1:4–5; Gal. 1:15 (Paul).

It was in my early adolescence, in the latter levels of grade school, that the goal of perfecting my mind rose to a high priority, clothed with a feeling of urgency and immediacy. The practical effect was to strive to do well in my academic studies—to excel to the best of my ability, shunning satisfaction in favor of trying to do better. The world is a big oyster, and there are many pearls far more lustrous than I, to the point that any comparison is a most humbling experience. Indeed, there are those within my own family whose academic records exceed my own. But in the course of my own four years in high school, those who do the calculation found that my record stood higher than any other in my class of one hundred twenty-five students, by the barest margin. Here, as in any competition, the winner is so often determined by a hair's breadth. I do not recall having had during those school years any feeling of competing with my classmates, and certainly I had no way of knowing who did what, save in the few instances where a classmate might spontaneously reveal information from a given class. In the "scrapbook" from my parents, there is not only a transcript of my high school academic record and copies of the eight semester report cards from the four years, but there is also a copy of the front page of the *Flora Daily News-Record,* dated May 23, 1950, with the headline, "Outstanding Members of Senior Class Recognized." Various honors recipients were named, with priority of listing given to the top academic students, as follows:

> In Senior Recognition ceremonies at the high school here this morning, the top ten members of this year's senior class were announced...
>
> For the first time in many years, a boy ranked at the top of the class, with Eddie Smith carrying off high honors on a 4.97 rating, out of a possible 5.00.

The courses I took in high school, by year, were:

Freshman (1946–1947): Mathematics (2 semesters), English I (2 semesters), Latin I (2 semesters), Geography (1 semester), and Health & Safety (1 semester)
Sophomore (1947–1948): Algebra (2 semesters), English II (2 semesters), Ancient History (2 semesters), Latin II (2 semesters)
Junior (1948–1949): Plain Geometry (2 semesters), English III (2 semesters), Physics (2 semesters), and Typing (2 semesters)
Senior (1949–1950): Advanced Algebra (1 semester), Trigonometry (1 semester), English IV (2 semesters), American History (2 semesters), Stenography I (1 semester), and Stenography II (1 semester)

It is hard to say which course or courses might have been the most valuable. I could say a lot for each one of them. Perhaps I gave more credit to the Latin than any one other, more out of an appreciation for its great value in word study than of a lack of appreciation for the other courses. It is my belief that vocabulary weighed heavily in a lot of the intelligence tests given as one moved on in various fields of study. Well I remembered being fascinated by the desire to increase vocabulary, to the point that I resorted to often reading the Webster's dictionary in search of new words and their derivation. In particular, I think that the college entrance exam, the LSAT (law school aptitude test), and the test given during the Korean War upon the results from which a four-year deferment for college depended (upon which I will comment at the appropriate point later), gave considerable weight to vocabulary, upon which I always did well.

Some brows may be raised as to why I would have taken stenography. Doubtless it was considered a course for girls, not boys. Why would any boy—any *real* boy—sign up for a girl's course like stenography? Aside from perhaps lack of aptitude, I expect a lot of fellows would have signed up for it had they considered that they would be surrounded by girls without male competition or interference. I was the only boy in my class of twenty-four, a really choice ratio I thought. But it was neither my own foresight nor that of my parents that prompted my signing up for stenography both semesters of my senior year. Rather, it was advice from Elberta Hubbell, the wife of the high school principal. The Hubbells were friends of my parents. Mrs. Hubbell said that it would be invaluable in taking notes during my college course work. And for certain classes during my early college years that turned out to be true. In the long run, however, the time taken to transcribe the shorthand back to typed transcripts was needed for other involvements and I let the proficiency eventually fade away. That I took to it enthusiastically though, among all the girls, might be evidenced by the fact that I was the only student in the first semester of Stenography I that was permitted to move, during the spring semester, to the second semester of Stenography II so as to emerge with the equivalent of having taken stenography for four full semesters instead of just two. Again I was the only boy in a different set of girls. I do not think this accomplishment (in stenography, not girls) meant much to the football coach, but it served an appropriate purpose of mine at the time.

Thanks to evidentiary detail assembled by dad in the "scrapbook," an activity that was surely indicative of much of my life activity to follow began to emerge. From its placement within the scrapbook itself, and in keeping with my refreshed memory, during my junior year I entered a nationwide essay contest on the topic "Why Democracy Works" sponsored by the Elks Lodge (Benevolent and Protective Order of the Elks). The sequence of progressive levels at which essays were judged were local, district, state, and national. The scrapbook contains a copy of the essay, three newspaper clippings sans date, and one Western Union telegram. The first clipping, a column at the top of the front page of the *Flora Daily News-Record* was entitled "Eddie Smith Wins First Prize in Elks Essay Contest," reported the local result and prizes. The first price was a $50.00 U. S. Bond (a more princely sum in the spring of 1949 than as I write at the end of 2012). It stated that winners of first and second prize would be sent to the district contest, but that the first place winner would automatically be sent to the state contest. Winners in the state contest were to be sent to the national contest. Prizes increased in amount at each successive level. The clipping concluded quoting "out-of-town judges" as saying that my essay "is outstanding in idea, principle, and phraseology."

The other two clippings, also without date, came from the two local newspapers that Flora then had (the aforesaid *News-Record* as well as *The Flora Sentinel*) and reported that I had won third place in the district contest, the *News-Record* saying, "There were 472 entries in district competition, with 30 high schools represented."

The telegram, sent from Springfield by the vice-president of the Southeast District BPOE, also announced my third place win in the southeast district of Illinois, and the award of a fifty-dollar prize. The latter two clippings as well as the telegram all indicated that I was to attend the award ceremony in Lawrenceville. Apparently, my essay won no prize at the state level.

There follows in the scrapbook, at what would appear to be the senior-year level, an essay entitled "What Is Americanism?" It is inserted within the same plastic page holder with the *News-Record* announcement of the previously mentioned clipping entitled, "Outstanding Members of the Senior Class...," but no indication of what it was written for or any result if entered in a competition.

Next in the scrapbook is a copy of my "Easter Sunrise Address—April 9, 1950," along with the *News-Record* clipping mentioning it.

Finally, inserted in the same plastic page as the Easter address is a copy of my essay on the topic "Peace with Honor for America," entered in the Illinois competition sponsored by the VFW Ladies Auxiliary and the Chicago Daily News. With it is an undated clipping announcing an 18-year-old Collinsville boy as winner of that competition and a 16-year-old Chicago girl as second-place winner. The newspaper from which this clipping was taken is not apparent, but it must have been either the *News-Record* or a paper from my area, for then a paragraph follows in bold print saying, "Eddie Smith, 17, of Flora, (Ill.) was third in the judging and received $50..." This clipping says "there were more than 3,000 entries in the Illinois competition," which was also preliminary to the national competition.

It appears that I seem to have been stuck at a $50.00 prize limit, but that was not a small amount in those days.

Interlacings through High School Years

Several events or factors were important during all or part of my high school years, yet do not fit snugly within any of the four "vertical" fields of activity, and in most cases not within any one year. My close companionship with Charley Rankin as well as a constant battle with acne commenced with my earliest teen year (thirteen) roughly with beginning of eighth grade, and both continued through high school.

My Upstairs Loft

My sister, Mary Anne, was born January 22, 1939, six and one-third years after my birth. My best recollection is that for most of the years between our births, our house had both an indoor bathroom and a basement. While I can remember the existence of the privy, I do not have any recollection of ever having used it or our not having an indoor bathroom. I do remember, vaguely, from a mental image during excavation and construction, the addition of the basement. That must have been in about 1936, or at least between then and Mary Anne's birth. The only entrance to the basement was by an outdoor stairway from the back of the house. It was immediately on the south side of the back porch, but I do not remember if the back porch was there when the basement went in or was put in years later as part of the construction of my upstairs loft.

In my earliest years, our living area comprised one floor of four rooms plus bath. We had a kitchen (with pantry), mother and dad's bedroom (the bath being between those two rooms), living room, and a fourth room that became mine, and then Mary Anne's and mine.

There was no privacy in our family, insofar as bathroom and nudity was concerned so long as it was just mother, dad, and me. That same condition continued during Mary Anne's early life. But at some point well before her menarche (puberty), probably toward the end of my grade school years, "our" bedroom became hers, and dad, hiring certain contractors, converted our attic to a wonderful loft for me that essentially extended over all four rooms of the house. The usable space was not, however, as great as that of the four rooms below because of the sloping roof that, similar to what exists in A-frame construction, closed off some of the outer areas of the floor space. The constriction of the slant was greatly diminished by the construction of three dormers, the two on the north and south being of considerable width, so that the usable space in these two dormers extended to the outer exterior walls of the house. The south dormer became my study area. The loft constituted one large room, plus closet and bath (sink, toilet, and shower). The stairway up to the loft came off of the south side of the then-enclosed back porch, which may have been added when the loft was put in. The back porch was never heated. We never had any air conditioning in any part of the house, as that amenity was virtually unknown in Flora in those days. The heat was provided by coal-burning furnace in the basement, later converted into an automatic stoker that fed the finer coal particles into the furnace based upon a thermostat-controlled upstairs temperature.

This loft was my kingdom. The heart of my academic activity occurred there. The study hours I put in up there were immense. Years later, at one of our high school reunions, my friend Don Walker summed it up pretty well. The reason for his mentioning it escapes me, except that I think it had to do with either justifying my lack of buddying around with "the guys" or with explaining how it was I had attained certain levels of accomplishment. Whatever his point, Don stood up and told all the assembled classmates that many was the night he would be walking home late from an outing with the fellows and would look up and see my light burning in the alcove where I studied.

J. J. Lynn

Aside from the early indications of my dad's health issue, the entrance of J. J. Lynn into our family life, and more subtly into mine in particular, was probably the most significant happening of my high school years. That it felicitously interlaced my high school years was touched upon at the outset of this high school section. It will be hard for the reader, prior to reading all the rest of this autobiography, and perhaps even a considerable sampling of my own writings from much later in life, to understand just how deeply this man seems to have influenced me. It is as though, without my having any comprehension of it at the time, something of a vital spiritual nature fed through to me from him. This is not to even hint that I could ever rise to his level in any sphere of mind or spirit, but only that in retrospect something seems to have emanated from him to me that had a significance that was not to come to flower for at least another forty years.

His life story is an astounding one of ascent, from impoverished childhood on a farm in Louisiana to the pinnacle of financial success in Kansas City, Missouri, all the while embodying the tenderest spirit that would become the spiritual successor of the Paramahansa Yogananda in the Western World. Gently and modestly his life bespoke both mental and spiritual genius. I am not in the least offended by the fact that his ascent in the Hindu tradition of the Yogananda differed from my own devotion to the Christ, for I've personally known no professing Christian whom I would take to be, or to have been, more Christ-like than J. J. Lynn. His own works literally show an immense admiration and devotion to the Christ through the medium of his commitment to the path of the Yogananda. He was driven, one might say, from the ostensible Christian path by the petty internecine squabbles within that faith at the time when the Yogananda's mission to the United States seemed to fill his heart with a divine peace and fulfilling commitment.

High School

His rise to the heights of material success faded in personal importance in his later years when it was transformed into complete and total submission of self and fortune to the spiritual realm. However, throughout his life, his kind and generous nature brought good things to all those who dealt with him. It is beyond my purpose here to go beyond this brief summary. More detailed accounts of his life story can be found in other publications.[1]

It was as though Lynn's benign and kindly light shone upon our family. Lynn was generous to our family during my dad's last illness, not only paying all his medical bills but also continuing his salary when he was totally unable to work and even raising his salary during that time, saying that dad's services had been exceptional, including procuring their most profitable oil and gas leases. That salary continued for years after dad's death while Mary Anne was still a minor, until Mr. Lynn's own estate was ready for distribution. His estate, beyond life support for his wife, was left to the Self-Realization Fellowship, the work of the Yogananda. Mr. Lynn himself died, as did my dad, from a brain tumor. Lynn died one year and nineteen days after dad, but he was fourteen years older at his death. Like dad, his illness plagued him for about four years, though unlike dad, Lynn is reported to have suffered no pain, and I believe I have read that his body after death did not decay.

Dad's brain surgery was in November 1950. Apparently mother had written to thank Mr. Lynn for paying the medical bills and had given him an upbeat report on dad's recovery to that point. By letter dated January 2, 1951, on his Kansas City letterhead but signed by him personally at a time when he was already spending most of his time in the southern California locale of the Yogananda's work and when he had himself begun to be ill, he replied to mother as follows:

---

[1] Sri Durga Mata, *A Paramahansa Yogananda Trilogy of Divine Love*; *Rajarsi Janakandanda: A Great Western Yogi:* The Life of Paramahansa Yogananda's First Spiritual Successor, by the Self-Realization Fellowship; see also Paramahansa Yogananda, *Autobiography of a Yogi* (first published in 1946).

Dear Mrs. Smith:

 Your letter of December 19 deeply touches my heart. I feel for Frank in his suffering and for you in your trials in caring for him and it is a comfort to me to know that what is done for you relieves your burdens and buoys your spirit.

 It is a great blessing to all of us that Frank is showing improvement and I feel that he will continue to improve and in a very large measure will have his health and strength restored.

 I wish for you and for Frank and your family all good things in the New Year, and with my blessing to all of you.

Sincerely,
(Signed, J. J. Lynn)

I met Lynn in person only once, a highly anticipated event. It was in the summer of 1948, shortly before my sisteenth birthday and the beginning of my junior year. The Lynn oil company had provided dad with a pretty blue Chevrolet auto for his work, which required much traveling. We still had a pre-war, 1937 Ford for family use. But Dad's supervisors had given him permission to use the company car for a family trip to southern California where Mother's eldest sister lived with her family—in the San Fernando Valley, north of Los Angeles. Mary Anne had never known having a new car, nor had I actually remembered having one either. When asked the color of that Chevrolet, she called it a "heavenly blue," and that moniker stuck within the family.

The meeting had been prearranged for Mr. Lynn to meet dad's family. Our family had come to love Mr. Lynn, if I may put it so, and to admire and respect him not only for his vast accomplishments, but also for who he was as a person. Mr. McReynolds, dad's immediate boss and liaison with Lynn's oil division, from the first had given us a good deal of information about Lynn. Among other things, the place we loved to eat when we were in St. Louis was the then-famous Forum Cafeteria in the midst of downtown, which was owned by Lynn—we had eaten there before dad went to work for Lynn. We had long known that Lynn did not smoke or drink nor permit anyone else to smoke in his office, a rather remarkable thing in those years. We, dad, mother, sister and I, were escorted into his oak-paneled office where Mr. Lynn sat calmly behind his immaculate desk. He put us to ease and I'm sure engaged us in personal conversation, but all I remember is being awed just being there. Not one word that was spoken can I remember.

Aside from being so successful himself, he had passed the bar exam at twenty-one years of age, and he had passed the C.P.A. exam at twenty-four with the highest grade on record, at which the authorities waived the twenty-five year age requirement for licensing in his case. I knew that I wanted to be a lawyer, and dad was already laying the groundwork for me to get an accounting degree first. Aside from my dad, Lynn was the highest role model I had or, for that matter, could conceive of at the time. Other than that he did not smoke or drink and was a vegetarian, I had no idea that he was already at such a high spiritual level. While McReynolds had certainly informed us of Lynn's commitment to the Self-Realization Fellowship in Los Angeles, we had no clue of the depth of his involvement there beyond significant financial support. Nor would I appreciate that depth for over four more decades in the future.

Dad's Illness

The earliest manifestation of dad's illness, his brain tumor, was clear in retrospect but entirely mysterious at the time. It was near the end of the regular basketball season in my junior year, in mid- to-late winter of 1949. Our team was playing at a town southeast of Flora, either Mt. Carmel or Fairfield. John Powless's dad, "Kayo," was driving to the game with dad in the passenger seat—just the two of them. Dad was reported to have had a seizure, maybe even to have slipped partially to the floor. I rather think Dad recovered enough that they went on to the game. I well remember him trying to think what might have caused this reaction. He thought it might have been caused by his exposure to some sewer gas in a part of the city water or sewer system in our neighborhood that he had gone into earlier that day. Why would he have been there? Whether on behalf of the city or because of a neighborhood problem or something else, I do not know. But he had been there and thought he might have inhaled noxious fumes. This event would have been almost precisely five years before his death. A lot was still to happen. During the course of that time he had many seizures of a sort. Well do I remember them. It was almost as though an electric current were passing through him, though less rigid and with body quiver, startled expression, and eyes flickering rapidly. I am unable to say for sure what portion of these instances occurred before we left Flora and moved to Wichita Falls, Texas. That something mysterious was happening was apparent. But nothing sufficiently definitive had occurred over the next sixteen months to abort the move. For at least a year before my graduation it had been planned that we would move forthwith upon that event. Dad had told his superiors that he would be happy to travel wherever they wanted prior to my graduation if they would let the family remain in Flora till then. In fact, he had spent an appreciable amount of time in Texas before we moved, though his travels included other states also.

While my high school years were not themselves much disturbed by these early symptoms, we were all obviously concerned, and the toll on dad and the rest of the family would become apparent not long after our move.

Washington D. C. and Gettysburg

Thinking that we would never again be as close to the East Coast as we were in Flora, Dad and Mother thought it well that we make a family trip back to experience our national capital before heading to the southwest. Mother's younger brother Richard, the one who had banged his punching bag before cleaning the chicken house, lived in Culpeper, Virginia. The trip would give us the opportunity to visit him and his wife Jackie also. Construction on the Pennsylvania Turnpike, which, as a route, probably went back to earlier American times, was started in the 1930s and significant early stages were completed before the war. By the spring of 1950, while still not the route it has become over the decades, it offered considerable distance of more convenient driving than slogging through the other existing roadways. We drove on this turnpike both going and coming. The very existence and novelty of this modern mode of transportation might have been an added enticement to the planning of this trip.

Through the years I have always considered that our parents made this trip for the benefit of my sister and me. Until now, as I write this, it had not occurred to me, or if so not in a way that stuck in my mind, that probably neither of my parents had ever been to the District of Columbia before.

The trip itself was doubtless worthwhile, but the most memorable and lastingly meaningful part of it occurred, insofar as I am aware, as something of an afterthought as we started for home. How the idea developed I do not know, or at least recall. I do know that I had studied American History for both semesters of my senior year. The Civil War was fresh on my mind, and as we left Washington driving up through Maryland, towns and villages on the map between Washington and the turnpike would have called to mind the various places that figured into the maneuvers of the two armies as they coalesced into position for this historically and tactically highly significant battle. While I may have simplified it in recollection, we were in a modest hurry to get on home to begin the move to Texas. When the idea of dropping over to check out Gettysburg occurred, it was with the thought that we would take it in quickly and get back on the road.

As it turned out, this was not to be. At that time, Gettysburg was still probably not so terribly different in layout and density of development from Civil War days as it has become over the last half of the twentieth century. At the visitor's center we engaged a tour guide who had been a history teacher in the local high school. He seemed to know every inch of the scattered battlefield and its various approaches and nearby towns, and the movement of the armies and development of the battle itself. It was magically captivating. We forgot the passage of time. I'm not sure how much farther down the road we got that night, but our plans to drop over for a quick look at the battlefield morphed into the most lastingly meaningful part of the trip. For me it was almost as though I was transported back to the approach and development of the three days of battle as they were happening. Its effect upon me will soon show up in my early college days. But the memories will last a lifetime. We took our three children back to Washington D. C. in the spring of about 1977 or 1978, the first of three annual trips that we did while our twin sons were in high school. Again we visited Gettysburg. It was so built up around it that it did not seem like the same place. No longer was it so easy to envision armies jockeying for position in the town's environs. But Gettysburg will always be Gettysburg, and so it is one of those priceless memories, one of the last of times we were to have as a family together before the ravages of Dad's illness began to reconfigure everything.

Korea

Upon returning to Flora, the movers packed our household furniture and belongings and we got in our cars and headed for Wichita Falls, Texas. I do not recall if Dad was still driving the "heavenly blue" or had another, but by then we had purchased our own red 1949 Ford, the acquisition of which had been a big event the year before. Doubtless it is the one we had just driven east.

We were on the road when the North Korean forces invaded South Korea, crossing the 38th Parallel on June 25, 1950. I would turn eighteen three months later (September 23) and have to register for the draft, not in the small town where I was raised but in the far larger city of Wichita Falls. My high school days were over and my hometown would never again be my domicile. A major stage of life was ending, and another was beginning.

College 1950–1953

Robert Frost mused on the road not taken. He closed his famous poem, "The Road Not Taken":

> I shall be telling this with a sigh
> Somewhere ages and ages hence:
> Two roads diverged in a wood, and I—
> I took the one less traveled by,
> And that has made all the difference.

Unlike Robert Frost, the decision to move to Wichita Falls was not made by me. Like Frost, however, as I look back at it from the perspective of an octogenarian, I judge that it has made all the difference.

Most of us cannot foresee the eventual consequence of life as we live it. Looking back now, as a matter of destiny, I see this move as having been among the most, if not the most, uniquely meaningful event of my life. The starkness of this imagination is brought into focus by the fact that the family moved down there and then, for all practical purposes, almost immediately moved back, leaving only me in Texas. The critical net result was not that I became a Texan, though of course that happened, but that I met Jo Anne. And behind that was the influence of her father, Thomas Hugo (T. H.) Myers, a chiropractor with a most unusual hold on some fundamental truths that took their own sweet time in taking hold of me. For now, I only lay this as predicate for what will come about as his influence plays itself out in my later years of life.

Thus it was that the most significant event of that summer by far occurred in the Sunday evening after-church youth activities at First Methodist Church. It was there I laid eyes upon Jo Anne Myers, a very pretty and personally captivating young lady who had just turned sixteen years of age. I did not work up the courage to ask her for a date for a while, but on September 9, 1950 that happened. I was driving the family car. With total lack of imagination or originality and with complete illogic I asked her, as the folk and square dances were ending, if she "needed" a ride home. Based on that question alone, she would have been justified in rejecting me as a retard. Her parents chaperoned these youth activities and had their car there, so my question was grossly awkward, but was apparently the best I could do. Perhaps she sensed I was bashful. She rescued me, saying that she did need the ride. It did not take long for us to decide that we were in love, but it was four years and one day before we were married, on September 10, 1954. Her parents were most supportive of our dating, and my parents let me know that she was the first girl that I had dated that had their whole-hearted approval. It was also auspicious for us that during the very short time that all of my family was together in Wichita Falls that the relationship between our respective parents was warm and friendly. My relationship with her and her family extensively interwove my college years.

Jo Anne still had two years of high school to complete as we started dating and, aside from her normal school work, was active in theater, the Footlight Players Club—later the National Thespian Society—as well as various other activities. My own schedule prohibited much time for dating. A lot of our time together was on the telephone, our conversations there usually being frequent but brief. By dating her through her last two years of high school, I got to know several of her classmates, especially her girlfriends, so that through the years I have enjoyed her high school reunions about as much as she has.

The Myers lived at 2126 Avenue J, their house being in the middle of the first east-west block from the southeast corner of Wichita Falls High School. During those years segregation was in full force in Texas and the rest of the South. WFHS was the only high school in the city except for Booker T. Washington, the segregated school for blacks. Flora had no black population during my life there,

College 1950–1953

though I played against black athletes in a few of the schools on our schedule. Nevertheless, having been raised in Illinois, the idea of legally segregated schools and public facilities in general bothered me greatly. The more respectful terminology used in those days was *Negro;* the term *black* came into preference only much later. All too often the odious term *nigger* was used. That always told me more about the moral character of the speaker than it did about the one spoken to or about. The term offended me worse than curse words. Thankfully, some things have gotten better through the years.

The Myers house was modest, but homey. It had six rooms and a bath; kitchen and dining nook on the north, a sitting room for lack of better description in the middle west, and living room in the southwest, her parents' bedroom occupying the southeast and the bedroom for Jo Anne and her younger sister Jean being north of that with bathroom in between the two bedrooms.

There was a small grand piano in the living room, which gave me opportunity to impose a bit of my playing upon them in the initial stages of our courtship. I've described the house at some length because some parts of it figured meaningfully into our courtship. Many luscious meals filled my tummy in the dining nook, and a substantial part of our courting took place on the sofa in the sitting room. Customarily, we would have a bit of a visit with the family and then, after a while, Doc and Mom, and Jean if she was around, would withdraw to their bedroom(s) and leave the west part of the house to Jo Anne and me. Only on few occasions did Doc come in to check on us as the hour got late. Normally I could not afford the time to stay that late, so I did not inconvenience him that way too often.

Jo Anne and I each always called our own mother, "mother." I called my dad, "dad," and she called her father, "Daddy." Neither remembers for sure what we called the other's mother before we were married. Possibly, in time, it was "Mom," and certainly was after we married. From day one I have always called her father, "Doc." Jo Anne's references to my dad were usually in talking to me since his time with her in person was too limited to establish a pattern.

Dad had made trips to Texas before the family moved. Well I remember him talking about the Southern Methodist University in Dallas and Robert G. Storey, dean of its law school who was fresh from serving as a prosecutor in the Nuremberg trials. Dad must have gone to Wichita Falls before we moved there if for no reason other than to find a place to rent. We rented a house on Tenth Street, which proved less than satisfactory but our family residence remained there for a number of months. Dad's health problems continued to hang like a cloud of concern over all of us.

Either on one of dad's earlier trips to Texas or promptly after our arrival he visited with James Boren, president of Midwestern University, who immediately told him that a full academic scholarship would be granted to me based upon my academic record in high school. Dad may also have talked to Billie Stamps, the football coach, because I remember walking with dad through the hall of the administration building in the summer of 1950 and meeting two recently graduated students who were talking to Coach Stamps. The coach introduced us to the two of them, Joe Dean Tidwell and Willie Bigham. Tidwell was a fullback and Bigham, of American Indian heritage, a big lineman. The 1949 Midwestern team had won its conference their senior year. The two were standouts. Tidwell went in the seventeenth round of the NFL's draft in 1950 as number 211, drafted by the NY Bulldogs, and Bigham went in the twenty-third round as number 296, drafted by the Chicago Bears. Coach Stamps had approved my walking on and playing as a freshman, but looking at them I wondered what I was getting into.

Because Jo Anne and I knew we could not get married before our education was complete and we could support ourselves, we got our degrees as quickly as we could. Jo Anne joined me at Midwestern while I was still there. She graduated from the Wichita Falls High School in the spring of 1952 and immediately entered summer school, then the regular school year 1952 to 1953 and summer school in 1953. In registering at Midwestern, she had used an SMU course catalog making sure that every course she took at Midwestern would count toward the degree she expected to complete at SMU while I was in law school there. We were hoping that I could get a scholarship at the law school there, for otherwise I would have returned to the University of Illinois. The scholarship was awarded and we both entered SMU in the fall of 1953. She went straight through school year and summer school, graduating in January 1955 with a Bachelor of Science degree in elementary education. But on this, I jump a bit ahead of my own account.

My Bachelor of Science degree was bestowed by Midwestern University in Wichita Falls in the spring of 1953. I had carried full loads (as much as twenty-one hours one semester), attended two full summer school sessions starting in the fall of 1950, and had taken one correspondence course from McMurry University in Abilene, Texas.

Of the four distinct activities from my high school years, namely church, athletics, music and academic scholarship, the last of these, academic scholarship, clearly dominated my three years at Midwestern. Although remaining significant, church activity was less while athletic and music endeavors were squeezed to relatively minor roles. I can quickly summarize these three activities..

Music activity included only singing in the church choir and such insignificant things as playing the piano accompaniment for hymns at Wesley Foundation meetings or perhaps Sunday school on occasion. I still could play enough in my early years of dating Jo Anne to give her and her family some idea that I had been a performer on the keyboard. Otherwise, I played no significant pieces in public.

Church or religious activity included regular church and Sunday School attendance on Sunday morning and choir practice one evening. Also, at least until the getting-acquainted stage of dating Jo Anne turned into a more serious relationship, the after-church activities on Sunday evening continued. I was also active in the Wesley Foundation on campus, as was Jo Anne during the year where we were both in attendance there. The staff pastor at the church who worked with the youth was Raybon Porter, who went by "Pop" Porter. Eventually, not only was he the minister who married us, but he also played something of a cupid role. The Methodist Church in those days convoked a quadrennial youth conference. It occurred after summer school in 1952 on the campus of Purdue University. Pop Porter had arranged for us to attend, and an important part of that arrangement was that it would give Jo Anne a chance to come back through Flora and see where I was born and raised. Chief Warden, a Methodist local preacher, was scheduled to do the driving on the trip. A boy named Vernon Snyder went as a delegate also. For reasons later mentioned, my parents were not in Flora at that time. Grandma Reaugh slept with Aunt Martha in the latter's bedroom and Jo Anne was given grandma's bedroom. I slept in the screened in porch at Aunt Mary's next door. Jo Anne remembers that night as the hottest experience in her life. There was no air conditioning, it was humid, and virtually no breeze moved through that bedroom. I did not do much better at Aunt Mary's. But love survived.

To get ready for football that first fall, I went regularly during the summer to the YMCA and worked in the weight room—regularly that is until dad reported having talked to Coach Stamps who said that I should not be working with weights as they impaired agility. Times have changed radically since then in that regard. I met Dustin ("Dusty") Fillmore at the "Y." He also planned to walk on for football so we did some workouts together. His dad was a lawyer with offices in the Hamilton Building. We thought we could build up stamina by taking turns getting on each other's back and climbing all eight or ten floors of the building's non-air-conditioned stairway—Wichita Falls is HOT in the summer. I got the best end of that deal. Dusty weighed only about 140 pounds, while I was 170. Many decades later I got to thinking that I did not remember Dusty actually being involved in any of our practices or games. I did an Internet search and located him as a lawyer in Fort Worth. He remembered those days in the summer of 1950, but with tongue-in-cheek he said Coach Stamps told him early on that he had no future in the NFL.

My athletic involvement in Wichita Falls consisted not only in playing football on the freshman squad at Midwestern in the fall of 1950 but also in playing on the First Methodist Church men's basketball team in the YMCA league that same school year. Having been fresh from a high school basketball career, I was able to make a meaningful contribution to that latter team's performance. My scrapbook also contains a certificate of appreciation from the Wichita Falls YMCA dated March 26, 1953, for service as "outstanding manager" of the Junior Basketball Team from First Methodist Church for the 1952 to 53 season. This was a team of junior high boys that did so well in the local competition that it represented the local "Y" at the "Tri-State" tournament in Dallas. I do not recall just what we did there, but my impression is that my team came out very well, perhaps even having won that tournament. One of the players who sticks in my mind was Joe Prothro, the grandson of Joe Perkins, wealthy oil man and founder of a prominent department store in Wichita Falls who also endowed Perkins School of Theology at SMU. Having tried to negotiate with him on oil leases, dad said he was hard to deal with. Certainly he could negotiate from a position of strength.

Of course, most of my energy and time in 1950 was spent on football. Coach Stamps had two assistants, Dixie White and Paul Brotherton. The latter was the basketball coach and he was also the coach of our freshman squad. The freshmen had their own schedule, playing against various Texas junior colleges within bus range. Our season ended a bit before the varsity season as I recall, but our practices did not. I got into some of the games, but do not remember a lot about them. I remember coming out of the backfield and catching a pass, and I remember carrying the ball through the line right at the goal line and fumbling away the ball.

The one other specific memory I have is the game where I had a miserable sick headache. It was not a game I played in since the coach knew my situation. During the game I went off the field, out behind our bus, and vomited. Our dinner on the way down to the game included a ham sandwich with a lot of mayonnaise on it. For years afterward, I could not eat mayonnaise, and still do not care much for it to this day.

In looking through the college annual for that year, it does not appear that there is a group picture of all the football team, varsity and freshman, and I only recognize two freshmen, Kenneth Buckley and Cleon Failes, who were individually pictured, who apparently suited up for varsity games. They were good backs, but the thing I remember most distinctly about either of them happened in English History class. Dr. Mitchell Smith was the professor. A textbook was assigned, but Dr. Smith said it was not necessary to read it because the answer to all test questions would be taken from his lectures. These he gave while continuously walking back and forth in an "L" shaped path from the entrance door to the far windows, where he elbowed in a left turn to the back of the room before turning around and retracing his path. The first row of chair desks may have been elevated above the lecture path; clearly each succeeding row was elevated above the row in front of it. Smith was somewhat intimidating in his manner of addressing students. He had a bit of the caustic in his high-pitched lecture style. The particular class session was underway, but Cleon Failes had not gotten there. All of a sudden the door opened and there was Cleon. He was trapped. His seat was in the upper corner diagonally opposite the elbow in the professor's path. He and Smith stood looking at each other across the room, the class holding its breath for Failes' dire situation. Finally, Smith said, "Land somewhere." Failes pointed to his seat in the most inaccessible spot. Smith said, "What is your name?" Failes said "Failes." Smith said, "Not a very auspicious name for this class." He eventually got seated, and all breathed a sigh of relief. In time I got acquainted with Mitchell Smith on a more personal level and found that his bark was worse than his bite. But he was a strict grader. Harold Harriger, an upperclassman friend then and over many decades, told me late in his life that he asked Mitchell Smith why he could never make an "A" in Smith's class. Smith said he only gave one "A" and Harold had the misfortune to be in the same class as Ray Marie Porter, Pop Porter's daughter, who got the "A." This was welcome news to me for I apparently later encountered the same problem as Harold.

One other memory from my 1950 teammates dealt with a fleet-footed back named Jimmie M. Crawley. While I remember him from our 1950 fall season, I am unable to determine from any of my three Midwestern annuals how he was classified as a student. He is not shown in any of the respective class student groups, the only two pictures of him being as a running back in the 1950/1951 annual and a whole page "In Memoriam" to him in the 1952/1953 annual featuring the same picture. My memory is that he was drafted during the 1950/1951 school year, perhaps even before the football season ended, for the Korean War that had started June 25, 1950. I also remember that he was killed in Korea. Under his picture on the memorial page are listed the following dates: October 3, 1929 to October 15, 1952. He must have been drafted after the 1950 fall football picture was taken and before the class pictures for the 1950/1951 annual were taken, hence he appeared nowhere else in my three annuals.

Aside from not having either the talent or essential desire, or both, to have been a good college football player, two things brought my football career to an end after the first season. One, which would have been sufficient in itself, was the realization that the time and energy demanded was out of proportion to the importance it held for me in relation to academic involvement in the college years, particularly when I was not getting any other benefit than the satisfaction of participating in the sport itself. My scholarship was granted based upon academic achievement. But the second thing was a more dynamic catalyst, particularly in conjunction with the first.

Dad's Illness Diagnosed

At some point between our arrival in Wichita Falls and the end of the 1950 football season, Dad had gone to the prominent Scott & White Clinic in Temple, Texas in an effort to find the cause of his seizures and general malady. When his problem was not adequately diagnosed there, he and mother went back to Barnes Hospital in St. Louis. He was given an encephalogram as a result of which a tumor was found in his left temple area. He went right into surgery for its removal. The date of this corresponded closely with the end of the freshman football season. His prognosis was for substantial recovery. In fact he did recover to an extent such that within the next few months they returned to Wichita Falls and we moved out of the house on Tenth Street and into a more satisfactory one on Hayes Street. We had not been there too long, as I remember, when his company wanted him to move to Abilene. This they did, renting an apartment. He tried to work but life was becoming quite miserable and he was unable to stay in Abilene for long. He and mother returned to Flora. Mary Anne had not moved with them to Abilene but returned to Flora to stay with grandma. When the folks moved to Abilene, they gave up the house on Hayes Street. Our neighbors there, Walter and Maisy Bachman, took the initiative in offering to rent their upstairs to me for a very reasonable amount. It was five dollars, but I cannot remember if it was weekly or monthly, probably weekly. It seemed generous at the time.

One incident that is related to this difficult time period happened as Christmas neared in 1950. Grandma Reaugh had come to Wichita Falls to stay with Mary Anne and me on Tenth Street until we were to return to Illinois for the Christmas holidays. We had planned that on the day after my last class at Midwestern I would drive the three of us to Flora in the 1949 Ford. Today Google gives the distance as 735.2 miles, on the interstates in a time of eleven hours and thirteen minutes. There were no interstates then, the highways went through towns, the roads in Oklahoma were notably poor, and

I recall the distance as being approximately 750 miles. There was no way that it could have been driven then in that amount of time, more likely twice that. Our church men's basketball team had a game in the evening of my last day of classes. I played that game virtually from start to finish. Amazingly, when I got home from the game that night I told grandma that I felt good so why did not we just start for Flora. We had things ready to go for the next day, but grandma raised no objection so we got in the car and started. I do not remember any discussion about the possibility of our staying in a motel. Avoiding the cost of that would have been an important consideration in those days, the thought of such a stay probably precluding any thought of leaving that night. So, when we started out, I planned to drive all the way without stopping, save for meals, gas or bathrooms. It was a foolhardy thing to do. As I recall it took a total of about twenty-two hours, and I was driving off the road sometimes before we got there. Grandma and Mary Anne were sitting in the back seat, and bless her heart, grandma, being the sport she was, never said a word. Nor did she ever criticize me, as I recall. I could have killed us all. But we made it.

The Need to Earn

If it had not occurred to me before then, it seemed obvious to me when dad's problem was diagnosed that I needed to devote the time and energy given to football to engaging in some kind of part-time work to help supplement funds for my living and incidental school expenses. During the rest of my days at Midwestern I had three jobs, two for the YMCA and one as an accountant. For the YMCA I served as lifeguard in its pool, which also entailed giving swimming instruction to youngsters. There would be times while I worked that no one would be in the pool. During those times I often spelled the person who worked the adjoining cage that passed out towels and locker keys to members needing them. Otherwise, during those spells, mastering boredom was the main challenge.

Bearing in mind that the YMCA was a male facility, except on women's night or other special occasions, all those entering the pool had to do so completely nude. It was always good for a laugh when some fellow forgot that women were in the pool and charged up the steps into the pool area stark naked before shocked awareness prompted hasty retreat.

The other YMCA employment was umpiring the YMCA men's evening softball games during league play in the summer of 1951. There were two games a night. I do not remember just how many nights there were games, but it was at least two. The pay was not high. For that matter it was not high in the lifeguard work either, but it was work that paid something. The one thing that was enjoyable about that umpiring job was that Fred Tewell was the other umpire. Fred was the speech and debate coach at Midwestern. I had taken the speech course the fall of my freshman year and was on the debate team all the way through Midwestern. From that beginning, we developed a lifelong very close relationship. One of us called from behind the plate and one worked the bases. The location of the base umpire varied, often being right behind the pitcher depending upon the bases that were occupied. We rotated positions so that each of us called behind the plate on only one of the two games.

Anyone who has spent much time in or attending officiated athletic events will have observed that sometimes players or fans become upset with calls that are made. On the night in question, a serious case of that developed. Most teams in the YMCA men's church softball league conducted themselves as good sports. That good demeanor did not require abstaining from notably disagreeing with our calls. Such things were just part of the game. I have a high regard for the Salvation Army, but its team, composed primarily of servicemen from Shepherd Air Force Base, was in this case largely a collection of hoodlums. Fred, who was stocky and not very tall, was calling balls and strikes behind the plate and I was standing, on the play in question, behind the pitcher with a pretty clear view of how each pitch crossed the plate. The situation was a full count, three balls and two strikes on the Salvation Army batter. The next pitch was right down the middle, clearly a strike. With the clear ringing voice of a decisive umpire, Fred yelled out "Ball, You're Out!" There really could not have been a question that the last part of the call was correct, but the outburst from the hoodlums was immediate and vociferous. It really never died down. Not long after that I made a call on them at second base that was equally disliked. They were giving us a very bad time. When that game was over, I took over behind the plate. All the hoodlums stayed around. Behind the plate they were saying to me (to both of us, but they were right behind me), "We are going to get you after the game, Ump!"

My transportation was a motorbike, not the more substantial kind of motorized bike on the market now but a bicycle with a motor mounted on it. Fred had his car. We both had to get to our transportation after the game, and I had worries of exposure on that bike after that. During the second game we visited with the men's teams that were playing and arranged for them to surround us with an escort leaving the game. It was tense, but it worked. I left carrying a softball bat. Both of us got out of there untouched, thanks to the support of the second game's players, some of whom followed me in their car for a distance.

My transportation during my Midwestern period comprised two different vehicles, that motorbike being one and the family's red 1949 Ford sedan being the other. During the times when grandma or my parents were there in Wichita Falls, I would have had access to the family car on a sharing basis with mother, and since we were not totally restricted from using the company car for some personal use when dad was home, I may have had access to the Ford for most all my transportation during those times. My parents were absent from the time of dad's surgery in the fall of 1950 until he was able to return sometime following the holidays in early 1951 when we moved from Tenth to Hayes Street. They stayed there for a few months until the company moved dad to Abilene, Texas. They took the Ford with them on that move, and we gave up the Hayes Street rental and I moved into the Bachman upstairs next door. It was at that time that I needed my own transportation and acquired the motorbike. Dad and mother rented an apartment in Abilene, and dad tried to work, but his days there were difficult because of the ravages of what he had been through and what, as it turned out, he still had ahead of him with the gradual return of the tumor. When they moved to Abilene, Mary Anne returned to Flora and lived with grandma and Aunt Martha for her seventh and part of her eighth grade. She was seven school years behind me, so that move was before the start of the school year of 1951/1952.

My job at the "Y" was in progress while they were in Abilene, my transportation in the big triangle between Hayes Street, Midwestern, and the "Y" being on the motorbike. But it was not too long after they moved to Abilene that dad's condition deteriorated to the point that they returned to Flora—for good as it turned out. On one occasion, as I was going home in the evening after work at the "Y," a group of boys or men drove by me and threw some type of a sandwich, perhaps a hamburger with all the trimmings, at me scoring a direct hit on my face. It did no damage beyond a generous deposit of condiments that came off easily back home. Perhaps it was after that and the incident at the ball diamond that my folks said they were worried about my safety and wanted me to take the Ford. It was doubtless sometime during the 1951/1952 school year. But I think that about the time they moved back to Flora, possibly a bit before, I had progressed far enough in my accounting studies to take a job in that type of work. I became the accountant for Wigington Brothers Transfer & Storage for the rest of that school year ending in the spring of 1953.

I lived in a condition of great frugality, calculating just how much I could spend on each meal. I could get breakfast at the school cafeteria, a bowl of oatmeal and toast for twenty cents. I could buy a large can of tomato juice, opening it with a "church key," drinking half of it in the evening while I studied and the other half in the morning before going to the school cafeteria. I had no refrigeration.

College 1950–1953

One morning as I drank the remaining tomato juice, I thought, lucky me, I have gotten a large piece of tomato which I masticated, until I suspected that it might not be tomato. It turned out to be a friendly cockroach that apparently also wanted some tomato juice.

I ate some meals at the "Y" where a bowl of chili or a salad and a glass of milk could be had for a reasonable fee of about sixty cents. My real salvation nutritionally was that on the weekends Jo Anne's mother prepared delicious meals, usually for Sunday after church, and I'm told that she always tried to prepare them with what I liked in mind. I ate of them lavishly to make up for a week of far less fare. Her green beans were the best I have ever eaten.

It is my recollection that my folks paid the rent for me on the Bachman apartment, and then they later gave me the Ford. Though I do not recall specifically, I feel sure they provided other support, but I did try to get by on as little financial help from them as I could in view of their circumstances. Though we had never done without, as a family, I knew that they could not have accumulated very much.[1] I was very touched in writing this to look back at a letter that mother wrote after she had returned to Flora. She said dad had been having spells just about every day but that before she got back to Flora dad had a seizure from which he was unconscious, the first like that which he had experienced. Mother had typed the letter, but there was a segment from dad at the end, also typed, perhaps even by him, and signed by him "Dad." He said he had been unconscious about an hour and had chewed his tongue pretty bad, and they had found him on the floor. He wrote six short paragraphs, part of which follow:

> It seems to me now that I didn't get to do much for you while there, I was so busy seeing to everything else all the time....
>
> I had written to your Mother before she started home and told her to tell you that, should your work make schoolwork

---

1 If my memory is correct, according to the inventory of dad's estate, the family net worth was about $16,000, which I believe also included the $4,000 of life insurance proceeds.

too much to carry on, that we could get along without your working. So, you can watch how things progress for you and then otherwise, feel free to use up some of the bonds we have purchased.

Thinking back on your birthday, I sure wish I might be able to double back for a 19-year period before jumping off into Texas. It would have been quite a lark then, but things are certainly different with me now, and I am beginning to wonder when something like a recovery will become accomplished.

Hope you will be happy with your new arrangement and I feel the Bachmans will make a nice place to stay. Each of you should be able to enjoy the other's company. If you have any needs in the future, let me know.

With best wishes for another good year at school.

The Lynn organization did not carry health insurance for its employees, but as described near the end of the high school section, it was unusually generous in the payment of all medical expenses and continuation of support for our family until long after dad's death. It did pay all of dad's medical bills and continued to pay his full salary, even giving him further raises after he gave up trying to work. Moreover, it continued his salary after his death for several years, considering that Mary Anne was still in public school. Mr. Lynn died about a year after dad, but the business continued to pay mother dad's former salary until the distribution of Lynn's estate was at hand. Then Mother went to work as secretary for the grade school principal, which continued till her normal retirement.

By the summer of 1953 dad's condition was deteriorating and clearly terminal if nothing could be done to remove or kill the tumor that was obviously growing back. Dad had made comments to the effect that he suffered so much from that encephalogram that he never wanted to go back through anything like that again, and it was almost recriminatory against mother for having put him through it the first time. But it seemed to me that he had not weighed that in the light of life itself. I had gone back to Flora to spend that summer between Midwestern and law school there in order to be with him.

Somehow or other I got from him an admission that he was glad he went through it since it did keep him alive, and I extrapolated that into an expression that if he had to choose between that again and certain death that he would choose the former. That was all I needed to hear. Mother agreed that I could make an appointment with Dr. Furlow, the neurosurgeon in St. Louis, and visit with him about what options dad might have at this point. What he had to say weighed heavily upon me. He told me that he thought at the time of the surgery that he had gotten the entire tumor, but that obviously it had returned. In regard to dad's chances in surgery, Dr. Furlow said that he felt dad in his present condition had a fifty percent chance of surviving the surgery and a five percent chance of anything like a normal life if he did survive. So many advances have been made since the early 1950s that I think he might have survived under pertinent medical practice as it is today.

I returned to Flora in a state of mental and emotional anguish, helpless to change dad's slide to the doorway of death. During that summer I painted our house, and then painted the newer house just to the south of us. While I was on a scaffold I had rigged up to reach the eaves of our house, I experienced such a burning itch all over that I jumped from the scaffold to the ground and rolled over in agony with an intense case of the hives, consequent upon our helpless concern for dad.

It was difficult for me to go back to Texas at the end of the summer. I'm jumping ahead of my college story, but continuity demands it. A full tuition scholarship had been granted to me to the SMU law school, the continuation of which would be dependent upon my maintaining a high grade average. I studied with intensity, but I found time to write to mother every day that semester, even if it was nothing but a postcard. I felt she needed a lot of moral support even though grandma and Mary Anne were both there. The entire grade in law school is based upon the written exam in each course at the end of the semester. Immediately after my last exam I got a phone call from grandma saying that if I wanted to see dad alive I should come to Flora immediately. Out of consideration for me, mother and grandma had held off calling till I had finished my last exam. I got there barely in time to be present as he died in convulsions. I'm convinced in my heart that dad's higher consciousness was with him as he approached the gate of death and that he held off passing through that gate until I had finished my exams and he knew, in his higher consciousness, that I was there with him.

It is normal to come to grips with the loss of a loved one. Dad's death still hurts greatly to this day. It has been a help to study the works of Rudolf Steiner over the last quarter century. With understandings from that work I'm reconciled to the loss, but tears of gratitude for the dad I had still flow.

Midwestern State University

During my years at Midwestern, from the fall of 1950 through the spring of 1953, the school's official name was Midwestern University. It started in 1922 as Wichita Falls Junior College, sharing facilities and faculty with Wichita Falls High School. In 1937, on a forty-acre campus it became Hardin Junior College. In 1946 it became a four-year institution, its name changed to Hardin College. Renamed Midwestern University in January 1950, in 1975 it became, and has remained to this day, Midwestern State University. Today its campus comprises 255 acres and 70 buildings and it offers a wide variety of academic programs.[1]

Academics

As mentioned, academics was my reason for attending college, and it intentionally dominated my years at Midwestern. It comprised three separate areas of emphasis, namely, course work toward a degree, writing, and debate. The first two of these were a continuation of areas of activity from my high school years. While larger

---

1 See http://aboutus.mwsu.edu/history.asp.

high schools, such as Wichita Falls High, offered interscholastic debate, such was not the case in Flora. Debate was a new activity for me, one that seemed a natural for pre-law students, and several of those on the Midwestern debate teams during my years there became lawyers.

The scrapbook that my parents had given me was a handy presence during my days at Midwestern. Up through that period I continued to use it as a receptacle for my items of interest from those years.

Course Work

My major was accounting, and my recollection is that my minor was in economics. Other courses were in English, history, government, biology, mathematics, physics, speech, other business related, and physical education. There is, in my scrapbook, an envelope dated June 1, 1953, from the Office of the Registrar at Midwestern containing transcripts of my academic work for all fall, spring, and summer terms with the exception of my final term in the spring of 1953. The absence of that final term's transcript must surely be explained by what was occurring as it ended. I had just taken the CPA exam and would have finished any final exams that we graduating seniors had to take, which were few, if any. I was eager to get my modest belongings loaded in the car and head for Flora. A note from Jo Anne on Wednesday night, May 13, 1953, to "Mr. And Mrs. Smith and Mary Ann" began, "Just a note to say that Eddie got off for Mineral Wells and the C.P.A. exam about three this afternoon. His accounting teacher told them not to be so pessimistic; they had a good chance of passing it. I do not know about the others, but I'm sure Eddie will pass some if not all of the parts he takes." Later she says, "I am sure that Mary Ann is quite excited about graduation [from grade school]. I am so glad that Eddie will be home for it." My recollection is that I was not interested in waiting around for my own commencement ceremony. I already had the scholarship from SMU Law School. Looking back I expect that getting that last semester's transcript for my files just was not that important to me at that time, and never became necessary or even important after that.

The transcripts indicate that Midwestern considered an "A" to count three points down to an "F" which garnered minus one point. However, since most universities seem to go on a "four-point" scale, I have calculated, from the existing transcripts I have through the fall semester, 1952, my grade point average on the four-point scale, considering that a "B+" is 3.2, and excluding the "B+" in the business law course taken by correspondence from McMurry and the physical education classes simply graded "S" for satisfactory. All my Midwestern grades were "A" except for a one-hour "B" in Freshman Orientation, a B+ in a Mitchell Smith history course, and a "B" in an economics course. My expectation is that my last semester's grades would have all been "A's," unless the economics professor who gave me the "B" the semester before that did it again. I do not remember the one where I got the "B" or who the professor was. Just showing up for the one-hour Freshman Orientation class doubtless earned a "B" and there was little possibility of doing better or worse than anyone else. Mitchell Smith was known to only give one "A" in his classes, so if he gave one, someone else got it when I took that course. Based on the 116 hours the included courses represented, thus excluding only as stated above, the grade-point average I calculate is 3.9448 out of a possible 4.0.

It is not hard for me to look back through my courses and judge which ones were most valuable to me, whether then, through life, or both. The speech courses had a direct relationship to the debate activities, which is treated separately below. Without a doubt, the most important courses were those in accounting, being the area of my degree major. Inasmuch as I had long anticipated going to law school, in considering what to study for pre-law dad had made the statement that in his opinion "a lawyer without an accounting background is just an office boy." Considering the many great lawyers who did not have that background, the latter part of dad's statement was obviously hyperbolic for effect. He and Mr. Lynn had both studied accounting, and to this day I continue to think it is almost without peer as the most valuable undergraduate degree for most, though not all, walks of life. Our daughter followed my advice and got such a degree, passing all four parts of the CPA exam right out of school without any practice. After practicing successfully with a major accounting firm for two years she told us that she did not really care for accounting, whereupon, following some aptitude tests, it was apparent that she was entirely oriented toward medicine which required that she go back and get all the normal premed course work. She is a practicing physician now. Even so, I do not think she has any regrets at having acquired the accounting background.

Still, one other course in particular I place up there, right under accounting, as my most valuable. It was the two freshman English classes designated with a W: English 113W and 123W. The "W" indicated Writing, specifically as was the case of Creative Writing. Based upon my academic record, including essay work, in high school, I was permitted to take this course. Not without significance is the effect the professor in that class, Saralyn Daly, had on me. Dr. Daly was small in stature, with short black hair, bangs, glasses, and, in my subjective observation and inspiration, the appearance and manner of speaking that suggested to me the dreamy imagination so critical for creativity. Even now, as I look back at her picture in the annual I see these qualities and remember so fondly and gratefully that class.[1]

Writing

Midwestern's School of Graphic Arts published a quarterly magazine called the *Owakiya*.[2] As my first fall term started, the *Owakiya*

---

1   Dr. Daly earned her PhD from Ohio State University in English in 1950, so this was her first teaching assignment. She appears to have had a successful career; see http://en.wikipedia.org/wiki/Saralyn_R._Daly#cite_note-1 and http://www.whoislog.info/profile/saralyn-r-daly.html.

2   Doubtless *Owakiya* is an Indian word. Midwestern's school symbol was "Indians" and had been since its founding days in the 1920s—it was not changed (to "Mustangs") till required to do so by the NCAA in 2005. On pages 2 and 39 of the 1953 annual, reference is made to Midwestern's being

sponsored a freshman essay contest. Right off the bat, as a starting freshman in Dr. Daly's class, and having but recently been transported back to mystical involvement in the Battle of Gettysburg, whether or not also in fulfillment of a class assignment, I entered a competition by submitting an impressionistic account of my experience entitled "Sacred Battleground," reminiscent of Lincoln's recognition of that hallowed soil in his Gettysburg Address. An article in the campus weekly newspaper, *The Wichitan,* as well as in *The Locust Log,* published by the journalism department in the Flora High School, reported that "Eddie Smith's "Sacred Battleground" took unanimous first-place honors in the freshman essay contest sponsored by the…campus literary magazine." Big stakes were involved in the contest. *The Wichitan* reported that my award for first prize was $2.50.

The *Owakiya* sponsored another freshman contest, the results of which were published, presumably by *The Wichitan* based upon a truncated clipping in my scrapbook. My short story "Game Time" won first place in that contest and appeared in the Spring issue.

The fall 1951 issue of the *Owakiya* contained my short story entitled "Conflict." I expect that this was written during the latter part of my freshman year in fulfillment of an assignment in my writing class, but not for a contest and not submitted in time for that semester's publication. I have no clipping or other indication than that it appeared in the following fall issue.

Two further essays won contests during my second full year at Midwestern. The first one was doubtless "The Dawn's Early Light." A clipping from *The Wichitan,* dated October 26, 1951, bears the title "Essay Prize Goes to Eddie Smith," the first paragraph reading, "First prize in the Homecoming essay contest has been awarded Eddie Smith for his essay 'The Dawn's Early Light,' submitted by

---

"received into the Kiowa tribe," and on the latter page appears a stunningly beautiful Indian lady in tribal dress. The Kiowa tribe is today headquartered at Carnegie, Kiowa County, Oklahoma, ninety-five miles straight north of Wichita Falls.

Phi Theta Kappa." Apparently, based upon an article mentioned later from the same newspaper dated January 16, 1953, that contest was to be on the flag.

It also appears, based upon such January 16, 1953, article, that my last writing, aside from class assignments, was in a contest my sophomore year. The article says that it was a "Sophomore Class Essay Contest." More definitively, Madge Davis, chair of the English Department, wrote in a letter to me dated November 9, 1951, "It is my happy privilege to tell you that your essay has been awarded first place in the sophomore entries in the Father and Son Essay Contest sponsored by the Featherston-Edwards Company of this city...The checks will be distributed by Mr. Featherston at his office...He likes to have a visit with each winner." The subject of the competition was "My Dad, The Ideal Man." My submission was entitled simply "My Dad." Dr. Davis's letter indicated the results would be published in *The Wichitan*. If so published, I have no copy.

As I write this, it has been six decades since my three years at Midwestern, all of which fell within the span of the Korean War, while the memories of the Second World War were also still fresh on my mind. Something in most of these writings can be seen to reflect those times.

Debate

Probably none of my Midwestern activities left me with so many favorable memories as those of the debate team, and perhaps no activity was more important over the long run. Certainly it ranked up there with accounting and writing as the truly salient aspects of my undergraduate college experience. My times and activities with Jo Anne were the most important element in my college years. That aside, activity on and with the debate team was the most memorable of my college experiences.

Strangely, I do not recall having had any awareness, prior to attending Speech class in the fall of 1950, of debate being a competitive college activity, and certainly had no expectation of being involved in it. Probably I signed up for Speech thinking that it would be a good pre-law study. I was the only student who was active on the team for the full three years I was there. Others came and went, some older, some younger. My relationship, though always pleasant, with the members of the team seemed to start and end with our mutual participation in that activity. No member became a lifelong friend, and no personal contact with any of them survived my graduation. The one warm and meaningful relationship that lasted was with my professor and debate coach, Fred Tewell. It continued until his death from a brain tumor in 1993. He moved from Midwestern to Oklahoma State University in Stillwater, Oklahoma a few years after I graduated. I was able to confirm that, just as with my Creative Writing professor Saralyn R. Daly, my freshman year was Tewell's first year as a college professor.[1]

Debate was apparently not much of an activity, if any at all, at Midwestern before Tewell started it. A page of the annuals my second and third years was devoted to the debate team, but it got no coverage there my freshman year.

Unfortunately, my account of the activities must be based upon nothing more than my memory and four newspaper clippings, all undated save as can be inferred from their content.

The universities where I remember attending debate tournaments were East Central University, Ada, Oklahoma; Southeast Oklahoma State University, Durant, Oklahoma; Texas A&M University, College Station, Texas; Louisiana State University,

---

1 Though suspecting that the fall of 1950 was his first year there, I was only able to confirm that by finding that his son, the professional golfer Doug Tewell (http://en.wikipedia.org/wiki/Doug_Tewell), was born August 27, 1949, in Baton Rouge, LA. LSU was where Fred Tewell got his M.A. degree. Fred and wife Marjorie lived in Marchman Hall, the athletic dorm, serving as dorm parents that first year he was at Midwestern. Doug was an infant. They found that all it took to get him to sleep was to put him in the car and drive him once around the block.

Baton Rouge, Louisiana; and Baylor University, Waco, Texas. At least some of us also went to Jackson, Mississippi to take part in a "Congress" that was to be held in the legislative chambers in the capitol but was moved to another local venue since the legislature was still in session.

Several meaningful impressions from these trips remain. While the two Oklahoma campuses were small, they were pretty in the spring, and their tournaments were competitive. I remember walking for relaxation among magnolia trees at one of them. Probably these debates were during my freshman year, though perhaps repeated. My reason for placing them in the first year has to do more with the fact that my debate partner my first year was George Deen. It is hard for me to express how pricelessly joyful and poignant the memory of those brief days with George were. No other partner was so stimulatingly delightful to be around. An electric energy seemed to radiate from him. Small of stature, with sharp countenance and penetrating eyes, his face seemed instantly to light up with thought or idea. His speech was crisp and rapid, never protracted, and usually incisive.

While incidental to debating, we participated at these Oklahoma colleges in both extemporaneous and impromptu speaking. In impromptu, a general area of interest was chosen from which a slip was drawn. Three minutes were then allowed for reflection before making a five-minute speech on the indicated topic. Seeing George emerge from a presentation, while heading to our next engagement, I inquired how it had gone. "I'll tell you the sad story later," he replied. As thus related, he had chosen American writers. A quick glance at the slip indicated to him that he had drawn Zane Grey. He knew Grey only by reputation as a writer of westerns, from which wealth of wisdom he elaborated an entirely fictional and erroneous account. As he said, "I saw astonishment before a smile crept over the judge's face. Only afterward," he said, "did I see that my slip read, 'Zola Gaines.'" Such were the wonderful, fleeting days with George.

To finish the account I must jump both back and forward. The Korean War was raging as the 1950 fall term began. Science and ministerial students were generally deferred to complete their studies. George, whose father was a local chiropractor, probably intended even back then to go to medical school. Not desiring to be so limited, however, George sought a deferment in the same manner as I and thousands of others, namely, by sitting for a general intelligence test. A high enough rank was the basis for granting a four-year deferment. Based upon the results, deferment was granted to both of us. My four years expired in the middle of the first semester of my second year of law school, when I stood at the top of my law class at SMU. Having just married, and with that record, I conferred with Colonel Schwartz, head of the Wichita Falls draft board in the hopes of being able to complete law school before military service. Schwartz made it clear that my four years were up. It is what he said in our conversation that is relevant to the George Deen matter. Schwartz told me that I had the second highest score among the eight thousand who had taken the exam in that jurisdiction. Possibly I inquired who ranked number one. It was George Deen, my cherished debate partner, whose association for me had been fun from the start.

Several years later, while we were each in graduate school, I in law, George in medicine, I learned to my complete surprise that he had married a girl I knew only casually. Total shock gripped my mind and heart a short while later when news came that he had hung himself. It has pained me to this day when I ponder how profound the loss of this incredible fellow, debate partner and friend. My scrapbook contains a page from "*The Golden Key* [magazine] of Phi Theta Kappa," with a picture of, and message from, George as national president.[1] Apparently too involved otherwise, George did not participate in debate after that year. Both busy, we only greeted each other in passing on campus.

---

1   Phi Theta Kappa is an honor society for two-year college students, but the chapter was still active at Midwestern even though it had become a four-year college in 1946.

College 1950–1953

In my second year of debating, my partner was Larry Robinson, who was a year ahead of me in school, and during my third year it was James (Jimmie) Cash, a freshman. At each tournament, each debate team of two debaters participated in a number of debates. In some, probably most if not all, of the tournaments, at least in those where there were too many teams for each team to debate each other team, the practice was to tally the wins and losses of each team and then to match the teams with the best won-loss records in final elimination round(s).

Each year a national organization, taking into account the national and world situation, would establish the resolution to be debated in colleges and universities for that year. According to newspaper accounts the debate topic my third year was: RESOLVED, that the Congress of the United States should enact a compulsory fair employment practices law. During the course of a tournament, each team was obliged to argue each side of the question, affirmative and negative, generally balanced equally between the two. Each debate lasted one hour, equally divided between the teams and the speakers, forty minutes for presentation of cases in chief and twenty for rebuttal, each speaker thus getting one-fourth of these totals. A set, but short, period of time was allowed between debates for the teams to get to their next debate location. Judging reports were posted as available during the day. A tournament usually took place all day Friday and until noon or shortly thereafter on Saturday. My memory is skimpy on this, but I seem to recall that the elimination rounds may have gone into the afternoon. Generally, though, we were through and ready to head home by mid-afternoon Saturday.

Since Tewell had earned his master's degree from LSU, the tournament there was high on his list for our participation. I'm assuming that we did it all three years. It was also high on the list of us men's team debaters, for we always left Baton Rouge by mid-afternoon headed for New Orleans and its bawdy French Quarter. Two memories from that first visit stick vividly in my mind. The first was

Felix's Oyster Bar, just off of Canal Street before reaching the action on Bourbon Street. The memory of the fisherman's platter with fried oysters, shrimp, and other delectables from the locale still makes my mouth water, though as so often happens, visits decades later cast a more common light on it. The second memory is what an eye-opener Bourbon Street was for this eighteen-year-old only recently from the Bible Belt of Southern Illinois. Again, decades later, sated by the sexual revolution of the 1960s, it seemed pretty tame, but that was not the case at the start of the fifties. At that time of my life I had never had a drink of beer, wine, or hard liquor, so the delights were all in taste and sight. Years later, with Jo Anne, we found the nearby, historic Monteleone Hotel with its famous rotating Carousel Bar.

While it was my destiny to carry away most of the team honors from my debating years, including the Philip Khoury Trophy my second year and, as I recall, the most valuable debater designation my third year, modesty compels a more realistic assessment. It was and is my impression that a team's most effective speaker almost always speaks last. Thus, my debate partner was always the second of us to present, George Deen my first year, Larry Robinson my second year, and Jimmie Cash my last year. While I was fairly effective at organizing and presenting our case, and thus went first, the knockout blow was typically dealt by the second speaker. It is not my intent to belittle my own capabilities, but simply to recognize how fortunate I was to have a talented partner following up. I've already told about George. Larry Robinson was superb. He went on to law school and practiced in Wichita Falls. Tragically, he was killed in a small plane crash in Arkansas in the early 1960s. A clipping from *The Wichitan* following our winning LSU debates in 1953 says of Cash that he "was a member of the national champion debate team of Adamson High School of Dallas in 1950." For a freshman college debater, my take on him is that he was immensely gifted. He fell off the edge of the world for me after that year as I have inquired and been unable to determine where he went or what he did. I do not have the 1953/1954 annual to see if he stayed at Midwestern. At Jo Anne's sixtieth high school class reunion in Wichita Falls in 2012, I visited with Jimmy Cowles, still then a prominent Dallas attorney who was also on the debate team as a freshman my third year. He knew of Jimmy Cash as having been a debater at Midwestern but could offer no further information as to what became of him. I feel sure, if he escaped fates like my first two partners, that he has amounted to something significant in later life.

My scrapbook contains no news clippings from my first year of debating, though I recall that George and I were winners of most of our debates. There is one clipping from *The Wichitan* following the Texas A&M tournament in year two. Larry Robinson and I were the "junior team" from Midwestern and Larry Lambert and Roy Epp were the senior team. The article reports that the junior team placed first and the senior team placed second in their respective divisions. It also quotes Tewell as saying "This makes the third first place trophy which Midwestern has won in speech tourneys this year." I doubt it was the first Larry and I won, and perhaps not the second.

Year three, with Jimmy Cash, was a stellar year. Three clippings speak of it, one each from the tournaments at LSU and Baylor and one about a Midwestern-West Point debate. The latter appears to be from the Wichita Falls newspaper. On LSU, the report includes, "James Cash and Eddie Smith, Midwestern's Senior Men's Debate team, tied for first place in the [LSU] debate tournament in Baton Rouge last week.…The Men's team tied with Southwest Louisiana Institute of Lafayette, La., for first place. Each team won four debates and lost two. The Midwestern team was defeated by S. L. I. 163 to 162, and by L. S. U. The L. S. U. contest was the first debate ever staged by Cash and Smith as a team. Later in the meet they defeated the L. S. U. Team." Referring to Tewell's comments, in addition to touring college campuses, we saw the Louisiana State Capitol and "many points of interest in New Orleans"—a euphemism. "The orators also visited the only leper colony in the United

States at Carville Marine Hospital, Carville, LA." I remember also that from the stage in their auditorium we spoke to the assembled patients about the debate topic for the year.

The last clipping was captioned "Debaters Place in Baylor Meet," and read in pertinent part, "MU senior men's debate team—James Cash and Eddie Smith advanced to the finals in Baylor tournament last week. They were defeated by an SMU team....Fifty schools competed in the Baylor Tournament [there were thirty-two senior men's teams] including the University of Texas, University of Kansas, Texas Tech, Texas Christian, and Oklahoma University."

The team from SMU were law students, one of whom, Bill Bryce, was a remarkable speaker. Bryce, a bit heavy-set, drew natural sympathy as he approached the podium with a simulated limp and began speaking with a calculated lisp, both, having served their purpose, disappeared as his golden voice emerged with devastating effect. There were five judges in that championship debate, the vote being four to one favoring SMU. I was surprised we got a vote from one judge, perhaps one who knew too much. Bryce was president of the SMU student body and was still in law school while I was there. His well-known high political goals flamed out even before leaving school, surely from failure to heed the wise counsel for modesty in Proverbs 25:6–7 and Luke 14:7–11.

In the margin of the Baylor tournament clipping, I wrote, probably a few years later, "Greatest success for any M. U. team so far."

The clipping from the Wichita Falls paper, captioned "MU-West Point Debate Set," reported:

> Debaters representing the United States Military Academy at West Point, N. Y., will meet Eddie Smith and Jim Cash, crack debate team of Midwestern University...at 8 p.m., in the MU speech auditorium.
>
> The public is invited to attend. No admission will be charged. The MU team will argue the affirmative of the national intercollegiate question for 1952–53, "Resolved, that the Congress of

the United States should enact a compulsory fair employment practices law."

The two West Point cadets, whose names were not available here Monday morning, come to Wichita Falls in the course of an extended tour of the South....[comments about Cash and I and our debating victories omitted].

Last spring Smith and a Duke University debater were named the outstanding debate speakers of the entire South.

Fred Tewell, debate coach at MU, urged Wichitans to hear Monday night's discussion of a hotly contemporary political question.

The penultimate paragraph above referred to the Southern Speech Association Tournament and Congress 1952. My scrapbook contains the association's certificate to "Eddie Smith, Winner of Superior in Bill—Senate" signed by the association's director and tournament director. This was at the "Congress" in Jackson, Mississippi referred to earlier. I presented there a bill, and argued its passage, supporting our country's taking part in completion of the St. Lawrence Seaway. This had been a joint dream of Canada and the U. S. for a long time but our Congress had never gotten behind it. Unwilling to wait longer, the Canadian government "decided over the course of 1951 and 1952 to construct the waterway alone...However, the Truman and Eisenhower administrations considered it a national security threat for Canada to alone control the deep waterway, and used various means—such as delaying and stalling the Federal Power Commission license for the power aspect—until Congress in early 1954...out of concern for the ramifications of the bilateral relationship, reluctantly acquiesced."[1]

An article appeared in the January 16, 1953, issue of *The Wichitan* entitled, "With Interests, Eddie Can Debate Any Subject." The subscription under my picture reads, "Let's Argue—Eddie Smith, senior from Wichita Falls, combines all of his many interests into one—debate. Eddie was a principal member of the Midwestern

---

1   See http://en.wikipedia.org/wiki/Saint_Lawrence_Seaway.

debate team last year and won the Phil Kouri Award as outstanding member of the team."

The article itself is a journalistic rendition of my involvements set out above, focusing upon their versatility in combination. It also references my membership in Phi Theta Kappa, the Alpha Chi National College Honor Society, and the Omega Rho Alpha English honors society as well as my serving as vice president of the senior class and representing Midwestern in *Who's Who in American Colleges and Universities.*

"Doc"

Near the beginning of this college section, I spoke of the influence of Jo Anne's father on me. That will emerge more fully much later, but on the cusp of our team's departure on one of our more important debate trips, I came down with a serious malady—the flu, bronchitis, or comparable disability. It would not have been possible for me to have made the trip without Doc's having taken me through a two-day healing extravaganza, the lurid and austere agenda of which, under less demanding time constraints, one would normally have preferred to avoid. As it was, with but one day of pampered travel following, I was in good shape for our mission. This trip was either the one to the Congress in Jackson, Mississippi or one of the LSU debate tournaments, for we drove eastward out of Texas.

Finishing Up

During this third year at Midwestern, I enrolled in the LaSalle Extension University's CPA Coaching Course. It was a correspondence course dealing with all four parts of the CPA exam—theory, auditing, business law, and practice. The full exam took two and a half days with a half day devoted to each of the first three parts and a full day (two half days) to the practice portion. Even though at that time the candidate could not sit for the practice part until after a year of public accounting experience, I wanted very badly to pass the other three parts before getting into law school. Consequently, I applied myself diligently during that spring term, taking those three parts shortly before the end of the school year in the now empty, but then prominent, Baker Hotel in Mineral Wells, Texas. It was with much joy later that summer that the report came that I had passed all three parts. With my plans to enter law school, I had no clue as to when, if ever, I would gain the experience to sit for the practice part of the exam. That, for the time being, was to be left in limbo. Little did I know that the dreaded draft call would later provide that opportunity.

Years later, when Fred Tewell was a special guest at my 1982 Steinway Dedication Concert, he told Jo Anne that "Eddie was the best student I had in my years at Midwestern." Doubtless that was influenced in large part by the depth of our personal, mutual affection.

A somewhat related remark came from O. McDonald, a prominent Wichita Falls businessperson in connection with my application to sit for the CPA exam. He had received from me a form letter dated March 10, 1953 provided by the Texas State Board of Public Accountancy in which I stated my desire to become a CPA and that I had applied to take the accounting exam. It also told him that the Board required "the endorsement of three substantial and representative business men as to moral character." Mr. McDonald returned to me one of my signed copies of the letter, indicating that he had sent it in on March 12, writing in his own hand a "copy of notation I made on form":

> Eddie Smith is, at the moment, the most promising young man of my acquaintanceship. I have offered him employment but he has a worthy goal he is pursuing wisely in my opinion—[signed]

During that last semester at Midwestern I was also attempting to secure a scholarship to the SMU Law School. A letter dated March 2, 1953, from Roy R. Ray, Chairman, Scholarship Committee, read:

Dear Mr. Smith:

I am pleased to advise you that our Scholarship Committee has selected you as one of our Regional Law Scholars for the year 1953–1954. This scholarship will be available in the sum of $250 per semester to be applied upon your tuition [that was the full amount of the tuition].

I congratulate you upon the fine record you have made at Midwestern University, and we are looking forward to having you here in the School of Law.

If you should be in Dallas at any time I trust that you will drop by to see me at my office.

Cordially,

[Signed as above]

There is a clipping from the newspaper in Flora captioned "Flora Boy Receives Scholarship to Southern Methodist." It is a lengthy article, remarking on my record at Flora, reciting the receipt of the scholarship, and then copying substantially the entire article from the Wichita Falls paper on the debate with the West Point cadets. The latter was prefaced, "Later word about the debate said that Eddie had won the unanimous decision of the judges." They were, of course, from Wichita Falls, but there was never any doubt in my mind that we had indeed won decisively. However, those fellows from West Point were good representatives of the school and our time together was warm and very friendly. It was a relaxed and pleasant way to wrap up my debating career at Midwestern.

The final semester at Midwestern was ultra-busy but highly productive. Jo Anne and I had our plans laid to attend SMU together in the fall with her in a campus dormitory and me in the Lawyer's Inn residence hall in the law quadrangle.

As these busy but happy days of anticipation were ending, my mind and heart knew also a heavy side as I prepared to spend the summer with my family in Flora, my last with dad as I fairly well knew.

Law School till Marriage and Military

The summer interlude between Midwestern and law school was achingly poignant, as though something vital to me was being slowly ripped away. Mother was a pillar of strength, but her heart had to be breaking as she cared for her life mate, watching him suffer while losing ground. Jo Anne and I were in constant communication by mail. Phone conversations were too costly, but we each wrote at least every two or three days. Even when there was not much new to be said, mail was eagerly awaited. I may have written to her on the typewriter, but her messages were always in her beautiful handwriting. Aside from painting our house and Gene Stanford's next door, I spent some nostalgic time on the farm, some with my older friend Charlie Rankin, but some just alone with my thoughts and memories. It was as if the river, gently flowing, was an eternal connection between dad's life and my own.

My return from Flora to Texas was ambivalent, leaving dad for probably the last time, yet heading into law school and the future as long anticipated. My destination was the law quadrangle at SMU, more particularly the law dorm on the quadrangle known then as Lawyers Inn. So far as I then knew, it would be my residence for the next three years. It was a most desirable residence, though my time there lasted only for a year, the fall, winter, and summer terms that constituted the required discipline for entering first-year day students.

Situated at the northwest corner of the campus, the law quadrangle as it existed then and for several years thereafter comprised three buildings, a very impressive array shaped like a horseshoe opening onto Hillcrest Boulevard, the western boundary of SMU.

Lawyers Inn was the bottom of the horseshoe at the east end. It was "a modern version of the British-revered Inns of Court."[1] Florence Hall lay on the south and housed classrooms and the courtroom. On the north lay the large, impressive Legal Center Building. It housed the administrative and faculty offices, four libraries including the large "Student Law Library," an auditorium, law review and legal aid clinic offices, and a basement lounge where students and occasional faculty typically gathered after a tough day of classes, sharing joys, miseries, or humorous anecdotes to lessen tensions before going separate ways. In 1971 the massive Underwood Law Library opened, filling in the west end and converting the horseshoe into a full rectangle.

Jo Anne's parents took her to SMU, helping her check into her Peyton Hall dormitory room. Well I remember the day I checked into Lawyers Inn. I learned that my roommate was an entering first-year student from Camden, Arkansas named Richard E. (Dick) Miles. Arriving first, I chose the north half of the room and was lying on my bed, in a lazy doze, when he came in. My first impression as he entered the room is still vivid. He was tall, dark-haired, and far more handsome than I had expected. He looked to me like Ronald Reagan, host of the General Electric Theater TV program that mother, Mary Anne, and I had enjoyed so regularly that summer. He put his bag down and we greeted warmly. A happy, congenial relationship was born. We usually called each other "Roomie," with a touch of affection, and still do. Otherwise, I was always "Eddie" to him and he was either "Dick" or "Miles" to me.

Today I recognize that my entry into law school in September 1953 was a major transition in my life. It was the first time Jo Anne and I had both been away from the home of our parents for good. Never again did I expect to see dad in his earthly conscious state.[2]

---

1 SMU 1954 Annual, 64.

2 I did return home for the holidays. Dad was not unconscious, but he was in bad condition, and we knew he could not last long. It was a somber holiday season for all of us.

My general schooling was over and the study for my lifetime profession was beginning. But on a deeper level than I could appreciate then or for several decades thereafter, I became an adult in the ancient tradition—I reached the age of twenty-one years. The first three seven-year periods (septenaries) of my life, those ending respectively at second dentition, puberty, and adulthood, had done their work on me. Now my adult "I Am" was in charge. A very busy decade, probably my most intense and demanding, was beginning, laying the groundwork in both profession and family.[3]

At some point, obviously, I had to take the Law School Aptitude Test (LSAT). It was generally known that an applicant's results on the LSAT, together with undergraduate scholastic record, were, as they still are, used in granting admission, perhaps also in granting scholarships, or in making judgments on the prospect of continued enrollment. That I had done well on the LSAT was made known to me, though if I ever knew the actual result it has escaped me and I have no record of it. When I took that exam is beyond me, though it must have been no later than the first few days of law school. What was clear to me, however, was the importance of ranking well up in my class in order to maintain the vital scholarship.

Time with Jo Anne was greatly restricted once the fall term started. I would walk over to her dormitory to visit her, but as she remembers it I would only stay for thirty-five minutes, precisely at the end of which I would leave. We attended church together at Oaklawn Methodist Church. Funds and time were both carefully husbanded, so outings together were infrequent. We did, however, manage to find a fairly decent sparking location in an area north of Loop 12. It was acreage that had been laid out with some roads for development but on which construction had hardly started. Many

---

3 The term *septenaries* and phrase "I Am" are not terminology I would have used or understood in those years, nor, in fact, would I until my discovery of the works of Rudolf Steiner in 1988 and the study of them in my life since then.

years later I learned that its location was almost smack-dab in the middle of the yard in the upscale area where John Wilson, one of our neighbors in Colorado and one of my best hiking buddies up there, then lived.

The first semester's classes were Contracts I, Torts I, Personal Property, Jurisprudence I, Legal History, Criminal Law, each of which was a three-hour course except Jurisprudence (one hour) and Legal History (two hours). Even though the entire grade in each course was based upon the one exam at the end of the semester, I studied from day one with great intensity. Such was not the case with everyone. A rather humorous observation was that when we got to the part of the criminal law course that dealt with the crime of rape, the library was overcrowded with every student in the class, each eager to read in careful detail all the cases cited by the professor. It is well to remember that this is still in the early 1950s, a decade before the sexual revolution began.

Along with study there was the feeling that I must write either a card or letter to mother every day. I wanted her to know that she and dad were constantly in my mind and heart.

There was a good bit of camaraderie among students, particularly those of us who lived in Lawyers Inn, where we also had our meals. Much like military experience, there is close and meaningful association during the time of the experience itself, yet few friendships that remain meaningful in later life. "Roomie" was one of those, as was Horace "Mitch" Mitchell, who later lived in Lubbock.

Grades in law school are by number, not letter. At SMU, the average grade level for cum laude recognition was 85, magna cum laude was 88, and summa cum laude was 90. I'm only aware of one previous SMU law summa cum laude graduate prior to the time I entered, namely, Harvey Davis from many years before who was a law professor while I was there. Jess Hay, a student in the class just ahead of me (the class of 1955), attained that rank upon his graduation. The third one I was aware of was in the class I would eventually graduate with after my army days.

The greatest feeling of pressure I experienced was in preparing for and taking the final exams at the end of that first semester. My average for that semester was 85.4. There was, I believe, a general understanding that grading the first semester was rigorous, weeding out those who might not have been destined to do well over the long haul.

Today, fall terms, whether called semester or trimester, seem always to end before the Christmas holidays. During all of our college years, the fall semester did not end, and exams were not taken, till January. Today's practice of ending before Christmas is more humane.

Within only a few hours after the last exam I got a phone call from grandma telling me that the end was near for dad and that if I wanted to get there before he passed I should come immediately. I did. I got home and to the hospital barely in time to be with him as he died in convulsions. It was February 1, 1954. He was forty-eight. He died almost exactly five years from the appearance of his first tumor symptoms on the way to my basketball game in Fairfield or Mt. Carmel, Illinois in 1949. His funeral was February 3. I drove mother and Mary Anne home from the service. The day was overcast and gloomy, or so it was to me. It is an image of quiet sorrow and emotional suffering together, forever etched in my memory.

As I look back upon the whole of my life, February 1 is the most significant day of the year and it never passes without my being acutely aware of it. Three February 1's establish that judgment, the first and by far the most foundational, was February 1, 1954. The second is February 1, 1959, the day I began practicing law in Lubbock, Texas. The third is February 1, 1993, the day we closed the sale of Resthaven of Lubbock, Inc. to Service Corporation International (SCI), a funeral and burial service company listed on the New York Stock Exchange that was among the big winners for Peter Lynch, legendary manager of the Fidelity Magellan Fund.

Once the grades were in, the legal fraternities Phi Alpha Delta and Delta Theta Phi got invitations out to the survivors. Roomie and I both joined Delta Theta Phi. Their gatherings were fun. It was in these where I got my first exposure to hard liquor. They were a refreshing break from the grind, and I enjoyed them that semester. My draft notice for the military came before the time for the next year's pledge activities.

An interesting thing happened one morning early in the spring, 1954 term. It occurred in Florence Hall in the class on Equity being taught by Professor Jack Riehm (pronounced "ream") a native of Peoria, Illinois, World War II Air Force pilot, recently from the prominent New York City law firm Cravath, Swain and Moore. Riehm was a natty dresser attired as though still in New York City—dark suit, vest, with tie under buttoned-down collar. He had either a tic or an ingrained habit whereby he moved his head, led by a jut of his jaw to the side and upward, sometimes simultaneously adjusting his tie with his hand. He spoke with clear and commanding diction. His demeanor suggested the power to bring down a lightning bolt on demand as needed, doubtless the inspiration for the student-ascribed moniker, Blackjack Riehm.

The large Florence Hall classroom was dissected by a walkway, dividing front and back, the back part in gradually elevated rows, a long table in front of each row of chairs. On the occasion in question, Miles and I were sitting next to each other at the right end of the first row behind the middle walkway, Miles being to my right. Riehm had just finished a brief monologue narrative and paused for student comment or observation. I raised my hand and began with precisely these words, "Are you trying to say..." Miles' reaction next to me spoke for everyone there. He put his face down on the desk with hands over his head waiting for the thunder and lightning to strike. Nothing of the kind happened, our dialogue continuing as though my inept words had been most appropriate. Leaving class Miles said, "My God, Roomie, I cannot believe you survived that," and others concurred. Class ended and we returned to our room in the Inn. It was not too long before our phone rang. Whichever one of us picked it up, the female voice on the other end said, "Professor Riehm would like for Mr. Smith to come to his office [at thus and so time] this afternoon." Roomie and I looked at each other as though my end as a law student must surely be at hand.

Nothing could have been further from the truth. Jack Riehm was something of an expert in Federal taxation and had been engaged by the Rabkin-Johnson tax service to update its current loose-leaf service. Riehm knew of my accounting background and apparently of my hope to specialize eventually in Federal tax law, and he knew my academic record and the results of the first semester of classes. The purpose of his calling me to his office was to propose that I work for him in updating each text or footnote citation in the service with the latest authorities pertinent to it, saying he could pay me so much per hour for my service. I jumped at the opportunity with an immediate acceptance. It was the best of all worlds. Roomie's jaw dropped when I got back to the room and told him how wonderful the lightning bolt had been. My relationship with Riehm was always super, including after he became dean of the law school. After serving as dean for a term, he returned to New York and a varied and successful career.[1]

Professor Arthur L. Harding, was "Colonel" Harding to the students, though his military background, if any, was not trumpeted enough to be known to me. He was a square block of a man with a carefully trimmed, two-part mustache, each side extending to the outer longitude of the mouth. Harding did not teach any class in our first year but did teach one of the mandatory summer classes, Agency and Partnership, as I recall, between the first and second year. Whether intended by the administration or not, Harding's imperious carriage and persona were calculated to cast fear into the heart of every student. After turning in the grade-determining final exam

---

1   Riehm, born in 1920, a longtime resident of Bronxville, NY, died at his home in Tucson, AZ on August 26, 2011, apparently after a period of illness. I had no contact with him after he left the law school, but always carried a warm gratitude for my happy relationship with him. See http://www.legacy.com /obituaries/dallasmorningnews/obituary-print.aspx?n=john-riehm&pid =153307134

paper at the end of each course, students would leave the examination room individually. It was customary for many as they left an exam to cross over to the student lounge in the basement of the Legal Center Building to relax, refresh, and rehash the exam with other survivors. There was a large square support pillar located at approximately the east boundary of this relaxation area. It was wide enough on each side for a good size person to stand behind. One of our classmates, who as I recall was named Bill Jackson, may have been primarily a night student, but in any event was probably one of those struggling both to stay qualified and to have enough financial wherewithal that he and his wife could survive. He had an outgoing type of personality, always worth a pleasant conversation. In fact, I believe he later became a representative in the legislature from Dallas and seemed to do quite well financially during that time—this latter is hearsay reported to me later by my roommate Miles who, by then, was practicing law in Fort Worth.

In any event, Jackson finished the exam in Harding's class and headed to the student lounge to relax and rehash the exam. He came in shaking his head and said, "If that Colonel will just give me a passing grade on that exam, I will kiss his ass at the corner of Main and Akard and give them a half hour to gather a crowd."[1] Jackson almost had heart failure as the colonel who, upon Jackson's outburst, peered around the corner of the big support pillar to see who was so eager to honor him in that manner. Unbeknown to Jackson, Harding had come in from the exam earlier and was standing hidden from Jackson behind the pillar, perhaps talking to someone who was visible to Jackson.

Pranks were a fact of life, enhanced by the need to lighten up from time to time from serious study.

Jack Ferrell started law school in the same class as I. Jack liked a good time, sort of playboy like—later a car dealer, among other things. Miles and my room 305 was at the south end of the Inn,

---

[1] At that time, the corner of Main and Akard was the epitome of downtown Dallas.

while Ferrell's and his roommate Ronnie something (who did not make the cut) was on the north end, both on the top, third floor. Only an attic was above that floor. As the final exams neared at the end of that first semester, study review became even more intense. The attic was essentially dark, though there were switches for light, but it had one irresistibly inviting feature. It had a large green Ping-Pong table with a green-shaded light hanging down above it, as one might expect to see in a shady, perhaps Mafia-like, type of business setting. But it was a perfect getaway for quiet, uninterrupted study at that critical point in the term. On the occasion in question I had retreated up there and was sitting at the pool table, black darkness all around save for the green-shaded light close above. I was completely absorbed in what I was studying, oblivious of anything else around. All of a sudden there was a horribly loud blast right behind my head and my head was being lathered with something white and wet. It was not just a sharp blast but a continuing one. I felt my end might have come. I put one hand over my face and waved my other one trying to put an end to whatever my attacker was doing. My mood was hostile as I turned to see Ferrell holding the big fire extinguisher and gushing with laughter at the sight of me.

Next to Ferrell's room lived my lifelong friend Horace (Mitch) Mitchell, son of a Methodist preacher, with his roommate Steve Condos, of Greek heritage. One day Steve or someone in cahoots with the two of them ran down to our end of the hall yelling that Mitch had just been beaten up by some guys over in front of the Toddle House across Hillcrest Avenue from the campus.[2] The harbinger of this evil deed said that Mitch was on the bed in his room bleeding badly. I immediately ran down, saw the blood, and headed out of the Inn running toward the Toddle House. I have no idea what I would have done had the hoodlums still been there, but, perhaps with a good deal of relief, I ran back to report that I had been unable to find any of them. When I got back, Mitch was up in good

---

2 See: http://en.wikipedia.org/wiki/Toddle_House.

spirits, completely cleaned up and none the worse for wear. It had been a prank. When I had first seen him, Mitch had been lying there as though in bloody trauma. The blood, it turns out, was catsup. A good laugh on me was had by the perps.

The most unique prank was pulled on me. It was such a good one that I became one of its perpetrators on the few that had not been initiated by, or heard about, it. The lead on the prank would brag to another classmate that he could lift the classmate and any two others then in the vicinity. There were always at least a couple of others around, by prearrangement. The chosen victim would invariably call the prankster's bluff, choosing two of the bystanders to join him to constitute the three to be lifted. The classmate was instructed to lie on his back on the floor with the other two lying beside him, one on each side. The prankster would then say that in order for him to get a grip for lifting them, they would have to form a rigid threesome. This was to be done by the classmate extending an arm around the neck of each of the other two who would then, with both hands, tightly grip his extended arm. Then each of the classmate's legs was to be caught in lock grip by the two legs of the one nearest that leg. Then, to get a grip on the center-point of the total weight, the prankster would put one foot on each side of the classmate, then bend down and unzip the fly of the classmate's pants. He would then say to another bystander to please hand him the red lipstick or fingernail polish with which to decorate the genitals. Of course, none was ever applied, and perhaps there was not even a container, but by this time the classmate was either laughing his head off or fighting mad. There was only one of the latter in my experience, but I had been the prankster in that instance and had chosen him because I thought he was too serious and needed to lighten up. I do not think he ever liked me after that. Many years later I was appointed by the Federal Court in Lubbock to defend an indigent charged with a violation of Federal Gun law.

This former classmate was prosecuting for the U. S. Attorney and was furious with me for not stopping my witness examination when he stood up (even though he had not spoken at the time—very picky I thought). He angrily accosted me in the hallway while the jury was deliberating. The jury acquitted my client. The classmate was not a happy camper. While we were never close friends, it seems obvious that the door to friendship was closed between us at the time of the prank and cemented shut at the trial in question. I should not have pulled that prank on him—it was a bad choice of target and bad judgment on my part.

To end on a much happier prank. My friend Mitch was the target on this one. Mitch has always had a fabulous sense of humor, and everyone enjoyed this one. It happened in the main lecture room in Florence Hall, probably during our first semester. We had one professor that everyone, without exception, loved, and who seemed to love everyone and was extremely solicitous that each student should learn. He was warm, friendly, and helpful in every way. He was Professor Clyde Emery. He taught the class on personal property law. All first year students were in the large class. Mitch had deposited his books at his place on the long row table and stepped out of the classroom. He returned in time to see Ferrell and Condos take his books and place them on an architecturally ornamental balcony outside a window at the side of the large classroom. To reprieve the books, Mitch had to climb out the window, get the books, and then climb back in. Just before Professor Emery walked into the classroom, Ferrell and Condos closed the window with Mitch outside. Class started. After a while there was a knock on the window. Emery looked up to see what it was. About that time Ferrell and Condos got up and opened the window and Mitch climbed over the sill and into the classroom. When Emery burst out in laughter, the room erupted with it. A good time was had by all. To a student, we all loved Professor Emery.

Emery was tall and skinny, probably cold natured for he always wore a vest sweater under his suit coat. He had been a distance runner in track in his student days. He was a powerful advocate for an effective note system. Every student will remember seeing him often stroll in his comfortable, long-legged gait across the quadrangle, stop dead still for a moment as if in deep thought, then reach into his coat pocket, take out a pencil and pad, and write a note to himself.

SMU Law School has been a center for foreign students to study international law. During my first year in law school, our third floor on Lawyers Inn was peopled by us first-year students in both the north and south portions, but the middle of the building housed German lawyers at least most of whom, I believe, had served in the German army during WWII. We did not have a lot in common as they sort of stuck together, but there was one of them who seemed congenial whom I visited with a time or two. He was strong. When he went walking he wore shorts that displayed strong leg muscles. He had been on a motorcycle, an officer I believe, during the days when the Allies were advancing on the continent in the European campaign. I remember a statement he made, "The Americans were filling the air with iron."

These Germans were getting ready to go back to Germany as the spring semester was coming to a close. We American students were staying up nights studying. Rowdyism was subdued as concern possessed us all with our studies. On the day in question we kept seeing the Germans carrying in boxes of beer and liquor. That the Germans loved their beer was not news, but the supply of that and booze that was coming in was enough to put every one of them in a drunken torpor, if not more. As the evening wore on, so did the crescendo of celebration sound. The floor plan of the top two floors of Lawyers was in the shape of an exaggeratedly broad "H" in which the vertical sides of the H were stubby short and the connecting horizontal hallway was very long. The Germans occupied most of the middle portion of that long hall. Soon the sounds of celebration gave way to the sound of crashing cans and bottles, accompanied by yells. The door of our room 305 opened looking out easterly into the length of the short east-west hallway at the south end of the floor. At the south end of the long connecting hallway was a fortification of chairs and room furniture, visible from our doorway. Behind this barricade were Germans who were rising to throw empty containers at the others who were doing the same behind a similar defense works built at the other end of the hall. It was bedlam. Concentration was impossible. But none of us had yet displayed the courage to challenge these inebriated warriors. Near the opposite end of our short east-west hall resided a good-natured, campus-wide popular, third-year student named Jack Cole. He was tall and big, not fat, just a good-size fellow. He seemed to sleep like a bear in hibernation, and who, if waked from that state, could act like one. Pretty soon, as the sounds became impossible to sleep through he came staggering out his door going straight for the gang behind the southern barricade. He spoke loudly in a peremptory and commanding way saying, "There will be no more of this tonight!" And there was not. The only sounds after that were slamming doors as the inebriants apparently started sleeping it off in their rooms. As I recall, most of us at our end tried the best we could to clear out the cans and sweep up the bottles, mostly broken. I'm not aware of any disciplinary action taken by the administrators against these rowdies, nor can I blame them for letting the incident go. But it was highly disruptive that evening. The next thing we knew, all the Germans had gone home.

Following that summer term, when the grades for the first two semesters and summer school were tallied, by a very small sliver I stood academically at the top of my class with a cumulative grade point average of 85.56. It had been 85.4 at the end of the first term and 86.53 at the end of the second term, having scored very high in the spring term. The dear Colonel Harding had blessed me with a score of 75 in Agency and Partnership, five points lower than the lowest score I had made up to that point, and the lowest I would make at SMU—this brought my average down. However, the entire class probably had a similar experience (even aside from poor Bill Jackson). The class leader through each of the regular year terms had been Bill Masterson, son of one of our very good professors, W.

D. Masterson, Jr. Professor Masterson was highly respected by all, including the Dallas bar in the field of oil and gas law. Since I seem to have passed Bill in cumulative grade average by virtue of summer school alone, his summer must also have been more humbling. In any event, allegedly because he and I were still so close together, the Dallas law firm Carrington, Gowan, Johnson, Bromberg & Leeds, which annually gave the top first year student after the summer term an engraved watch, elected this year to give a watch to each of us. It was an elegant gold watch engraved on the back as to the award. I wore it proudly through basic infantry training, the rest of the army days and for a good while after that. It had a leather strap that eventually wore down and I think I shelved it after that and have long ago ceased to possess it, its disposition not noted.

Marriage, Law School, and the Draft

A major event happened that summer. Jo Anne and I broke up, supposedly for good—four years of serious dating disappearing down the drain. Neither of us can now remember what caused this flare up. Whatever it was, I went out and bought three cans of beer. I had never yet drunk a full can of beer, so by my estimation three cans were enough for me to drown all my anguish. I took them to our room, where I was alone at the time, and as I poured each down I threw the empty can with all my might across the room. I'm sure something over there was shattered into a mess—on Miles' side. Once all three were down I collapsed on my bed. At length Miles came in, took one look and uttered, "God, Roomie, what happened?"

Not much time passed before we got together again. Neither of us can remember just how that happened either, but it did. But in the process, it seems apparent that we decided it was just time to get married. We were not having enough time together, had long been in love, and the time had come to go to the altar. Doubtless we talked first to Jo Anne's folks, then to my mother. None of our three parents had any objection but seemed immediately to go with the idea. Doc and Mom were committed to providing the cost of Jo Anne's one remaining semester, after which she would be qualified to teach school—and teachers were in demand. Jo Anne says that her dad was pleased with the arrangement because now my 1949 Ford would serve us both and he would not have to provide a car for Jo Anne when she started teaching. Jo Anne also remembers that he planned to give us $50 a month toward our living costs.

Since the wedding was not planned far in advance and needed to occur before fall classes started at SMU, we immediately immersed ourselves in the necessary preparations. Our wedding date was set for Friday evening, September 10, 1954, in the sanctuary of the First United Methodist Church in Wichita Falls, with reception to follow at the Women's Forum. The senior minister at First Methodist was Dr. Alfred Freeman (honorary doctorate), whose preaching my dad had enjoyed. But, while we were on the best of terms with Dr. Freeman, and his son Dick (Richard) had been a high school classmate of Jo Anne's and a friend of mine, "Pop" Porter was the natural choice to perform our wedding ceremony. There was the matter of choosing the wedding party, those who were to be involved in the wedding itself, what they were to wear, planning the rehearsal dinner and wedding reception, selecting rings, planning (more confidentially) the honeymoon, arranging a place to live, and doubtless other details.

The wedding party consisted of Jo Anne's younger sister, Jean, as maid of honor, my sister as her bridesmaid, my roommate, Dick Miles, as best man, and my friend and fellow accounting major at Midwestern, Al Guinn, as groomsman, and four other men as ushers. These latter included Ted Anderson, a friend from Midwestern, Paul Myers, Jr., Jo Anne's first cousin, Bob Pace, a law classmate who was from the small town of Iowa Park near Wichita Falls (and whose father owned the house my family had rented on Hayes Street), and Malcolm Drummond, a neighbor of Jo Anne's. Some girl friends of Jo Anne's were also helpful serving at the wedding reception. As is so often the case as one moves through life, those who are part of one's life at one stage cease to be as one moves from stage to stage, as a rather natural drifting apart or divergence of life's respective paths. Such has been the case in all instances, in varying degrees, and some have died over the years.

Seeing no need for engagement rings, Jo Anne and I chose, for her, at Sterling Wholesales Jewelers in Dallas, a platinum wedding ring set with diamonds. Our recollection is that it cost about $600, which, also as I recall, was pretty much identical with the balance

I then had in funds. Ours was a "single-ring ceremony." I had a powerful aversion to the wearing of any kind of ring, one that has remained with me all my life. I had bought a class ring at some point in my public education, probably when I graduated from grade school. I found myself constantly twirling it around my ring finger between by thumb and my little finger, and it never felt natural on my hand. It was a great annoyance to me playing the piano. The idea of any kind of a ring on any finger has continued to be unthinkable for me. And that is pretty much true with respect to jewelry of any kind, for me, though I am pleased for Jo Anne to have whatever she wants. Fortunately, her wants have not made me uncomfortable in these respects or otherwise. And that has generally been the case in the acquisition of material things of any kind. How fortunate I was on this in the selection of a mate.

Before we left Dallas, we found and rented an apartment to return to after our honeymoon. It was on the south side of Potomac Street in Highland Park, just a block or two west of Hillcrest Avenue and one block north of Mockingbird Lane. The intersection of Hillcrest and Mockingbird defined the southwest corner of the SMU campus except that Highland Park Methodist Church occupied the large corner property, at the northeast corner of the intersection, just south of SMU's Perkins School of Theology.

Constrained by both time and funds, our honeymoon was spent in a rustic cabin at the Lake Murray Lodge, south of Ardmore, Oklahoma, some eighty-six miles east-northeast of Wichita Falls. Weddings are tiring events, especially so I think for the bride and her family. Jo Anne was so worn out on our wedding night that after the reception, as I drove to Ardmore, she very soon laid her head in my lap and slept till we got there. We may have stayed only over the weekend. If that is the case, then it must have been Saturday afternoon that she got in the shower. As soon as she got lathered with soap, the water to our cabin area was shut off, an event of which we had no advance notice. Upon my reconnoiter, the only water conveniently available was a pitcher of cold water in the refrigerator. I climbed up on a chair to get above the top of the shower stall and poured the water slowly and carefully so that she could get all the soap off with the limited quantity available. It was invigorating for her and devilishly enjoyable for me. On Sunday afternoon we drove into Ardmore and saw the new movie "The High and the Mighty," featuring a cast headlined by John Wayne, about a commercial airliner in trouble over the Pacific. We drove back to Wichita Falls on Monday, gathering some of our wedding gifts and heading for Dallas, our new apartment and our married life together.

Our apartment was one of two on the first floor of a two-story house. The second floor was rented to other tenants. The other apartment on the first floor was occupied by the owners, a friendly couple but who seemed pretty old to us. There was one bathroom on the first floor, with a door into it from each apartment. Some type of a signaling system was worked out to avoid unwanted intrusion when occupying that facility.

Jo Anne and I had no more than gotten back to Dallas after our honeymoon than my best man, roommate Dick Miles and his girlfriend Karen McVeigh, came to us and said they had decided during our wedding events to get married, and they wanted Jo Anne and me to be their attendants, Jo Anne as Matron of Honor and I as Best Man, with no other attendants. They married in the chapel at the Oaklawn Methodist Church, where both of us couples attended, and it occurred nine days after ours, on Sunday, September 19. They promptly rented one of the upstairs apartments above us, theirs being on the east side and ours on the west. The one above us was never rented during our time there.

The Miles had not been dating nearly so long as Jo Anne and I, but long enough. An email to Karen as I write this, to inquire as to "approximately" when they had met, brought this reply: "It was at 8:30 p.m. Tuesday, February 8, 1954."[1] One morning before class

---

1 This date was exactly one week after my dad's death in Illinois. His funeral was on February 3, 1954. I must have hastened back after the funeral for the start of classes.

(doubtless the morning of February 9, 1954), and probably even before breakfast, while Roomie and I were still in our Lawyers Inn room, he went on about the "doll" he had met the night before. It was Karen. She had been raised near Pittsburgh, Pennsylvania and was doing modeling work there in Dallas. That marriage, like ours, has stood the test of time and they are still happily together in Fort Worth.

I have baked one pie in my life. It was an Eagle Brand lemon ice box pie with graham cracker pie crust, all of which I made from scratch during our short tenure in this apartment. It was a stunningly luscious success. I quit while I was ahead.

The armistice in the Korean War, which had started on June 25, 1950, was signed July 27, 1953. My four-year deferment for school had started with the fall term in 1950. By the end of the summer in 1954 it was ending. But with the armistice and my marriage, I thought perhaps I might be able to miss being drafted, or at least defer it till I could finish law school. With that thought in mind, as I said in the college years segment above, I went to the draft board in Wichita Falls and talked there with its director, Colonel Schwartz. Schwartz thanked me for reporting these things to him, but said that I was on the next draft call from Wichita Falls. He did tell me that I could arrange to report with the next group that was leaving from the area where I was living at the time, namely, the Dallas area. Whether from him or otherwise, I learned that a student required by the draft to report for military service during a semester of law school would, if departure was after the mid-point of the semester, be given credit, at his or her average grade, for all the courses in which enrolled for that semester, and this would be without any kind of an examination. Whether this practice was unique to SMU Law School or not I do not know, but it was a definite palliative if caught in the draft. As it turned out, there was a group leaving from Dallas one day past the mid-point in the semester, and I was able to arrange departure on that precise day. Ironically, in no other term of school did I ever take courses more directly involved in my chosen focus of Federal tax law than in that term. Included in that group were Income Taxation as well as Trusts & Estates. To the extent that one had to review all the fields covered that semester in preparation for taking the bar exam, the shortcoming was somewhat allayed but it was, in any case, not seriously detrimental to my later law practice. Course work in law school is important, but one learns an area of law practice by actually practicing it. The quip has made the rounds about the client not wanting to hire a lawyer who was still just "practicing" his trade, but the client will have a hard time finding a lawyer who is not then still just "practicing."

As soon as Schwartz informed me that my draft number was up, I tried to pull a few strings to get my reporting date deferred till the end of law school. Former Texas Attorney General Price Daniel had just been elected in 1952 as the new United States Senator from Texas. Though his position on various issues would later become increasingly inconsistent with my own views, at the time, I had been an enthusiastic supporter. I wrote to him expressing my situation at the academic head of my class, the armistice in Korea having been signed, and my willingness to serve after completing law school. He wrote a letter to the Wichita Falls draft board suggesting that my draft call be reconsidered. As I recall, it was reconsidered, but it was confirmed that my number was up and that I was to report on the next call.

Recognizing, finally, the reality of the situation, one day as I was walking from school to our apartment on Potomac, perhaps noting a military plane in the sky, I pondered the possibility of preemptively joining the Air Force and seeking flight training. The thought, fleetingly glamorous for a moment, quickly vanished as I came to my senses.

On the more practical level, Professor Riehm told me that I should visit with a night school law student, a licensed CPA, who was currently in military service assigned to the Army Audit Agency in Dallas. It was a most marvelous suggestion, which I followed. The student, whose name I do not recall, was most helpful in describing the agency and what qualifications it was looking for in those serving in the military. Having a degree in accounting and having passed the three parts of the CPA exam that I was permitted to sit for, I was delighted at the possibility that I might actually be able to accomplish something in my own long-range plans while serving in the military. Indeed, that was to come about, but that story belongs in the Army segment to follow.

Army

Basic Training

Wednesday, November 24, 1954, was one day past the middle of the fall semester in law school, one day before Thanksgiving, and the one day on which I had arranged to report to Love Field in Dallas for induction into the U. S. Army pursuant to my draft notice. Upon being there sworn in, I and others in that reporting group were loaded onto a commercial airliner for flight to El Paso, Texas, the headquarters for Fort Bliss, where my eight weeks of infantry basic training was to occur. As I write this, almost six decades have passed since my basic training in the U. S. Army; doubtless the manuals and requirements have changed. What I report may or may not be consistent with basic training today, but I write as I remember it from the mid-fifties as active fighting in Korea was subsiding.

My memory for the details of that day is scanty. Early formal steps in processing in included assignment to quarters, issuance of uniforms and gear, and receiving an extremely cursory physical and inoculations. Aside from the assignment of quarters and issuance of sheets and blankets for our cot, I believe these processes occurred on the day after Thanksgiving, the 26th rather than the 24th. What is certain is that we had a place to sleep that night, and it was the place we would be sleeping for seven of the next eight weeks, the one other week being that of bivouac.

Shortly before the Japanese bombed Pearl Harbor, in late 1941 the organizational structure for infantry divisions was changed from "straight" (fourfold unit structure) to "triangular" (threefold), the former fitting the needs of military action in WWI but not suited to the type developing by 1941. Thus, a division of four brigades or regiments (approximately 20,000 men) became a division of three (or 15,000 men)—brigades were generally a bit larger than a regiment, but the main difference was that a brigade was commanded by a brigadier general at brigade headquarters while a regiment was commanded by a colonel. A brigade comprises three battalions where a regiment comprises two or more battalions. However, I believe that for our basic training purposes the fourfold "straight" organizational structure prevailed because I know we had four companies, A, B, C, and D in our battalion, known respectively by their then military alphabetical names Able, Baker, Charlie, and Dog. While numbers vary in actual practice, my sense is that there were approximately 192 men in each company with each company comprising four platoons of 48 men, each platoon having four squads of twelve.[1]

My company was "Charlie Eight" or "C-8." I was in the third company (Charlie) which was a component of the eighth training battalion. Although they were so far above me that I only saw them in rare parade formation review, we did have a colonel (commanding

---

[1] My personal expertise on these matters is limited to my own company, so I rely largely upon information describing the "triangular" structure of a division as set out in http://www.mnstarfire.com/ww2/history/land/division.html as follows:

    Corps (Lt. General) = two or more divisions
    Division (Major. General) = three Brigades + Divisional HQ (10,000 to 18,000 men)
    Brigade (Brigadier General) = three Battalions + Brigade HQ
    Regiment (Colonel) = two or more Battalions
    Brigade & Regiment are nearly equal (Brigade generally being larger than a regiment)
    Battalion (Major) = three Companies (700 men)
    Company (Captain) = three Platoons & HQ Section (111 men)
    Platoon (Lieutenant) = three Squads & HQ (33 men) - a Tank Platoon is 3 to 5 tanks.
    Squad (Sergeant) = ten men (10 men)

the regiment) and once I saw a brigadier general (commanding the brigade). The latter was somewhat like having a glimpse of God. But from a lowly recruit's standpoint, even a PFC (private first class, with one stripe on the arm) represented commanding authority, something I learned the hard way from a medic while moving at a snail's pace through the physical check-up line.

The quarters for all the infantry inductees, at least for all of our battalion, and I'm sure many more, were huts that we understood had been condemned for use to house prisoners of war in World War II. Each hut housed five trainees, assigned in alphabetical order. There were five cots in each hut, one on the side opposite the door and two on each side next to the door. I do not recall that we had any heat in the hut, but if there was a heater in the middle it was not to be used because of possible asphyxiation and may not have had a fuel line connected. My cot was the one opposite the door. All heads and feet had to be in the same direction in such way that one man's head had to be next to the feet of the one alphabetically following him. The beds must have been assigned on a clockwise basis from the door, for the man whose feet my head was privileged to rest near was named Smithhisler (the pronunciation of the second "I" being long). Smithhisler was not a bad guy at all but he was not a man of high culture, and his boots and sox, which after a day of training activity were profoundly odiferous, were required to be placed at the foot of his bed very close to my nose. Fortunately my nose was almost always covered by my wool blanket, a necessity anyhow because of the very cold nights without heat in a hut whose paperboard walls welcomed in the cold outside air of Logan Heights, the portion of the eastern slope of the Franklin Mountains north of El Paso used for our basic infantry training at Fort Bliss. If we had been training in the summer's heat, the miasma rising from Smithhisler's boots would surely have asphyxiated me.

There was at least one other Smith in our company for a while. His name was David Smith. While he was with us, his cot was on the other side of me from Smithhisler. David was far more cultured, but the account of his departure comes in due course. John Smart was on the other side of David Smith, nearer the door.

My recollection is that aside from finding our quarters and making up our beds (cots), little was demanded of us on the 24th. Things were pretty lax, winding down for Thanksgiving the next day—nothing remotely military-like, other than sleeping on a cot. We may have been given a time for lights out, but there was no early bugle call on Thanksgiving. That day was incredibly leisurely and we were lavished with all the traditional Thanksgiving fare that was so fabulously good it would have honored royalty.

My thought as I retired on the evening of the 25th was, this army life is not at all bad. It was a study in contrasts. Our bliss at Fort Bliss was shattered by the bugler's reveille at 4:00 a.m. on the 26th.

The rigid aspects of military organization gripped us. Falling out from our huts, we were ordered to assemble in front of our company's administrative office, an elevated yellow building on the uphill end of our rows of huts. The administrator was a staff sergeant. When we were called to assemble, we were to do so in platoons and squads. Each of the four platoons, starting with Able and ending with Dog were lined up in rows of twelve-man squads (four squad rows per platoon). When the officer or enlisted man who was in charge of the assembly emerged from the administrative office, he shouted his information, instructions, and/or commands either from the platform outside the door or from ground level after descending the stairway from the platform down.

According to the divisional structure given above, each company was to be headed by a captain and each platoon by a lieutenant. Whatever may have been the case in other companies, our company did not to my knowledge have its own captain, but we had two lieutenants, and both of these were "real men" as I will shortly describe. The staff sergeant administrator was the only sergeant I can recall for our company, whereas structurally each infantry squad was to be led by a sergeant. Our drills were almost always under the command of a corporal or sometimes a PFC. So, obviously, for basic training purposes, the structure for combat was not pertinent.

One of our lieutenants was regular army and no one doubted his physical and leadership capabilities. It seems to me that he held a higher status than the other lieutenant did, probably by virtue of being a first lieutenant with the other being a second lieutenant. The latter, however, was respected as having been on the University of Tennessee football team that had been victorious in the Orange Bowl not too many years before. My intuition was that no recruit would have wanted to test individual combat capability with either of these.

As I recount my experiences in basic training, I will be using language as it was used there, lest their reality be diluted.

At the end of the organizational lectures on the morning of the 26th, we were lined up at the chow hall for breakfast. This was usually pretty good. Never before or since this eight-week stint were pancakes something I really liked much, but I must say that those served during this time were the best I've ever eaten—maybe because the weather was cold and I was always hungry.

After breakfast, still being in our civilian clothes, we were ordered by our corporal to police the grounds of the company area. The order instructed that we were to pick up anything below the animal kingdom, no matter how small, that did not grow in the ground, especially cigarette butts. This was our first of many occasions to police the grounds. As we broke ranks to scour the corporal shouted, "I don't want to see anything but assholes and elbows." We would hear this often.

The next thing was a trip to the quartermaster buildings where we were outfitted with both fatigue and dress gear. I was particularly fond of the field jacket. It was standard during the winter season and provided a surprising degree of protection from the weather. I hated to leave it behind when we had to turn it in at the end of basic. The more memorable part of our clothing allowance were the dress shoes and the boots. We wore the boots most of our waking time. For obvious reasons, boots have always gotten high priority as infantry gear. The foot soldier lives in them and boots that are not a perfect fit can turn into a real problem. Consequently, both the length and width of the foot are carefully measured and the proper size of both shoe and boot handed over. At an appropriate point in this gearing-up process a duffel bag was issued. When we left basic training, save for what we then had on, all our clothing, military and civilian, would be jammed into that bag.

A word about my shoes: I have a high arch and very wide feet that are short. My measured foot size required a size 8 triple E. My footgear was so short and wide that I looked like Donald Duck walking down the street. But whatever its stylish shortcomings, these were the most comfortable footgear I've ever worn. Especially did I hate, in later decades of hiking mountain trails and climbing peaks, not having those boots available.

Next came the infirmary building. There we were given a superficial physical exam and inoculated. For infantry engaged in the thick of mortal combat, surely the medic must be one of the most cherished personnel. Not so entering basic training. The lines for the several inoculation shots were long and slow. The medics seemed to enjoy demonstrating their authority in moving the troops through. I must have said or done something wrong in one of those lines, because in the process I ended up doing pushups. The medics injecting the needles seemed to get sadistic satisfaction in their work, rather as if they were playing a game of darts, targeting each soldier's arm or buttocks. The visual exam seemed a farce. The hapless recruit was placed before customary optometric chart, with the big "E" at the top, and asked if he could read what was at the top of it. Upon identifying it as an "E," he was waved on with some comment like, "Man, you've got eyes like a hawk."

But one part of this physical was the most memorable. A line of us recruits was stretched from wall-to-wall and told to turn facing away from the medic in charge. We were ordered to undo our belts and drop our pants and shorts to the floor and then bend down with head near the floor. This ridiculous posture evoked a sense of anxiety. The inevitable wise cracks earned a series of pushups. But things got worse. We were ordered to reach back with our hands and pull our cheeks apart. One by one the medic walked behind the line of troops bending down to inspect the center of each full moon. The word spread abroad that if he could see daylight at the other end, the recruit passed. I've often wondered how many pushups, or worse, would have been demanded if some fearless recruit had dared to squeeze off a jet of gas at the inspector. Considering the brevity of our physical exam, surely the purpose of subjecting us troops to this indignity was to instill in us the idea of total obedience to authority.

Two recruits in our company had recently graduated from law school and passed the Texas Bar exam. Upon receiving their draft notice they had applied for direct commissions in the JAG, the Judge Advocate General's Corp, the branch of the military concerned with legal matters, including military law and justice or other legal matters affecting the military or its personnel. Their applications were approved, but not before one of them, David Smith, my hut mate mentioned above, who seemed to have an effeminate nature, had "boloed" on the rifle range.[1] The problem was that a JAG commission started at the first lieutenant level. At least one of our lieutenants, the Tennessee football player, was a second lieutenant which meant that after David Smith's commission came through, if the two of them met on the grounds, military protocol required the company officer to salute David Smith. I heard this company officer say that if he saw David Smith coming he would cross to the other side of the street. Sadly, in later years, information came to me suggesting that David Smith, a civilian lawyer at the time, had taken his own life.

---

[1] The term *bolo* was military slang that, as used during our basic training, meant the failure of a recruit to qualify on the rifle range, and in the case in question involved numerous shots that did not even hit within any of the circular rings of the target, let alone the bull's eye.

The other JAG commission came to a recruit from some other platoon of our company who fancied himself an opera singer. He was by no means effeminate, quite the contrary. On a memorable occasion, he was in the structure that housed the company showers and latrine. While showering he was rendering some bold aria when someone on the latrine side yelled, "Someone step on it before it multiplies!" I think the company officers would have saluted him though, after his commission came through, had the occasion called for it.

By the time Thanksgiving was over there were not many days left in the week that I reported for duty. It must surely have been the next week, perhaps very early in it, that the staff sergeant stepped out his door onto the platform and one of the most urgent of his messages was, "Is there anyone in the company who is a good typist?" A piece of wisdom that more than once had come to my ears before I entered the service was, "Do not volunteer for anything!" Realizing that some others in that company surely considered themselves good, or at least adequate, typists, it hit me that now was the time for a quick decision, do I or don't I? Typing had always come easy for me. After one year of typing my junior year in high school I had a corrected speed well over sixty words per minute. But typing was also a required course for a business degree at Midwestern and I had a semester of it there where I attained an eighty-five words per minute speed. This is for accurate typing, where five or ten WPM were subtracted for every error on the paper over a set period of time of at least several minutes, no less than five. And this was in the day when there were only mechanical typewriters where the operator reached the right hand up at the end of every line and threw the carriage back to the left margin. Piano playing had probably benefitted me greatly in finger dexterity, still there was the matter of not having to think each letter but seeing the word with the fingers flying to the right keys immediately, meaning that accurate reflexive spelling was part of the equation. Typing from printed pages required a virtually spontaneous conversion from the printed word to the proper keys on the keyboard.

In any event, my gut told me that this is something I should volunteer for—quickly. I did. I got the job. I do not remember if there were others who volunteered. Perhaps if there were, the sergeant interviewed all of us as to our qualifications. In any event, I ended up working a good bit in the administrative office. This did not relieve me from participating in the events that were required in the training manual for basic training. But it did give me something a bit more pleasant to do at times when my fellow recruits were waiting in those endless slow lines or marching out to required training events or obediently displaying only their "assholes and elbows." On the occasions when a required training event was to occur, I would stay in the office doing any necessary typing or other work until shortly before the designated event was scheduled to occur. The sergeant would then put me in his car and haul me out to the event. Perhaps in some cases he even got me in the front of the line to do the event and then hauled me back, but I think sometimes I would merely arrive and he would leave and I would finish the day with the troops. Needless to say, I felt a sort of special relationship with the sergeant, who, I suspect, could not type worth a hoot and desperately needed office help for all his reports. There was one aspect of it that I did not care for. I really liked to march distances with the rifle and day pack on my back. I've always liked to walk or run and this part of the "benefits" of working in the office deprived me of that, especially was this so on the week of bivouac. That march was longer, seven miles as I recall, with a much heavier pack. That week had some special events that I could not miss, but I'm assuming, in thinking back, that the sergeant probably worked it out to come get me once or twice during that week—although perhaps not, since maybe he did not have the normal quantity of office work that week.

Whatever else might have occurred before, or even during, the third week of basic, that third week involved interviews and questionnaires specifically for the purpose of determining the MOS (Military Occupational Specialty) that a recruit would be assigned at the completion of his basic training. This is where I made sure that my accounting training and CPA testing came through loud and clear, as well as legal and other educational background. It would not be known whether it would get me to the Army Audit Agency (AAA) or not until our orders for where to report next were received at the end of basic training.

After I was humbled by the medic during the infirmary processing, there is only one aspect of the applicable rules and orders that I recall violating, and that was during the week of bivouac as will be recounted. In most other respects, during my eight weeks of infantry basic training, in my own immodest judgment I was a model soldier (given that I spent some otherwise killable time in the company office). But there is one thing the army failed to teach me. It became painfully obvious on the occasion of our first major dress inspection. We were admonished that the inspection would be by our battalion commander, a major, walking in front of every recruit in every squad in every platoon in the entire company—very formal. We were to stand at attention the entire time. After a squad was inspected, it took a step forward to make ample room for inspection of the next squad. We were in our winter dress uniforms—shoes and brass (on collar, jacket lapel, and belt buckle) clean and shining like the sun, uniform clean and pressed, same with shirt, collar, and cap, tie smartly and correctly tied and placed.

The object of all this was to select *the* model soldier from each company to represent it in later dress inspection at higher levels, each such model soldier to be written up in the publication of the regiment.

When the major had inspected all 192 of us, he returned and inspected a few, then finally just two. I was one of those two. He did a thorough look at both of us up and down. Then he came to me and said, "I pick this man, except for his filthy brass," and then he walked to the other man and said, "I pick this man."

The army never was able to bring me to the point where I could get my brass clean, shiny, and free of fingerprints; and this, even though I put in an inordinate amount of time trying; one of my life's great failures.

Obviously, in preparing for this inspection we were expected to expend some funds for cleaning and pressing uniforms, buying Brasso to clean and shine our brass, shoe polish, and other supplies. There must have been a place on the base for laundry and the cleaning and pressing of uniforms. The other supplies could be bought for very reasonable prices at the "PX" (Post Exchange). But this took cash. Where did that come from? I do not recall what the situation was about bringing money with us at induction. We were paid for our military service, and perhaps we might have had one pay period before this dress inspection.

Military pay for recruits is not going to make anyone rich. The lowest rank in the army, which is the recruit's rank for the first several months, is that of E-1 (enlisted first level). The pay at that level was seventy dollars ($70.00) per month. But if the recruit was married, forty dollars ($40.00) of that was withheld as a "Class Q Allotment" to be mailed to his wife. The net pay coming to the recruit could be picked up at the disbursing office on the base. After the required number of weeks (or months), the recruit became an E-2, and the pay went to seventy-eight ($78.00) per month. After that the next rank was PFC, and that is the exalted rank to which I rose in the army. Jumping momentarily forward, I did get into the AAA, and for the first sixteen months I was in the AAA, not a single promotion came through for military personnel in any of my San Francisco region's offices. We were there during a time when Eisenhower was strictly controlling non-essential military expenses. The AAA was not a military line outfit so it was very low on the totem pole for promotions. By the time I got my PFC stripe, my remaining enlistment period was far too short for me to satisfy the "time-in-grade" requirement to make corporal.

Recruits who, at the end of our eight weeks of basic infantry training, were classified with an infantry MOS were ordered into further and more advanced infantry training, doubtless increasing experience with weaponry not included in the first eight weeks of training. The weaponry that was involved in our eight weeks included primarily the Garand M1 Rifle, recognized as the finest infantry weapon in the world. In addition, we had training in the hand grenade, bazooka, and bayonet. While we were exposed to machine-gun fire, we were not trained in the use of any such weapons.

Hand grenade practice had to be conducted in a way that did not expose the troops to shrapnel from the exploding grenade. The grenade facility that provided such safety was a series of horseshoe-shaped concrete or sandbagged walls about waist high with a sump ditch lining the inside of the walls. The recruit who was to throw the grenade was accompanied by an officer or an otherwise-qualified drill instructor. In my case, it was our company officer who had played football at Tennessee. There were probably about six of these stations, all filled at the same time with a recruit prepared to throw. All personnel within one of these embankments lay flat on the ground within them except the recruit who was next to throw and his instructor. Specific motions were to be followed. A right-handed recruit would turn ninety-degrees to his right to face his instructor, firmly holding the grenade with handle depressed in the left hand while pulling the pin with the right hand. When the pin had been pulled, the handle was released and the recruit counted to a certain number in measured rhythm, then threw the grenade at the targeted area. He and his instructor then immediately fell flat on the ground within the wall and trench. In the event the grenade, for any reason, was dropped or could not be thrown after it was set to explode in due course, it was to be kicked into the sump ditch and the two men were to immediately fall flat on the ground encircled by the ditch, facing away from the grenade. The ditch had vertical walls and was deep enough to keep the path of the explosive force and shrapnel flight from hitting them.

Before any grenade was thrown, instructions were shouted for all to take cover. As I was preparing to throw, but had not yet gotten to the point of pulling the pin, I saw a grenade in flight while my officer, facing me, had his back to the launched grenade and could not have seen it. I immediately said, "There goes a grenade!" He said, "Get down!" We did, just in time to avoid the explosion. I could hear a chorus of singing shrapnel as it shot by above our heads or glanced off of nearby obstructions.

Each of us got to fire the bazooka, or rocket launcher, at an old tank a few hundred yards away. Before we could do so, the instructor warned us of the tremendous force of the retro blast from the back of the tube as the rocket was fired. He demonstrated by putting an empty wood crate on a stand directly behind the bazooka. The box was shattered when the rocket was launched. The danger was particularly to the one who assisted by feeding the rocket into the back end of, and arming, the bazooka for firing. The one firing was to wait for the "all clear" signal from the one assisting. Obviously, everyone else was warned to stay clear from the back of any rocket launching. Fortunately, we had no mishaps on the bazooka that day.

The main weapon training was on the M1. Every recruit was ranked as to his rifleman status, and everyone had to pass the minimal level of skill or go back through the training again. I do not recall the various levels, except that I believe the top level was "expert rifleman." The score for that was high, requiring at least some in the bull's eye. The primary distance between the firing line and the target was three hundred yards. What was surprising to me is the degree of precision that could be gained by the use of the strap on the bottom side of the rifle.[1] Use of the strap was required. By entwining that strap tightly around the arm that held the rifle to the shoulder, a steadiness could be attained almost equivalent to putting it in a vice. The rifle had a sighting system whereby the rifleman was to put the sighting pin near the end of the barrel so that the top of the pin was both in the center of the sighting circle on top of the rifle barrel and squarely on the target. Firing was to be done

---

1 See the picture of the rifle that has the strap on it, at http://en.wikipedia.org/wiki/M1_Garand.

from three positions, standing, sitting (with rifle elbow braced on raised knee), and prone. The lower two postures were more accurate than standing, thanks to greater stability. The recruit with adequate eyesight and attention to instructions should be surprised by how accurate his shots could be.

A recruit's day on the rifle range was divided between the firing line and target trenches. Each circular target, with the round bull's eye and three or four concentric rings expanding sequentially beyond it, were mounted on wood frames with handles extending downward from each side. Each recruit fired some number of eight-round clips from each of the three firing positions. The targets were raised from and lowered into trenches. Those recruits not assembled on the firing line were in the trenches. After a round of eight shots had been fired at a target, it was pulled down into the trench and a black circular indicator some inches in diameter was plugged into the hole made by the cartridge. These indicators could be seen from the firing line. A long pole could be used to point to them if needed, particularly those in the bull's eye. From these, the recruit's score on the rifle range was tallied and he was assigned the proper grade.

The most remarkable phenomenon to me of doing target service in the trenches was the impression made by the sound of the projectile smacking sharply through the target and then being followed by the crack of the rifle up range. It was a wonderful demonstration of the fact that sound moves dramatically more slowly than the speed of a bullet or fired projectile. This impression stuck with me from those days in the fall/winter of 1954–1955 to the summer of 1964, the second time I climbed the 14,305-foot Uncompahgre Peak in Hinsdale County, Colorado. I and my two climbing companions, standing as much as twenty-five feet apart, enshrouded by a cloud, were all knocked to the ground by a moderate lightning bolt. It felt like a ballpeen hammer on the crown of the head. The hit on the head was followed by the related sharp crack of thunder nearby. That sequence instantly registered in the reflexive part of my nervous system and instinctively flashed to me the reactive thought, "Some son-of-a-bitch is shooting at me."

How did I rank on the rifle range? My recollection is that I qualified in the second highest level. If I had not tried to show off, I was positioned to qualify as an expert rifleman. I had fired, in order, my clips standing and sitting, and two of the three lying prone. But just as I was ready to hit the ground for the last clip, the company commander approached my position. In my eagerness to get with it, I failed to get strapped carefully before firing. My score on that clip pulled me down. My guess is that a soldier new to a combat unit might, when face to face with the enemy, have a somewhat similar experience, but not from trying to show off.

In addition to the weapons used, we had training in the use of gas masks. I do not recall that we were actually exposed to any type of gas, though perhaps some non-lethal type, such as tear gas, may have been involved.

It was probably in about the sixth, or perhaps the last, week when we were required to undergo physical testing. This would go on our record. The testing involved push-ups, sit-ups, pull-ups (chinning on a high bar), and running. It was all done wearing full fatigue gear, including boots, except that only our T-shirt was above the belt. The testing was done on the gentle slope that prevailed on the mountainside. Both push-ups and sit-ups were done with head downhill and feet uphill. Each was to be done within a time frame that was fairly generous, but resting was to be done only while holding the up position (in push-ups) and the sitting uphill position (in sit-ups). I do not think that there was a time limit on chinning, which sort of imposed its own limits and required a drop to full arm extension between each one. Running was a timed event, done in sixty-yard bursts turning around a stanchion at each end, and I think the total distance was about three hundred yards. My recollection is that I did very well on all tests, and it seems to me that I did twenty-five chins which, with boots on, was one of the higher, if not the highest, number attained in my platoon, if not in the full Charley eight (C-8) company.

Army

Everyone anticipated the big week, the week of bivouac. It started with the seven-mile march with rifle and fully loaded backpack, including bedding gear, half of a two-person pup tent, mess kit, and many other items. I rode out in the sergeant's car, but think I had the opportunity to march back with the troops, which would have made me happy. Some aspects of the week were particularly memorable. It was very cold. During the entirety of basic training, daily shaving was required each morning. This was a gruesome task on bivouac in early January because our water supply, which hung in a fabric-covered tank, was frozen most every morning. We had to dry shave. Perhaps the numbing cold helped a little, but having to start the day in the dark by cutting off the day's growth with a safety razor without soap or water was not fun.

The cold was sufficiently severe that by the end of the week, half our company was put in the base infirmary. I was not one of those.

John Smart, from our hut, was my tent mate. On that I was fortunate. He was a tall, congenial fellow from Midwest City, Oklahoma (Oklahoma City complex), who had played football as a lineman in a junior college or small college in Oklahoma. The nights were cold in those tents. One yearned for a bit of warmth. The only method of doing that was by burning a can of Sterno in the tent at night.[1] The practice was specifically prohibited. This is the one rule I knowingly and intentionally broke, carrying a can of it in my pack and lighting it one night for warmth. John was happy for me to do so. But it backfired on me. In order to protect us from it getting against something flammable, I removed the plastic helmet liner and lit the can of Sterno in my steel helmet. How many nights I burned Sterno I do not recall. But on one night it must have gotten slightly tipped during the night, for in the morning, the fire had burned the chin strap where it was attached to the helmet. This must have been right at the end of the week, for I do not remember getting any reprimand for it and probably used the helmet without the strap for the short

---

1 See http://en.wikipedia.org/wiki/Sterno.

time remaining before shipping out, and the quartermaster did not make any big deal about it when I turned it in. One thing is for sure, I had that chinstrap tightly fastened during the infiltration course.

Bayonet training was during bivouac week. Another activity of that week was a simulated nighttime engagement with the company divided up into opposing forces. I remember the event, but its details escape me.

The big event, anticipated by all with anxiety, was the infiltration course. This was a course of some length, perhaps over one hundred yards. It had the type of obstacles that an infantry unit might be expected to encounter. There were pits with explosives going off resembling artillery or mortar shell blasts and tangled wire. But most of all, there was live thirty caliber machine-gun fire with tracer bullets three feet over ground level. The course was carried out at night, probably so that the tracer bullets above us would be frightfully obvious. We were required to emerge from trenches with our rifles in the face of that fire and crawl through these obstacles to a point not too far from the machine-gun embankment. In front of those guns was a barrier to keep stray bullets from coming closer than three feet to the ground; but who was going to test that level? The moment we were ordered out of that trench onto that course was the most unforgettable moment of the entire eight weeks. I hugged the ground so closely while crawling forward on elbows and knees that I ripped a gash in the front of my cherished field jacket. I later patched it with thread, but the prominent tear could not be concealed.

My time at Fort Bliss not only included Thanksgiving but also encompassed the entirety of the Christmas holidays. Christmas that year was on Saturday. We were all given a three-day pass for the holiday, Friday through Sunday. Across the Rio Grande from El Paso lay the Mexican city Juarez, a worthy tourist attraction in those days, and troops from the base normally enjoyed its haunts on the very few occasions when a pass was granted. Later in the training time the sergeant offered to give me a three-day pass, but I was

Army

not interested in going off base by myself. The most important time was at Christmas. My three-day holiday pass started precisely one month after I had left Jo Anne in Dallas. Her parents drove her and her younger sister Jean to El Paso and we all stayed in a motel there for the duration of the pass. Jo Anne and I had our own room and her folks left us pretty much alone, except perhaps for some meals together. We probably also crossed over to Juarez to experience that briefly, neither of us, however, being certain of that.

Juarez was an attractive place to visit in those days and for some years thereafter, not at all like it became as the drug lords took over and killings and kidnaping virtually closed it down as a tourist attraction. Some years after my army days, Jo Anne and I lodged in the famous Camino Real resort in Juarez and then later took our children in the camper to El Paso and went over to Juarez and the area surrounding that resort. Many happy memories remain to this day from those experiences, and it has been with great sadness that we have deemed Mexico unsafe to visit in more recent times.

At the end of the last week at Fort Bliss, each recruit received his orders giving him his next duty station and when he was to report there. It was a happy day. I was to report in San Francisco. While my pay station was at the Sixth Army Headquarters at the Presidio, I was to report to the Army Audit Agency office on Montgomery Street in the downtown financial district. The very idea of San Francisco was enchanting. My family had gone to southern California in 1948, but never had I been in the Bay Area.

I think we were given a travel allowance to get home or to our next duty station, and I was given a few days before being required to report. Some man had a station wagon and was offering transportation from Fort Bliss to Dallas for ten dollars. I took it. The vehicle was full, with five or six of us, the driver, and our stuffed duffel bags. That day was when I discovered how far it was from El Paso to Dallas. Google gives it now as 635 miles requiring eight hours fifty-four minutes, but that was at today's speeds on today's highways. It was a very long day.

The only thing I remember between that day and the day we left driving to San Francisco was when we were packing all our belongings that were not stored in Jo Anne's parents' attic into our 1949 Ford. I had the car parked at the curb out front. We got everything stacked out there on the sidewalk or grass next to the car. My distinct memory is that Dick and Karen Miles were standing there with Jo Anne, all three shaking their heads at me and saying that I could not possibly get all of that stuff in that car. I rose to the occasion and proved them wrong, but aside from the trunk, things were piled in the back seat higher than the tops of the front seats, with the ironing board lying at an angle loose on top of it all.

Fortune could not have smiled more brightly on us in respect to the timing of my arrival home and Jo Anne's completion of her final semester at SMU. They were essentially simultaneous, at the end of January, on the cusp, as it happened, of the first anniversary of Dad's death February 1, 1954. I was now out of basic, ready to put my accounting training to good use and Jo Anne was qualified to be an elementary school teacher, a qualification that was in critically short supply in both California and Texas.

California

While both of us had seen the Grand Canyon with our own families long before we met, we planned our route out to go by the South Rim of the Grand Canyon. It required a considerable detour off of US Route 66. We drove north out of Flagstaff to Cameron, then west to connect with the most southeastern points of the national park, driving thence along its south rim to the famous Bright Angel Lodge. That drive was memorable for at that elevation the ground and top portions of the canyon were snow covered. Though it was night it was clear and picturesque. It remains vivid in our memory. We stayed that night at the lodge. Jo Anne remembers that as we left the next morning, a huge icicle extended from the lodge roof to the ground. From there we drove south to Route 66 at Williams, thence west on the long road through the California desert and roads up to San Francisco.

The Army Audit Agency was originally established on November 12, 1946, by General Order No. 135 at the request of the Under Secretary of War, with specific accounting and auditing services pertaining to the U. S. Army and the American Red Cross.[1] Its responsibilities were refined and clarified over the years and it remains an active and significant arm of the U. S. Army.[2] During my service in the Agency (February 1955–September 1956), it was my understanding that AAA reported directly to Congress so that our functions were not under the command of lower military authorities, such as the Sixth Army, even though AAA branches were located within the army areas and pay stations were from those areas. It appears that this information given to me was not correct but that we were always an arm of the top levels of the U. S. Army to which we reported and were responsible. The existing organizational structure continues to reflect the essence of our responsibilities in the 1955 to 1956 period. More simply stated, we had audit responsibility for both "internal" and "contract" auditing, the internal referring to the audit of military installations themselves and contract auditing referring to the auditing of contracts entered into by the army with commercial establishments under the procurement laws and regulations then in effect. Our governing manual in contract auditing was known as ASPR, the acronym for Armed Services Procurement Regulations. The name of those regulations may now be the Defense Acquisition Regulation.

When I reported to the AAA office on Montgomery Street, it seemed that they did not quite know what to do with me. Someone handed me a copy of ASPR and said to study it, which I did for the three boring weeks I was in that office. Sitting in that office for three weeks with nothing to do but study that manual was driving me batty

---

[1] See http://en.wikipedia.org/wiki/United_States_Army_Audit_Agency.

[2] See http://www.army.mil/aaa (AAA Organization Structure).

with frustration. They had informed me that none of the auditing was done directly out of that San Francisco office, for it was just the regional office with jurisdiction over the four active branch offices in the Sixth Army area. Those four branch offices were at Oakland, Seattle, Salt Lake City, and Los Angeles. In one manner or another I learned that a big part of the work at the first three of these was on internal audits at military installations. That was of no interest to me. What I found interesting were the audits of defense contracts at companies manufacturing goods for the army. These were heavy in cost accounting work. The one branch where the heaviest concentration of contract auditing was done was in Los Angeles. Probably I made my wishes known, for whatever good that might have done.

But no orders were issued for me to report anywhere for three weeks. It turns out that the office there (or at the Presidio) was waiting for Washington to issue the order and apparently Washington was either unaware of that or was waiting for the order to be issued from San Francisco. Finally, the order came from Washington and, to my great satisfaction it was to the Los Angeles branch located at 1206 Santee Street, Los Angeles, my home station, as it turned out, for the rest of my enlistment up to the processing out that was done at Fort MacArthur in San Pedro south of Los Angeles.

During off duty hours, Jo Anne and I were able to enjoy the sights of downtown San Francisco, but not any part of it that cost money. As yet her class Q allotments from November 24 on had not caught up with her and she was not yet where she could even apply for a teaching position. Our funds were limited and were diminishing rapidly. We were staying in a downtown hotel, and although not the most costly it was taking our cash balance down too quickly. We could only walk the streets, and look in the windows, for increasingly as time went by we spent only for necessities. An added anxiety was that our car was parked in a lot directly across the street from the hotel with all our possessions still loaded in it, and the right back door would not lock. How times have changed. Not one thing was taken from it during the entire three weeks.

Army

One wonderful thing occurred to us while in San Francisco. There was another recruit named Dick Levy lolling around the Montgomery Street office while I was. Dick was a Jewish fellow from New York City. I rather think he was assigned to Los Angeles also, but if so we did not have any memorable assignments or association together there. However, while in "Frisco" he spoke highly of a fashionable new food that was then popular in New York called pizza pie.[1] We had never heard of it. He had either eaten at a place that served it in Frisco or found out about a particular one. We had a car there. He did not. So we invited him to go with us to this place. The back seat was loaded nearly to the roof, with the ironing board on top, so all of us had to ride in the front seat. I drove, Jo Anne sat in the middle, and Dick sat next to the passenger-side door. Anyone who has driven certain parts of that city knows that there are hills there that are so steep up and down that, when going over their top in an automobile, the street below cannot be seen by those in the car that is about to plunge down. As we began that steep downward plunge the ironing board slid off its perch in the back seat and clipped Dick about where a guillotine blade would land. It was not fatal, and given a spell to recover from shock and manageable pain, a good laugh was had and we proceeded to the pizza parlor where all unhappy thoughts were dispelled. The atmosphere was cozy and very Italian, with overhead trellis and the aroma of oregano and tomato sauce wafting throughout. When our pizza was served, somehow the aroma of all that melted cheese, tomato sauce, and oregano was so obnoxious to me that I did not think I could get it past my nose into my mouth. But once there, I was forever addicted. The only problem is that I've never had another pizza that wonderful. We did find a little shop, pretty atmospheric, in Eagle Rock, once we got to the Los Angeles area, that was almost as good. When mother visited us out there, we took her and she loved it as

---

1 May the San Franciscans forgive me for this abbreviation, which I have understood is not so popular among them. The full name is lovely, but a burden to spell out each time in frequent usage.

much as we did. Sadly, even the best pizza these days seems not to have that magic combination of tomato sauce and oregano, and I'm seldom able to even detect the presence of oregano—very sad.

Aside from learning a bit about ASPR in San Francisco, I was also enlightened by a seagull. To help kill a weekend, Jo Anne and I went to the beach south of the Golden Gate Bridge and the Presidio. We did not go to swim. The Pacific Ocean always seemed too cold, and besides it was February. I went for the purpose of fishing. We packed a picnic lunch. Jo Anne took a book and settled down on a blanket to read and watch me fish. From my days in Flora I had an old rod and reel of the type used up there mostly for bass fishing, which I did not do much of. For bait, I bought a sack of shrimp at the Fisherman's Wharf market. After we had spread the blanket I assembled my fishing gear and put a shrimp on the hook. Moving the sack a bit closer to the water I then walked twenty or thirty yards north to begin my happy quest. Not long after my first cast, I heard Jo Anne yelling, "Ed, Ed—the seagull." Looking to see what the yelling was about I saw her pointing toward the sack. A seagull was plucking away at it with purpose. I threw down my fishing line and ran toward the gull yelling and frightfully flapping my arms to scare it away from my sack of shrimp. The gull took one look at me, calmly picked the sack up and flew several yards down the beach sitting the sack back down. My fearsome charge continued as fast as I could go in that sand. The gull calmly repeats the procedure, and this may have gone on one or two more times before the gull finally picked up the sack and flew out a good ways into the ocean before setting it down and pecking it open and consuming all my shrimp. I caught no fish but learned a bit about seagulls.

When my orders came through we immediately headed for L.A. Except for reporting to my duty office, the immediate necessity was finding a place to rent. On that we were fortunate. In general we wanted to be somewhere in the Glendale-Pasadena area, several miles on the expressway north of downtown L.A. In those days I had close relatives living in the San Fernando Valley. Having an apartment in the chosen area would be intermediate between work and family. The smaller city of Eagle Rock lay on the famous Colorado Boulevard midway between Glendale on the west and Pasadena on the east.[1] The north-south Eagle Rock Drive crossed Colorado Boulevard in the center of Eagle Rock. The ascending grade of Eagle Rock Drive up to Hill Drive was pretty steep. From an ad in an Eagle Rock paper or from a yard sign, we found a well maintained, but modest yellow duplex that was on the mountain slope just one lot downhill from the palm-tree lined Hill Drive that also ran between Glendale and Pasadena. We knocked on the front door. Presently a lady we judged to be in her late seventies or early eighties, with a distinct German accent and manner, appeared. Her name was Bauer—*Miss* Bauer. In time we learned that she had been an army nurse in NYC during the Spanish-American War (1898). There was a three-room apartment for rent above her three-car garage at the back of the house, which had an indoor stairway at the north end of the garage. It also had a small breakfast nook, where I studied. We were able to rent it for $45.00 per month. There were avocado and lemon trees on adjoining lots out our windows and flowers around the house and driveway leading back to our apartment. It was an ideal set up and we stayed there happily until we were in the process of coming back to Dallas.

Our days and activities there were interesting and varied, including the nature of my audit work in the AAA, the wonderful establishment of a meaningful connection with my California relatives, experiencing a small bit of the immense reality of Los Angeles and the San Fernando Valley in the mid-fifties, studying for and passing the one part of the CPA exam that I had not been able to take earlier, attending night law school, and experiencing the wonderful outdoors of northern Arizona from the Flagstaff area.

Promptly upon arrival in L.A., Jo Anne and I each immediately immersed ourselves in getting started in our respective jobs there.

---

1 See http://en.wikipedia.org/wiki/Colorado_Boulevard.

First, Jo Anne had to get a teaching position. That was virtually automatic. She was promptly hired by the Los Angeles Schools and for the duration of our stay taught second grade at the El Sereno School in East Los Angeles, an area of economically disadvantaged children.

My duty station was at the AAA office at 1206 Santee Street in downtown L.A. However, little of my time was actually spent in that office. Only in between audit assignments would I be there for a short period at most.

An anxious financial situation presented itself in our earliest days in L.A. My salary was still well below $100 per month, although I was given a per diem allowance for living off of a military base in the amount of $2.87 per day, or about $86.00 per month. Jo Anne's salary was $400.00 per month for the school year itself. We faced a scary squeeze, however, when we got down to only five dollars between zilch and us. Even in those days, that would not get us far. I did not want to ask our California family for help, and though our parents would gladly have helped, the logistics of that were problematic. The problem was that my pay day was not that close and Jo Anne had not reached her first pay check. But by then we also had four months of her class Q allotment of $40.00 per month, taken from my total pay of less than $100.00, none of which had ever caught up with her. We knew money had to start coming in soon, but until then we could not eat on that knowledge. Then, like manna from heaven, it all came at one time—her back class Q allotments and first monthly pay check as well as my paltry net monthly check. Never have I ever felt so rich as I did that day.

I felt so rich that I went forthwith to the Merrill Lynch office in Pasadena and bought twelve shares of a company I at least knew the name of, American Airlines, my first stock investment. We held it until Monday, September 26 of that year, 1955. Eisenhower had his first heart attack early Saturday morning, September 24, one day after my twenty-third birthday. While that was a shock, I felt some pride in thinking, "I believe his heart attack makes this a good time to sell my stock." Every one with a lick of sense and any experience, requisites I lacked, would have known that the market would have a hard time opening Monday morning. Indeed, trading did not start for a good while beyond the opening bell, and when it did there was an air pocket under stocks and they fell mightily. I had called before the opening and told my broker to sell all twelve of my shares. I apparently did not know anything about limit orders, so it was placed as a market order, which meant that it got crucified as it was executed at the time of the free fall. In the long run it probably was a reasonable tuition cost for its educational value. But I did not feel quite so rich anymore.

My first audit assignment in L.A. was in the accounting office of a small manufacturing plant in El Segundo, near the ocean between Santa Monica and Palos Verdes. Over the rest of my enlistment period I was in the accounting offices of many plants all over the area, including the large Firestone plant. Except for the very few internal audit assignments, discussed later, all my assignments were heavy in cost accounting work and involved, over the course of that period, each of the two major types of cost accounting, job order or process, as well as instances involving a combination of each. From the standpoint of one hoping to complete his remaining section of the CPA exam, it was priceless experience in a major area of accounting practice that was almost always substantially represented in the exam. As earlier indicated, in 1955 completion of the one-year practice requirement was a prerequisite to take the exam. Currently the Texas law permits one, having met other statutory requirements, to take the exam before meeting the requirement to have "one year of full-time work experience under the direct supervision of a licensed CPA," but the certification must await completion of the practice requirement. My recollection is that in 1955, the experience could be under either a CPA or a licensed "public accountant," and it seems to me that the Texas State Board accepted what it deemed to be the "equivalent" of such experience requirement. I could not have started the audit work in Los Angeles any earlier than sometime in the second half of February 1955, and I surely must have received permission of the State Board to take the practice part not long thereafter, for I took the exam in May or June and entered the night school of Loyola in downtown L.A. in the fall term of 1955. I can only speculate at this time on how I satisfied the Board on the one-year of public accounting experience requirement, but the fact is I did. Thus I was permitted to sit for the practice part of the examination, the last of the four parts and the only one I was not able to take while at Midwestern in the spring of 1953. Practice is the longest of the four parts, requiring two half days, while each of the other three was allotted only a half day. I sat for the exam later that spring. It was proctored by the California Society of CPAs and took place in a large building on the USC campus. I studied intensely for the exam. The cost of my CPA Coaching Course at the LaSalle Extension University out of Chicago had been paid for in 1953. The practice part of the course was still available to me, and to the extent of my available time I attacked that course of study vigorously when I learned that the Texas Board would accept my experience as soon as my year was completed. Just when that was to be I do not recall and cannot presently find the certificate, which was mounted on my law office all the years I practiced law. Joyfully did I read the congratulatory telegram that finally came that summer saying that I had passed. Licensing by the Texas Board followed during the year 1955.

The larger portion of the staff in the L.A. AAA office were Civil Service employees of various grade levels. At one point, and for most of my time, I noted that there were sixteen of us auditors who were military personnel. That group comprised nine Jews, four Roman Catholics, and three Protestants; an alignment I thought was probably not too different from the composition of the financial industry as a whole. It was simply an observation, for the working relationships were excellent. Some come back to mind as I reflect. The only one of the group with whom some relationship continued beyond my army days was an Oklahoma fellow named Clarence Vaughn.

He and his wife Marie once visited us in Lubbock on their way somewhere else and for quite some number of years we exchanged Christmas cards, normally including a note updating with the year's events. Two military auditors, a Gary and a Stewart (or Stuart) whose last names I cannot recall, climbed a mountain with me during an internal audit, and one civilian employee, Cal Root, who at forty-four was almost double my age, hiked with me into the Grand Canyon in the summer of 1956.

The auditors who were military in our office were mostly buck privates like myself, but we had a few lieutenants who were either fulfilling an ROTC commitment or had received a direct commission in finance at the cost of a three-year enlistment. Rank had no effect whatsoever on work assignment. One of these officers was named Nader, as in Ralph Nader. That name became meaningful to Jo Anne and me much later for the late Sam Nader, a native of Lebanon, though much older, was our close friend and pastor at First United Methodist Church in Lubbock for about sixteen years.

Jim O'Brien was one of the more memorable of these assigned military personnel. He was a tall, handsome, blue-eyed blond who appeared in the office one day and immediately impressed me as someone I would be interested in working with, if possible. A new assignment for me was in the process of issuing. At my request, the auditor in charge (AIC) asked personnel to assign this new man to our upcoming audit team. The request was granted. Jim O'Brien, was an Irishman from Boston, a buck private who had just graduated with an MBA degree from the Harvard Business School. Jim had been on the Harvard hockey team for four years starting in the 1950/1951 season, and not long after he joined our office he accepted an invitation to try out for the U. S. Olympic Hockey Team, and was granted leave to do so. As he reported to me later, he felt he had made the cut but in the last scrimmage before the cut was announced, he disqualified by breaking his arm.

Harvard's business school is preeminent. Its training must be rigorous. But I had to chuckle at an incident that occurred right at the first of that initial audit assignment of his. He came over to me, out of the presence of the AIC and said, "Ed, what did he (the AIC) mean when he told me to foot this column of figures?" Every beginning accounting student in my more mundane accounting training at Midwestern quickly learned that to "foot" a column of figures meant to add it up. It was, of course, decades before computers automatically kept a running total for you. Obviously, it seemed, these little practical niceties of the trade had not penetrated the lofty heights of instruction at the Harvard Business School.

My mother's eldest sibling was her sister Ruth, born March 16, 1898. Ruth's husband, my Uncle Everett Colclasure, was born and raised in Xenia, IL, some seven or eight miles west of Flora on U. S. Route 50. He served in the U. S. Army in WWI. They were married August 15, 1920. Uncle Everett was a victim of poison gas which was used by both sides during that war. It affected his health for the rest of his life. He was advised for medical reasons to move to a drier climate than that of southern Illinois. The family moved to Albuquerque, NM. Their son Bryce was born in Flora July 30, 1921, before they moved. Ruth Ann was also born in Flora, on April 19, 1923, but they had moved between those births, and Aunt Ruth had returned to Flora to deliver her baby. As I write this, Ruth Ann, who is in a nursing home, is the only one of my generation, or higher, on either side of my family, older than I.

Bryce was said to have been a very good baseball pitcher, but a limit was placed on his future in baseball because he had some apparently congenital heart defect, from which he died on April 21, 1984, at the young age of sixty-two. His heart defect kept him from serving in WWII, but he found employment in the aircraft industry in California and soon found work there for his dad, prompting Uncle Everett and Aunt Ruth to move out there also. By the time we visited them in 1948, they lived in separate houses very near (front and back) each other, separated only by a garden, in the San Fernando Valley north of L.A. Aunt Ruth had a sewing room back of their garage off to one side between the houses. It also served as a small guest room on occasion. Upon our arrival in L.A., Jo Anne and I stayed in that room until we found our apartment in Eagle Rock.

It was almost as though there had never been those long years of separation. The affections ran deep between all of us. From our standpoint, it gave us family nearby and we spent holidays and other times together in warm, familial relationship. Bryce and his wife Judy, lived back behind Aunt Ruth and Uncle Everett. They had two young daughters, Kathleen, who was probably about five and Barbara, about two. One of those events that is memorable to all of us was the Christmas morning when we were around the tree at Bryce and Judy's house and were opening packages. Judy opened a gift from Bryce. It was a pair or pairs of fancy panties. Barbara grabbed them, got in the middle of the floor, and began putting her legs through them. We all laughed and it was remembered by all. We still talk about it six decades later.

Before my tour of duty was over, we invited Aunt Ruth and Uncle Everett to take a car trip with us over into the vast and sometime scenic country beyond the Sierras into Nevada, including a drive through Death Valley, experiencing its unique, barren beauty in moderate temperature, visiting also its notable Scottie's Castle. The whole trip with them was fun. There was a good bit of laughter. What it was about neither of us remembers. It was some significant inconvenience I think, and it prompted Uncle Everett to jovially remark, "It is just another chapter in the book." Funny how little things like that flood back in happy memory.

Family from both Illinois and Texas came to visit while we were in L.A. Mother and Mary Anne came and spent at least a month, perhaps two, in the summer of 1955. We had furnished our apartment with economical ingenuity, including borrowing some things Aunt Ruth was not then using. Aunt Ruth also provided us two roll-away beds upon which mother and Mary Anne slept, though they also spent some time, as Jo Anne and I had, in Aunt Ruth's little sewing room. Jo Anne's sister Jean came out for Christmas, 1955. Bryce and Judy's young daughter, Kathleen, and Ruth Ann's somewhat older daughter Camille, spent a week with us also. Jo Anne's parents and her own Aunt Ruth and Uncle Frost came out in the summer of 1956 and they caravanned with Jo Anne when she drove back at the end of my enlistment. The California family participated in all these visits from Illinois and Texas family in a way joyful for all.

The family days in California were rich and those relationships have continued warm and loving ever since, even as older generations have moved on to higher realms. Uncle Everett died first, on June 10, 1970. Aunt Ruth followed on April 5, 1979, Bryce on April 21, 1984, and Judy on April 22, 1991. But life goes on, and their descendants have flourished in both number and continued relationship.

It was either near the beginning of the 1955 fall or the 1956 spring term that we received word from a mutual friend that Richard Miles and his wife Karen were really struggling. They had married on September 19, 1954. Karen quickly became pregnant which brought an early end to her work as a model. With the increased expenses and loss of one earner, Dick had started working a forty-hour week on the night shift for the post office while continuing to carry a full-time load in law school in order to graduate on schedule in 1956. But they were struggling to make ends meet and the stress on my former roommate and best man was immense. Jo Anne and I talked it over. By then we were getting by pretty well on our combined incomes. By agreement between us we sent them some funds. Roomie responded saying that we would never know how much that meant and at what a critical time it arrived. He was able to buy books for the courses he was beginning, which otherwise he simply could not have done.

It was a tight squeeze, but I was able to enroll in night classes at the Loyola Law School in downtown L.A. for its fall 1955 term, and then for the spring 1956 term. I took the following courses there: Business Associations (Corporations), Legal Profession (Ethics), Conflict of Laws, and Evidence. But my twelve hours of

Army

credit there were recognized by SMU, though only grades made in courses taken at SMU were taken into account in calculating the cumulative grade average.

By having taken these major courses while in the service, I was able to finish law school at SMU only one year behind the class I started with, while having fulfilled my two-year enlistment obligation. My actual time served ended, however, on September 17, 1956. Thus, I served in the army one week less than twenty-two months. A recruit who desired to enter a fall term of college or advanced education could apply for an early release if his enlistment ended within less than three months after the start of the relevant school term. If granted, he would have fulfilled his full time obligation.

The front cover of *Time Magazine* dated August 8, 1983, featured the picture of a man identified as "National Security Adviser William P. Clark." The related cover story was entitled "The Man with the President's Ear" and called him the "most powerful man in the White House" next to Reagan. Anyone remotely connected to national events at that time knew Clark's name and that he was Reagan's closest, most trusted, and influential adviser, going back to their days as neighboring ranch owners and Reagan's political life in California. Clark had become Governor Reagan's highly effective chief of staff, and Reagan, though criticized for cronyism and lack of candidate qualifications, had later appointed him to various judicial positions including as an associate justice on the California Supreme Court where he served from March 23, 1973, to March 24, 1981, when Reagan called him to Washington. It was not that I had not generally been aware of all this. But the name William Clark, or the more casual Bill Clark, while not as common as Ed Smith, is not at all an unusual name in our country. But when I saw the picture of him on the *Time* cover, the name and the face coalesced into a memory of a fellow night law school student I buddied with in the evenings at Loyola Law School in the spring of 1956. I thought, "Could this possibly be the Bill Clark that I knew back then? I hesitated at the thought of writing to someone in that elevated position. Yet it was possible and the strong urge to put the matter to rest prompted me to write to him. Essentially I described to him the situation when I knew a Bill Clark in night school at the Loyola Law School in L.A. Whether or not there was some slight mention in that article of him having an interest in classical music, having myself only the year before, as will appear later herein, played a Beethoven piano concerto with orchestra, I enclosed a cassette tape recording of the concert.

Clark soon wrote back to me saying, in words indelibly inscribed in my mind, "Yes, we were outlanders and brown baggers together." And he commented that he and his wife Joan loved classical music and often went to the Kennedy Center to hear it performed.[1]

Nothing between 1956 and 1983 caused me to ponder at any great length on Bill Clark. Without a doubt, however, he was the only person, other than one or two professors, of whom I had any memory from that semester. It actually felt to me like we reached out to each other as though there were no others for either of us, which was pretty much true for me—at least that was and is my perspective on it as I reflect back, and it seems to fit not only his quoted response above but also his personal circumstances at the time. It was unthinkable that I should write anything at all about my Loyola evening classes without mentioning that relationship, and in doing so I googled the name William P. Clark and in the process found and immediately ordered the book *The Judge: William P. Clark, Ronald Reagan's Top Hand*, a 2007 publication of what was both a biography of him and surely the most intimate and informative of all articles or books on Reagan and his presidency.[2] Clark was the only one, aside from Reagan himself, who could possibly speak of events in the light of those many sessions where only those two were

---

1   He and his wife Joan had a "mutual love of Mozart," infra *The Judge*, 50.

2   The book was written by Paul Kengor and Patricia Clark Doerner. Doerner was a cousin of the William P. Clark in question (there was one other William P. Clark in the family, though their middle names were different).

present, especially on the most trying issues of the day where only the President's most trusted adviser was consulted.

What so amazed me is that my erstwhile friend seemed so modest and likeable, not in the least way one to put himself forward.[3] He was one of the easiest I've ever met to feel instinctively completely at ease with from the first. It was just hard for me to imagine how such a non-self-assertive and modest person could be one and the same as this prominent figure on the national and world scene.

Between 1983 and my reading of *The Judge*, I had assumed that Bill could be so modest because he came from a prominent landed family who had ranch property next to Reagan and that Bill, in spite of his seemingly humble status in night law school, had risen quickly as a lawyer in the years before being appointed by Reagan to high judicial post in California. But it seemed odd that one coming from that family background would be going to night law school rather than attending as a prominent day student. Something did not quite fit. My disillusionment came as I read his background in *The Judge*. Actually times had been hard for his family, and the ranch was one he acquired later with help. But what really astounded me is that from an academic standpoint Bill had apparently laid a firm foundation for modesty. He had left Stanford because it "was not right for him, socially or academically."[4] After a year at an Augustinian seminary in New York and two years of pre-law in a Jesuit college to bring his grades up to a "respectable level" sufficient to be admitted to Loyola law school in Los Angeles, he "headed back to Southern California in his 1931 Model A Ford and spent the rest of 1952 and most of 1953 at Loyola.[5] He was drafted in late 1953.

---

3 Prov. 25:6–7.

4 *The Judge*, 46.

5 Ibid., 49–50.

At twenty-four years of age [in 1955], Clark returned to his goal of becoming a lawyer.[1] He enrolled at Loyola Law School, taking evening classes and worked full time during the day, earning income as an insurance adjuster...in downtown Los Angeles. He also performed odd jobs when he could get them.... As costs mounted to an uncomfortable level, Clark left Loyola before completing the requirements for a degree; he had, however, earned enough credits to qualify for the bar exam.[2] After studying on his own for a year, he passed the California bar on a second try in 1958.[3]

Clark would hold a number of prominent posts in Washington during the 1980s, but he was first nominated by Reagan January 23, 1981, as the number two person, behind Alexander Haig, in the State Department, which required confirmation. Robert G. Kaiser, in a Washington Post article January 24, 1981, said that Clark "had to withdraw from Loyola, an evening law school, because of poor grades."[4] Clark's appointment was eventually approved by split vote, but on February 16, 1981, "Time magazine introduced Clark to the American public in this way: 'He dropped out of Stanford University with poor grades. He flunked out of Loyola University Law School." It may all be a case of spin, but Clark's significant qualifications seem not to have been academic in nature (though he spoke German

---

1 Clark was born Oct. 23, 1931, eleven months to the day before my birth.

2 Clark was a devout Roman Catholic. He met Joan, an East European refugee in West Germany, while he was serving in the army counter-intelligence corps in Mannheim, Germany. They married May 5, 1955, in a Catholic Church in Basel, Switzerland. He was discharged in September 1955, returning with bride to California where he entered night law school at Loyola in L.A. The first four of their five children were born in 1956, 1957, 1958, and 1959—the fifth in 1963. Understandably, "his costs mounted to an uncomfortable level" which, suggestively, is why he withdrew from law school, and also possibly why his grades may have suffered, if such indeed was the case. *The Judge*, 55–57.

3 *The Judge*, 56.

4 Ibid., 107–108.

and served in the army's Counter Intelligence Corps).⁵ Indeed, the irony is that Clark, who seemed to have few recognizable qualifications for his various high positions, may have gotten there to a remarkable degree as a natural result from his own modest and self-effacing nature. While I personally feel the passage has a deeper meaning, the words of the beatitude come to mind, "Blessed are the meek for they shall inherit the earth."⁶ It must surely have been that magnetic quality, without respect to any academic prowess, that pulled me toward him as a friend at Loyola. The relationship was as comfortable for me as an old shoe. But alas, as with so many others one meets on the way, it was there for a while and then disappeared with the ever diverging pathways of life. Clark's last years were difficult. In 2005, his wife Joan was diagnosed with a form of dementia and he with Parkinson's Disease. She predeceased him. He passed away August 10, 2013.

Jo Anne and I managed to work in a bit of time not only to be with my California family but also to see a good many things of interest in southern California and experience its life and atmosphere. It was a long and tiring day to drive to the beach from Eagle Rock, but we did it on occasion. We took in the new Disneyland, and took our guests there. We visited the aquarium. We made one weekend trip to Las Vegas. We attended Sunday worship services at the First Methodist Church on Colorado Boulevard in Pasadena. But study was always a fact of life for me between basic training and discharge.

It remains only to say a word about my few assignments on internal audits. As did most of the staff, I lived in dread of being assigned to Fort Huachuca, near Sierra Vista, Arizona, fifteen miles north of the Mexican border, or to the installation at Yuma in the southwestern corner of Arizona. I never was so assigned, but barely escaped being ordered to go to Japan in the middle

---

5   *The Judge*, 50.

6   Matt. 5:5; Ps 37:11.

of my semester of night law school. I got word while out on an audit that the office would have to send someone to Japan, and that they had put my name down for it after someone else got his name removed. I called the office and told them about my situation in night law school and what a hardship it would be. They moved me off of that assignment and put another recruit down for it. The one who ended up going was Jim O'Brien. Perhaps he was selected because he was single, but it seems that he actually volunteered for that reason to go. Before he left, he asked if he could send us anything from Japan. Jo Anne made a suggestion, and he followed through and sent us an attractive set of Japanese coffee cups and saucers. I've often wondered what happened in Jim's life after that. Recently, after nearly six decades, I've been trying, without success, to locate him, if still living.

Internal audits of military installations were, for me, a gigantic bore, having no recognizable relationship to civilian or commercial accounting, but they were part of the landscape of our mission. Fortunately, I had few and can only remember one at Edwards Air Force Base and two at the Navajo Ordnance Depot (NOD) west of Flagstaff, Arizona. The only memory I have from the Edwards AFB audit was the scare I had leaving the base office one day. Not familiar with the place or its protocol, I drove my car directly across the runway squarely in the descending path of a landing jet fighter plane. I experienced what a rodent under a large hawk or Eagle's beak, claws, and wings had to feel. The pilot buzzed me, applied his jet power, and started around again. I flinched imagining the epithets hurled at me by tower and pilot—but save for that scalding I got away unscathed (I did not have much rank to lose anyway, short of dishonorable discharge).

Near the end of my AAA days, likely before I left for NOD and my last assignment, an offer was extended to me to remain with AAA, at the end of my enlistment, as a Civil Service employee at a G-11 grade level. I appreciated the offer and thanked them for it, but explained to them that my army time had interrupted my legal training to which I desired to return. Doubtless the office knew that beforehand but made the offer as a matter of formality on the basis of my service there.

Probably few people are aware of what a major part the Navajo Ordnance Depot played in all our twentieth century wars in the Asia-Pacific region.[1] Essentially all ordnance for those engagements went through the NOD, shipped in for storage in hundreds of widely dispersed earth-covered concrete bunkers available for shipping out by rail to ports for shipment to meet the combat demands in those far regions. This covered WWII, the Korean Conflict, and the Vietnam War. While it was also used in the Persian Gulf War, it has since been deactivated and is currently used as a munitions storage and training site for the Arizona National Guard units.

In the mid-1950s, Flagstaff was a small town. Today it is a fair-size city. Both the town and NOD of that time exist today only in nostalgic memories—treasures for me.

Aside from workday boredom the two NOD assignments were among my most pleasant experiences and memories. Each was in the summer and lasted about six weeks as I recall, long enough for weekend outings among the many natural sights and wonders. With a per diem allowance for expenses we stayed in a modest Flagstaff motel and ate off-duty meals in restaurants there. Jo Anne went with me in the summer of 1955. We imbibed together the natural ambrosia of the Grand Canyon, Painted Desert, Indian ruins, Oak Creek Canyon, and Sedona.

We also took a guided mule train ride down Bright Angel Trail all the way to the river. The vertical distance from the Bright Angel Lodge at the south rim down to the river is nine-tenths of a mile. The horizontal distance from the south rim to the river is not much greater than it is to Plateau Point, from which the vertical drop to the river is precipitous. The trail down from the rim divides at the Indian Garden Campground, the Plateau Point trail going off to

---

[1] See John Westerlund, *Arizona's War Town: Flagstaff, Navajo Ordnance Depot, and World War II.*

the left and the river trail to the right.¹ Guided mule train rides are available from the lodge to either Plateau Point or the more grueling one all the way down. The animals move slowly and deliberately and the guest's legs must stay paralyzingly astraddle the animal the entire way. Toward the end of the day the desire to bring legs back together and pamper the posterior becomes dynamic passion. Several times I have greatly enjoyed hiking these trails and others on foot to the river, and once all the way across to the north rim in two days. These were all less punishing for me than that mule ride. My advice to those contemplating a mule ride is, take a shorter trip than to the river and back.

The lure of Humphreys Peak in the San Francisco Mountains just north of Flagstaff was irresistible. The Gary and the Stewart (or Stuart) mentioned earlier were among the group I promoted to climb it. In climbing it from the west, we were exposed to several false tops. Approaching each, I urged the guys on because they could see we were near the top. After topping a few of these only to see another still higher my hold on credibility with them was slipping. When finally I could hold back no longer, I started on up alone for what appeared to be, and was, the peak. I got there quite a while before they did, looked out at the Grand Canyon many miles to the north and at the Painted Desert far out to the east. Felt like Moses on Mount Sinai, but finally lay down on my back covering my face with my cap and waited. The peak is the highest natural point in Arizona, at 12,637 feet. It was the first mountain I had ever climbed, but it was not the last. I was addicted.

Jo Anne did not go with me to Flagstaff in 1956, for the circumstances that year were very different. My enlistment was ending on September 17, 1956. NOD was to be my last AAA assignment after which I would report to Fort MacArthur in San Pedro for processing out. At or near the time I left for Flagstaff, Jo Anne left with her folks caravanning back to Dallas. She had a contract lined up with

---

1   See the topographical map of Bright Angel Trail and surroundings: http://www.u.arizona.edu/~sandiway/hikes/grandcanyon/.

the Dallas Independent School District to teach fourth grade that fall in its Rufus C. Burleson Elementary School in southeast Dallas, again in an economically disadvantaged area. She needed, among many other things, to find and rent an apartment and get ready for her own start of classes at the new school. I had tried to get back to Dallas shortly before the law school's fall classes started. However, my release was timed to permit me to get back only before the deadline for late registration. Classes had started, but I beat the deadline, barely.

While I missed her presence in Flagstaff, it turned out to be a blast of a summer. In addition to the Humphreys Peak climb, Cal Root, a Civil Service auditor, took me up on my invitation to hike from the south rim down Bright Angel Trail to the river. There is virtually no breeze down there and in mid-summer it gets very hot. Leaving early for the eighty-one mile drive to the starting point, we made it down to the river without difficulty. But we had not gone far on our climb back up when Cal, who as previously stated was then forty-four years of age, looked up to me as he panted for breath and said, "I'm a damn fool for doing this." But he was a good sport and we made it up okay, especially after getting out of the stifling, breezeless heat and humidity at river level.

Flagstaff did not then have a lot of decent eating-places to choose between. There was a fellow I frequently saw in these. We visited and found that we had a common interest, hiking the many luring attractions in the region. Each of us had cameras and occasionally shared pictures. As my time in Flagstaff was drawing to a close, he told me about the hike he had made into a very special part of what is now in the western part of the Grand Canyon National Park, but was then, I believe, called the Grand Canyon National Monument. He called the place the Havasupai Indian Reservation. His description of it made me drool. In my enthusiasm I suggested that he and I take that hiking trip the coming weekend. He reluctantly declined, saying that he had promised himself that he would not make it again unless he had more than two days. It occurred to me that the coming weekend was Labor Day, a three-day weekend. He said, "By golly, I'll go with you." "Great," I said. Not having previously exchanged names I extended my hand saying, "My name is Ed Smith." The quizzical look on his face prompted me to ask, "What is the matter?" He said, "That is my name too." All of my life I have run into, or been confused with, other Ed Smiths, but none so coincidentally as this.

I picked Ed up very early on Saturday morning. We drove west on U. S. 66 from Flagstaff through Williams and Seligman to a wide spot in the road called Peach Springs, a distance of 115 miles, then turned north on an unpaved but decent road a distance of sixty miles to Hualapai Hilltop, on the rim of the canyon. The only indication of civilization on that road was a lumber mill about midway, unattended that day perhaps because it was Saturday. A website about Peach Springs informs that "It is the nearest town to Hualapai Hilltop, which is the trailhead from which hikers descend the 8-mile (13 km), 3,000-vertical-feet (900 m) trail to the town of Supai, Arizona, from which the renowned Havasu Falls and three other waterfalls can be visited."[1] I believe there are only three falls in total, and the first one downstream from the town is not so notable. Near it was what we called the Indian Passion Pool, where it appeared there may have been a fair amount of mating (at least of sorts) going on among the youngsters in the tribe. On downstream from the Passion Pool were two grand falls, the first one, Havasu Falls, was the most idyllic and beautiful. On downstream from that was Mooney Falls, the name of it deriving from the legend that an explorer named Mooney came upon it from upstream and, finding no other way down the steep canyon walls, decided to anchor a long rope to the nearest thing he could find with the other end around his waste, then himself go over the falls. Unfortunately, the rope was not long enough and he dangled in the midst of the powerfully falling water till he was no more.

---

1   See http://en.wikipedia.org/wiki/Peach_Springs,_Arizona.

The trail down from the rim was steep at first, then moderated as it gradually descended toward the village, a lot of it going through the bottom of beautiful arroyos. A moderate distance before coming to the village we noticed that the ground off to the right of the trail was becoming increasingly moist until it became a trickle and then a streamlet and then the beautiful color that gives the tribe its name Havasu, meaning blue-green water, appended by "pai" meaning people, or blue-green water people. Its coloring made it opaque but it was otherwise clear, especially till its volume increased to the point of obscuring its bed. We observed, growing wild, vegetation that gave us a sort of Garden of Eden feeling. Memory of it includes figs and what looked like celery.

Even in 1956, through the Indian Agent or otherwise, one could get word down to the village to have horses brought up to take a traveler down. However, Ed and I were enthusiastic backpackers and disdained any such mode of getting down and back. For many years now visitors to the village number in the thousands each year. Such was not the case in 1956. Of course, it was Labor Day weekend, when summer travel in rugged country naturally slows down. But it is indicative that for the entire weekend, the only white people on the trail or in the village and waterfall areas were Ed and I and the resident missionary and his pregnant wife. We made arrangements to stay in what the Indians called their armory—a modest vacant structure as I recall it, where we pitched our sleeping bags and what we would not need on the hikes on down to the two lower falls.

When, off to the right from the trail, the Havasu Falls setting came into our view, it was breathtakingly spectacular. Over time the water's lime content mineralized, accreting onto the cliff wall overlaying leaf-like formations over which the water plummeted into a series of pools below. Natural walls that had been formed by the same mineral build-up segregated each pool from all of those around it. We saw no tribe members or other humans below the Passion Pool, so it was without the least hesitation that we stripped nude and luxuriated in these warm swirling pools of color, while ever raising our eyes aloft to the colorful rising cascade of canyon walls above and around us.

At length we emerged from the pools, sun-dried on the strip of sandy, grassy creek-side, and made our way back up to the trail and on down it to Mooney Falls. Unlike Mooney, we did not have to risk our lives finding an original way down. Though precipitously steep, right through the canyon wall a tube-like tunnel, with steel railing and steps, had been engineered from trail to creek below the falls. Again, it was a beautiful area, with a considerably higher falls, but it did not have the absolutely stunning attractiveness of Havasu Falls and ponds.

There are two pillars balanced at the top of the canyon wall across from the village. It is the tradition of the people that the tribe will continue to exist as long as those two pillars remain perched on the wall. There are many other things I could say about the people and our experience. Few experiences of my lifetime have impressed themselves so meaningfully and indelibly into my memory.

At some point not long after Jo Anne and I moved into our 57th Street house in Lubbock in late 1962, Ed and his mother stopped to visit us for a day as they were making a car trip. Except for that he and I have not seen each other since I left Flagstaff in 1956. But there has probably never been a year since then that we have not exchanged correspondence at least once, usually initiated by him but always with a grateful response from me. Typically I will hear from him when he has something to send me or just needs to update on his situation. Aside from numerous editions of Arizona Highways, he has sent me books, magazines, pamphlets, or other literature on Arizona and/or Havasu. Ed remained in Arizona, moving a couple of times, until a decade or so ago when he searched out a retirement facility to move into. He found one in Midland, TX only 118 miles south of Lubbock. In those recent decades, and even a bit before, his health declined and he is subject to several ailments now. He is a bit older than I. But our exchanges continue and I keep telling myself I need to drive down there and visit him in person. Trouble is, we might neither one recognize the other, as many moons have come and gone since we hiked the Havasu together. I have in my library, and have read, two meaningful books on the Havasupai.[1]

Labor Day in 1956 was Monday, September 3. My two-year army enlistment was ending on Monday, September 17, pursuant to the grant of my request for early release for the fall term of law school at SMU. Between Labor Day weekend and my departure from the military on September 17, I would have completed whatever else remained for me to do before departing the NOD, driven from Flagstaff back to L.A., completed any necessary procedures at the AAA office, and reported to Fort MacArthur where I processed out and left on the 17th. However and whenever it was accomplished, I would have loaded into my car such of our belongings as Jo Anne and her folks had not taken back to Dallas.

My only specific memories from the time period between NOD and departure for Dallas are the last nights I spent back in the L.A. area. Reconstructing events, I feel sure Jo Anne and I closed out our apartment lease with Miss Bauer when she headed back to Dallas and I to Flagstaff. Whenever I got back from Flagstaff, I stayed in the detached guest room at Aunt Ruth's house until I began to process out at Fort MacArthur. Desiring to avoid staying on base, I must have spent Thursday night at Aunt Ruth's, driving to the base and back on Friday. That day of driving the one hundred mile round trip (fifty each way) between her house and Fort MacArthur, prompted me to get an issue of bedding and spend my last night before discharge in the base barracks. So I probably stayed Friday and Saturday nights at Aunt Ruth's and Sunday night in the base barracks.

My first real day in the army was November 26, 1954, the day after Thanksgiving. It started with bugle call at 4:00 a.m. followed by our picking up cigarette butts to the shouted command, "I don't

---

[1] Stephen Hirst, *I Am the Grand Canyon: The Story of the Havasupai People*; Tikalsky, Euler, and Nagel, *The Sacred Oral Tradition of the Havasupai*.

want to see anything but assholes and elbows." September 17, 1956 started with reveille at 4:00 a.m. followed by our picking up cigarette butts to that same command, the humbling and irreverent alpha and omega of my army days, "I don't want to see anything but assholes and elbows." I was smiling from ear to ear as I drove away from the base on the 17th for I was not showing them my elbows.

Conclusion

Writing as an octogenarian with many more years to look back at than forward to, I see things differently now than I did in the late summer of 1954 in regard to my draft call and its timing. The four-year deferment that let me get my college degree and some law school behind me first was fortunate. But in that draft notice and its timing, my stars were actually guiding my path in a very beneficent way.

Many good things happened as a result. Most are obvious from what I've recounted above, including being able to complete licensing as a CPA that probably would otherwise never have happened; generating, through early experiencing, a lifelong love of the natural beauties and challenges of the northern Arizona environs; and bringing into full bloom a family relationship, long previously limited by geography and the times, that probably could never in later years have been so meaningfully and lastingly developed.

But perhaps only as I wrote above of my basic training days did it really begin to dawn on me how meaningful it was to have experienced, in a minimal way, the rigors and demands of army life in general and infantry life in particular. By no means was my military service heroic, especially when measured against the extreme sacrifice of that generation, often labeled the "greatest," whose youngest were only six years older than I.[1] To them, with tears I kneel in

---

1 Tom Brokaw, *The Greatest Generation Speaks: Letters and Reflections*. Ed Haney, survivor of the early June 6, 1944, landing on Omaha Beach and the

Army

gratitude. But just having served, carried the soldier's pack, fired his rifle, thrown his grenade, launched his rocket, fixed his bayonet, and crawled under his live machine-gun fire, invested in my conscious soul something it could not otherwise have acquired. For this I'm grateful. It only took eight weeks—but as with life, its value is not measured by length of time.

---

continuously bloody but ongoing mission of the 29th infantry division till V-E Day, sent his personal (marked-up) copy of this book to me as a gift in appreciation for our visit with them in March 2013 and my interest in him and his account. It is a treasured part of my library.

Wrapping up Law School

The SMU Law School environment that I returned to in the fall of 1956 was a different world from the one I had left in late 1954. The physical premises remained, but the classmates I had "hit the beach" with in 1953 were no longer around. Those I was with now had only been in school for two months when I entered the army, so while our relationships during the year were cordial there was no broad base of shared experience between us. Moreover, not only was I married but I also took a part-time job with a CPA named Don Turner on Lover's Lane north and west of the campus, so I spent little more than class time on the campus. Time serving as one of the editors on the Southwestern Law Journal was not extensive, and time spent working on my own article for publication was not a social activity.

The class of '56 that I left in 1954 was one that I stood atop of academically. The class of '57 that I was to graduate with had two outstanding members who stood higher than I in grade point average, one graduating magna cum laude and one summa cum laude.

Aside from completing course work and contemplating the bar exam upon graduation, third year students inevitably are increasingly mindful of the job market they will be entering. This latter is one of the major changes in milieu to which I returned. The general goal of any student upon completion of his second year is to seek summer employment as an intern at one of the local law firms, of which there were many in Dallas and environs. Typically, if the student performs well it is an avenue into the firm upon completion of the bar exam. This is the route I had anticipated taking with the tax department of some firm. The army eliminated that possibility, and by the time I got back the positions I would have chosen had already been filled. As will appear below, I had to consider other alternatives.

My scholarship was still available without the anxiety of the early years in regard to maintaining it. We were able to do reasonably well financially. Jo Anne had her teaching salary, which, though not as high as in Los Angeles, was our highest source of support. The Korean War G. I. Bill had not yet ended at my discharge. That brought in about one hundred dollars a month for the school year, and I earned a modest amount working for Don Turner.

In the course of preparing this autobiography, I ordered a copy of my law school transcript from SMU. While the reports at the end of each of the first three terms of law school had indicated the cumulative GPA to that point, I was disappointed to see that the full transcript did not give my final GPA. Clearly the hours from Loyola were not to be taken into account, but the question is, were the courses for which credit was given for the fall term of 1954 to be taken into account at the previous cumulative GPA, or were they to be excluded in computing the GPA? On the transcript no grade is assigned to them, but only the fact that credit was given. Taking the cumulative GPA of 85.56 at the end of the summer term in 1954, I have made calculations with the additional information from the transcript for the final two semesters after the military service. If the courses for the fall 1954 term were taken into account at the GPA of 85.56, then according to my calculations the cumulative GPA upon graduation was 86.36. However, if the fall 1954 semester was simply credited and no grades attached to them (as the transcript shows), then the cumulative GPA was 86.53. A score of 86.50 would have been exactly half way between my graduating cum laude and magna cum laude. The transcript does indicate cum laude. Interestingly, the GPA for those final two semesters was 88.04.

An essential activity of the spring term was studying the traditional bar exam review materials in preparation for taking the exam more or less contemporarily with the end of class work or graduation. The exam that June was given in the student union building on the University of Texas campus in Austin. The grade on the exam is not something to which one attached much significance so long as it was passing. Mine was. Though respectable, I do not remember or have any record of that detail.

Doubtless as is the case with most persons approaching any level of graduation, course work and the regular school grind became almost anticlimactic. So it was with me in the spring semester of 1957. Of considerably more importance was lining up some type of employment.

It came to my attention that Joe E. Estes, Federal District Judge for the Northern District of Texas in Dallas, had an opening for a law clerk at this time. Estes had been appointed by Eisenhower in July 1955, during my military service. The details of how we came to agree on my appointment have escaped me, but I do remember well that, in connection with it, the judge invited Jo Anne and me to join him and his wife at his nice residence in north Dallas for a relaxed social visit, no doubt with cocktails. Jo Anne and I both remember it as a most pleasant occasion. The judge made one statement that sticks vividly in my mind. I remember only the statement itself. The context that gave rise to it must surely have involved some aspect of my economic prospects down the line as a lawyer. Essentially, the statement was, "Oh, you will become wealthy." My sense is that he said this as though it was merely incidental to other aspects of the profession and my future. In those days, I had the conscious thought that, if I ever attained a net worth of one hundred thousand dollars, I would be very well off. As in almost everything else, six decades have dramatically changed that prospect. In any event, it was settled that I would become his clerk after taking the bar exam. As things worked out, however, I never did.

Not long after that, it was announced that Marvin Collie, who headed up the tax department of the large Houston law firm of Vinson, Elkins, Weems & Searls (VEWS, now Vinson & Elkins), was going to be interviewing at the law school for a new associate for his department. Without being too immodest, I felt that I was the best uncommitted candidate in our class for such position. I did the interview and was promptly offered the position. Of course, I had to deal on the matter with Judge Estes. Whether I talked to him about the prospective job before the interview or after I cannot be sure. What remains clearly in my mind is his immediate and wholehearted recommendation—namely, that it was an opportunity I could not pass up, and that he would certainly release me from any obligation to clerk for him. There was, I think, a personal reason that he was so readily recommending I take the law firm position. David Searls, one of the four partners in the firm name itself, was a close personal friend; they had been, as I recall, roommates somewhere in their own schooling.

This change of plans was a relief to me in one other aspect. It seemed clear that a substantial anti-trust case involving the A & P grocery chain (Atlantic & Pacific Tea Company) was heading for his court. I could envision that litigation consuming a lot of the court's time and, consequently, my own clerking period. I had taken the course in Business Regulation (anti-trust, etc.) and had some concept of the complexity of these contests. It was not a quagmire into which I looked forward to becoming entangled.

My starting salary at VEWS was to be four-hundred seventy-five dollars ($475.00) per month. To the best of my information, this was the highest starting salary for any member of my graduating class who accepted employment with a Texas law firm (New York may have been otherwise). Professor Riehm seems to have taken an interest in me, and, though wishing me well, he seemed almost disappointed when I accepted employment in Texas rather than letting him land a position for me in his former New York firm Cravath, Swain & Moore.

Just what the timing of these employment matters within the spring term was, I have no independent recollection; but I'm assuming that they were pretty much completed no later than sometime in April because Jo Anne and I thereupon consciously began to try to start our family, and our twin sons, Mark Edward and Michael Reaugh, were born at Methodist Hospital in Houston, a slight bit early, on January 1, 1958.

So, with Jo Anne's extensive help, I got a good bit accomplished in my final semester of law school.

Looking Forward from 1957

At the beginning of summer 1957, three months shy of my twenty-fifth birthday, I was a licensed lawyer, a certified public accountant, had served two years in the U. S. Army, had a job awaiting at a prestigious law firm in Houston at a relatively good starting salary, and was an expectant father. My childhood, youth, and years of preparation were over, and it was now up to me, along with Jo Anne's participation and support and the circumstances of fate, to see what I would do with all of this.

Many strands comprise my life—even more, it seems, in the part that began in 1957 than in my youth, though probably the latter's natural product. They can, I believe, all fall within the following five classifications:

Most Major Classifications (the "A" Group)

1. Family
2. Law Practice
3. Investment & Business
4. Other Involvements
    A. Charitable/Civic/Political
    B. Travels
    C. My "Irrational Dreams"
        I. Running
        II. Music
5. Journey of Spirit
    A. The Cornerstone Class
    B. Rudolf Steiner and Anthroposophy

In my judgment, the development of each of these categories separately will be better understood with this approach than by trying to treat them all together as they progress in tandem through the years. Perhaps calling this a vertical rather than horizontal presentation is appropriate. But it will often be helpful to refer incidentally to what is then happening in other areas. The Chronology of Self and Family at the end of the book should aid in this.

Family

Family is listed as the first classification because it is what it is, my family, though my time and effort were generally committed much more heavily to the other activities indicated. Jo Anne devoted far more time to family matters than I, and to her goes the greater credit for all that falls within the term family—and this includes our extended family, my side as much as hers. When our family needed serious attention from me, hopefully I always gave it. There were times, when we traveled, or engaged in out-of-doors activities, especially on trips or in Colorado, when my involvement with our children rose to a high level.

This is an autobiography for our descendants. It is being written to fulfill a promise to Jo Anne to that end. If it is of interest to others, I will be most pleased, though the initial, and still primary, ones for whom I write are our issue. While primarily for them, clearly it is an autobiography and is not about them—other than Jo Anne whose life has been entwined with mine and with everything I've been involved with since we first met in the summer of 1950. Children have been a vital part of our lives and thus must be part of the account, but only with economy of information. Just as with every parent, there are countless precious memories of each and every child. There are also joys and anxieties with each and every child. Those areas are off limits. The children will appear incidentally in the account of the other categories covered.

Looking Forward from 1957

Jo Anne and I were in agreement, from the first, that four children would be our goal, ideally equally divided between girls and boys. As it turned out, we could have only three. As we left Dallas, we pretty well knew that our first child had been conceived, but deferred selecting a doctor until we got to Houston. Jo Anne was ahead of the game in expansion. At about four months, the doctor listened for a heartbeat, heard two, and said there might be a third that he could not hear. Getting two or more for the price of one was exciting. The targeted due date was January 15. At about noon on New Year's Eve, Jo Anne called me at the office and said that her water had broken and that the doctor said the babies would be born before the New Year. Not so. We did not leave for the hospital till after midnight. Our sons Mark Edward and Michael Reaugh were born about twenty-four hours after Jo Anne had called me. They were the first babies of the New Year 1958 in Bellaire, Texas, an incorporated city within the greater Houston area. We were showered with baby merchandise by the merchants in Bellaire, but I would rather have had the two tax exemptions that we just missed—not the best tax planning according to my fellow members of the firm's tax department.

Twins are a blast. While Jo Anne might have had some reservations, I was hoping that our second pregnancy would also be twins.

We planned both of Jo Anne's pregnancies, and in each instance conception promptly occurred. We moved from Houston to Lubbock, Texas in early 1959. Our daughter Jill Michelle was born June 14, 1961, in Lubbock. Again, Jo Anne's water broke well before expected. I was at the office of the appellate division of the Internal Revenue Service in Dallas, planning to go on to Washington for the swearing in of John Tower as United States Senator.[1] Jo Anne's doc-

---

1   Well before my family moved to Wichita Falls, Tower's father had been pastor of First Methodist Church there where Jo Anne's family worshiped. They knew John, who also became a professor of government at Midwestern University. I was in his class, and the relationship was close because of these connections.

tor had examined her right before I left Lubbock and said that the baby would not be born within the next several days, which was plenty of time for me to complete this travel plan. Jo Anne called me while I was in the Dallas conference to inform me that the doctor said the baby would be born that day and that I should catch the first plane home. Upon concluding the conference, I headed to the airport only to learn that the next plane to Lubbock was full. The airline, recognizing my plight, made the announcement in the plane of my situation and asked if anyone would volunteer to give their seat to me. One wonderfully kind gentleman did, whom I thanked profusely and who congratulated me and wished us well as I rushed past him to the plane.

Jo Anne's mother and sister had driven to Lubbock upon learning what was happening (it was about a four-hour drive from Wichita Falls to Lubbock). It came to a point that if I was not on that plane or was delayed in getting home, she was going to take Jo Anne to the hospital as the delivery time was clearly nearing. As soon as I drove in, we loaded Jo Anne in the car and headed for the hospital emergency room, whence she was taken directly to the delivery room and Jill very soon made her entry upon the world stage.

Jill was jaundiced. A blood change by transfusion was necessary. When a mother is Rh-negative and the child is Rh-positive (from the father), there are problems. Today those problems can be dealt with during pregnancy. But at that time such treatment was not available. We first learned that we had this Rh incompatibility when we had the blood tests required for issuance of a marriage license. When it was explained to us then that there could be problems limiting our ability to have children, Jo Anne cried and asked if I wanted to go through with the marriage since children were in the picture we had talked about together. I assured her that I loved her and that we would get married and take our chances. Normally the condition is not a problem on the first pregnancy. But where the elements are so diverse as they were in our case, which was an extreme diversity, the second pregnancy can be affected, as Jill was and even greater danger exists after the second. Because of this, and because this was her second pregnancy, Jo Anne's gynecologist inquired urgently if she had ever been pregnant other than with the twins. Following Jill's birth, we were told that if we had any more children they could either be stillborn or have serious problems. Sadly, we took steps to avoid further pregnancy. We were grateful that the first pregnancy produced twins.

Ironically, while Jill was only one child, she would give birth much later to twins. Later in life Jill changed her name to Jillian. She liked that name and her brother Mark had married a Jill.

Each child is well educated, happily married with children, and well-established in a rewarding career of his or her own. Each is of a responsible nature with strong work ethic and manifests a serious interest in the deeper aspects of life.

Mark has a bachelor's degree and a master's degree in business administration (MBA) from Texas Tech University, and has for many years been employed in the home office of DuPont in Wilmington, Delaware. He is married to the former Jill Summerville from Hagerstown, Maryland and they are the parents of two children.

Michael has a bachelor's degree in mechanical engineering from Texas A&M University with a master's degree in engineering from the University of Texas in Arlington (UTA). He has been with Bell Helicopter in Hurst, Texas from shortly after graduation at A&M in 1980. Until recently he held more patents at Bell than any of their other personnel. He is married to the former Stacey Kelley of Dallas and they have six children and two grandchildren, with another grandchild on the way.

Jillian has a bachelor's degree in accounting from the University of Texas. Out of concern that she should study in college something that would qualify her for employment in most any community, we suggested she consider either teaching or accounting. She chose the latter, became a CPA, and practiced with the accounting firm now known as Ernst & Young in Dallas for two years. Then, though doing well, she decided that she did not want to spend her life in the field of accounting. An aptitude test strongly indicated that she should go into medicine, whereupon she went to the University of Texas in Arlington (UTA) for her necessary premed courses. She is a graduate of Southwestern Medical School and for more than a decade has practiced, with great satisfaction, psychiatric medicine in Bucks County, Pennsylvania. She is married to Donald A. Rauh, MD, PhD, originally of Springfield, Illinois, who also practices psychiatry. They have two children. They live in Newtown, Pennsylvania.

Jo Anne always said that the goal of any mother should be, and hers was, to work herself out of a job in the sense that her children become independent and capable of caring for themselves. I've often accused her of over achievement in that respect, for each has been almost fiercely independent. That has been most satisfying for us, though occasionally each of them has taken a path contrary to what we would have chosen for them at the time.

We've often commented both between ourselves and with them how extremely fortunate we are to have the three children we have and how proud each has made us. Garrison Keillor, in concluding each of his Lake Woebegon monologues, says it well, "and all the children are above average."[1]

Above all, we feel a mutually strong, loving relationship exists between each of them and us, and collectively between all three of them. It extends in each case to and from their spouse and children.

---

1 Keillor's fuller conclusion is, "where all the women are strong, all the men are good looking, and all the children are above average."

LAW PRACTICE 1957–1984

One of the things Professor Riehm said to me when I told him I had accepted employment at the Houston firm was, "Just remember that on average a lawyer makes two moves before he finds the right situation for himself." In my case, at least, it was prophetic, as follows:

> Vinson, Elkins, Weems & Searls:
> July 1957–December 1958
> Nelson, McCleskey & Harriger (Lubbock):
> February 1959–February 1961
> Self-employed (including firm additions later):
> March 1961–August 1984

The first of these three is the only law firm situation that was not a happy and successful one for me.

VINSON, ELKINS, WEEMS & SEARLS

While on the one hand helpful and considerate, it was also probably indicative of the culture of Vinson, Elkins, Weems & Searls (VEWS) that, upon my arrival, I was informed that we should live within a certain defined sector of the city. While there were ample mid-level homes in the sector, the larger region also included River Oaks, the most exclusive section of Houston—homes way beyond anything a non-endowed beginning lawyer could sanely acquire. We were also advised that a good place to buy clothes was Norton Ditto, where the least expensive suit cost almost half as much as my monthly salary. Whether we were told by our superiors or not, it was obvious that we should also wear hats. I did not own one, but bought one. There was a saying among the lawyers in town that if you saw a lawyer at coffee wearing coat and hat he was from VEWS; if wearing a coat but no hat he was from Baker & Botts; and if he was there in shirt sleeves he was from Fulbright, Crooker, Freeman, Bates & Jaworski. These were the largest three firms at that time, and probably in that order. I was given number eighty-nine (89), but learned that it had belonged to someone else before me.

In my observation, VEWS hired young lawyers for one, if not both, of two reasons, family prominence or good academic standing from a respected law school. I was only in the latter category. They were, and probably still are, the pre-eminent law firm in Texas, if not the nation, in representing the oil and gas industry, but also represented numerous large public corporations and wealthy families. Typical among the latter was Allan Shivers, who had just completed seven and a half years as Texas governor on January 15, 1957, as well as the Shary interests. Already a state senator, in 1937 Shivers had married Marialice Shary, the only child of John and Mary O'Brien Shary of South Texas, who had adopted their niece Marialice (born January 2, 1910) as a teenager. Bushman, under whom I worked, gave me the assignment, subject to his review, to draft the wills for the Shivers, whose substantial wealth was doubtless largely from the Shary family, John Shary having died in 1945. Perhaps, though I have no reliable memory of it, Bushman may have briefly introduced me to the Shivers when they came in to review and execute their wills.

During my time at VEWS, the tax department was under Marvin Collie. Below him were three mid-level personnel: R. P. "Pete" Bushman, Columbia Law school (with tax specialty); John G. Heard, Baylor Law School; and Clyde L. Wilson, Jr., South Texas Law School. Below them were Albert "Al" Hamilton and myself. All of the tax department, I believe, except Collie and Bushman were also CPAs. I worked under Bushman and Al worked under the other two.

Bushman's practice concentrated on wills, trusts, estates, and retirement plans. Most of my time was thus spent in these areas.

At least on one occasion I was solicited to research and prepare a memo brief for an older experienced lawyer whose office was situated near the far end of our firm offices from our department. He was most complimentary of my work. Such was seldom the case in my relationship with Bushman. More often he was critical of any shortcomings, especially on my imperfect proofreading of instruments that I had drafted. Most of the instruments were take-offs from some sort of form that had been developed in the office. But in those days as many as an original and eight carbon copies of a will would be prepared. The wills were usually eight to ten single-spaced (within paragraphs) pages on which there could be no corrections. Any page corrected, even for a single letter, had to be completely retyped. Being very labor intensive, accuracy in the initial preparation and first proofreading was important. He found many errors in my work and was very vocal about them. Almost from the first it seemed to me that a wall came down between us. He was always correct in pointing out my errors. To me, his manner in doing so seemed abrupt and condescending, rather than patient and helpful. This was increasingly so as time went on. Putting myself in his situation and considering the unspoken pressures within the firm, I can understand. I do not remember many occasions on which he complimented me or expressed appreciation. Perhaps I did not deserve it, but it might have improved my performance.

John Heard generally handled corporations and partnerships and related tax litigation. Clyde Wilson seemed generally to specialize in oil and gas tax work. My relationship with each of them was friendly and comfortable. While unfortunately I did not work for either John or Clyde, the atmosphere around them seemed to me to be quite different from that around Bushman, but my lot was under Bushman. He was a large, though not obese, fellow with a boisterous voice that could often be heard, especially laughing, from far down the hall. He was, as noted in a VEWS history, an associate whom Collie seemed proud to have hired. Bushman may himself have come from a prominent family in the northeast, but his wife's father had been, or was, chair of one of the large corporations on the New York Stock Exchange. Bushman was competent, but we seem to have come from different worlds.

It was a stressful relationship that was not to last. Toward the end of 1958 I was called to the office of one Mr. Shepherd, managing partner of the firm. He said that my situation with Bushman was not working out. He offered for me to move to another section of the firm outside of the tax department. I told him, whether then or soon after, that since taxation was the area of my greatest interest, I appreciated his offer but preferred to seek other employment. My pay may have continued through January 1959 but probably went only through year's end.

Indicative of the sensitiveness of the firm to our basic needs, immediately upon the news of the birth of our twins January 1, 1958, my pay was increased to $650 per month. Then later there was the annual increase to at least $750 or $800 per month.

My inclination, with which Jo Anne agreed, was to seek to become a bigger fish in a smaller pond. In particular I wanted to take a look at four mid-size cities in Texas: Waco, Abilene, Lubbock, and Wichita Falls in that circular order. This I did in the course of one week in December 1958. My objective was to visit with one lawyer, one CPA, and one bank trust officer in each city. I would drive there, check into a motel, study the yellow pages to pick out before bedtime a person in each of these capacities to visit, contact and visit with them the next day, then drive to the next city and repeat the process. My Lubbock visit ended the process, for I knew that Lubbock was a prime prospect from the first. It was in an expansive mode, especially in irrigated cotton farming. All over the area farmers were putting down irrigation wells into the Ogallala formation. The entire area was moving into the irrigation of crops, especially cotton. Lubbock had doubled in size from 1940 (31,853) to 1950 (71,747) and did so again from 1950 to 1960 (128,691).[1]

---

[1] Since then it has consistently increased each decade but at a less rapid pace. Its 2010 population was 229,573.

Texas Tech had just entered the Southwest Conference in 1958. Reese Air Force Base was an added factor. Farmers and those who served them were acquiring moderate wealth and comprised countless estate planning prospects with virtually no competition in my field of experience and interest.

From Lubbock's yellow pages I saw the unusual name Harriger (Harold) in the firm Nelson, McCleskey & Harriger (NMH). Jo Anne and I had known Harold and his wife-to-be, Rebecca "Becky" Craig, in Wichita Falls and had even double dated with them, though they married in 1950. He was four years older than I, but had been in the service at Shepherd Air Force Base in Wichita Falls before college. We were in the same church and he also was attending Midwestern as a sophomore or junior while I was a freshman. In addition, the eldest son, Burt, of the senior partner, Hobert Nelson, following his enlistment period in the Air Force, had been behind me in law school at SMU and we were in the same legal fraternity there.

The firm and I struck a deal while I was in Lubbock. I was to come to work for them as their tax man for two years. The three partners with Burt and me comprised the five lawyers in the firm. It was agreed that at the end of that time, if all worked out as expected, I would be offered a partnership interest. My starting salary was to be a bit less than what I was then earning at VEWS and would increase periodically during the term. I was to start February 1, 1959. I did go on to Wichita Falls but not to do the previously anticipated interviews. It was not greatly out of the way to go through there on my return to Dallas, and I wanted to share my news with Jo Anne's parents, who knew "Skip" Harriger and "Becky" Craig before and after the latter married in Wichita Falls. After I left Doc and Mom they called Jo Anne saying that I spoke to them in glowing terms of Lubbock and the new situation. Indeed, it was the beginning of the happy remainder of my law practice days.

But let us return to finish the story of our lives in Houston.

Before I left the firm in Houston, I made copies of all the types of documents I had been involved with while there as I knew they would come in handy in fashioning instruments in my Lubbock practice. In addition, I applied myself intently on reviewing the other areas of the Internal Revenue Code that had largely been outside the sections I had worked with at VEWS, those areas that would have been handled by John Heard and Clyde Wilson rather than Bushman, especially corporations and partnerships. The firm in Lubbock was promoting me, in a proper way, as its tax expert, and I entered upon the undertaking with enthusiasm and confidence. My experience at VEWS, while not the most pleasant, had been priceless as a learning experience, and I intended to make the most of it.

When I first arrived at VEWS, my predecessor was in the process of clearing his things out of the office I would occupy next to Bushman. He had taken a position with another firm somewhere. His name escapes me. I've often wondered what his reason was for leaving. It did not seem appropriate for me to inquire at the time, and he did not bring it up. Before I left, my successor, Jim Brelsford, had arrived. He was a decent sort and seems to have made good there, at least for several years after I left.

Finding a place to live in Houston was high priority. We rented a unit in an apartment complex on Bancroft Lane off of San Felipe Street until we could locate a house. We had to have a house before the babies were born. We found a satisfactory house on Evergreen Street in Bellaire and moved in some time around Thanksgiving. Jo Anne's mother did not want her doing a lot of lifting, so she and Doc came down to help us move in.

We did not have enough money for the down payment. With great misgiving I talked to mother about it. She loaned us five thousand dollars. I do not remember just how soon we were able to pay that off, but it was a matter uppermost in my mind and we repaid it, with interest, as soon as we possibly could as I knew her resources were limited—she had gone back to work. In all likelihood, the majority of it was repaid when we sold the Houston house, with any remaining amount being paid off fairly promptly.

Al Hamilton had alerted us to the fact that the house we ended up buying was, or was about to be, for sale. It had not yet been listed. It was next door just west of his. On the other side of us, we later learned, was a most congenial neighbor who was also an attorney named Frank Barnes, and his wife. He practiced law by himself. It was a happy arrangement being next to Al. His wife was Lucy. Both were from Mississippi. Except when our individual schedules prevented, Al and I would usually drive to and from work together, alternating cars. One of Al's tasks was helping prepare personal tax returns for some of the top partners. I am not sure whether he also did the firm's return. One day driving home he said that preparing those personal returns almost made him want to go communist. He could not divulge any further information. But he did tell about trying to reconcile one senior partner's bank account as part of his task. For some reason the bank statement was approximately one hundred thousand dollars less than it should have been if everything had been handled correctly. When Al pointed it out to him, the partner said, "Yes, I thought that account was *a little bit* low." Obviously, those in the higher levels made a lot of income. But I would not have traded the future I had for such a position. It was just not a fit.

Al later left the firm for one in Midland where I thought he was doing well, but family-wise apparently not. He left his wife and two daughters. Though it gradually waned over the years, until contact was lost, Jo Anne stayed in touch with her for decades. We do not know what became of Al. Lucy, who seems to have come from a cultured family, was understandably bitter. It was a sad situation.

About the time we went to Houston, the head pastor of First Methodist Church in Wichita Falls, Dr. Alfred ("Al") Freeman, whom dad had enjoyed in the brief time he had been there, became head pastor of St. Paul's Methodist Church in Houston. We joined there. Al even had me come to his house and prepare their income tax return while we were in Houston. Al's wife Carolyn began teaching a young married couples' class which we also joined. It provided many friendships. Several of we fellows got together fairly often and played penny ante poker. I learned it and loved playing it in that group. The rule was that the maximum raise was three cents and the maximum number of raises was three. Winning or losing two to three dollars a night was about as extreme as it got. I've not played poker since we left Houston. Too much money is always at stake.

The climate in Houston did not appeal to either of us. It did not seem to get either as hot or as cold as other places we had lived, but it was much more humid. Combining the situation at work and the climate, my memories of Houston are not that pleasant. But it was most worthwhile and it all worked out very well in the long run.

Nelson, McCleskey & Harriger (Lubbock)

January 1959 was a very busy month. We had to find a place in Lubbock to rent for a while, make arrangements for moving our furniture, and put the Bellaire house on the market. My arrangement with NMH, apparently in keeping with the firm policy for each lawyer, required me to furnish my own office. That had to be selected and moved in by February 1. A complicating factor is that our twins both got sick in Houston in December. Jo Anne took them to Wichita Falls to be with her family and care for them there. It was there that they were diagnosed with mononucleosis. It was not till about March that they were well enough for her to return with them to Lubbock.

Harold Harriger was an immense help to us in finding a house to rent on a month to month basis and getting moved in. He found a small house (about one thousand square feet) not far west of College Avenue on 64th Street.[1] Jo Anne left the boys in Wichita Falls for a while and came to Lubbock to help get furniture moved in and

---

1   When Texas Technological College was renamed Texas Tech University in 1969, College Avenue was also renamed University Avenue.

placed in the house and to help me select office furniture. The house had tile floors. When we got to the house, Harold had rented a polishing machine and was there polishing all the floors before we moved in. Clearly the friendship with the Harrigers that had been meaningful in Wichita Falls carried over in Lubbock. Harold was known as "Skip" Harriger in Wichita Falls, but only as Harold in Lubbock. His wife Rebecca was known only as "Becky" in Wichita Falls, but only as Rebecca in Lubbock (except to us). We often exchanged baby-sitting with them. Becky died of a brain tumor several years before Harold, who himself died June 5, 2012. Harold was born and raised in what was called "Harriger Hollow" in western Pennsylvania, and he maintained his interest in and enthusiasm for that property the rest of his life. He had a wonderful personality and was widely loved and admired in Lubbock.

My two years at NMH were a joyful and productive time. My relationship with each of the other four was super. They had some clients waiting for me, but I also lost no time in generating other clients on my own, especially in estate planning. Frequently I spoke to the gathered agents in several life insurance agencies on matters of estate planning, and business usually followed. Other independent agents also heard of my work and became acquainted, referring countless clients. Quite regularly, as scheduled by these agents, I traveled to the homes of prospective clients in towns or on farms within a fairly wide radius of Lubbock. Many accountants in Lubbock and from surrounding towns or cities referred clients to me on tax issues or for business or estate planning service. There were also estates to be administered. It was a busy and exhilarating time, especially coming as it did on the heals of the VEWS experience. But to a great extent it was that Houston experience that paved the way for my transition from law school to a successful legal career.

It would serve no meaningful purpose for me to give details of practice in all these areas during my two years with NMH, even if I remembered it, which I do not other than as previously summed up. However, there were two cases that stand out in my memory. One was the landmark Marvin Shurbet water depletion case. The other was the Clark Wood matter.

The Shurbet case involved a claim for refund based upon a deduction taken for depletion of the cost of water under Shurbet's farmland. It was a test case as the issue had never been presented or judicially decided before, nor to my knowledge had the Internal Revenue Service (IRS) been faced with it before. With the increasing cost of farmland, a big part of that cost was based upon the estimated recoverable water from the Ogallala below the farm in question.

When I began practice at the firm, the plan was taking shape to fashion a test case. George McCleskey not only had some farmland but had become something of a local expert on water law. Just how the idea of such a test case originated I can only imagine. By the time I got to the firm, the picture had partially developed. The firm was very happy now to have a "tax man" as part of its team. In the thick of all of it was the High Plains Water District (HPWD), formed under Texas law in 1951, the first groundwater conservation district created in Texas. It encompassed all of eight South Plains counties and parts of eight others. Its purpose was to conserve, preserve, protect, and prevent waste of, groundwater within its district.

Whether the catalyst was McCleskey or the water district I do not know, but surmise they were essentially involved symbiotically in the birth of the initiative. By the time I arrived on the scene, the prominent Austin firm Graves, Dougherty, Heron & Moody had also been associated on the case, Chris Dougherty being the primary one involved from there. The chief justice of the Texas Supreme Court at the time was Joe Greenhill who, before election to the court, had been a partner in the firm. Since the case was a Federal case, there was no conflict with him being also involved in some of our meetings, which added an element of interest for me as he was not only prominent and highly respected but also most personable.

The general manager of the HPWD was named Tom McFarland. He was all business except when he was all play, and he emanated gusto in each in its time. He was a strapping fellow, man-sized in a good way. Whether as a marine or sailor, he was on a cruiser that was torpedoed and sunk off of Luzon, Philippines, in January 1942, one month after the Japanese attack on Pearl Harbor. He was promptly captured by the Japanese and was a prisoner until rescued after the official surrender of Japan on September 2, 1945. He both witnessed and experienced brutality, including as slave labor on the Burma Road. Surprised that he survived, I asked him how he did so. By sheer will power and determination to get through it, he said.

All forces gathered in one location on occasion to strategize. One incident illustrates Tom's playful side. All parties were to gather at the Adophus Hotel, 1321 Commerce Street in the heart of downtown Dallas. For some reason, I was a bit delayed arriving beyond the designated meeting time on the first evening when they gathered. No sooner had I gotten into my room than the phone rang and Tom said, in a voice adequately lubricated, "Where in the hell are you?"

"Just got into my room," I replied.

"Get over here!" (Tom).

"Where are you?" I said.

"At the theater lounge."

The Theater Lounge was located a block or two south of the hotel on a parallel street. I knew of it while in law school but was not there during those years. It was a well-located and patronized stripper lounge. Well I remember Oscar Mauzy, later a state senator and two-term associate justice of the Texas Supreme Court. A local attorney, he was an alumnus of the Delta Theta Phi legal fraternity that Roomie and I had joined. Candy Barr, Theater Lounge's prominent headline performer, was one of his clients.[1] The word went out to all of us that at our upcoming DTP gathering Oscar would have Candy there. Attendance was very good, all being in a high state of anticipation. Arriving with Oscar she was fully, well, and even surprisingly modestly, dressed. She did little more than say hello, but in

---

1 For Candy Barr, see http://en.wikipedia.org/wiki/Candy_Barr.

the midst of all her fame she had been there for a few moments—no performance and few words, the "perfect lady." But, palpably, the air in the anticipatory balloon had lost some of its pressure.

The next week a letter came to all of us who had attended the Theater Lounge enclosing a clipping from the Fort Worth Star Telegram. Judge Greenhill had been on the stage of some sort of event in Fort Worth the day after our evening at the lounge. The clipping was a picture of those seated on the dais. Greenhill appeared to be dozing. His comment with the enclosure read, "See what you guys did to me."

These occasions added color to the seriousness of the water depletion case. The group had selected Marvin Shurbet, a taxpayer who farmed in the area of Petersburg, Texas, a small community northeast of Lubbock. Marvin may have also been a board member of HPWD at the time. This is the stage to which the planned tax case had progressed when I became involved. It was a no-brainer that the case would be filed in the Federal District Court rather than in the Tax Court, in order to try it before our own district's jury. I was involved in a number of important preparatory procedural matters, as well as the several conferences.

Though I attended the trial, I did not participate in the courtroom in the trial. There were much older and more experienced lawyers from both firms to handle the trial itself. Aside from my inexperience in actual trials at that point, this case was a very visible one in our entire area and George McCleskey was understandably going to stay in the public eye in actually trying the case. Chris Dougherty was a Harvard lawyer with years of practicing in the state capital. I judge him to have been more or less a contemporary of McCleskey. While the local McCleskey was the lead, obviously Chris had to participate in it also.

The evidence and law were actually remarkably simple and clear, with one exception. The big fact question on which we presented considerable expert testimony, and as I recall the government presented little or none of it, was whether or not the water level was irretrievably declining, or whether it was subject to recharge. Our witnesses testified that it was rechargeable only in geologic time. Instruction on the law was given to the jury, which then decided the case for the taxpayer. The HPWD worked with the IRS in establishing certain guidelines, and in each case a claimant would have to set out, subject to challenge, the portion of his cost basis in the land that was properly allocable to the water. That was subject to challenge, but in most cases it was probably not a matter of strong contention if not patently excessive, for clearly the recoverable water was valuable and measurable.

The second of the two more memorable tax cases mentioned earlier involved taxpayer Clark Wood. He had a ranch in an area southeast of Lubbock. It had been infested with mesquite trees. He had spent a considerable sum for aerial spraying to destroy as much as possible of the existing growth. His option at that time for destroying the mesquite trees was either the spraying method he used or the dragging, between two bulldozers, of a large, heavy chain that literally broke the trees off around ground level. On his tax return he claimed it as an ordinary expense of his ranching operation. The IRS denied the deduction, claiming that it was a capital improvement to the land, proposing a deficiency. Hobert Nelson brought him in for me to represent on the matter. Any cost that permanently improved the land could only be added to his cost basis. Any expense that was of a recurring type, and thus an ordinary and necessary expense of operation, could be deducted. I was faced with how to prove that it was of such latter nature. In my research it came to my attention that the Texas A&M Extension Service had published a study on controlling mesquite, indicating that eradication was not possible but that control methods were available. New growth will emerge even when all existing above-ground growth is killed. When that publication was provided to the IRS appellate division in Dallas, the proposed deficiency was eliminated.

As the end of 1960 drew near I had high expectation that I was about to become a partner in this firm where my two years had been such a happy and successful experience. Never during that time did it occur to me that I might not become a partner. As it turned out, I never did. The first two months of 1961 were among the most draining and stressful periods I have lived through. While light finally appeared at the end of that tunnel, it was dark in the passage through. An evening routine began for me that helped burn off adrenalin and alleviate stressful anxiety. It was the seed that grew into my distance running career, but that is a story for a separate section to follow.

Toward the latter part of 1960, as the two-year probationary period was nearing completion at the end of January, it seemed to be assumed by all that I would be offered a partnership interest in the firm going forward from February 1, 1961. There was no written partnership agreement. The substance of our discussions as I was employed included their expectation that I was not coming aboard to establish a local base and then leave the firm to practice alone or with another firm, and that subject thereto, if all went well during the two years, I would be offered a partnership interest in the firm. Legally, that hardly constituted a binding obligation on either party, at least not insofar as determining the nature and extent of the partnership interest was concerned. Implicit in that, I felt, was the condition that I would be fairly treated in the partnership share and arrangement that was offered. The firm's commitment was not sufficiently defined, nor was mine. Nevertheless, it was clear that a partnership interest of some kind was in the mind of all parties as the critical date approached.

What the firm offered was a percentage that, based upon expectations from 1959 and thus far in 1960, would have produced an income for me in my first partnership year, 1961, of approximately twelve thousand dollars ($12,000). That percentage was not acceptable to me. I had kept good records myself and compiled from my charge book a total of about thirty thousand dollars I had billed for the year 1960 (at a billing rate of twenty dollars per hour, when based on hours spent), of which considerably more than twelve thousand was billed to clients that I had brought in that had not been firm clients before. Moreover, my own personal clientele was in a growth phase, while that from existing firm clients was probably static at best.

I do not remember meeting with any of the firm partners prior to December 1960 or January 1961, although perhaps one or more of them might have met with me before then. All I remember is my distress and utter disappointment when I learned what the percentage interest they were offering me was and applied that to the net firm income for the year 1960 after adding back my salary for that year. I expressed my dissatisfaction in the hope that they would make some kind of an increase. Whether they asked me what it would take or not, I cannot be certain, but I am pretty sure they did not and I was determined that I would not give them that even if they asked for it. Apparently they felt that by sitting tight I would come around. It did become obvious that they were fitting me into a set scheme to move up gradually over time, starting from a low entry point. The end of January was approaching with nothing resolved. Whether it was then or later, I cannot be certain, but my sense in thinking back is that our final meeting did not occur till toward the end of February. Our contractual period had run out on January 31 without us coming to any agreement on my status going forward into February. I continued to work through substantially all of February in the hope that something would give. I did not expect to be paid for work in February if nothing was worked out, nor would I have accepted any. None was offered. As the month of February unfolded, more and more of my time was devoted to the many preparations for opening my own office. Up to the point where I had to commit to other arrangements, I had made up my mind that if they budged and increased the proffered percentage in any amount, however otherwise inadequate, I would stay at least for another year. It never happened. They never budged.

At one point before the end came I was in Harold's office. Perhaps I was talking about the partnership situation, but maybe it was on something else. In any event the matter did come into the conversation. I remember Harold, in his generous-spirited way, saying that whatever I worked out with the two senior partners would be fine with him, but he added, "I just hope it does not hit me too hard," or something to that general effect. It was not Harold where the problem lay.

When I also did not budge from the fact the amount offered was not satisfactory, we met together in the library behind closed doors. Hobert and George were both there, and I think Harold also was although he did not speak during the meeting; the other two did. Hobert, whom I had gotten along with so well and still liked, was pretty hard on me, although in retrospect it may well have been primarily George McCleskey's decision. In the context of whether or not I had broken a binding agreement not to leave the firm if I was offered a partnership, and minimizing the question of fairness of the offer, Hobert said, "We'll see about that." To me, this was a threat to sue for breach of an employment contract. That statement pretty well ended the meeting for me, and I left it. I do not recall if the others stayed there to confer.

The law seemed clear to me that an employee cannot be forced into continued employment or partnership, the damages from breach by the employee being of monetary nature only.

Anticipating that the firm would sue me, I promptly contacted Tom Milam of Crenshaw, Dupree and Milam, Lubbock's largest defense firm (the Milam in the firm title was Jim, Tom's older brother and essentially the highly respected dean of Lubbock lawyers). Tom thought NMH would not sue and would not have a cause of action against me if they did. But he agreed that he or his firm would defend me if they sued. They did not.

While it could not have been known at the time I had to make the critical decision to leave based on the unfairness of the proffered partnership share, the justness of my position seemed to me in retrospect to have been supported by the fact that in the first year of practice after I left the firm my net income, after all expenses, was approximately $24,000, twice the estimated amount I would have earned under the share offered.

NMH replaced me in 1961, hiring Clarence P. Brazill, Jr., also an SMU Law graduate previously with the IRS Regional Counsel's office.[1] Hobert Nelson's son Burt, one of the five of us while I was there, left the law practice for good soon after I left the firm. He became an entrepreneur who, through ownership in several banks and a large beer distributorship in San Antonio, accumulated wealth beyond anything he could have expected in practicing law in Lubbock or probably most anywhere else. Burt and I remain friends, as is also the case with his younger brother, George, also a Lubbock lawyer.

From the very early days of my Lubbock practice, one of the CPAs who was particularly supportive of me and referred many clients, was the late Crayton O. Campbell. Our relationship became sufficiently close that I confided in him the likelihood that I would be leaving the firm and probably opening an office of my own. He said to me, "Ed, if you are concerned about making it, I will pay all of your expenses for half of your profits." Of course, such an arrangement (sharing of income with one who is not a licensed attorney) would have violated one of the firm rules of ethics of the Texas Bar Association and subjected me to sanction if not disbarment. But clearly he was most encouraging. As it worked out, his continuing support as well as that of virtually everyone else I had worked with during my employment period made it immediately obvious that my prospects for success appeared high. As indicated, such prospects were promptly confirmed the ensuing year, and the level of net income continued to increase with each passing year.

---

1   The firm name was changed to Nelson, McCleskey, Harriger, Brazill & Graf in 1970. Nelson's name was removed in 1977 after his death. Though it has many more lawyers today, it has remained McCleskey, Harriger, Brazill & Graf since then. Only Graf survives at this time, Brazill having died in 1990, McCleskey in 1997 though inactive for health reasons well before that, and Harriger in 2012.

Support for my opening my own office was also strong within my own family. Though we had the young twin sons and were expecting another birth in June, Jo Anne said, in all seriousness, that if it became necessary she could go back to teaching. In addition, Doc, my father-in-law, said that he would make our house payments if needed.[1]

I owed a bit of money on a small new station wagon we had purchased. We knew that Jo Anne was pregnant with targeted due date in June. Most of the furniture I would need had been purchased two years earlier. A bank loan for books, shelving, and some other items, would be essential. Getting it turned out to be no problem. I was banking at Citizens National Bank and at the same time was negotiating with them for rent of a single office in the Citizens Center, an adjoining single-story building owned by the bank that essentially covered all of the balance of the rectangular block not occupied by the multistory bank building itself.

I leased an office in the Citizens Center at 1313 Ave L. The office was one in a suite of offices comprising a reception area off of the street, and four or five single-room offices. For a short while, attorney and friend Bill Parsley occupied the office straight across the hall from me. The others were occupied by the Larry Hibler Insurance Agency. At first we all shared a receptionist-secretary, but my need for a secretary of my own became obvious fairly soon. Later, Parsley and I visited about the fact that I was negotiating in the late spring of 1962 to bring a younger lawyer into the practice with me. Happily the timing was perfect for Parsley who was in the process of running for the Texas legislature, which he did and was elected that fall. We

---

1   Our house was then on 65th Street. After we had lived in the rented house on 64th Street for a few months, the owner wanted to sell it. We found essentially the same floor plan a bit further west on 65th Street. We bought it with virtually no down payment and a favorable interest rate, using the long-term loan available under the Korean War G. I. Bill. The house, which was new and backed up to open cotton field, cost approximately ten thousand dollars for approximately one thousand square feet of living space plus adjoining covered car port with small enclosed storage area at the rear.

moved my new junior partner into Parsley's vacated office at the end of August 1962. But on this as well as our later addition of lawyers and office space I jump a bit ahead of the story.

Most of the office furniture I would need to open my own office I already owned. For bookshelves, I bought, sanded, and varnished raw lumber boards (1 x 8s as I remember), laying them on white solar blocks standing on end. Several rows of bookshelves provided the space for my most basic books. I also had a cabinet by the side of my desk where the Prentice-Hall Tax Service could be quickly accessed from my desk. To occupy the other shelves I bought and subscribed to Vernon's Texas Civil Statutes and the Tax Court Reports. It was a minimal library, but the county law library was within walking distance.

During my tenure at NMH, and for some years thereafter, the firm occupied the second floor of the Central American Life Insurance building at Broadway and Texas Avenue, which occupied the northeast corner of the block diagonally across from the Lubbock County Courthouse to the Northeast. Many nostalgic memories remain to me of parking my car just off Texas Avenue on Sixteenth Street and walking the four blocks north to our offices. Late in the evening of Tuesday, February 28, 1961, when all others had left the offices for the day, I entered it with a professional mover. All my belongings were removed and transported the few blocks to my new office at 1313 Avenue L. As I've generally done when vacating any location that occupied a significant segment of my life, when all of my things were out of the firm offices, I went back in to take one brief but private, contemplative moment. It had been a wonderful place, with people I greatly enjoyed. But it was finally over and a major new and salient segment of my life was about to begin.

My Solo Practice
(March 1, 1961–August 15, 1962)

My readers may wonder at the fact that I do not remember a lot of the detailed content of my law practice during this exciting period, a time that rewarded me financially and with an even more fulfilling sense of worthwhile accomplishment for client, self, and family. My many detailed hand-written charge books were retained for many years but, taking up limited storage space and with my having no thought of their later usefulness, they have long since been disposed of as some of life's accumulated baggage that, once vital, no longer justified retention. They would have been a godsend in bringing back the names of clients and work performed for them. Now I have only the diminished memory available to me as I pass through the early years of my ninth decade. Such detail occurred more than a half century ago. Nor would most readers appreciate having to labor through it had my recall been perfect. It is the more salient aspects, the more defining characteristics of those years, as I recall them, that I share here.

The nature of the actual legal work I handled did not significantly change in the transition from the NMH to my own individual practice. It was the enhanced sense of authoritative control and ultimate responsibility with which the work was generated, accepted, and executed that was wonderfully different.

One memory from the first several days I was on my own is how I wanted to silently utter a prayer of thanks for every item of business that came in. Confidence in how things were working out increased regularly so that I took incoming business in stride after a while. From those days and extending throughout my entire legal

My Solo Practice (March 1, 1961–August 15, 1962)

career, it seemed like feast or famine; that is, either I was under stress to get the work done that had piled up, or I was concerned that I did not have much backlog of work to be done. It seems like it was usually one or the other, though there were intermediate times when things seemed to be balanced about right.

Typically I left for the office around 7:00 a.m. and left the office around 6:00 p.m. Coffee breaks were not part of my day, though several cups were consumed during the day from the coffee pot in the offices. My impression is that even as other lawyers were added, I continued normally to be the first one there in the morning and the last one to leave in the evening; though this changed in later years during my lengthy early morning distance runs or piano practice. When I left the office in the evening, unless I expected to return later, I almost always carried a brief case of reading material, digests of current cases and rulings from the various courts or other authorities applicable to my type of practice.

By the time I got home in the evening, Jo Anne would have had a full day tending to the affairs of the house and the children. Except on the rarest of occasions, it was my job to give the boys their bath every evening, and to help in the process of getting them bedded down for the night. Some evenings I would read to them, although I think more of that was done by Jo Anne while I read legal materials and the daily newspaper. At some time during the evening, sometimes shortly before bedtime, I normally went out for exercise, continuing the anxiety relieving practice that I had started in my last months at NMH. However, when there was serious research to be done for a brief or letter opinion or legal memo, I would often return to the office and work into the late hours while it was quiet and without the disturbances of the day.

Jo Anne understood the importance of my taking care of these matters, especially in those early years in my own office. Not only was she helpful in that way, but even with her responsibilities for the children, from early in my days in Lubbock she was active in ways that not only gave her outlets into the wider community but also tended to help further my own name recognition there. Her community activities, along with mine, are the subject of a later section.

Earlier, in the NMH section, my speaking to agents in several life insurance agencies on matters of estate planning was mentioned. Among those agencies were those headed by Robert G. (Bob) Schuster, Del Burkhart, Gerald Davis, and Terry Condrey, the manager of the Investors Diversified Services (IDS) office. Individual agents who referred numerous clients included Schuster, Charles Gray (of Ralls, Texas, originally from Schuster's office), Gerald Davis, and Chuck Diegl. Other agents also referred clients, if not so regularly as those named. These references, even when commenced during the NMH period, continued after I opened my own office. I like to think it was beneficial to the agents also in seeing that their clients' estate planning was handled in a manner that was in their best interest.

The problem most commonly addressed dealt with the fact that the net worth of a married couple had increased to more than the Federal estate tax exemption, which in those years was sixty thousand dollars. If one spouse died leaving a community one-half interest outright to the survivor, a tax would be due upon the second death on that part of the total value on the second death which exceeded that decedent's one exemption. A testamentary trust for the first community half that provided for the support and maintenance of the surviving spouse in the standard of living to which they were accustomed at the first death, even when the surviving spouse served as the sole trustee, would not be included in the taxable estate of the survivor on the latter's death. The problem addressed thereby was almost universally present with these referred clients in the Lubbock region. Each case presented its own circumstances, and the wills or trusts were prepared to address those beyond simply the estate tax matter.

My practice certainly stretched well beyond this immediate type of service, but the type constituted the most basic bread and butter support. Beyond that, business proprietorships, partnerships, and corporations were significantly in the picture. Areas that I avoided

My Solo Practice (March 1, 1961–August 15, 1962)

were divorce, personal injury, non-tax criminal, bankruptcy, patent law and selectively other situations that might arise.

Two significant clients that came in were Gene Hancock (of Hancock Manufacturing) and R. C. (Bob) Johnson, Jr. (of Johnson Manufacturing). The Johnsons, R. C. and R. C. Jr. (Bob), had been clients of NMH for whom I had worked, and I was pleasantly surprised when Bob came in for services. He stayed for a while, but as time went on he felt that no one firm should be handling the matters of both these manufacturing operations. Both of their principals were building earth-moving equipment. Hancock Manufacturing was later to become a publicly held corporation and a while later be absorbed into Clark Equipment Company. Johnson Manufacturing would later be acquired by Eagle-Picher Corporation. But while I was practicing alone, Hancock held patents that it felt Johnson was infringing in the earth-moving equipment area. While the controversy was outside my practice area, Bob's discomfort with being represented by his potential adversary's lawyer was most understandable, as he explained to me upon withdrawing. Probably this was after Brazill had replaced me at NMH.

One particular gratification probably came to my attention for the first time during this year and a half I practiced by myself. It was the Martindale-Hubbell (M-H) rating.[1] It is a peer review rating of lawyers by other lawyers. The review starts only after one has been admitted to the bar for three years. It is based upon a lawyer's own specified area(s) of practice. The waiting period means that my review probably did not appear in the M-H publication until I had opened my own office. How pleasing it was, on the first occasion I had to inspect the publication, to see that M-H had awarded me its top rating. It was to continue after a partner was added and included the firm rating from then on. The publication itself, available, I believe, only to lawyers or law firms, was too expensive for me to subscribe, but could be examined at the county law library

---

1 See http://www.martindale.com/Products_and_Services/Peer_Review_Ratings.aspx.

when needed. It is useful in finding lawyers in other cities or areas when service in those regions is needed.

While I handled, during this period, client controversies with the IRS both before and after deficiency notices had been issued, I do not recall that any specific litigation was instituted during this short period, though some of the later litigation may have had roots going back to this time frame. Some litigation cases recollected will be mentioned in the partnership period to follow.

As the years and decades slipped by, my accumulation of historic financial records, including financial statements, income tax returns, checkbook stubs, bank statements, credit card statements and others, excluding active and closed files at the law firm, grew at our residence to the point of requiring an increasing amount of storage space. Illustrative of my reluctance to throw any such record away was the fact that I even had the checkbook stubs from my college days at Midwestern. The accumulations began encroaching into areas that introduced severe competition with higher priority needs. Selectively I began to eliminate some categories that were justified only by my pack rat mentality's hesitation to jettison anything. The real test came when, in April 2004 we moved out of the house on 57th Street where we had lived for more than forty-one years and into our commodious apartment residence in Lubbock's top senior life care campus. At that time, all this remaining accumulation was either trashed or recycled except the year-end financial statement for most years and our tax returns for six years back.

While it is beyond the scope of this autobiography to set out detailed financial information through the years, without a doubt these annual statements are a helpful prompt in refreshing memory and sequence of some events as they unfolded.

Up to the time I opened my own office, I made only a few small investments to the extent I could pay for them without borrowing. I did borrow money from the bank to get my office opened, and though I think it was merely a signature loan, possibly the bank took a lien. The earliest financial statement I prepared, based upon

My Solo Practice (March 1, 1961–August 15, 1962)

my retained records, was for the date of March 31, 1962. Thereafter I generally prepared quarterly statements up till the time I ceased needing bank loans, after which statements were prepared as of the end of each calendar year.

That my first retained financial statement was for March 31, 1962, corresponds with my memory as to what was happening by then. That was a year after my income level had jumped with the opening of my own office. It was the beginning of a new era when law practice and investment activity lived happily in symbiotic growth. While "Investment and Business" is the subject of a separate segment in the period of my life following 1957, it is helpful to share the substance of my first financial statement when my law practice itself was the mother that gave birth to significant investment activity. It was beginning in 1962. Here is the first financial statement I prepared:

FINANCIAL STATEMENT MARCH 31, 1962

ASSETS

Capital in law practice		$11,696.32
Investments		
Investors Diversified Services	450.00	
Central American Life Ins. Co. Stock	90.00	
American Founders Life Ins. Co. Stock	6,050.00	
100 shares Transitron Electronics	1,300.00	
Equity in Houston apartment—partnership	350.00	
100 shares Plains Mortgage Corporation	2,000.00	10,240.00
Cash value of life ins. ($99,000 permanent life)		750.00
Cash in State Savings & Loan Association		400.00
Equity in home		500.00
Personal automobile		750.00
		$24,336.32

Liabilities and Net Worth

Income tax payable	$1,688.80	
Employers taxes payable	173.00	1,861.90
Net worth		22,474.52
Total Liabilities and Net Worth		$24,336.32

The American Founders Life Insurance Company stock investment is a story in itself that will be told in the "Investment & Business" segment. The date of this statement, as the first of many that continues to the current writing, confirms that my period of borrowing for investments was getting started. Looking ahead to the December 31, 1963, statement indicates a net worth of $90,160.43, net of liabilities for bank note ($44,336.00) and income and employment tax payable ($3,723.99). The growth from the earlier statement to this one, from $22,474.52 to $90, 160.43 ($67,685.91), resulted from the excess of law firm earnings over living expenses as well as appreciation in American Founders stock, both that stock reflected in the earlier statement and additional purchases since then.

We lived frugally and I squeezed everything I could out of my law practice earnings to take to the bank and pay on my (our) loans for investment. These were numerous over the years. My practice of paying them down as fast as I could continued, and I was never turned down in any request for loan. The loans were generally collateralized by the investment itself as a perfunctory process.

It is appropriate to say that in addition to all her other wonderful qualities, Jo Anne was a cooperative, low-maintenance wife through those years.[1] And she has so continued, in relationship, of course, to our ability to afford more and more as time went on. It was a philosophy of life on which we have always been most compatible. Not all men (or women) are so fortunate. It enhanced our capacity for

---

1 "Low maintenance" is a description I picked up from a grandson in reference to his switching from one girlfriend to another, whom, happily, he was later to marry.

My Solo Practice (March 1, 1961–August 15, 1962)

both accumulation and related generosity and happy opportunity for a modest taste of philanthropy. But on this I leap ahead.

This first financial statement doubtless coincided with a significant event that was happening in 1962, probably early that year. W. B. Rushing, a man with whom I would retain some connection for the rest of his life (he was almost twenty-three years older than I), walked into my office one day accompanied by J. C. Chambers and Jack Kastman. J. C. was a talented, gregarious and popular fellow, frequently receiving well-deserved public acclaim, an outstanding local agent for Massachusetts Mutual Life Insurance Company. Jack Kastman was an outgoing realtor. He was a former SMU basketball player who met there and married an heir of a prominent Lubbock area grain operator and oil investor. Rushing himself was doubtless Lubbock's most successful commercial real estate operator and investor both then and until his death. He got his start owning and operating the Varsity Book Stores adjacent to SMU and then Texas Tech. He will appear from time to time later herein. Rushing had just then recently purchased the prime, sizeable tract of land occupying the southwest corner of the intersection of the arterial Avenue Q and 50th Street in Lubbock, as well as the triangular property on the southeast corner of that intersection. His plan was to develop a shopping center on the larger southwest tract, but he wanted to charter a new Texas savings and loan association to be located at the corner of the intersection. His brother-in-law, Max Tidmore, also his partner in the development of shopping centers in Wichita Falls and Lubbock, and soon to become mayor of Lubbock, would hold the larger shares of the new association's stock, along with other board members. A majority of the association's stock was to be in the hands of its board of directors. The rest of the stock was to be sold in small parcels to young go-getters or the scions of older wealthy and/or prominent citizens of the area. Rushing proposed that we bring in about one hundred of these who would each hold one hundred shares of the new stock, constituting in total a bit less than fifty percent of the outstanding stock. Rushing's idea was to compose the board of himself, as the largest shareholder, Max Tidmore as the next largest, with four other up-and-coming young men. Of these four, it appears that I was the last to be selected, as an attorney that also fit that category. Chambers and Kastman obviously were selected before I, but equally obvious was that Rushing's young employee Henry Huneke fit the mold, especially in real estate involvement. The Texas Savings & Loan Commission, or the Federal Home Loan Bank, required that two more be added who were not affiliated with any of the other board members. In addition, the newly hired president and vice president were to be board members.

Rushing had the name of the association already picked out. It was to be Briercroft Savings & Loan Association. It represented a significant activity and investment from that time period until sold just in time to avoid the disastrous plunge that all savings and loans were to experience with the general collapse of that industry in the eighties. But the story of Briercroft is for the "Investment and Business segment." It is related above only because Rushing entered my own life activities during this short period of my solo law practice and became a significant client in it as well as associate and friend in my life from then on till his death.

By the spring of 1962, word came through the grapevine that those back at the SMU Law School heard that I was doing pretty well in my solo practice in Lubbock. Ken Hobbs had been a first year SMU law student during my senior year there. I believe he was a bit older than I, but had been in the oil and gas servicing business in the Texas panhandle before entering law school. In the spring of 1962 he was working in the law office of another local lawyer. Ken called me to speak favorably of one Norton Baker, whom I had known in school only casually. Norton had been in the same class as Ken, two years behind me my senior year. Ken seemed well informed on Norton, who was licensed as both a lawyer and CPA. Ken said that Norton had been working after law school in the tax department of the big international accounting firm of Peat, Marwick, Mitchell & Co. (P, M, M & Co.) in Dallas when his reserve unit was activated

My Solo Practice (March 1, 1961–August 15, 1962)

during the Berlin Wall crisis. Ken spoke highly of Norton as a good man and capable law student, saying also that he was born and raised in Lockney, Texas, in Floyd County. Floyd County lays northeast of Lubbock County. The two counties touch at the corner. According to Ken, Norton's reserve unit had just completed its tour and he desired to come to Lubbock to practice law, especially Federal tax law.

Norton did come soon after that to visit with me about the possibility of practicing with me. He seemed flexible and agreeable and we came to an oral understanding while he was there. It seemed a timely addition for me. My practice was growing and some capable help was a welcome development. His limited time with P, M, M & Co. was good tax experience, but he had not yet had experience in the type of work that was my bread and butter, or in handling matters generally in the overt practice of law. The thing that made the arrangement ideal for me was his flexibility in a participating share of firm income. I knew that I could feed work to him, so it was not a matter of identifying billings at that stage of our practice. He told me candidly that he had some outside income, primarily I suppose from farms in Floyd County or perhaps income from bank interests—his father either was or had been a banker as well as landowner. He understood that I would be reviewing his work carefully until he had gained the necessary experience and confidence to move forward without supervision. It was agreed that he would come to work, and that our partnership would start, on August 16, 1962, under the firm name *Smith & Baker*. We worked out a procedure for the division of income and for his building up a capital account. My retained records contain the Smith & Baker year-end balance sheet and operating statement for each year ending December 31, from 1962 through 1966. They appear to reflect that starting in the last quarter of 1965 we began sharing net income equally and by the end of 1966 our capital accounts in the partnership were equal. I have no Smith & Baker financial statements after the close of 1966. At some point, perhaps after we began adding others, a different method was agreed to for sharing of firm income that reflected a lawyer's billings above overhead and a modest percentage return on capital accounts. From my own year-end financial statements, it appears that we incorporated as Smith & Baker, Inc. as of October 31, 1971, under the professional association legislation that had been enacted in Texas, each of us holding fifty percent of the association stock.

From March 1, 1961, through August 15, 1962, except for the preparation of billing statements by my secretary taken directly from my daily charge book, I had done all of the bookkeeping for my practice. Happily, whether or not by our agreement at such initial meeting, Norton was quite willing and able to take that over immediately, and on it he did a very good job.

Thus did the propitious and stimulating seventeen-and-a-half-month period that I practiced alone come to a close. It would have been hard to imagine at that time the warm and lifelong relationship that was then being established between us, but such it was to become.

The Smith Firm Years

The firm that came into existence at the conclusion of my time as a sole practitioner never bore the name "The Smith Firm," but always started with the name Smith, followed by from one to three more, until the firm split into two groups several years after my retirement. "The Smith Firm Years," as discussed below, will cover the period when Baker joined me in 1962 until my retirement in 1984. The discussion will cover the following four interpenetrating subject areas that played out, from my perspective and involvement, in those years:

1. Evolution of the firm
2. Pension and Profit Sharing Plans
3. Litigated cases
4. Winding down and Farewell

Evolution of the Firm

Omar Khayyam said it well, "The moving finger writes; and, having writ, moves on...."[1] Such is the nature of created being, and so it was with the law firm spawned by my solo practice. Within that progeny, my patriarchate ascended, crested, and descended in a way that, reflecting upon it, seems the pattern of earthly life itself. The firm evolved, and so did I, each in its own way. My days in the firm comprised twenty-two years plus sixteen days, August 16, 1962, through August 31, 1984.

---

1 From *The Rubaiyat of Omar Khayyam*, verse 51: "The moving finger writes; and, having writ, / Moves on: nor all your piety nor wit / Shall lure it back to cancel half a Line, / Nor all your tears blot out a word of it" (cf. Dan 5:5, 24).

That firm evolution can be seen to comprise three stages during that twenty-two plus years:

1. The Smith & Baker years, the firm consisting of only Norton and me (August 16, 1962 till August 1972), the firm name being Smith & Baker;
2. From August 1972, when Mike Field joined us until June 30, 1978 when I sold my stock in the firm equally to Mike Field and Karl Clifford; even though lawyers were added during this six-year period, the firm name remained Smith & Baker;
3. From the 1978 sale of my firm stock, at which time the firm name was changed to Smith, Baker, Field & Clifford, until my retirement August 31, 1984, during which six-year period more lawyers joined the firm.

Following the "firm years" as I have defined them, being the above-segmented twenty-two plus years, the firm continued under the same firm name, Smith, Baker, Field & Clifford until the year 1991 when the firm split into two different firms. Three of the members, Norton Baker, Debbie Brown, and Mark Thompson, left the premises on Indiana Avenue moving into the new location in the Plains National Bank (now PlainsCapital Bank) building at 50th Street and University Avenue, where it has practiced under the name Baker, Brown & Thompson to this day. All the other lawyers stayed at the Indiana location, and the name was changed to reflect its new status. Whatever that firm name has been between 1991 and the summer of 2013 as I write, the current name of the firm is Field, Manning, Stone, Hawthorne & Aycock (P.C.). It has ten stockholders, one "Of Counsel," and four associates.

Up till the time of the split in 1991, I was listed "Of Counsel" to the firm. It was gratifying that upon the split each of the groups expressed the desire to continue listing me in that status. The State Bar would not permit the double listing, so I had to make a choice. While I had warm feelings for both groups, it was a no-brainer for me that I must stick with Norton's group. Up till that time and for a while thereafter I believe I had complied with the State Bar's annual

CLE (continuing legal education) requirement, thus remaining licensed to practice law and qualified to be carried as "Of Counsel" by a law firm. Meeting the CLE requirement each year became increasingly burdensome since it became obvious that I would not be practicing in the future in the absence of some financial catastrophe. At that point I took inactive status, after which I could only be listed by Norton's firm as a "Retired" member of the firm. Somewhere in those years I took inactive status also with the Texas State Board of Public Accountancy. While dues payments, even for inactive status, continued until age seventy, I no longer thereafter had to pay dues, though I continued to be listed as a Texas lawyer receiving the monthly Texas Bar Journal (which I read mainly for the memorials), and I continued to voluntarily contribute each year to the Texas Access to Justice fund sponsored and administered by the State Bar and Supreme Court to fund help for the indigent in need of legal assistance.

My own evolution as a lawyer during the firm years followed roughly the same three stages, time wise, listed earlier. The nature of my practice within the firm also seems to have moved through different types of legal work within the overall framework that the nature of our practice involved. In the earlier portions, estate planning (wills, trusts, estates) continued, but in the first couple of years Norton was with me I was sending work to him and going over his work with essentially the same intensity that Bushman had gone over mine at VEWS. Maintaining quality of product was vital. But I like to feel that the sense of close relationship with which we worked together on these things was more constructive, more in the nature of pointing out things that, though detailed or involved, were important and needed further attention. I did my best in this relationship to avoid overbearing or caustically critical comments or the display of exasperation. Norton needed to learn these new things he had not yet had experience doing. He was a willing and enthusiastic learner. It seems that maybe for about two years he continued to seek my advice on things even as he began to need less and less of my intense review of everything. This was a gratifying observation for me.

And then the day came when Gene Hancock needed added financing in a dimension that could only really be met by going public in a way that would require registration under the governing Federal and State securities laws. I had my hands full and did not want to get into that time and paper consuming undertaking. By then I had gained sufficient confidence in Norton's capabilities to the point, as I well remember, of walking into his office and saying to Norton that we had the choice of referring it to Dallas securities counsel or undertaking the massive project ourselves, but that I did not want to undertake such a registration myself. Without hesitation he said he would like to take it on. He did, and he did a very good job. Hancock was then and thereafter his client and not mine on all matters, business and personal.

It was a watershed event. Norton had reached maturity in our practice. In some respects, John the Baptist's words seemed to fit, "He must increase, but I must decrease" (John 3:30). The young eagle had spread his wings and was beginning to soar on his own. More and more, over time, I observed that clients who had been mine opted to bring new work to Norton. He also had a clientele of his own, especially from Floyd County where he and his family had roots and numerous acquaintances. Then I began to notice that at least one or two life insurance agents who had brought business to me, such as Gerald Davis, were bringing in new clients not to me, but to Norton. Others were working with both of us rather than just me. The same phenomenon was happening in some cases with accountants on tax matters. I was pleased to see how well Norton was doing, but I must confess that the extent of the shift was a bit of a blow to me after the early years of exhilarating creation of my own community stature as a lawyer and otherwise.

This ambivalence caused me to reflect. For one thing, I could not ever reveal that I had this blow to my own self-esteem. It was necessary that I recognize things for what they were. Norton had a "bedside manner" that people loved and that made them feel totally comfortable being in his hands. Seemingly, he was willing to give them the day if they wanted it. On the other hand, I normally felt the need to get the information and bring the conference, whether in the office or on the phone, to a close and get back to work. My own sense is that I was the more intellectual of the two, more creative in planning and in the preparation of instruments that Norton and I would both then work from. I seemed to have a greater eagerness to dive into arrangements that seemed sustainable on the law and facts if challenged, and to undertake litigation. To some extent these things would eventually come for Norton, but such was the state during the period of his transition from learner to master.

In fact, as will later be described, things were happening in my own practice, as well as in the other realms of my life, that were demanding, fulfilling, and often exciting. This general shift in the nature of our relationship came off in a positive way. Never did we ever, to my knowledge, have a cross word with one another, and our relationship was one continually on the increase as time went on. We, and our wives, are about as close even today as friends can be. We attend men's and women's basketball games at Texas Tech with seats together, and the same at Lubbock Symphony Orchestra concerts. We have traveled together joyfully. It was a way of growing together, even if on different personal paths, that was healthy and wholesome not only for the firm and our relationship but also for each of us individually.

Well after I had eventually retired from practicing law, I either heard him say, or learned that he said to one who reported it to me, that the best years he had practicing law (to that point) were the years he and I practiced alone together as Smith & Baker. That priceless remark made it all worthwhile. He and I shared some philosophies about billing clients and about rewarding the younger lawyers who joined us that were more generous both to clients and to the younger associates than seemed to be the case as the firm expanded and the younger ones sometimes had different views on these things.

The firm's expansion was more a result of natural growth than the product of any goal to expand for the sake of expansion itself. Neither Norton nor I desired to head up a large firm because of any assumed merit or prestige therein or hoped-for economic gain therefrom. Our goal was to take in highly qualified individual attorneys as they were available and so long as our expectation of adequate, if not plentiful, clientele persisted. We both recognized that, if properly managed, there are some economies of scale in the spreading of fixed overhead expenses, though most firm expenses, notably office space and secretarial help and equipment, tended to have a positive relationship to the number of lawyers in the firm. Library costs would be a bit less directly proportional to personnel size. For our first ten years together, we did not add any other lawyers. On October 31, 1971, we incorporated as Smith & Baker, Inc., a professional corporation. In August of 1972, Mike Field joined the firm. In the summer of 1973 we were able to hire the top three graduates that year from the Texas Tech law school, being Karl Clifford, Don Collier, and Elgin Conner. It was soon mutually agreed with Elgin that our firm was not the place for him and he left. Actually Don Collier (Robert Don Collier) got a master's degree in taxation at NYU in 1974, then practiced a year in Dallas before joining us in 1975. He was highly capable and was a big fish that got away from us within a year or so after returning. He went to Dallas and has done exceedingly well there. We were in the vanguard of Lubbock firms hiring women lawyers. Deborah (Debbie) Brown, one of the top graduates of Texas Tech Law School in 1977 joined our firm and one of her classmates, Deborah (Debbie) Welch, also a very good law student who had clerked for us in the 1976/1977 school year, was offered a position upon graduation, but opted to take a position with the large Underwood law firm in Amarillo.

On June 30, 1978, I sold all of my Smith & Baker, Inc. stock equally to Mike Field and Karl Clifford whereupon the firm name was changed to Smith, Baker, Field & Clifford. Between that date and my retirement on August 31, 1984, the following lawyers joined the firm: Steve Krier, Steve Stone, Nevill Manning, Mark Thompson, and Steve Crain. A few other lawyers joined our firm during our period of expansion and did not stay for long for one reason or another. All of us except Mike Field, Nevill Manning, and Mark Thompson were involved in some significant way with the field of taxation.

Thus, upon my retirement on August 31, 1984, there were ten of us, the following eight in addition to Norton and me: Mike Field, Karl Clifford, Debbie Brown, Steve Krier, Steve Stone, Nevill Manning, Mark Thompson, and Steve Crain. Steve Krier had a masters of taxation from NYU. He was the son-in-law of Bub and Writ McDonald who were clients of mine in the cotton gin business in Lamesa. Steve Crain was also licensed as a CPA, but soon after my retirement he moved to the Texas valley to practice.

Our ability to hire top graduates from Texas Tech Law School, as well as others, was due, I believe, primarily to two things. One was that we had a good reputation in our community. Perhaps, however, the other was the most compelling, namely, our method of compensation. At least, I believe, until I sold my stock in the firm, our policy in taking in younger lawyers was to pay them all of the amounts they billed, after allocating to them their part of firm overhead expenses and a return on our capital of six percent per annum. Since we were providing work to them, over and above any they might be able to bring in themselves, this was a very generous way of paying beginning lawyers. Essentially, it was exactly the way Norton and I were sharing. How soon this changed after I sold my stock I do not remember, since I was not then involved in such decisions, being highly involved in other activities in those years. It is my understanding, however, that at some point the decision was made to go to the more conventional method of hiring young lawyers, which normally anticipated that the firm would make some profit from the work product of the new hires until such time as they became co-owners on an established sharing basis.

The firm practiced in three different locations during the Smith Firm years. The Smith & Baker firm continued at the offices I had rented in the Citizens Center Building, our location therein being at 1313 Avenue L in downtown Lubbock. The firm took over the rest of the suite that had originally been occupied by Bill Parsley, the Hibler Insurance Agency, and me. As we took on new lawyers we rented a significant part of the area to the north of our original suite and remodeled everything into office space compatible with law offices, secretarial space, and library.

Briercroft Savings & Loan Association, with which I was involved, had been very successful and had added two new buildings adjacent to its original permanent structure at 50th Street and Avenue Q. The southern most of the three buildings was primarily to be rented to other tenants, and Smith & Baker would occupy the first floor. The firm moved into that location under a five-year lease starting in 1975. Toward the latter part of that lease term it was obvious that the firm needed more space. Also significant was the state of the savings and loan industry, which was facing tough times and an uncertain future. I was no longer a stockholder in the law firm, so the matter of what to do at the lease expiration was in the hands of others than myself, but I was not averse to a change of location under the circumstances. The decision was made to acquire a rather prime bit of real estate three blocks south of the Tech law school at the corner of 19th Street (the south boundary of Texas Tech University) and Indiana Avenue but still in the eastern edge of Lubbock's main medical district as it existed at that time. The location was at 2212 Indiana Avenue (intersection of 22nd Street and the arterial Indiana Avenue). An impressive new masonry office building was constructed and ready for occupancy at approximately the time of the lease expiration. While I was not a stockholder, I was accorded a prime office and secretarial area in the northeast corner of the building. I was quite content with the state of things, for they accommodated the needs of my other interests during those years.

Pension and Profit Sharing Plans

One of the areas of law practice in which I had some experience at VEWS that I brought with me to Lubbock was in the preparation and qualification (with the IRS) of pension and profit sharing plans. While I have no specific recollection of having worked in that area from my first days in Lubbock, I know that I would have done some of that work, especially for clients with controlling ownership of corporations. Few, if any, other local lawyers did work in this area. It is not an area of practice that I transferred over to Norton so far as I can remember.

Two major developments in the laws governing pensions and profit sharing plans occurred during the days of the Smith firm. The first was the enactment of the Texas Professional Association Act, which I believe took effect on June 18, 1969. This permitted professionals, such as doctors, lawyers, and accountants, who previously were not able to secure the personal tax benefits of these retirement plans, to do so by forming such P. A.s. This was a major development, and because of my familiarity with that area of practice a substantial number of doctors came to me for the formation of such a professional association and the establishment in it of a retirement plan that could cover their own compensation as well as that of their employees. It was a field of practice that filled in quite nicely for the bread and butter estate planning work that Norton was getting more and more of.

The second of these major developments was Congress' enactment on September 2, 1974, of ERISA, the Employers Retirement Income Security Act. It covered all types of retirement benefits, not just pension and profit sharing plans, but its practical effect for my practice was in these two areas. It was a major piece of legislation that was complex and spawned voluminous output of new regulations. I appeared on a program sponsored by the State Bar at the University of Texas Law School dealing with this new legislation. While this area of practice was productive of a substantial amount of legal work and fees, keeping up with it as a special field in addition to the other areas of practice became increasingly burdensome. By 1978, when my outside activities were taking more time and energy and I was targeting a reduced level of law practice, I transferred all of this work to Karl Clifford. He was exceptionally good at it and it represented for him a lucrative area of practice.

Litigated Cases

The twenty-ninth anniversary of my retirement from Smith, Baker, Field & Clifford was close at hand as I began writing this litigation section. The entirety of my years of law practice, right out of law school, until retirement in 1984 was only a month or two over twenty-seven years, the first three and a half of which were in the employee of other firms before opening my own office.

Litigation was a part of my practice, but not a dominant part. While I have been able, with some concentrated effort, to recall some twenty-five litigation cases within the period from the opening of my own office March 1, 1961 until retirement, it is usually only hazy shards of recollection that I must rely on; like trying to see a distant object through unforgiving clouds. Law firm records or files that might in earlier years have helped refresh memory have either ceased to exist or are, practically speaking, no longer available to me. Nevertheless, some memories exist in varying degrees of specificity. Notes from our annual personal financial statements have helped in two or three cases. Otherwise, a general idea on each case is about all I can offer, for which limitation, doubtless, my readers will be grateful.

Only cases that occurred after opening my own office will be listed, and I believe that none of those reached the stage of litigation before Norton joined me, even if in a case or two they might have had their roots before that joinder. With the exception of the Briercroft and Williams cases, I cannot remember any other lawyer in our firm being involved with me in any of the litigated cases. In the Clanton case, Austin Deaton, an Ada, Oklahoma lawyer served as co-counsel with me, and on several cases Dean Carlton, a Dallas trial lawyer, and I were co-counsel. At least three Lubbock lawyers and I were co-counsel, namely, Charlie Jones (in one case), J. R. Blumrosen (in two cases), and George Gilkerson in the Banta tax evasion trial.

Other than in a general way on some cases, I will not be able to give either the sequence of these cases or their dates of involvement.

While I was licensed to practice in any state court in Texas, and some of my cases were in Texas courts, it is important to note that Federal tax cases, which were central to the bulk of my practice and litigation, cannot be tried in any state court, but are limited to the Tax Court, Federal District Court, and Court of Claims, with appeals to the prescribed Federal Courts of Appeal, and beyond that, in rare instances, with Supreme Court review. In any state, including Texas, trial practice is predominantly in the state courts. Jurisdiction of the Federal Courts is strictly limited to cases that fall within the established rules for some Federal court jurisdiction. As a consequence of the prevalence of my practice being related to Federal tax matters, I did not find myself opposed by other local lawyers in most cases, but rather by government counsel, either from the Treasury Department's regional counsel's office, in Tax Court cases, or from the office of the Justice Department's U. S. Attorney, in the Federal district court or Court of Claims (centered in Washington, DC).

Of the twenty-five cases coming to mind, only fifteen will be numbered and described from my memory. However, in each of two of the numbered cases another case will be appended to it that is closely related to it in nature or involvement, so that seventeen of the twenty-five will be described. The other eight will be mentioned with brief comment but without elaboration.

Numbered Litigated Cases

1. *W. B. Rushing*: This was probably the first, and it was by far the most famous, of my cases. As such, a bit more detail is

warranted than normal. Almost certainly in 1962 not long, as I remember, after Rushing came to my office with J. C. Chambers and Jack Kastman, in the formative days of Briercroft Savings & Loan Association (discussed earlier and in the following investment section), Rushing, or "Dub" as he was known, along with his brother-in-law Max Tidmore came into my office with what they seemed to assume would be a simple corporate liquidation matter. A corporation they jointly owned had been hired by the landowners (the Parkers or their own corporation) of a prime piece of real estate in Wichita Falls, Texas, to develop upon such land what was to became known as the Parker Square Shopping Center, which is still a thriving center with that name today. The Rushing and Tidmore corporation had performed under its contract and had received as compensation a note in the amount of $1,500,000.00 with interest payable periodically and the principal being payable on maturity ten or fifteen years from the date of the note.

Section 337 of the Internal Revenue Code, sometimes called the "twelve-month liquidation" section, provided that if a controlled corporation adopted a plan of liquidation under which it would liquidate within twelve months from the date of adoption, then gain to be otherwise recognized on disposition of its assets would not be recognized at the corporate level. The aim of the section was to avoid double taxation of gain, once at the corporate level followed immediately by the recognition at the stockholder level to the extent the value of what they received on liquidation exceeded the cost basis in their stock.

When Rushing and Tidmore entered my office to ask me to do the liquidation for them, there were only about ten or twelve days remaining within the twelve-month period during which they had to liquidate the corporation. The problem was that even though gain would not be recognized at the corporate level, if liquidation was completed within that remaining ten or twelve days, all of the gain would be immediately recognized to the stockholders upon the liquidation. This would not have been so bad, except that the note would not be paid for ten or fifteen years, but each of them would have tax to pay on approximately $750,000 of gain upon the liquidation. I apprised them of this terrible consequence and told them I would try to figure something out.

Many things had to happen quickly, and they did. The first thing was that I had to figure out a solution. The best I could come up with was for them to form trusts for their children, using a bank as trustee, and then negotiate with the bank trustee to sell their stock to the trusts in exchange for the trusts' note payable to them over essentially the same period as the note held by the corporation the trusts were buying. Rushing and Tidmore would elect installment reporting on the note received from the trusts for their stock. They asked me to proceed with the necessary arrangement with the trust department of the Citizens National Bank, prepare the trust instruments and get them executed by my clients and the bank, and then prepare the sale of stock, note instruments and consummate the corporate liquidation before expiration of the twelve-month liquidation period. I prepared and had executed all the necessary documents.

Rushing and Tidmore, and their respective wives, filed their tax returns reporting the sale of their stock on the installment basis. Their returns were audited and the arrangement I had set up was challenged as, in substance, a liquidation, triggering immediate recognition of gain, by Rushing and Tidmore and then the sale of the corporation's distributed note to the trusts.

The IRS audit was far more extensive, however, than just on this Parker Square transaction. Rushing and Tidmore were involved in many commercial real estate activities and had a number of corporations equally owned by themselves, the same as on the Parker Square corporation. When one corporation would need money that was in another corporation, on many occasions they simply caused loans to be made from one corporation to another. The loans were recorded on the books of each corporation, and repayments were made according to their terms and so recorded. The IRS challenged these loans between brother and sister corporations, contending that they were, in substance, dividends payable by the lending corporations to their stockholders who then contributed the moneys to the borrowing corporations as additional capital.

The issues could not be settled without litigation. Accordingly, deficiency assessments were proposed by the IRS and I filed a petition with the Tax Court to contest all of these issues. Because I had very little prior exposure to actual trial, I got Charlie Jones, for whose capability as a trial lawyer I had great respect, to serve with me as co-counsel at the Tax Court level. I did most all of the assembly of evidence, and in fact, as I recall, Charlie's actual courtroom activity was pretty limited, since there were not a lot of heavy evidence matters in serious dispute, but rather the legal consequence of evidence as admitted. Charlie's value to me was just being there, and we often conferred before trial on the evidence and its consequences.

The trial judge assigned by the Tax Court from Washington, DC, was Judge Fay. He ruled in favor of Rushing and Tidmore on both of these major issues. The government appealed the case to the United States Court of Appeals for the Fifth Circuit. I handled all of the appellate case by myself. The Fifth Circuit affirmed the Tax Court on both issues. I do not remember if the government sought Supreme Court review, but I must assume that it did not.

Countless things flowed from the case.

First, the *Journal of Taxation,* popular with all tax practitioners, published, in succeeding issues, two articles I wrote on Rushing, the first on the trust sale transaction, and the second entitled essentially "Brother-Sister Inter-Company Loans; Are they Loans or Dividends?" I felt rather certain that by far the more significant of these two issues, as legal precedent, would be the inter-company loans. It turned out to be dramatically the other way around. The "Rushing Case" began to appear as a lead presentation at essentially every tax institute or program in the country. With one possible exception, I was not invited to speak on any such program. But as part of fulfilling the CLE (continuing legal education) minimum annual requirement of the Texas Bar Association, I attended a tax conference put on at the Intercontinental Hotel on the "gold coast" in downtown Chicago. When the lecturer was at a certain point in the "discussion" following his presentation, I rose to mention that there were some critical evidence matters in the case that were not in either opinion, Tax Court or Fifth Circuit. In fact, though I do not remember exactly what they were, I do remember that they were evidence and/or argument that I was highly concerned about and greatly relieved that focus was not brought to bear upon them. Such a statement could only have come from one intimately familiar with the trial itself, and indeed I did confirm that I had been the one planning the arrangement and trying the case. Every eye in the auditorium turned to me—I was probably half way back in the audience.

Later, I was at some type of tax conference at Texas A&M University, being on the program in some capacity. It was likely either a discussion of "the famous Rushing case" or a seminar on the new ERISA legislation. In any event, the tax professor at Texas A&M who had been involved in planning and holding the conference spoke to me afterward saying that the Rushing case was the most prominent case in the tax field since it was handed down several years before. He was probably right, for the tax citator continued to have numerous cases listed that had relied upon the Rushing case as precedent on the trust sale issue, and it was the subject of much writing in the tax literature.

The irony of it is that Rushing became important not in the setting of Section 337 liquidation matters but in certain other transactions set up for tax avoidance purposes. The Internal Revenue Code of 1984 specifically recognized the legitimacy, and thus vindicated the result, of what I had accomplished in Rushing under Section 337, but put an end to the use of Rushing to accomplish the types of avoidance schemes that had successfully relied upon Rushing up to that point.

One other result of the Rushing case and the two articles I had published in the *Journal of Taxation* was that Prentice-Hall, publisher of one of the two major tax services practitioners used, invited me to write a book on some aspect of the field of taxation. It was gratifying to be so invited, but it was not an invitation I had the least temptation to accept.

2. **Big State Grain (O. A. Webb)**: This case started while I was with NMH. O. A. Webb owned a corporation that had a metal grain storage warehouse just east of the Lubbock-Amarillo Highway in Abernathy, Texas. At issue was the allowable life expectancy of the warehouse for purposes of the depreciation deduction. The corporation claimed a ten-year life. I do not remember whether the case got to the litigation stage or not. In fact, I do not remember what the resolution of the issue was. I mention the case only because of an interesting connection it had with other taxpayers, but also, and primarily, because I could not discuss my law practice days without telling about O. A. Webb.

The case had to have arisen while I was still with the NMH law firm because I made certain inquiries on it while in the office of Superior Manufacturing Company, of Amarillo, Texas (Superior). Coleman McSpadden was a client of Hobert Nelson, and on his behalf I had done some work in setting up the corporate structure of Superior. The latter corporation manufactured anhydrous ammonia tanks used for agricultural fertilization in the West Texas area. The company was apparently selling tanks to Billie Sol Estes, of Pecos, Texas, who was quite an operator. Among Estes's enterprises was an astonishingly large assembly of huge metal tanks for the storage of grain, mainly milo or sorghum on the highway between Hale Center and Plainview, Texas. And he seemed to be keeping them full. O. A. Webb was very suspicious that Estes was getting improper political help in keeping his storage bins full, thus generating huge payments from the government for the storage. Of these things I was keenly aware while in the Superior offices on an occasion when the officers of the corporation were talking on the phone with Billie Sol Estes. I had mentioned to them my grain storage depreciation issue (for O. A. Webb) and the officer on the phone asked if I would like to talk to Billie Sol. I jumped at the chance, knowing that he had massive grain storage facilities. I learned nothing of value from him, though not surprisingly he was congenial in agreeing that my contention on the depreciation was appropriate.

Later, after I had opened my own office, it came out that Billie Sol Estes and Superior Manufacturing Company were complicit in the criminal act of borrowing large sums of money purportedly secured by Superior-made tanks that were in fact non-existent. Estes and McSpadden both served prison terms, as did one or two other officers of Superior. When all this surfaced, I was shocked to learn of these events, having worked with McSpadden and the other Superior officers, and talked to Estes by phone. Never did I have any inkling whatsoever that any nefarious deeds were taking place, if indeed they had been undertaken that early in the process—I'm a bit doubtful that such fraud had yet been committed at the time I was working with them. The life and involvements of Billie Sol Estes make a lurid story. His actions touched negatively upon the lives of other clients of mine, but his story is too long and too well known for me to say anything further on him here.

It is O. A. Webb who leaves me, to this day, with many warm and wonderful memories. If I had any inward impatience in spending time with clients, hoping to get on with my work, that was never the case with O. A. Webb. Thinking back, it seems fair to say that I had a real love for the man. He followed me from NMH to my own office and conferred and visited with me there many times. Jo Anne remembers him well, for he would often call for me at my house when she would answer the phone. His was the slowest, most deliberate, and uniform introduction on the phone that I ever heard. And for her, it was "Mizz–zuss Smiiiithhh, t-h-i-sss iz Ohhhh Aaaaa W-e-b-b," and he would say it in such a gentle and rhythmic way that she would be mentally trying to help him get through it after the first syllable he pronounced. He had some degree of wealth. It is my understanding, which I think I may have visited with him about, that he got his start playing poker. He must have been very good at it. But once he had accumulated his stash, he had the wisdom and will to gamble no more.

Even though, as I recall, I prepared wills for him, I have no recollection of the approximate size of his holdings, though I always thought he was most comfortable—and he seemed to live simply. He was probably not over sixty-eight to seventy inches in height, tending to a stocky build, always appearing very comfortably and simply dressed, with hair sort of messed up. I do not think he wore a hat, but if so it was not western and would have been well worn. He would come in and deposit himself in a chair across the desk from me and we would talk. Oh how I would like to sit down across from him again and talk. My research indicates that he was born January 18, 1909, and died June 1, 1979, at seventy years of age. Surely, if I was in Lubbock at the time, I would have attended his funeral—it would not have been at Resthaven. As my section on business and investment will indicate, he died in the middle of a very significant time for me at Resthaven. I do not remember handling his estate, even though I'm pretty sure I drew one or more wills for him. Probably I did not see him too much in the late years of his life. He left a wife and I think another relative may have lived with them on Twenty-Second Street, but he left no children. I'm saddened to think that I have no more detailed memory of his last days. But memories of the times he was with me are vivid and priceless.

3. *W. D. and Gertrude O'Brien:* Soon after I opened my own office W. D. O'Brien and wife Gertrude consulted with me. They had no descendants. As directed, I prepared and they executed a declaration transferring a substantial part of their wealth to a trust providing for their own support and maintenance in their accustomed standard of living for the rest of their lives with remainder upon the death of the last of them to die to designated charities. They served as trustees of the trust. In their joint income tax return for the year of the declaration, they took a deduction for the value of the charitable remainder interest based upon tables promulgated by the Treasury Department relevant to joint life estates and remainders.

The evidence showed that their income normally exceeded the cost of their support and maintenance.

The IRS issued a proposed deficiency assessment based upon disallowance of the claimed charitable deduction. I filed a petition in the Tax Court and decision and judgement was rendered in the O'Briens' favor. The case had value as precedent in the tax field.

About the same time as the O'Brien transaction, Ross and Evelyn Daniels, of Colorado City, Texas, being very similarly situated as the O'Briens, followed the same plan. The IRS did not challenge their situation, possibly because of the O'Brien precedent. They are mentioned here only because in the summer of 1970 Ross Daniels died, I probated his will in Colorado City, and on my drive home the stage was set for my next interesting bit of litigation.

Following the probate Mrs. Daniels and I had eaten lunch together, where I had a chicken fried steak, mashed potatoes and white gravy, and other trimmings. Colorado City lies one hundred ten miles south of Lubbock. While driving home, half way between Snyder and Post, Texas, with the radio playing music, I went to sleep at seventy-five miles an hour (in a 70 MPH zone), totaling our new Buick LeSabre but not doing much physically to me. The seat belts doubtless saved my life as I had only a small chip in a vertebra in my neck that never gave me any trouble. The courteous and otherwise helpful Texas Highway Patrol officers gave me a ticket charging me simply with "Unsafe speed." When I asked them what speed they considered safe when one is asleep, they just chuckled.

It did not appear from that charge or anything else on the ticket that it presented a chargeable offense. The case was a spoof. The prospect of paying for a moving violation was not itself the least problem. What bothered me was that when a moving violation went onto your driving record, it significantly boosted the annual insurance premium for a period of time free of other moving violations. To avoid that I chose to contest the ticket. A trial was sought in the Justice of the Peace (JP) Court in Post, Garza County, Texas. Not wanting to ask a favor of any Lubbock lawyer, and not being aware of any lawyer in Post, and not caring to incur a lot of lawyer fees in any event, I made the proverbial idiot's decision to represent myself and requested a jury trial. In JP trials, the number of jurors seated was to be six. The applicable rules of procedure relative to picking a jury provided that the defendant (myself), in addition to any challenges for cause, was entitled to a certain number of peremptory (arbitrary) challenges—I think the number was three in the JP Court. The problem was that the entire panel of prospective jurors that showed up was seven. Out of an overwhelming generosity, the county attorney graciously said that I could have the one and only challenge possible. Not wanting to prolong the contest by continuance till a full panel of prospects could be seated, I made no objection to the procedural shortcoming.

This was the first of my cases where I lost the battle but won the war. The jury verdict was guilty and the penalty it set for my violation was one dollar. I had damaged no state property and had probably cut a pretty good swath of weeds for the highway department on my way to the culvert.

Trials in JP Court do not have a court reporter who prepares a record for appeal, but appeals from JP Court judgment are to the county court in what is called a "trial de novo," meaning that the case is simply tried all over again, or "de novo," at the county-court level where a record is made by a court reporter. I appealed the JP Court judgment to the Garza County Court.

Two aspects of the case, one in the JP trial, and one in regard to the appeal, are worthy of note.

Regarding the JP trial, I went to the men's room during the jury deliberations and discovered that the jury room lay on the other side of the entirely non-acoustical wall between the men's room and the jury room. Not only so, but the one commode was conveniently situated right next to that wall, making for a comfortable spot to sit and listen to the jury deliberations. I closed the stall door and did the same. Both of the highway patrol officers were residents in the small town of Post, and the jury all seemed to know them well and spoke of them by their first names. I, on the other hand, was "Mr. Smith." I did not hang around to the end of the show in the jury room, having gotten the feel for how it was going.

The other aspect of the case is that the county judge was Giles Dalby, the son of Arno Dalby, the well-to-do owner of a freight trucking company headquartered in Lubbock that had gone public. Arno's regular lawyer had engaged me to do estate planning for Arno Dalby, and in the process I also did the same for Giles, who happened to be the same age as myself, give or take a month or two. The name Giles was a name of prominence in the history of Post, and I believe that one or both of the Dalby parents had likely come into something of an inheritance to begin with. Giles loved the ranching life, and, as I write this, has only recently passed away having served Garza County and the Post community for many years. Having lodged my appeal in Giles's County Court, I merely waited for it to be set down for hearing. That never came. The appeal is now forty-three years old, the judge has passed away, and my driving record has never reflected a traffic violation as a result of the "unsafe speed" I was allegedly driving.

But I paid plenty for my accident as I only carried liability insurance so we had to pay the cost of another new car out of our own pocket. I had felt that if our car was damaged, it was not likely that either of us would be at fault. The accident cured that arrogant assumption.

4. A farmer near Post, Garza County, Texas: This case never went to trial because it was resolved with the local IRS special agent. But special agents got my attention because they were the ones assigned to investigate for the purpose of criminal prosecution for tax evasion. The agent in question was named Nichols. He was well known and respected locally, and was called "Nick." He was about to recommend the case for prosecution. It involved a retired and rather elderly farmer (Farmer), whose name I cannot recall, who lived with an unmarried son on a farm northwest of Post, Texas. Nick suspected tax evasion because Farmer had living expenses that could not be accounted for by any income reported for income tax purposes.

The matter had reached the serious stage when the son brought Farmer in to consult with me on the IRS investigation. Farmer's story was that he had raised his family on brown beans (pinto beans) on a marginal farm over in eastern New Mexico during the depression and dust bowl days when the banks had failed and so many, perhaps also himself, had lost their money. He said he quit using banks and kept his money in tin cans buried in his yard, not only while they lived in New Mexico but also after they moved to Post. It was easy to imagine how that story would fly with Nick. Out of curiosity I asked Farmer if he could bring me some of the money from his buried stash so that I could examine it. He went home and brought back several bills, each for one hundred dollars dated in the 1930s. I made a machine reproduced copy of one or two of them and took them to Nick's office. He took one look at them and accepted the old man's story—end of story—except Nick told me that in copying that currency I had violated Federal criminal laws relating to counterfeiting. Stupid me, I had not even thought of that, so he immediately got my attention. But I think he was getting his bit of amusement out of the situation because he promptly said that nothing would come of it this time but that I should not do it again. I have not—but then I have not had another such case like that one.

5. **Willie Teeter**: He was like a ray of sunshine. Not only did he have a titillating name, but he had a face of bright and childlike innocence that resonated with the name. He was a farmer in Hale County, the county just north of Lubbock County. I formed a corporation for his farming operation and arranged a salary for him, perhaps also setting up a profit sharing plan, but in any event seeing some overall tax advantages from the arrangement.

To my great surprise, the IRS challenged the setup, though I do not remember if it was a challenge to the substance of the transaction as a whole or to the reasonableness of the compensation, or some other aspect. Whatever it was, I felt the agent's action was not supportable. A deficiency assessment was issued. Willie paid it and I filed a claim for refund which, when denied, prompted my filing of a suit for refund in the Federal District Court in Lubbock, followed later by our demand for trial by jury. The assistant Federal district attorney who handled the case was Herb Kendrick. I had known the Kendrick family from Brownfield and was friendly with Herb, a bright young fellow who later published a treatise on certain aspects of Texas law.

Joe Dooley was the judge in the trial of Teeter's case. Dooley had practiced law in Amarillo, Texas. He was appointed to the Federal bench by Truman in 1947, became chief judge of the Northern District of Texas in 1959, assumed senior status in 1966 and served till he died on January 19, 1967, at the age of seventy-seven. Unbeknown to me, Dooley had apparently become so hard of hearing by the time of the Teeter trial that microphones were placed on the counsel tables and at the witness stand, and anything said by the lawyer out of the immediate range of these microphones would apparently not be heard by the judge. I was not aware of this disability or the necessity of speaking into these microphones and proceeded to put on our case standing, for the most part, in the open space between these two microphones. As soon as I rested, government counsel Kendrick rose to his feet prepared to present whatever he had to present as the government's evidence. Judge Dooley told him to sit down for the Court was going to instruct a verdict against the plaintiff on the grounds that it was not lawful for the owner of a corporation to employ himself in this manner. I was aghast, wondering if Dooley had taken leave of his senses. Kendrick obeyed the court and sat down. The trial was essentially over and a verdict and judgment were to be entered against my client.

As soon as the judge left the courtroom, Herb came over to me and apologized, acknowledging that the court's action was nonsensical. I immediately said to him, "I assume then that you will have no objection to my motion for a new trial?" Herb's response was that he had no control over that, for it would have to come from Washington.

It never came, so I had to pay for a transcript of the trial record, prepare the papers for appeal to the Fifth Circuit Court of Appeals, then prepare a brief and have it printed (in Dallas). My brief was filed. The time came for the government's reply brief, and it was only then, after all this effort and expense on my part, that the government confessed error by the trial court and the case was remanded for retrial.

By that time, apparently Dooley had died, for the case was handled by his successor, Judge Halbert O. Woodward. I tried the case again and the jury awarded us one hundred percent of what we claimed.

Feeling that I could not charge Willie for all the time I would need to spend on the trial of the case, never having anticipated that IRS would challenge the set up, I originally agreed with Willie to take a contingent fee of one-third of the tax refund. I think the refund was something like $4,500.00, because my recollection is that I got $1,500.00 for all the effort. I think Willie did pay for my out-of-pocket expenses. So far as I recall, Willie was fully satisfied, and the sweetness of his personality never disappeared during the whole dismal affair with IRS, the Court, and the government. Sometimes screw-ups like that just happen.

Nevertheless, the happy memory of Willie Teeter was sufficient compensation for me.

6. Federal Court appointment to defend on a gun control indictment: Halbert O. Woodward succeeded Tom Dooley as Federal District Judge in Lubbock on July 7, 1968. It was probably not too long after that when I was appointed by Woodward to defend an indigent who had been indicted under the Federal gun control laws. He had been stopped when driving his car and had been arrested when an unregistered handgun had been found under his driver's seat. His story was that he had loaned his car to another person a day or two before his arrest and that he did not put the gun there and did not know it was there. I have no recollection of why he was stopped or of my having raised any objection to the legality of the search. The government's case was based upon the bare evidence of the arresting officer who found the gun under the accused's seat and that the gun was there in violation of the gun-control laws. The only part of that which I countered was that my client was guilty of the violation. On cross-examination, I had brought out that even though the gun had been in control of the arresting officer and the prosecution from the time of the arrest, no finger print tests whatsoever had been performed on the gun. I argued that the government had not proved its case beyond a reasonable doubt because it had full control of the gun since the time of the arrest and had not even tested the gun for my client's finger prints—or those of anyone else. It was evidence that could and should have been produced in rebuttal of my client's clear testimony.

There were several interesting sidelights to this case.

The first was that the assistant district attorney prosecuting the case was the fellow I pulled the "lifting-three-men" prank on, as related earlier in the discussion of my first year in law school at SMU. His anger was rekindled at me when he let this case get away from him.

The second is that word came back to me from other attorneys that Judge Woodward was using my handling of this case as an example of the kind of diligence that attorneys appointed to represent indigent defendants should give to their assignment. In that regard, changes in the appointment process have been made that give greater safeguard to these defendants, for the Court began, I understand, to appoint attorneys who engaged in criminal defense work rather than those engaged primarily in other fields of practice. Apparently this change was made in the local state courts also, for I had been appointed in one case there earlier, arranged a satisfactory plea bargain, and was never again appointed.

The third is that word sure spreads fast in these circles when a court appointed lawyer gets an acquittal for an indigent defendant. The day after the verdict, this defendant came back in with some other legal "business," and within ten days or so I got a letter from an inmate who was in solitary confinement at the Federal prison in Leavenworth, Kansas, wanting me to file a writ of habeas corpus on his behalf. Not being that hard up for business, especially of the non-paying kind, I passed up these opportunities.

7. **Roby, Texas auto repair shop owner tax evasion indictment**: The first I ever heard of Roby, Texas, was during the summer term following my first year in law school. During that first year, just down the hall from my room in Lawyers Inn lived a third-year student named Roscoe Elmore. Upon graduation, he accepted a job in the office of an older lawyer in Roby, the county seat of Fisher County, the older lawyer probably being the only lawyer in the county. During the summer term following that first-year, a letter came to the Inn from Elmore signed, "The Roby Rocket," saying that he could stand on top of the court house and throw a stone in any direction and it would fall on farm land. Hyperbole for sure, but not by much, for Roby's population was roughly eight hundred souls in 1954 and shrinking. Roby lies one hundred twenty miles SE of Lubbock, thirty-five miles east of Snyder, and twenty miles north of Sweetwater where the annual round up of rattlesnakes is held. It did not take Elmore long to conclude that there was no fortune to be made in Roby, whence he departed shortly.

While the firm still officed on Avenue L, a tax evasion case from Roby came to me. I do not remember how the case got there but it did. A young man operated an automobile repair garage there. He was probably still in his thirties, married and with children. He either had already been, or was about to be, indicted for evading taxes by failing to report all of his income from the garage operation. No specific income was identified, but rather the special agent was using the so-called "net worth method," by which he determined that the living expenses for the taxpayer exceeded any income he reported. In fact, I do not remember if my client even filed returns, since it appeared he was just getting by feeding his family.

The judge assigned to the case was Leo Brewster, whose chambers were in Fort Worth. The venue of the case was in the Federal courtroom in Abilene, Texas, one hundred sixty-five miles SE of Lubbock, but only fifty-three miles SE of Roby. Judge Brewster was sworn in as Federal judge March 17, 1962, served as chief judge of the district from 1972 to 1973, the year in which he took senior status but continued to serve until his death in 1979. The Roby case was thus between 1962 and 1973 since he had not yet taken senior status.

A preliminary proceeding was held in the courtroom shortly before the trial was scheduled to start. Well I remember objecting, at that hearing, to the imposition by the court of certain expenses on my client. What was memorable was the chewing out the judge gave me there in open court for such a "trivial" objection. It did not seem trivial to me considering the non-thriving nature of the garage operation and the client's family needs.

In the brief intervening time before trial I came back to our library to try to find some authority to support my feeling that the net worth method could not be used because no beginning net worth for the year(s) of the alleged evasion period had been determined by the special agent. I found a case squarely in point and, the trial date being imminent, prepared a motion for dismissal of the indictment to be filed before the trial began. Upon reading my motion, the assistant U. S. Attorney requested a recess to consult with his superiors, presumably in Washington. When he came back in he moved separately on behalf of the government to dismiss the case. The judge immediately granted what was now a joint motion for dismissal and called me to meet with him in his office following the conclusion of the case.

When I walked in, he told me to have a seat. I did. He looked at me and said, "You did a hell of a job for your client in this case." I felt wonderful not just for myself, but also for my client. Roby is not a likely place to make a lot of money repairing cars.

It was not the only time I had been emphatically criticized by a Federal judge and then later been emphatically complimented by that same judge. Woodward, with whom I had a reasonably warm personal acquaintanceship, had done the same to me in Lubbock, though I do not remember if it was all in the same case. It is the name of the game in Federal court, in my experience, and I think also in that of most other attorneys. Federal judges are appointed for life, require Senate confirmation, and thereby rise to a significant level of independence in the conduct of their court.

8. **GOBSC (Great Oil Basin Securities Corporation)**: The City of Odessa lies one hundred forty-six wide open miles SSW of Lubbock and twenty miles SW of Midland. A man named McAdoo had been a client of mine for wills and/or estate planning. He had operated, or perhaps still did, a Chevrolet dealership either in Odessa or in one or more communities between there and Lubbock. He, as well as a man who was known as "Judge Byers," a former county judge as I recall, whose given name also I do not remember, consulted with me in relation to the affairs of a corporation named Great Oil Basin Securities Corporation, which understandably went by the acronym GOBSC. Whether that was its original name, or whether that was the name it bore as a result of events that gave rise to this case, I do not know. In any event, that was its name by the time McAdoo and Byers consulted with me on its behalf. They were the main, if not the only, stockholders of the corporation.

The only asset of any significance in GOBSC when they contacted me was a shopping center in Odessa, and what prompted the contact was that the real estate involved purportedly secured a loan that was in default and the property was in the process of being foreclosed. It was often said, in those days that Midland was where the oil operators lived while their oil field workers lived in Odessa. Things were not swell in the oil patch in 1970, and the center was thus not prospering at the time. But there were serious complications in the case beyond these simple facts.

In rough outline, a man from New York named Ezrine (phonetically correct if not correctly spelled), who apparently fancied himself a financial whiz, had finagled himself into the corporation's affairs in such a way that he purported to encumber the corporation's real estate as part of his scheme. Recognizing the immediacy of the need for some type of restraint on the foreclosure, I got in touch with Dean Carlton who joined me as co-counsel on the case. Alleging the invalidity of both the debt and the encumbrance on the basis of lack of authority of Ezrine to act on behalf of the corporation, we were able to secure a temporary restraining order (TRO). This would have been some time after I had met and engaged Carlton on another case, mentioned later, in 1970. The TRO was the first volley in a litigation war that was to stretch over approximately ten years through various trial courts and one or two Federal courts of appeal, or perhaps just two appearances before the United States Court of Appeal for the Eighth Circuit, sitting in St. Louis. The jurisdiction of that Circuit was based upon some involvement in the Federal district court in Little Rock, Arkansas, presumably because the lender was based in Arkansas. We came out okay on a few of the skirmishes, but in the end we finally lost the case. However, while we eventually lost the battle (the case), we nevertheless won the war, for had the foreclosure occurred at the beginning, nothing could have been salvaged in GOBSC, whereas by the time it was finally resolved, roughly ten years later, the oil patch had heated up, the property was worth substantially more than the debt against it, and our clients ended up with something worthwhile to show for their efforts.

9. *Nelson Canode v. Amarillo National Bank*: Nelson Canode was a loquacious, colorful, and entertaining client. Emerging, however, from within all his colorful embellishment, was the indication that certain valuable property in Amarillo had been held in a trust created by Nelson's parents of which Nelson was a substantial beneficiary and that the bank as trustee had dealt with the property in a way distinctly unfavorable to Nelson and suggestively favorable to the bank or others having some affiliation with it. In short, the distinct possibility of a breach of the bank's fiduciary duty seemed to exist.

Whatever investigation into, or negotiation on, the matter might have intervened, as Canode's attorney I filed suit against the bank, again bringing Dean Carlton in as co-counsel.

Amarillo National Bank was not a weak adversary. The bank had been founded in 1892, and apparently was even then managed by B. T. Ware, who purchased the bank in 1909 and the Wares had owned it and largely run it since that time, still true in the fifth generation in 2009. It was probably at the time of Canode's suit, and still today, Amarillo's largest bank, based on deposits, and it was one of the country's largest independent cattle lenders.

At the conclusion of pretrial discovery by both sides, it was time to get serious about the probable outcome of trial. The facts as Canode had given them still appeared to have some color of merit, but we had enough concern about plaintiff's case that, in the final analysis, we negotiated a compromise settlement and Canode agreed to it.

In what follows, my memory was refreshed from my financial statement notes.[1] My 1979 statement indicated that I held an undivided 1/6 of approximately 15.94 acres in Canode Park Addition in Amarillo received as legal fee in June of 1979. I valued the property interest for income tax purposes that year at a precise amount suggesting some then current basis for estimating fair market value. Before finding the financial statement note, I had not recalled that I had co-counsel on this case, but this footnote indicates so and it would have had to be Dean Carlton. That I had a one-sixth interest in the land suggests two things: first, that the legal fee was a one-third interest of whatever could be recovered to be split equally with Dean; and second, that the settlement with the bank called for well-situated land to be distributed to the trust beneficiaries rather than being otherwise disposed of by the bank as trustee.

The land was carried again at that tax base value in the 1980 statement. Thereafter for the next few years it was assigned a constantly higher value based upon the improving indications of what it

---

[1] These year-end financial statements go from 1962 through 2012, but there are no statements for 1972, 1981, 1984, 1988, 1989, 1992 (but I have March 31, 1993), 1994, and 1997. Probably no statements were prepared for these missing years, and in most, if not all, of these years, existing circumstances would understandably account for a statement not having been prepared.

should bring on sale. In the 1983 statement, my interest was valued at 3.58 times the 1979 valuation, with footnote reading, "The land seems to be in an appreciating mode. It is on a direct line between the regional medical complex and the regional shopping center in west Amarillo near I-40." In September 1983, I received option money for a six-month option at a price indicative of a value 5.36 times the 1979 valuation. The statement for 1984 is missing and the tract is not on the 1985 statement, apparently having sold in the interval. For what final amount I do not know. For many years now we have driven through the heavy traffic around this shopping center on the west loop around Amarillo on our way to Colorado.

10. **Hi Plains Hospital:** Hi Plains Hospital (HPH) was and is located in Hale Center, Texas, forty-eight miles north of Lubbock and twelve miles SW of Plainview, on the Lubbock/Amarillo highway (now I-27). The town's population was 1,964 in 1970; 2,297 in 1980, and 2,257 in 2011. HPH is a charity qualified as such under the provisions of section 501(c)(3) of the Internal Revenue Code (IRC). It operated, within its premises, a pharmacy. The nearest pharmacy otherwise was in Plainview. If a qualified charity produces income from what is called an "unrelated business," the income is called "unrelated business income" and the charity must pay an income tax on that income. The IRS determined that HPH's income from the operation of its pharmacy was income from a business not related to its charitable function as a hospital. Notice of deficiency was issued by the IRS for one or more years. The year or years in question were almost certainly sometime in the decade of the 1970s. On behalf of HPH I filed a petition in the Tax Court to set aside such deficiency.

Finding that the lack of any other pharmacy conveniently available to the doctors and patients at the hospital or the residents of the Hale Center area made the operation of the pharmacy something important to the mission and purpose of the hospital upon which its charitable status was based, the Tax Court rendered judgment in favor of HPH. The government did not appeal the decision.

This HPH decision later served as helpful precedent in the last litigation I was involved with before my retirement. Lubbock lawyer J. R. Blumrosen brought me in as co-counsel on the case. He represented most of the cooperative entities (co-ops) in the area, including the small cooperative hospital in Amherst, Texas. Amherst was a town of less than one thousand population and lay 47 miles NW of Lubbock, on what we call the Clovis Highway, and nine miles NW of Littlefield, the county seat of Lamb County. Like HPH, the co-op hospital operated a modest on-premises pharmacy, the nearest pharmacy otherwise being in Littlefield. The Lamb County Tax Assessor-Collector had brought the suit to collect the tax that had been assessed against the hospital property. The main issue was whether the pharmacy operation nullified the hospital's charitable status. The issue in the case was basically the same as the issue in the HPH case, but with one considerable difference. HPH involved the question of whether the income from its on-premises pharmacy operation was "unrelated business income" under the IRC, while the Amherst hospital case involved the question of whether the hospital was a charity exempt from property tax in Lamb County.

The case was tried before the district judge in Littlefield without a jury. The Court rendered judgment in favor of the hospital, and the tax assessor-collector appealed to the Amarillo Court of Civil Appeals, which affirmed the lower court, relying heavily upon the decision of the Tax Court in HPH.

What made this property tax case special to me was that it became the lead case in an ALR 3rd (the *American Law Reports, Series 3*) analytical review of all prior authorities that have some reasonable connection to the critical aspect such lead case depicted. My guess is that the percentage of lawyers who ever had a case appear as lead in the ALR series is very small. Not a bad one for my legal career to go out on.

11. **Clanton estate**: Charles Clanton was a farmer in Crosby County, the county just east of Lubbock County. He consulted me soon after I had opened my own office, and I did estate planning and

wills for him and his wife, and perhaps other legal work. Beyond simply farming he had a venturesome nature. He moved his family and farming operation to the Ada, Oklahoma area before the issues involved in this litigation arose. A few years later he was murdered in Mexico under the most bizarre circumstances imaginable, which led to the litigation in question.

Clanton's will, which I had prepared for him, was admitted to probate in Ada, the county seat of Pontotoc County, Oklahoma. The attorney for the estate in Oklahoma was Austin Deaton, of Ada, and since there was also property in Texas I was employed to handle the estate's affairs in Texas. We worked in constant cooperation on the Clanton matters, particularly in the litigation stemming from a life insurance policy and the murder.

The details, especially as they involve the geography and canyons of Mexico are again given as closely as I can recall them, but the issues in the litigation were clear. The venture that led to this litigation involved a corporation apparently located in a Texas town not far from the Texas-Mexico border. It's apparent formation and purpose seemed to be to investigate and try to acquire a silver mine or mines somewhere in Mexico. The stockholders of the corporation were Clanton, a Mexican (Latin One) and his Mexican associate (Latin Two), collectively "the Latins." Latin One's father-in-law (Latin Three) was also incidental to the story. One or more of the Latins may have resided in San Antonio. Latin Three may have resided across the border in Mexico. The corporation had as yet few, if any, assets other than ownership of a one-million-dollar insurance policy on Clanton's life on which, strangely enough and for some mysterious reason, the named beneficiary was Latin Three.

On the night before the murder, Clanton and the Latins were staying at an inn or motel in a Mexican city not far from a precipitous canyon skirted by a highway over which they had apparently planned to travel within the next day or so. Whether the canyon in question was part of the massive Copper Canyon (Barranca del Cobre) SW of the city of Chihuahua, or some deep and precipitous canyon near Saltillo, our information was that it was a major canyon. The Latins got Clanton thoroughly intoxicated and the three of them traveled in two vehicles, Clanton's red pickup truck and one other, out of the city to a point near a steep drop off where they placed Clanton alone in his pickup, then put it in drive causing it to plunge over the precipice. They then drove the other vehicle back to their evening's point of departure. The place where Clanton's plummeting pickup and body came to rest was obscured from ready detection. The Latins apparently indicated that Clanton had been drinking and got in his vehicle alone and drove on the highway that skirted the canyon. It was in the summer and neither the pickup nor Clanton were found for a period of at least two weeks. A more careful search along the canyon rim detected something that looked like the victim's red pickup. A search team went down and found a body and the red pickup. It seems highly likely that the search that spotted the wreckage was orchestrated by the perpetrators who could not make a claim on the insurance policy without proof of death, and only they would have known where to focus their search, while still feigning their lack of prior knowledge of it.

Deterioration was extensive. Clanton's remains were beyond recognition except that there was a small patch of copper-colored hair on the back portion of the head, the same color and shade as Clanton's. Because of the patch of hair and his pickup being found nearby, the remains were determined, probably by a family member, to be those of Clanton.

The remains were prepared, to the extent possible, by a mortuary in Mexico. It casketed and shipped them to a funeral home in Ada, Oklahoma. The family had a burial plot in the memorial park in Lubbock, Texas, known as Resthaven and opted to have Charlie's remains returned there for interment. The funeral home in Ada shipped them to the funeral home on the grounds of Resthaven, which I (and Jo Anne) had owned since 1964.[1] The sealed casket

---

[1] The history and structure of our ownership is covered in the investment and business portion of this autobiography.

arrived and was interred without being opened by the Resthaven funeral home. All of this occurred before the filing of claim, by Clanton's estate, to the insurance proceeds on his life, the claim that led to the litigation here involved.

The law in Texas, and generally elsewhere, is that one who criminally causes the death of an insured person cannot receive any of the benefits provided by the insurance policy. It was on that basis that Austin Deaton and I, on behalf of the Clanton estate, made a timely filing of claim against the insurance company for the proceeds under the policy. The insurance company resisted the payment on the grounds that the policy had been fraudulently taken out in the first place, a legitimate defense if the facts supported such a finding. If fraud had been involved, Clanton certainly could not have participated in it, the perpetrators being the Latins. Perhaps that had some bearing on why the beneficiary named was neither the corporation nor the Latins, but Latin Three, the father-in-law of Latin One. In any event, we took the position that they were all lassoed together, as should have been fairly self-evident from the relationships involved—in fact the father-in-law may have been completely ignorant of the arrangement but did not himself make any claim on the policy, probably out of fear of prosecution. Nevertheless, the Latins themselves filed for the benefits in some capacity.

By our making claim against the insurance company and the company declining to pay within a specified period of time, the face amount of the benefit was increased in a major way if the claim eventually stood up. I believe that the amount in question thus became $1,500,000.

In order to recover, we had to prove that the Latins criminally brought about the death of Clanton, but our burden of proof was only to the level of a preponderance of the evidence, not the criminal burden of proof beyond a reasonable doubt. However, if we were to prevail on that issue, it would essentially prove that the insurance company had been defrauded in the issuance of the policy and would thus owe nothing to anyone. If we failed in that proof of criminal killing by the Latins, they would be entitled to the insurance proceeds according to the beneficiary arrangement, which was really substantively for them through the sham of being payable to the related and ignorant Latin Three. So what we were faced with was the checkmate condition of a true Mexican Standoff.

All parties recognized this and the essential impossibility of anyone winning on the facts of the case, so a settlement was reached whereby the $1,500,000 was divided three ways. Austin Deaton and I had taken the case on a contingent fee basis, so ended up being generously compensated in terms of the value of the settlement in dollars four or five decades ago.

However, there is a significant Epilogue. Deaton and I endeavored to bring the authorities, of either the state of Texas or the FBI, into the investigation to assist in the proof of murder, but they were not sufficiently motivated since any murder occurred out of the country. There was some reason we either could not try or were not successful in getting a disinterment ourselves for the purpose of furthering our factual investigation. Probably the family did not want to bear any of the cost of disinterment, pathological study, and re-interment, or perhaps were simply not interested in causing further disruption of the remains. We got nowhere in trying to have the investigation done by the authorities. However, approximately ten years later, after the matter had been settled on the Clanton case, and after I had retired in 1984 from practicing law, the family was contacted because the Federal authorities had become intensely interested. The Latins had pulled the same stunt in some other distant western state. The Feds got the order to disinter, did disinter, and discovered that Clanton's body was in the casket, but his head was not in there. So far as I know, it was never determined whether the head was removed in Mexico or Ada, but my money was on Mexico. The Latins were put away for good though on that sick and similarly patterned but ill conceived and executed venture.

12. Briercroft Savings & Loan Association: During the 1970s there was a steady and appreciable increase in interest rates leading to the very difficult times by 1980 when the interest rate curve was severely inverted, short-term rates being higher than long-term, making life increasingly difficult for savings and loan associations having older loan portfolios and paying short rates far above portfolio yields. Loan commitments of any length were increasingly dangerous for lending institutions to enter. Doubtless at the time that the prospective borrower in the present case applied for a loan the contemplated interest rate was appreciably lower than it was at the time the borrower wanted to close its loan under the alleged commitment. It was not in the interest of Briercroft to close the loan, and it denied that a binding commitment had been made.

Briercroft was sued in the district court in Dallas County to require it to fulfill its obligation under the alleged loan commitment. Briercroft denied that it had effectively committed to make the loan. Plaintiff demanded trial by jury. Dean Carlton was employed as co-counsel with me for the trial. Under the instructions given by the Court, the jury returned a verdict for the plaintiff and judgment was entered accordingly.

Karl Clifford from our firm worked with me in trial preparation and was present at the trial in Dallas. He recently reminded me that the trial judge told us in chambers, "The only thing he disliked more than out-of-town lawyers was people who did not honor their commitments."

I filed notice of appeal, which was assigned to the Eastland Court of Civil Appeals. Eastland was a town of about 4,000 population 96 miles WSW of Fort Worth on Interstate 20, and 224 miles ESE of Lubbock. Carlton was not involved with me on the appeal. The chief judge of the Court was Austin McCloud, a fellow my age raised in Colorado City, Texas who had started law practice with Fulbright, Crooker, Freeman, Bates & Jaworski (later Fulbright & Jaworski) the same summer of 1957 that I started with Vinson, Elkins, Weems & Searls. I knew McCloud casually while we were both in the Houston firms, but knew him primarily by the nickname "Digger"—he was Digger McCloud. We were friendly. I think he married a girl in the Kelly family from Colorado City, and I'm sure he knew my clients, Ross and Evelyn Daniels, as Colorado City is one of those small communities where everyone knows everyone.

I prepared and filed the brief and argued the case on appeal. The Eastland Court reversed the trial court and rendered judgment that no enforceable commitment had been made by Briercroft to the plaintiff/appellee in the case.

One thing stands out vividly in my mind. At the time I was working on the appellate brief and preparing for oral argument, our new young attorney, Don Collier, assisted me. He was with our firm only a short period of time before going to Dallas where he has had a stellar career in the practice of tax law.[1] His remarkable capabilities manifested themselves to me in the excellent work he did. He was an extremely valuable sounding board as we studied and discussed the issues involved in the case. His decision to leave Smith & Baker and go to Dallas to practice tax law disappointed me at the time, though we understood and wished him well. Having myself retired from law practice in 1984, I had no contact with Don after he left for Dallas. But as I was working on this portion of my autobiography, I sent an inquiry to Don on his firm's website "contact" button hoping to jog my memory on some aspects of his time with us. His memory for the details of the case is far better than mine. Here is his gracious email reply:

> Ed,
>
> I graduated from Texas Tech Law School in 1973 and was in the same class as Karl Clifford and Elgin Connor. I then went straight to NYU, graduating in May 1974. I then practiced in Dallas for approximately one year. I joined you at Smith & Baker in the summer of 1975, and we achieved the Briercroft victory in February 1976.
>
> I will always remember the Briercroft case and the opportunity you gave me to work on it at a very early stage in my career.

---

1 See meadowscollier.com.

It was also the first big victory in which I participated. Seems now like it involved a lot more than $225,000.

I have been very fortunate in my practice in Dallas. I have thoroughly enjoyed my career and my clients have treated me very generously. One of my Partners and I recently completed a 12-year battle with the Justice Department over an estate tax refund claim. We achieved a major victory at the trial court and at the Fifth Circuit, which resulted in a refund of over $150,000,000 to our client, a career high for both of us. Most people, however, do not realize that my appellate experience started in Lubbock with you and Briercroft. Thanks for all that you taught me.

Don

13. **Banta tax-evasion indictment:** Banta was a resident of Brownfield, a town of about 10,000 population located 39 miles SW of Lubbock. He was in the insurance business, and perhaps others. He was indicted for income tax evasion and came to me for representation. As usual, my memory for case details is very hazy, but certain things remain firmly in mind. The case presented a challenge for the defense, requiring the talents of a skilled criminal defense lawyer. The late George Gilkerson, considerably older than I, was such a lawyer. George was a good-sized fellow who had been a lineman on the Baylor University football team. He had been an effective prosecutor as Lubbock County's district attorney years earlier, and he was then currently still a criminal defense attorney, though not exclusively. I called upon George to serve with me as co-counsel in defending Banta.

The case was tried in the Federal District Court in Lubbock before a jury. At the conclusion of the trial, the jury returned a not guilty verdict.

Jo Anne and I were associated with George and his wife, Louise, in other ways also. Jo Anne had served on the advisory board of Sherick Memorial Home, a privately well-endowed home for elderly women of which George Gilkerson was one of the well-paid trustees with controlling authority. So while the relationship with George was quite close on a personal basis, working with George was often a frustrating and trying (no pun intended) experience for me. He was hard to reach by phone and he had developed to a high level of perfection the art of putting things off till the last minute. My mode of operation was to get prepared as fully and as early as possible, while George, as did many effective trial lawyers, held off till the last minute. Dean Carlton was a bit that way, though not as totally as George. Dean used to say that by putting things off till the last minute there are some bridges that you end up not having to cross. There is some truth in that. I think it works well, though, for attorneys who practice that way to be associated with others, like myself, who do a lot of pick and shovel work getting ready, even if some of it might have been avoidable in the end. In any event, George and I ended up successfully defending Banta.

George served as lead counsel in the trial itself, with me at the counsel table assisting. When all the evidence was in and the parties had rested their respective cases, the Judge recessed for a brief period to give all participants a break and let the lawyers make final preparation for closing argument.

As we broke, George told me to outline his argument for him while he went to the rest room. I carefully prepared the outline of our case on its merits, writing it down on a yellow legal pad which George later picked up and held in his hand as he argued. Each side was allotted a set amount of time for argument, the government splitting its time between opening and closing. The total time for the defense was likely one hour. But whatever it was, George spent the first 90% of the period without looking at the outline I had prepared for him. I was squirming, wondering if he was ever going to get to the facts of the case as I had outlined for him at his request. He was arguing, as most all criminal defense lawyers do, on the point that they must each determine "beyond a reasonable doubt" every element of the prosecution's case against Banta. And George was an expert in that argument, his stock in trade. When he finally got down to the outline, he did not have much time left to deal with it, but he spit it out quickly and closed, and the jury apparently all ended up agreeing that not all elements of the alleged crime had been proven to that high level of certainty. George had put on a clinic.

14. **Williams competency**: Yoakum County, Texas lies SW of Lubbock and borders the New Mexico line. Just inside the state line is a "town" called Bronco, home to well under 100 people. The only other towns in the county are Plains, population about 1,450, the county seat, and Denver City to its south, population about 4,000. The county population is about 7,800.

The only lawyer I knew who practiced in Yoakum County at the time of this litigation was Paul New of Denver City, who represented the many children of my client in this case, most if not all of whom resided with their families in the county. Plains is 71 miles SW of Lubbock and 32 miles west of Brownfield. The trial was held in the middle of the winter, with roads a bit treacherous. I opted to rent a room in one of the town's two motels, the one that seemed to be the least primitive, but to say that it was modest was an extreme overstatement of its amenity. It had a phone in the room, a party line that anyone in the motel could pick up and listen in on at any time. Debbie Brown assisted me at the trial, but opted to drive back and forth rather than rent such a room. Debbie had joined Smith & Baker in the summer of 1977, and if my information is correct my client, whom we will call A. O. Williams, born May 6, 1901, died in November 1982.[1] So the case took place between the summer of 1977 and November 1982.

---

1 Without historical records, I'm winging it on flimsy memory. The last name was, I am pretty sure, Williams. Of the first name I am less sure, but it comes to mind as A. O. A search of the death records of all persons named Williams who died in Plains between 1980 and 2000 revealed four hits. Only one could have been my client, and he was one Albert Williams whose birth and death information was as above indicated. Actually I would have thought Williams would have been a bit older, but my memory is that he and his wife had married as youths. Aside from the possibility that the name or other record is not correct, the facts otherwise are essentially as previously stated.

Williams' wife and the mother of his eight or so children had died after they had been married for about sixty years. They had been a farm family, living in the country near Plains. Williams was deaf and legally blind. In spite of the fact that he and his wife had managed to accumulate a certain level of life's comforts, his physical condition was not such as to make him a hot prospect for many single women. But he had always lived with a woman (his wife) and wanted a woman in the house. Somehow he acquired one, a lady who had a young female child. While he showed some affection to the child, and probably to her mother, never was there any indication by any party that the relationship went further than the fact that he needed a helper and she needed a source of shelter and support for herself and her child.

Williams was not able to tend to his routine banking needs, so the lady took care of those, including making deposits and writing checks, but he endorsed all incoming checks and signed those in payment of their expenses. His signature was not picture perfect and only approximated being on any available signature line provided, but no claim of forgery on her part was raised. No claim was made that she had ever appropriated any of his funds or violated the confidence he placed in her in handling these matters.

Somebody, perhaps even one of his children, drove him to Lubbock where he came into my office in a dither. Paul New, representing his children, had filed a petition in the court in Plains to have Williams declared incompetent and a guardian appointed over his estate—but not his person.

It was completely obvious to me that Williams was not legally incompetent to manage his affairs. He had arranged someone he trusted to handle them for him, but from the standpoint of the children, considering that he could neither see nor hear, he was vulnerable to being financially abused. Actually, he probably had some peripheral vision, though legally blind, and he could hear if one spoke to him from a close proximity and sufficient sound volume.

Williams came to me because he needed a lawyer, Yoakum County's Paul New was on the other side, and I had done estate planning and wills for Williams and his wife some time before. The case was not one I relished taking, but sometimes one takes a case because it would be unthinkable not to do so on behalf of an existing or former client.

It would not be far off to say that everyone in the courtroom—judge, jury, court reporter (probably), petitioners' attorney Paul New, and any spectators—was well acquainted with everyone else in the courtroom, with the exception of Debbie and me. I could not have picked a jury that was free from these relationships and friendships. Request for change of venue was not feasible and would not likely have been granted.

The jury returned a verdict for the petitioners, though the decision of the jury was not, and did not have to be, unanimous. One of the jurors, who had not voted with the majority, told me afterward that some comment was made by others in the jury room that Williams was surely well represented.

In counseling my client after the trial, I expressed confidence that, with the record that had been made, the verdict in the trial court could be reversed on appeal, for the facts as shown fell far short of establishing any lack of mental capacity, only the limitations of seeing and hearing and the obvious financial vulnerability. No showing of wrongful action on the lady's part was made or attempted. But physical vulnerability simply does not establish lack of mental capacity.

However, the family matter was soon resolved to Williams' satisfaction. He had first told me to proceed with the appeal, but later got in touch with me saying that he and the children had worked out an arrangement that was satisfactory to all concerned. I told him I thought that was the best resolution possible.

Sidebar to My Experience in Trying the Williams Case

The discomforts of the available lodging in Plains reminded me of an incident told, in my hearing, by a prominent and capable Lubbock plaintiff's lawyer, the late Bob Huff, then of the firm Huff

& Bowers, during the early days of my law practice in Lubbock. Bob drove a cream colored Rolls Royce automobile. Because he handled so many cases out in the boondocks, such as in Plains, he also owned a medium size Airstream trailer. It served as a most comfortable lodging for him wherever he went. He told about being in some small county, maybe even up in Oklahoma, trying a case. During the noon recess one day, to kill a little time and get some fresh air after lunch, he was walking around the courthouse and took note of the bronze plate on the cornerstone that gave the names of all the county commissioners that served on the building project, one of whom had died during the process. The decedent's name was listed last and read "[Decedent's name], died during erection." And so it goes, out in the boonies.

15. **Jimmy Holloway**: Holloway and/or his family had, I think, been a client of mine on earlier matters. Holloway had consulted with me regarding a partnership his Holloway Construction Company (HCC) was in where the relationship had turned sour because HCC had advanced considerable funds that he felt had been mishandled. As in the Canode case, my recollections on the details of the case were most hazy until my memory was refreshed by a footnote to my 1980 financial statement. Most of what follows came from that.

Carlton again served with me as co-counsel with a contingent fee agreement for one-third of whatever we could recover for Holloway in resolution of the partnership. In October 1980, the 137th District Court in Lubbock County granted judgment in excess of $1,000,000 for HCC against Robert Genho and Lasertron Company, the latter being a partnership between Genho and HCC. The judgment became non-appealable on February 1981. Primarily because of such judgment the partnership was in bankruptcy in Houston, and the partnership was the debtor in possession with HCC having the right, as partner, under such judgment to wind up. The main assets were laser patents and some equipment and inventory relating to laser manufacturing. The judgment's value depended upon what could be recognized from these assets after paying partnership debts. On my 1980 statement, I assigned only a nominal value to the potential under our fee contract, there being so many contingencies. We made no appearance for our client in the bankruptcy proceeding. I had no retained statement for 1981, but a footnote to the 1982 statement recited the fact that Genho was murdered in January 1982, and some $634,000 of insurance on his life became payable. The owner, and doubtless the designated beneficiary, of such insurance was Holloway Contracting Company, but the insurance company had paid the policy proceeds into such 137th District Court to determine the possibility of rival claims between Genho's children as next of kin and Holloway Contracting Co. On HCC's behalf we filed suit against Genho's children and next of kin seeking a determination that the insurance was payable to the partnership rather than to Genho's estate or his heirs. Presumably the insurance company followed this procedure to avoid liability to the Genho children in case HCC, through its owner, was implicated in the murder. No such assertion or claim was ever made. Holloway convinced us that he was in no way involved in Genho's death, and I know of no investigation by any authority of Holloway in that regard. I do not recall where the murder occurred, but I think not in the Lubbock area. Holloway seemed an entirely credible person about whom I had no personal doubt on the matter. Proper service of summons was made upon the named defendants, who filed no answer within the time prescribed, whereupon we filed a motion for summary judgment supported by affidavit of the facts supporting our cause of action. The court ended up granting our motion for summary judgment, which was never challenged, and upon entry of final judgment Holloway proceeded to settle matters and make distribution. Dean and I ended up with payment that seemed adequate for the time and effort put into the case. Holloway seemed happy with the resolution.

The Other Eight Cases

(1) **Myra Robinson**: This was a gift tax case based upon a gift tax return filed to test the consequence of a particular transaction.

The decision went against my client in both the Tax Court and Fifth Circuit. My relationship with this client has been one of the most richly rewarding experiences of my years practicing law. She successfully led the Robinson Drilling Company, of Big Spring, from the time of her husband Bob's death in the 1960s, and was distinctly recognized and honored in the industry within the Permian Basin.

(2) **Farmers' Cooperative Gin**: This is not the name of the client, which I do not remember. It was located in some community south and west of Lubbock. J. R. Blumrosen referred the case to me. The case involved an issue of interest in the taxation of farm cooperatives. The Tax Court's decision was favorable to the individual co-op and served as precedent for farm cooperatives.

(3) **Cardinal Life Insurance Company**, owned by W. B. (Dub) Rushing, claimed to be taxable as a life insurance company, but on facts that made it a tough case to win. Paid tax, filed claim for refund, and filed suit for refund upon denial of claim. Federal District Court ruled in Cardinal's favor, but upon government's filing of notice of appeal, the Fifth Circuit reversed the lower court per curiam, a peremptory action with no filing of briefs or oral argument.

(4) **E-Systems**: I bought its bonds based upon a promotional flier. Precipitous loss of value occurred based upon facts not disclosed in flier. Dean Carlton was recommended to me for the purpose of filing suit against the company. Ended up settling the case when Federal Judge Joe E. Estes denied our petition to certify it as a class action suit. Recovery in settlement was less than my loss, but this is where I began the association with Dean Carlton that was a positive collaborative relationship for the rest of my law practice days.

(5) **Amarillo pension issue**: I remember very little about this case except that it was contemporary with the Canode case, and involved a different client in Amarillo, a lady who, based upon my best guestimate of the issue, felt entitled to benefits from an ex-husband's retirement plan based upon the enhancement of such benefits during their

marriage. The case was tried in Federal District Court in Amarillo. The decision adverse to my client was affirmed by the Fifth Circuit. The case was a tough one to begin with as it came under the scope of ERISA, which clearly pre-empted conflicting state law. Not surprisingly, I was unable to establish an exception to that pre-emption.

(6) **Alton Taylor case:** This case involved Taylor's claim to a ten-percent interest in the partnership that owned and operated the ideally located Lubbock Inn. I lost this case by failing to use one of my peremptory challenges to strike the lady who ended up swinging the jury around to my opponent.

The early balloting in the jury room heavily favored my client, but this lady held out and in the end brought enough jurors around to my opponent that I lost the case. This lady worked in the district clerk's office. My opposing counsel, Orville Smith, of Crenshaw, Dupre & Milam, was a man I greatly admired as a consummate gentleman and good trial lawyer. He would have been well known and liked in that office. I handled few cases in the local district court, and did not recognize the danger she was to my client. He told me afterwards that his client was very lucky to win.

(7) **Bob McKelvey:** This was a tax case involving the consequences of certain distributions from a "subchapter S corporation."[1] The issue in question was a challenging one involving many complexities. Anticipating that the position of the Fifth Circuit, to which appeals would lie from the Federal district court or Tax Court, might be less favorable to my client on the issue than the Court of Claims in Washington, I opted to go that route.

The Court's decision written, as always, by one judge and concurred in by three more, comprised several pages and held for the government against my client. One judge, Byron Skelton, dissented with an opinion considerably longer than the Court's opinion. Obviously, I felt the dissenting opinion was correct and far more astutely perceptive. Indeed, such was the information coming from

---

1 See http://www.s-corp.org/our-history/.

Judge Skeleton's son-in-law, the now late Texas Tech engineering professor Jerry Ramsey, a close former friend of ours. The Ramsey's, both now deceased, had been in the same Sunday School class as Jo Anne and I were in, and Judge Skelton and his wife had visited the class with them on one occasion. Judge Skelton later sent word through the Ramseys that he thought my case was good, but dealt with a very involved section of the IRC and the issue was of such a complex nature that the four other judges, none of whom were tax specialists (nor was he), did not fully understand and did not take the time necessary to fully comprehend. What it all said to me is that when the judge or jury in a case knows you, he, she, or they, while not violating their own best judgment, will give your presentation a full and fair evaluation, and perhaps in cases that could reasonably fall either way might be influenced in their consideration by that full attention given to your position.

(8) **Doctor X**: This case involved a particular type of partnership arrangement that I had set up for Doctor X under which his wholly owned professional association, rather than he as an individual, became a partner. The question was whether that partnership structure would be recognized. The arrangement offered several tax advantages to the doctor. It was a novel issue on which there was as yet no specific judicial precedent. For some reason unknown to me or any of my associates, when the arrangement was challenged by the IRS, Doctor X employed a different law firm to handle the case. The Tax Court sustained the objectives I had sought in the arrangement. Until the decision appeared in the reports, I was not even aware that Doctor X had been challenged on the issue. It was pleasing to me to know that my judgment in setting up the plan was vindicated, but it was an issue that I would like to have had the opportunity to defend. I've long been puzzled as to why I did not have that opportunity. The arrangement has been widely used by practitioners since then. But I did not dwell long on the disappointment, for as I recall I was then in the process of bringing my days of law practice to a close.

Winding Down and Farewell

By the late 1970s it seemed to me that a secure economic base for my family and me was falling into place and that there were enticements in other areas of activity that were increasingly attractive to me and demanding of much time and effort. I had a sense of wanting to "slow down" my practice to make room for these involvements. In reality, a lot of the work that I had done before was flowing naturally to Norton as well as to the other younger lawyers. As things developed, there seemed to be more times when I was not covered up with legal matters demanding my time. On the one hand it bothered me, while on the other hand it was working in a providential direction on my behalf. The nature and extent of these other activities and involvements will become apparent in the parts of this writing that follow.

The law practice had been wonderful to me. It had opened many doors, generated countless highly meaningful relationships, and provided generously for my family, and now it was graciously opening the door for me to pass through into other walks of life.

The spring and summer of 1984 was a period of transition for me. As later indicated, I made the recording of my last piano recital on April 24, 1984, the end of a priceless, signal period of my life, freeing much of my time and energy for other applications. If I remember correctly my legal secretary, Jerry Bryce (later Jerry Saffle), was nearing a change in her own life and I would be facing the need to hire a new legal secretary. Most significantly, the time demands that our Resthaven operation were making upon me were steadily increasing, including a significant amount of time managing its investments from my law office. But the greatest factor in motivating me to retire from law practice and move my office to Resthaven that summer had to do with a change in the top administrative office at our Resthaven operation. Our son Mark had been working in Denver as a project accountant for a Canadian company that constructed high-rise buildings. Whether or not he had been notified of an end of his job, it was becoming obvious to him that he needed to make a move in employment because a significant drop in that company's building activity was developing by 1984. The timing turned out to be ideal, for Phillip Welch, the young man who had been serving as president of Resthaven, was making noises about the need to return to his family's similar operation in Big Spring, Texas. When we were talking by phone with Mark and his wife Jill, I mentioned to him that it appeared we would be having to look for a successor, and I wondered if Mark might be interested in that position. The suggestion clicked and the decision was promptly made that he would take over the reigns at Resthaven, with a bit of overlap before Phillip left.

In due course, and in order to have an orderly shift of client files and make other necessary rearrangements, I had made my thoughts known to Norton and the other lawyers and a meeting of all the firm lawyers was held to discuss what would be involved. At the meeting, concern was understandably expressed by some of the younger lawyers that I might at some point return to the practice of law locally, competing in a sense with the existing firm, especially in regard to clients whom I was then representing or had previously represented. In the strongest way possible I assured them that, as meaningful as my days of active law practice had been, they were coming to an end. There was not the slightest reservation in my mind about that. Hopefully they felt some assurance from that. In any event, in all that followed, they were each and every one most gracious, and the maintenance of a positive relationship with every one of them has remained of great importance to me to this day.

The date set for my retirement was August 31, 1984, a bit over three weeks prior to my fifty-second birthday.

The firm planned a retirement dinner party for me, and Jo Anne of course, to be held in a meeting room at the upscale Lubbock Club. They presented me with an elegant, heavy black leather briefcase, which I used to much advantage for many years. While new and different briefcases have found there way into my service since that time, the one the firm presented that night remains, and will remain, a tangible reminder of that night and those relationships.

One of the more memorable aspects of the retirement party was opening of the floor to those who cared to say something anecdotally about me, particularly those describing one of my many foibles, humorous in retrospect.

One partner told of the time he came out into the hall to see blood streaming down my forehead. I had gone to the bathroom from the library carrying a law book that I was still studying as I emerged and headed back down the hall to the library whence I had come. Miscalculating the location of the library door, I had made my turn with nose still stuck in the book and walked directly into the door casing headfirst.

Another told of going by the coffee-break room and seeing coffee running across the floor. Anyone was free to make a fresh pot of coffee any time. Upon investigation it was determined that I had gone in to do just that, emptied the filter out of the holder and put a new filter in, put in fresh coffee grounds, poured a pot full of water into the top, then set the empty pot down on the counter. As the fresh coffee ran through, it fell onto the hot plate and onto the counter, and then commenced its journey across the floor toward the door.

There were others along this vein, normally exhibiting absent-minded preoccupation. It was a warm, meaningful, and memorable evening.

And with this my twenty-seven plus years of law practice came to an end.

Epilogue

A humorous note. About a year after I had retired from the firm and had an office on the Resthaven premises, one of my former clients called the law firm saying to the receptionist, "May I speak with Mr. Smith please." The receptionist, new since my departure, replied, "I'm sorry, Mr. Smith is no longer with us. He is out at Resthaven." The caller, with solemn voice, responded, "Oh, I'm so sorry. I didn't know."

A note of sadness. Karl Clifford saw it before I did and sent an email. The December 2007 *Texas Bar Journal* memorial reported the death of Dean Carlton on October 13, 2006, at age 77. He had been just three years my senior. He and his wife Mary Ellen had lived in Richardson (NE Dallas), but his memorial in the TBJ listed his residence as College Station, where Texas A&M is located. Dean was a rabid Aggie who did not even smile at Aggie jokes and whose twin-engine Beach Bonanza aircraft's number contained the letters AM and the year of his graduation. Dean and Mary Ellen had been in Colorado with us one summer before Jo Anne and I bought our summer home there, and both of them were among the out-of-town special guests at my 1982 piano concert. I called Mary Ellen upon receiving the news of Dean's death. She said that Dean's death was unexpected, though "he paid no attention to doctors' advice and ate every greasy cheeseburger he could get his hands on." He collapsed while speaking before a zoning board meeting in College Station. She said he had "a ruptured aorta in the stomach area and could not be saved."

A happy note. In December 2005 Karl Clifford and Steve Krier contributed equal amounts to the Texas Tech Law School Foundation to endow the Edward R. Smith and Norton Baker Tax Award to be given annually to a law school student who has shown an interest in tax law. The first award was made in the first part of 2006, and it was the great pleasure of Jo Anne and me to attend the awards ceremony in the reception room of the law school when that and the other awards were presented. An annual award had been equally funded by the two of them for some years prior to 2005, but that is the year they equally funded the endowment, and they have made additions to the endowment some years since then.

Karl was the top graduate in his class of 1973, and Steve was an adjunct professor of taxation at the law school, giving them each a strong and ongoing connection to the school. Words alone beggar any effort to express what this spontaneous and generous endowment in our honor by these two younger partners means to us.

Mary DeLong
(Grandma Reaugh) at 16

Grandpa Reaugh holding Eddie

Mother (2nd from right) visiting sister, Ruth Colclasure, and family in Albuquerque, ca. 1931

Section of Images

Dad with Eddie swinging on a trellis

Granda Reaugh (probably mid-1950s

House at 152 Meyer Street, Flora, Illinois, about 1988

Grandma Reaugh at our first Lubbock house, 1959 or 1960

Dad with Eddie on the running board

Eddie at 8 or 9 years old

Family on 1948 California trip

Section of Images

Bridge over the Little Wabash River flowing through farm

Grade school basketball team (Eddie with ball)

1948 FHS Championship team in *Chicago Daily News;* Eddie over center

*Eddie at field
after football practice, 1949*

*Donald Ray Brown holding
Eddie; study loft in background*

Section of Images

Jo Anne's deb presentation, spring 1952

Eddie during college years at Midwestern

Jo Anne and parents with Eddie at Ciro's in Hollywood, 1955

Eddie and Jo Anne at duplex apartment near SMU, fall of 1956 (I was always called Eddie until I graduated from law school, May 1957)

Mother laughing with Mary Anne, Eddie, and Jo Anne

Section of Images

Jo Anne, Ed and the twins (ca. mid-1959)

*Daughter Jill (now Jillian)
at 18 months, December 1962*

*Ed at 20 miles in 1979
Boston Marathon*

Framed 1979 Boston Marathon memorabilia

Ed practicing piano for performance

Section of Images

Ed in tails for Steinway Dedication Concert March 23, 1982

Jo Anne with 1st 4 grandchildren in lakeside condo, summer 1987

Lake City, Colorado, house (owned from 1987 to 2007)

Section of Images

American Basin near Lake City, Colorado; Jo Anne and Ed, July 13, 2003

Jillian, Mark, and Michael at a restaurant in Philadelphia, July 20, 2004

Ed with Christopher Bamford, and Gene Gollogly in exhibit hall booth, SBL convention

Paul O'Leary (not named in book) and Ed in a New York City hotel during a SteinerBooks Seminar, March 13, 2008; deeply rooted in Steiner's works, a priceless friend, encourager, sounding board, and helpmate since we first met in 2004

Law partner Norton Baker and Ed on deck of Colorado house, August 19, 2007

Section of Images

*September 10, 2004, 50th wedding anniversary,
on deck of Colorado house*

Family Portrait August 2012

Investment and Business

Horald Eaton, husband of mother's younger sister Mary, and father of their five children, started out peddling auto parts from the back of his vehicle. By the time I was in college and law school Uncle Horald had become one of Flora's more successful business men. His H. W. Eaton Auto Parts store impressed me. One summer evening, probably the first summer after dad died, Uncle Horald and I were talking in his yard—he and Aunt Mary lived just south of grandma's house. Horald and Mary had always shown an interest in my activities, and now Horald was giving me something that probably qualified as fatherly advice. He said, "Eddie, one who never takes any chances will never get ahead." He probably need not have said that, for I believe that taking calculated risks, normally after due diligence but not always, was simply part of me. But I appreciated him saying it. It has been a recurring memory over the years.

From the twelve shares of American Airlines that I bought and lost money on while in the army, investing has been for me a regularity. Usually in the earlier and more creative years it was with borrowed money. Probably at least half of the investments turned out poorly. But the net result had been positive well beyond my early expectations.

My investment activity began in 1962, something over half a century ago. Looking back through the lens that I now use to judge these things, only three investments can I put in the really significant category, and all of them were made within the years 1962 through 1964.

Those three aside, any detailed recount of my investment activity through the years would show a fairly constant flow of what

I would call, in retrospect, incidental investments, a fairly regular pattern of investing, but would serve no other meaningful purpose. It is appropriate to mention, largely for the purpose of getting them out of the way, two popular types of investment in Texas; the first is oil and gas, and the second is farmland. I dabbled a modest amount in each without much success in either.

I took small positions in a few oil and gas working interests. Those entered into with my late friend Bob Schuster with the Coursons, who were clients of his in Perryton, Texas, were decent investments. While the tax deductions on the others helped some, the ventures never did well. My investment in oil and gas working interests were very modest in relation to the whole, and I bought no mineral royalties. Investment in securities of oil and gas companies or publicly held limited partnerships are not what I speak of here as oil and gas interests.

In early 1974 Don Cooper, the John Deere dealer in Perryton, Texas and I bought a section of irrigated farmland near Perryton, in Ochiltree County near the upper NE corner of the Texas panhandle. The year 1973 was a great year for farming and farmland. The farm was a good investment for a while, the value increasing notably for a few years before the market went south. My impression is that the farm operations themselves probably produced less net income than could have been derived from other sources on the same invested amount.

This brings me to one of Bernard Baruch's famous quotes. When he was asked the secret of his success, he said, "I made my money by selling too soon"; and closely related, "I never lost money by turning a profit."[1] These proverbial remarks suggest to me that most, if not all, investment media, in the course of its life, plays out the same pattern as everything else in creation. It either fails to begin with, or succeeds to some extent. In the latter case, what comes first into existence grows, crests, then declines and disappears. It

---

1 See http://www.goodreads.com/author/quotes/5768330.Bernard_M_Baruch.

is the life cycle of every created thing. One who invests, according to Baruch, should sell at or before the crest—and his other quotes indicate his agreement with conventional wisdom that trying to pick a top or bottom is folly. On the Ochiltree County farm Don and I violated Baruch's pattern for success. From the time of our purchase in 1974 value increased through 1982 when it crested, remained there through 1983, then declined annually thereafter through 1987 when it was valued below our 1974 purchase price. It was sold sometime before the end of 1990 for no more, and probably less, than its 1987 value.

On the first two of my three significant investments, I also violated Baruch's pattern for success by holding them too long. On the third, I demonstrated Baruch's wisdom. As I look back, it is what made each significant that puts it in this special category. The three are:

1. American Founders Life Insurance Company stock
2. Briercroft Savings & Loan Association stock
3. Resthaven of Lubbock, Inc. stock

American Founders Life Insurance Company stock

In the early days of my law practice in Lubbock, one of the insurance agencies where I was invited to speak on estate planning was American Founders Life Insurance Company (AFLIC), located at 3702 Avenue Q in Lubbock. Some of the agents mentioned how well the AFLIC stock was doing. It was in 1962 that I bought my first shares. My 1962 financial statement is dated March 31, 1962. It reflects a value of $6,050 for AFLIC stock, but does not give the number of shares held. There is no 1962 year-end statement, but the statement at the end of 1963 lists 682 shares at its market value on February 7, 1964 at $69,564, or $102 per share. The 682 shares is what I had accumulated by the end of 1963, at constantly increasing prices. The year-end holdings of AFLIC shares thereafter are as follows:

1964	750 shares @ 65	$48,750
1965	762 shares @ 48	$36,576
1966	762 shares @ 18	$13,716

No shares were held at the end of 1967. My cost basis is not reflected on my statements and my tax return copies for these years no longer exist. But my recollection is clear. At one point I had a $40,000 gain on paper. It was about that time that I decided to sell some, or maybe all, I held. Trouble was, no one wanted to buy, and everyone wanted to sell. The price was collapsing. I should have gone ahead and sold a bit earlier, but I did not—violation of Baruch's policy. Even then, I should have sold at whatever the market was, for it would have produced some profit, but I did not—further violation of Baruch's policy. I ended up selling in 1967, and my recollection is that my collective loss on the stock was about $10,000. I do remember that at its peak value, each share of the first batch I had bought, which the $ 6,050 on the March 31, 1962, statement doubtless included, was worth seven times what I had paid for it. One who, out of attachment to his or her holdings, cannot sell what has been a very good investment is probably going to do poorly on it in the end.

So, aside from illustrating a very important investment principle, why do I list this investment as the first of my three significant investments? The reason is that it gave me the necessary collateral to borrow what I needed from the bank to close the purchase, in the fall of 1964, of Resthaven stock. That I ended up losing money on the AFLIC investment fades into insignificance. It is what that investment made possible for me while I held it that counts. It is only in looking back that its significance becomes obvious. Call it luck or fate (i.e., destiny); most would call it luck, but to the extent that the two might differ, I see it more as fate, which becomes more obvious to me as it relates to the Resthaven situation.

Briercroft Savings & Loan Association Stock

Briercroft Savings & Loan Association (Briercroft) from beginning to end demonstrates the nature of created things mentioned earlier: "What comes first into existence grows, crests, and then declines and disappears." It so happens that the trajectory of Briercroft seems remarkably to have paralleled the days of my legal career from the opening of my own office in 1961 to retirement in 1984, except that the last years of Briercroft were difficult. Its coming into existence is described in the section "My Solo Practice" where I tell of Rushing, Tidmore, Chambers, and Kastman coming into my office in early 1962. Things moved rapidly from that meeting to the chartering of Briercroft. It was a thoroughly engaging and exciting experience. It is no exaggeration to describe Briercroft as a stunning success as it blasted off like an all-systems "Go" Cape Canaveral rocket launch. But then anyone at all familiar with the collapse of the savings and loan industry in the 1980s will know that Briercroft's last days had to be as trying as its early days were exhilarating.

But just as those who lived in the glory days of the southern Confederacy looked back upon the shambles of that society with a continuing affection in their hearts for what they once had known, so it is with me, and I think also with every one of the organizing group of Briercroft, that the memories of those vital, central years of our lives, and what Briercroft meant to us in those days, will never fade from our hearts. And the difficult days of survival as the life of Briercroft, ultimately a victim of the times, came to an end did nothing to extinguish the joy it had brought us in its earlier vigor. It is that story, and the place Briercroft occupied in our lives in that time frame, that prompt me to list Briercroft as one of my three significant investments.

Rushing and Tidmore were to have the largest number of shares, probably about double what the rest of us original board members were to have. Each of us put up $25,000 for 1,000 shares, and our goal was to bring in another hundred young go-getters and scions, offering each of them 100 shares at that price. Each of us original board members were to shake the bushes and come up with these stockholders, and we did, rather enjoyably and successfully. In terms of the number of stockholders recruited in this way, I may have brought in more than anyone else but there was no aspect of it that was competitive, and those brought in by the others included some very important local young folks. In those days, they were pretty much all male stockholders, but family involvement was invited and stressed so that wives were as much a part of the party and social aspect as the husbands. Our solicitation of these investors did not require a separate securities exemption, being subject as it was to regulatory oversight. The required number of commitments for stock was quickly filled and we were in the process of rather leisurely getting things ready to make formal application to the Texas Savings & Loan Commissioner. We knew there would be opposition, for in those days getting a new bank or savings and loan charter was far different from what it has been with the proliferation of new banks in more recent years.

As we were getting all the material together to prepare our formal submission, some of our group got word that we needed to get our application down to Austin immediately if it were to have any chance of success. Perhaps it had to do with some changes that were about to be made. In any event, J. C., Jack, Henry, and I were in Dub Rushing's office, pushing papers up to our necks one night, into the wee hours of the morning. I remember that Jack had his own plane and planned to fly four of us, him, J. C., Max, and me to Austin the next morning and hand deliver our filing to the Commission. We worked till 3:00 a.m. that morning getting all of it ready. When we asked Max if he had brought something to the plane that was vital, perhaps a check for the filing fee but in any event something we had to take with us, his memorable answer was, "I've got it in my pocket!" We were working on one of the top floors in the twenty-story Great Plains Building when we finished and went to the elevator to go home and try to sleep for one hour before meeting Jack at the airport. We stood waiting for many minutes on the elevator down, when it finally dawned on someone that we had not pushed the elevator button. It was so near breakfast time that we stopped at the Toddle House on 34th Street for a quick breakfast, then all headed home to get ready for the plane ride to Austin.

I hated long private plane rides, especially in the morning, and this one was way too long. I thought my bladder was going to burst before we landed. But we got there and filed our application before the deadline, whatever that was.

A date and time was set for the hearing in Austin. Every other local financial institution was there to speak against us. I spoke for our group. We had a lot of *esprit de corps*. We had chartered a bus and taken a full load of our young stockholders down for the hearing. So, in terms of numbers and enthusiasm, it made for quite a show. The Commissioner granted our charter. There were still hurdles, for we had to toe the line on the requirements of the Federal Home Loan Bank Board (FHLBB) in Little Rock in order to get our FSLIC (Federal Savings & Loan Insurance Corporation) approval for the insurance of deposits comparable to that offered by banks. The FHLBB told us there was too much affiliation among all the original board members and that we had to bring two more from the community onto the board. That was no problem, though the closeness still remained. Two were brought on board. One was Elmer Tarbox, who had been a star football player for Texas Tech in the 1930s and was, at one point, a local representative in the Texas legislature. The other was Bob Couch, younger brother of a high city official, who himself worked for Amoco Petroleum in the area to the west of Lubbock.

No sooner had we gotten our charter than we had a big overnight social bash at the Ko Ko Inn, a new motel with inside atrium and swimming pool that had just been completed by Rushing in a commercially developed triangle across Avenue Q to the east from the Dora Roberts estate property on the NE corner of which the new Briercroft premises would be located. Spouses were invited to the Ko Ko bash, and quite a rollicking good time was had by all. Enthusiasm carried from all of these out into the community and deposits poured in rapidly. I believe our growth was record-breaking among such Texas institutions in those early years of activity.

Our location was at that prime corner where so much of the traffic flowed between downtown and the active southwest residential area of town. We opened in a trailer on that corner and business boomed. In the meantime our board, particularly those most attuned to commercial real estate development, were working with architects on the plans for the new home office. It was essentially a replica, both inside and out, of George Washington's Mount Vernon home on the Potomac River. Adorned by much colonial and Revolutionary War memorabilia, the ambiance was striking. School tours were scheduled through the premises. There was an immense pride among our board members and stockholders in the awesomeness of this home office structure. It was a thing of civic beauty.

We were in business as technology was coming into vogue. It seemed like we would no sooner get a new accounting system installed and working than it would become obsolete and a new and larger system was needed to replace it. This was not just a development that was occurring generally in all businesses, but a factor in our situation was that we were growing at such a rapid pace that what was adequate at one time quickly became inadequate for the next higher level of activity. In any event, they were heady years, and all systems were on go.

Through the sixties and the first half of the seventies, our weekly board meetings, while tending to business, were nevertheless jovial good times. We all looked forward to them.

Everything was going along so well, but then, as time went on two disturbing trends were developing that were symptomatic of the decline and demise of our wonderful institution. Both were insidious for us, but they were of a very different nature. Lubbock was growing, and that was good. But in the case of our wonderful location, the town was growing to the west and south of us. Traffic patterns changed. What had been in the 1960s such a magnificent corner location was becoming a part of town left behind. That migration was of concern to us, but the other item was far more serious. It was the ruinous creep of interest rates upward as the yield curve "inverted," short rates becoming greatly in excess of long-term rates, especially the rates on already fully invested portfolios. We had a portfolio of loans at the formerly desirable yield of six percent per annum but were paying ten to twelve percent for deposits. It did not take a rocket scientist to see that we were headed for disaster. This was typical for the industry.

Faced with this industry-wide situation, the Federal Home Loan Bank Board set aside generally accepted accounting principles (GAAP), promulgating regulatory rules that in effect permitted institutions such as ours to remain officially solvent even as de facto insolvency became more and more apparent.

In the early stages of this insidious rate creep, Derrell Jones, the president of the association, and I began to suggest that we needed to consider selling our stock. This would have been in the latter part of the seventies. At first, it was just our voices. As the situation tightened its grip more and more, additional board members came around to our point of view. Finally it came down to just one board member being unwilling to cash in our chips, but that board member was W. B. Rushing, who seemed, almost uncharacteristically, to cling to the dream.

Jones made it known to me that there was a prospective buyer if at least 85 percent of all of the stock could be delivered. When this prospect, and indicated offer, were taken to the board, all eyes were on Dub. He finally relented.

On January 12, 1981, the directors signed a contract with George and Douglas Krupp, of Boston, Massachusetts for the sale of all shares of Briercroft, or for all that were tendered provided that at least 85 percent of the shares were tendered—and they were. Adjusted for stock splits and stock dividends since inception, the contract price per share was a multiple of several times the original cost of $25 per share. Closing was to take place in the early summer months of 1981. The contract contained several conditions to closing, and provided minimal liquidated damages if the Krupps failed to close. But at this point we thought the gods had been smiling on us when a capable purchaser appeared on the scene.

One might wonder who would be a buyer of a savings and loan association at this time, considering the state of the industry. The Krupp brothers had proven themselves adept at syndicating real estate packages, especially large apartment complexes, and either operating or marketing them. A savings and loan association with considerable assets, even when burdened by a relatively low-yielding portfolio, was nevertheless a tool they seemed to feel they could use to their advantage in their syndication ventures.

While the signing of the Krupp contract seemed a godsend, and perhaps was, it turned out to be the first in a long, arduous, and sometimes anguishing, journey to the end, with endless twists and turns to get our heads and some of the cheese out of the savings and loan trap before its final collapse. As the lawyer in our organizing group and on our board, I felt the pressures of this long working out of our interests, especially so because we felt a strong responsibility to the multitude of our smaller stockholders who had been with us from the first.

The contract of January 12, 1981, was canceled and renegotiated, and the sale was consummated on September 1, 1981. The price was only slightly less, due to some intervening losses, but the terms of payment were otherwise less favorable to us sellers. The purchase price was payable July 1, 1986, with no interest to accrue till July 1, 1984, and then to accrue at 10% per annum payable quarterly. Of the total purchase price of $6,073,415.69, the personal liability of the Krupps was limited to $1,500,000. The Krupp notes and related papers were held by trustees for the benefit of all the stockholders, and I was one of the trustees.

The contract provided that the members of the board would resign, with the exception of W. B. Rushing, J. C. Chambers, and me, who were to remain on the board at the Krupps' request. While Jack Kastman was not, I believe, included in that listing, through serving as insurance agent or in some capacity, he maintained some relationship to the association's activities, and did, I believe, sit in on at least some of the board meetings.

What became obvious in our board and loan committee meetings is that the buyers of our stock were rolling the dice with our money. That is, in order to keep Briercroft's head above the water, chances had to be taken that would normally have been beyond the type of activity a prudent savings and loan business would have engaged in. Because of the limited personal liability of the Krupps and the fact that losses on these transactions could wipe out anything we former stockholders might get under our contract, a conflict of interest was inevitable between the present stockholders and those of us on the board who also represented the former stockholders' interests.

At one board meeting where board approval for a particular transaction was presented, a vote was taken at which all the other directors present, including Rushing and Chambers, gave their assent. But on that transaction I voted against the resolution, and I insisted that I review the minutes of that board meeting and approve them, making sure that my objection was reflected in the minutes. It was. As a result of that action, I was asked to resign from the board, which I did. As I recall, Rushing and Chambers followed by resigning not long after I did.

Most of the details of these transactions that I've been able to relate have come from notes to my retained personal financial statements. The final note that gives any relevant details was in a statement dated March 31, 1985. It indicated that, "Due to some differences between the buyers and sellers regarding operations and security, the contract was renegotiated on April 5, 1984. A cash payment of $2,562,309.75 was made by buyers, for which they received credit of $3,416,413.00 against the original total price of $6,073,857.37, leaving a balance of $2,657,444.37 remaining. The buyers, previously personally liable for $1,500,000.00 of the

$6,073,857.37 have no further personal liability now. The balance is secured by all the stock of the Association under pledge requiring the meeting of all FHLBB requirements as to capital. Buyers are also now obliged to pay interest monthly instead of quarterly, and all payments are current."

I recall that at some point I gave notice to George Krupp that we were going to accelerate the note, meaning that the entire debt would become immediately due and payable, on the grounds that they were violating our security agreement by the nature of business they were engaging in. It was a somewhat chancy act on my part, as to whether I could have prevailed on such a legal argument, but it was a chance I thought had to be taken. Whether this action was before, and thus brought about the April 5, 1984, renegotiation or was after it, and resulted in another and final payment on the $2,657,444.37 balance, I am not completely certain. But my recollection, which the evidence does seem to confirm, is that it was after the April 5, 1984, renegotiation and thus garnered some additional payment on the balance due after that partial payment. What does appear is that by the time of my next retained personal financial statement, dated June 30, 1986, all had been paid by the Krupps that would be paid, for no balance was shown owing by them on this 1986 statement. It is, and has always been, my impression that we got a significant final payment as a sort of cliff-hanger final settlement on all amounts from the Krupps, and that it was received only about a month before the FHLBB shut down the Briercroft operation. If this is true, as I believe it is, then that final payment would have been after the one negotiated on April 5, 1984, for the note describing that partial settlement was on my statement dated March 31, 1985—too late to be descriptive of the final scenario of a payment one month before collapse. In any event, my threat to accelerate the Krupp note did produce some significant results and I received many expressions of appreciation from my other former board members and many of the smaller stockholders for having salvaged what it got for them.

Happily, the collapse of Briercroft apparently did not bring down the Krupps, for later word was that it had been a blip in the road for them and that they were continuing to do very well in their syndications and real estate business.

However, as is well known, there were many repercussions following the collapse of the industry where significant lawsuits were brought and recoveries were obtained, and in some cases convictions with prison sentences attained. The RTC (Resolution Trust Corporation) was authorized to pursue recovery on the assets of the failed institutions. I'm not aware whether it accused and/or recovered anything directly from the Krupps. However, I do know that the affairs of Briercroft during these latter periods were the subject of litigation and much discovery by these authorities. Depositions were taken of those of us on the board, specifically Rushing, Chambers, and me. I think Dub's deposition was taken here in Lubbock. However, these depositions were being taken during the part of the year when Jo Anne and I were staying at our summer home near Lake City, Colorado. I agreed to be deposed provided that it could be done in Gunnison, Colorado, fifty-five miles NNE of Lake City. J. C. also agreed to be deposed provided he could be deposed when and where I was, namely, in Gunnison. And that is what was done. No further actions were taken against any of us original directors.

Many were the nights I was thankful that the minutes of that directors' meeting at Briercroft reflected my objection and that I was then asked to resign. Otherwise, there might have been some sleeplessness during that time frame.

Not many years later the final desolating sacrilege occurred—the Mount Vernon of Briercroft was demolished, brick by brick, as if a promising youth struck down too soon. But just as there arose from the aborted lives of John and Robert Kennedy the poignant, etheric memory called Camelot, so is Briercroft the idyllic, bright and shiny place and time that lives on in the hearts of those of us who were involved with it.

Resthaven of Lubbock, Inc.

Table of Contents
- How It All Started
- History of Resthaven 1948–1964
- Formation of Resthaven Memorial Park, Inc. (RMP)
- Two First-Year Events
- Formation of Resthaven Funeral Home, Inc. (RFH)
- Operations of ROL (1964–1968)
- The Events of 1973/1974
- Norton's Sale to Me
- Refinancing the Brown Note
- The Complex of Other Middle Ownership Period Operations
- Reacquisition of the Funeral Home
- Operational Aspects
- Aspects Affecting Both Funeral Home and Cemetery
- Aspects Primarily Affecting the Funeral Home
- Aspects Primarily Affecting the Cemetery
- Low Turnover of Personnel
- Gifts of Resthaven Stock to Children
- Mark Pursues MBA Degree at Tech in Evenings
- The End of Family Ownership of Resthaven
- Epilogue on Larry
- Fund Investment Activity During the Resthaven Years

How It All Started

Philosophically, the capacity to understand the ultimate causes of anything is still well beyond the evolutionary state of human consciousness in its earthly embodiment. Practically speaking, however, we attempt to ascribe the beginnings of things in our lives. My acquisition of Resthaven, rather than reflecting personal investment acumen, was to me a matter of destiny, an event of karmic origin, not that I comprehend it otherwise. Thus, I ascribe the cause of my acquiring Resthaven to a certain traumatic occurrence.[1]

On the night of August 19, 1963, and for many days thereafter, I hovered at death's door with ruptured appendix and gangrenous infection throughout my peritoneal cavity. Twice, eleven days apart, the doctor told Jo Anne that there was little hope that I would survive the night. But I did not die, and three weeks later, in skeletal appearance, I emerged to take up where I had left off so unexpectedly. We were relatively new in Lubbock, having lived here at that time only four and a half years, but that was longer than we had lived anywhere else in our few years of marriage and all of my family members, living and dead, were in Illinois. Shortly after my leaving the hospital Jo Anne said she had spent those nights wondering where she would bury me under these circumstances, and she asked me where I would have chosen. My response, "Right here. This town has been good to me."

Without delay we went to Resthaven and selected two burial spaces, and began paying $5.00 per month on the $120 purchase price. Dan, the sales representative, shortly thereafter contacted me saying, in deepest confidence, that R. P. Brown, the owner, then sixty-three years old and without family members capable of carrying on the business, had been told by his doctor to dispose of the

---

1 Normally, I will be using the singular pronoun (i.e., I, my, or me) when describing affairs at Resthaven, even though all my involvement with it is for the community interest of both Jo Anne and me. The use of the plural option (i.e., *we, our,* or *us*) will so often be ambiguous as I will be dealing with others and have to clarify that I speak of our community rather than of the other persons with whom I am dealing.

Investment and Business

business. Dan informed me that he was authorized to talk to me about it and, if a sale could be consummated, he would be entitled to a commission. However, if it should get out that Resthaven was for sale, then it would not be for sale and he would get no commission.

I learned that Brown was asking $1,000,000 with $200,000 down and the balance secured by lien and payable, with interest, over a certain fairly extended period of time. I also learned, or perhaps already knew, that the CPA Crayton O. Campbell, who had befriended me so much in my law practice, was Resthaven's accountant and that he was authorized to make the books available to me for examination. I was sufficiently interested that I accepted that opportunity for examination and performed myself a cash-flow study to see if a purchase was practical based upon operating history to date and reasonable projections.

In the meantime, I did the "due diligence" study, considering a number of other relevant factors. The physical setting of Resthaven was not, at that time, anything like it was to become over time. I had the vision that these things were in the process of change in a favorable direction. The property contained ninety acres bounded by the obviously important 19th Street on the south, Frankford Avenue on the west, modest housing neighborhoods on the east, and the newly acquired public right of way for the future Loop 289 around Lubbock running northeasterly on the north. Nineteenth Street was a paved two-lane street at this western edge of town. Frankford Avenue was a dirt road that got muddy with rain. These two streets intersected at the SW corner of Resthaven. They were both section lines, destined to become arterial streets in the years ahead. The young Lubbock Christian College (now Lubbock Christian University) was only a block east across 19th Street to the south.

Only a small part of the property had been platted and dedicated for cemetery use up to that time. Improvements on the property were minimal, being a modest concrete block office building at the corner of 19th and Frankford, a maintenance shed midway up Frankford on the west edge, and opposite on the east edge an impressive indoor marble interior mausoleum, in which, however, most of the crypts had already been sold. A modest staff was in place, consisting of onsite manager, Gary Caffey, a bookkeeper, park maintenance and operation personnel, and some sales personnel. The essential cemetery equipment, tractor, backhoe, and some other items were on hand, and there was a respectable amount of accounts receivable. The other local cemetery was run by the City of Lubbock in an ethnic part of town across the tracks. While the history of burials in Lubbock had largely been there and many families were committed to it, it seemed clear upon any normal observation that Resthaven offered a far better future going forward. I confirmed that no other cemetery could be started within four miles of the city limits of a city the size of Lubbock. A small cemetery outside the four-mile limits to the south of town either was in its early stages, or would be within a few years, but did not pose a serious competitive threat at that time.

It was my feeling that the price was not the important thing, but rather the terms of payment were critical. I made an offer accepting the $1,000,000 price, but with conditions and terms on its payment that were very favorable from my standpoint as buyer. Brown declined my offer and the transaction appeared dead. And so it remained till the following summer of 1964 when Crayton Campbell called me saying that Brown had told him that if he could sell it for $900,000 with $100,000 down, Brown would pay him a $50,000 commission. Moreover, the $800,000 balance of the price could be paid on a non-personal liability basis, with notes bearing interest at four percent per annum payable semi-annually, both principal and interest being payable over thirty years from date of closing. Crayton told me that if I could find a buyer he would split that commission with me. Without hanging up the phone, I told Crayton he just sold it, as I would buy it, and I would happily take half of his commission to help wrap up the deal.

I worked it out with Campbell that I would take 70 percent of the stock if he would take 10 percent out of the other 30 percent with two older associates of mine at Briercroft, W. B. Rushing and Briercroft's president, Claude R. Meadows, Jr., each taking

10 percent. Norton Baker was a one-third partner with me in the law firm at that time, so he and I split the 70 percent in a one-third to two-thirds ratio, with the other 30 percent owned as above. Eventually, as will be described, I would acquire all of the stock.

The sale was closed that fall. As we were coming away from the closing, Crayton and I were in the car together and he said to me, "Ed, you may live a long time, but I think you will never make a better deal than you did on this." He was right.

It never was, however, simply a passive investment, for much of my life effort was dedicated to it. Ultimately I would end up owning and operating that investment approximately one year longer than I practiced law; about 28 1/3 years in it and 27 1/6 years in law. But the two areas of activity overlapped for almost twenty years, from October and November 1964 through August 31, 1984. Without what the law practice provided in family support and resources for investing, I could never have acquired Resthaven and guided its operation through its more formative and challenging period of development and emergence. In that sense, the law practice parented Resthaven for me, but as so often happens, the child standing on parents' shoulders reaches higher levels in a worldly sense. A significant reorientation of my own goals for Resthaven took place during the course of these 28 years. Initially, it was just an investment with the normal intent of making a significant profit. While the investment motive never fully disappeared, two things happened that minimized it in relation to the overall commitment. First, during the course of the 28 years, my economic situation, increasingly as a result of the Resthaven operation as compared with the law practice, improved dramatically. As this became true, the feeling of "enough is enough" outweighed any urge to keep pressing for ever more of the same. Second, as Resthaven moved steadily into the position as the dominant funeral and burial service in Lubbock, an awareness of the public service aspect of the business became increasingly important, guiding many aspects of the operation, and providing an increasing proportion in the personal satisfaction aspect of life.

Initially, I list at the first of this Investment & Business section only three investments that I considered "significant." That was true in a sense, but very misleading in another sense, for the lion's share of my investment activity from 1964 on took place within the corporate framework of Resthaven and its several related operational funds. In the early years, this was a relatively small activity in terms of funds to be managed, but it was like the mustard seed that in time would become a major aspect of the operation.

History of Resthaven 1948–1964

From the purchase of Resthaven in 1964 until 1989 I had very little knowledge about the cemetery's history prior to 1964. In the spring of 1988, a lady who identified herself as Doris M. (Mrs. Jack) Jones, a resident of an upscale north Dallas neighborhood, came to Resthaven in connection with a decedent then lying in state. I was in my office upstairs over the funeral home when a call came from the staff saying that a Mrs. Jones was there who stated that she was related to one of the original owners of the cemetery. Curious, I went down to meet her. She was modestly elegant, most pleasant, and we visited. She did not go into a lot of details other than giving me the name of Bill Curry, who was up in years but still active, saying that he would be happy to relate the founding and early history of the cemetery to me.

In retrospect, I am appalled that I did not put much priority on the matter and procrastinated in calling Curry for the better part of a year. When I called, he eagerly invited me to come by his home and visit, which I did on February 18, 1989. He lived in a modest house in central Lubbock. He was eighty-eight years old but emanated a warm and feisty zestfulness for life and my two-hour visit with him was both delightful and informative. The history below is almost entirely from that visit. Bill was looking forward to a dance that evening. Fortunately I did not put off that visit much longer, for he died within the next few months.

P. W. Curry, who owned cemeteries in Austin and San Angelo, was the founder and leader of Tech Memorial Park, Inc. (TMP), which was organized and started the cemetery in 1948. Initially he owned 51 percent of the TMP stock with the other 49 percent owned equally (16 1/3 percent each) by the brothers Robert (Bob) and Jack Jones and their brother-in-law, W. A. Worley, husband of their sister, all three from Austin. These three moved to Lubbock but P. W. Curry never did. P. W. Curry was chairman of the board and Bob Jones was President.

In 1950 Bill Curry retired after 22 years with the city of New York, first as a patrolman and then a detective. He moved to Lubbock, bought the stock of W. A. Worley, and took over the operations as president, though W. P. Curry remained as chairman. W. A. Worley then moved back to Austin.[1]

---

[1] Apparently there were three W. A. Worleys. It was the middle one of the three who had lived in Austin, who had for a short while been involved in TMP. An interesting sidelight of the Worley interest is that a few years earlier while I was practicing law, a W. A. Worley consulted with me in regard to a problem he was having with his grandson, the third W.A. Worley, who went by Bill, and who I well remember played safety for the Texas Tech football team a few years earlier. Young Bill seems to have come into ownership of the Midland cemetery operation also called Resthaven Memorial Park, and its Valhalla Mausoleum (W. B. Rushing and Max Tidmore had built and owned the Valhalla mausoleum before selling it). Bill Worley's father, the middle W. A. Worley, was married to the sister of Bob and Jack Jones. My new client, the eldest W. A. Worley, was fretting over the influence that Bill's mother (nee Jones), who may have married after her Worley husband's death (or divorce), was influencing Bill's handling of things. I do not presently recall precisely what my client was claiming, but I think it must have been an interest in the Midland operation, or a debt owed by it to him. I was a member of the Texas Cemetery Association and knew Bill casually through that, as well as having watched him play for Tech. My client authorized me to make claims against Bill or the Midland operation itself, which I did. The matter ended up being settled. Apparently I had to file suit first in order to make the settlement, for I seem to recall taking Bill's deposition in Midland. The whole case would have made a lot more sense to me had I known then what I learned from Mrs. Jack Jones and Bill Curry in the late 1980s. I doubt my client even knew all the TMP relationships, for he was never able to get me to understand them. My effort to understand them was only a matter of curiosity, for they were not relevant to the Midland case.

In 1952 the Jones brothers came to Bill Curry with a give-or-take offer to him and P. W. to buy or sell so that either the Currys or the Joneses would own all the stock. Bill called P. W. who said that by all means the Currys would buy, which they did. Bill made the comment that in buying their TMP stock, the Currys did the Joneses a big favor, for the Joneses went to Dallas and got into the lumber and development business in north Dallas and eventually sold out for many millions of dollars.[1]

When the Curry's bought out the Joneses, they brought another brother, James A. Curry, into TMP. He bought some of the Jones stock, though less than Bill who himself bought less than P. W. The exact amounts Bill did not remember. James Curry came from San Angelo where he had been running a cemetery which was also owned, at least in substantial part, by P. W. Curry.

In 1954 Bob Brown propositioned the Currys about a deal whereby he would build a mausoleum on the property and pay the Currys a commission on sales of its crypts. The Currys liked the drawing card aspect of the deal but their attorney required a $100,000 escrow. Brown got Mr. Reed, who owned a cemetery in Corpus Christi, to put up the escrow and they became partners on that project, which prospered. Brown and Reed bought TMP from the Currys in 1955 or 1956 for $200,000, asking Bill Curry to stay on as president. Bill turned them down but his brother James did stay as manager for about a year before going to Dallas. He, like Brown, was a lawyer. Mr. Reed came up often to oversee his investment. By around 1958, Brown and Reed were not getting along too well. Reed's health was not good and he wanted out and did sell to Brown. Bob often mentioned Mr. Reed to me.

TMP started out with only the south thirty acres, which it had bought from Olive Fluke, along with an option for an additional thirty which it later exercised before the sale to Brown and Reed. TMP later

---

[1] Doris Jones had told me the sale from the Jones brothers to the Curry brothers had occurred in 1951.

bought the north thirty acres from Olive Fluke, bringing TMP's total area to ninety acres before the sale of TMP to my group in 1964.

Formation of Resthaven Memorial Park, Inc. (RMP)

At the time of my group's purchase in 1964, the official name of the operating company was still TMP, though it had been operating for some time under the assumed name Resthaven Memorial Park. To close the purchase, my group formed a new corporation, Resthaven Memorial Park, Inc. (RMP) whose stock was divided among us in the proportions indicated earlier. It was the buyer from Brown of all the stock of TMP. The $800,000 due Brown after the $100,000 down payment was represented by RMP's two notes, one for $750,000 and one for $50,000, the amount of the Campbell commission.

When the time came for RMP to close the purchase, Brown said that for tax reasons he did not want to get all of the $100,000 down payment in the year 1964. He requested that payment of a significant fraction of it, probably half or more, be deferred until 1965. Collections on accounts receivable were so good between closing and early 1965 that we buyers did not have to put cash into RMP to pay the balance of the down payment.

Upon consummation of the purchase, TMP was liquidated into RMP, a procedure that permitted the buyer to step up the tax basis of the assets acquired on liquidation by allocating the purchase price among them.

The seller, R. P. Brown, continued to have a non-financial interest in the operation of the cemetery. It was non-financial in the sense that he did not have an equity interest. Of course, the major part of his selling price was represented by a long-term note secured only by the purchase money lien on the stock and first lien mortgage of all the corporate real estate. We had formed RMP, a new corporation, to purchase the stock and liquidate the old corporation, officially named Tech Memorial Park (TMP), so the obligation of our new corporation attached to the assets received in liquidation and our stock was pledged as additional security.

Brown was on the scene most all the time, just about as much as before, and I found myself developing a considerable fondness for and excellent working relationship with him. He was invaluable in so many ways. That continued for as many years as his health held up, though in time he began to phase out. He eventually passed away before the final payment on the note—and I believe his wife had also passed away before then so that the final payment was to the son and daughter, both of whom expressed so much appreciation that we had been so faithful in timely payment of all amounts as they came due on the note, the terms of which had been contractually changed in the 1970s as mentioned below.

Two First-Year Events

Two events stand out as dominant during the first year of operation, from acquisition in the fall of 1964 through the end of 1965. The first was the almost immediate commencement of planning, contracting, and initiation of construction of a funeral home on the SW corner of the property. Brown's brother-in-law, Merle Steele, was a successful funeral home owner and operator in San Angelo, Texas. Bob had developed the dream of having a combination cemetery-funeral home operation at Resthaven. It was not feasible for him to initiate such an undertaking in his own right in the years leading up to his sale to us. However, he was burning up with the idea of doing it. In fact, information provided me at my first meeting, and becoming acquainted, with William R. (Bill) Curry on February 18, 1989, shed a good bit of light on Brown's enthusiasm for the funeral home which, indeed, was the moving catalyst for our launching that venture almost immediately after the 1964 purchase. What Bill related to me in 1989 in relation to Brown's interest in putting a funeral home on the property was informative. Up till the time Brown and Reed acquired the cemetery, its sales office had been downtown across from Sanders Funeral Home, and all of the funeral homes in town, with the exception of Rix and perhaps Franklin Bartley, had been active promoters of the cemetery as against the City cemetery.

But Bob's goals for the cemetery to put a funeral home on the property were no secret, so that from the time he and Reed acquired the cemetery, the funeral directors' ardor for Resthaven (still TMP) went from very warm to increasingly cool. Of this, I was not aware until Bill related it. However, Brown's enthusiasm had been obvious to me.

George Young was the developer and owner of the increasingly prominent Restland Cemetery and Funeral Home in Richardson, Texas (Dallas metropolitan area). He had a daughter attending Texas Tech University. Bob arranged for George to visit with us during one of his visits to Lubbock, giving us helpful insights on starting a funeral home based on his own experience. The thing that stands out most in my mind from that meeting is his statement, "When you open a funeral home on your cemetery, you will go from being a good guy to being a son-of-a-bitch" to the other funeral homes. He was right about that, except that I did not realize that their ardor had been cooling even before our 1964 purchase.

If Bob ever told me about the Currys and their organizing group, it did not make enough impression for me to remember it. The critical event that led to my learning so much detail about how TMP, the forerunner of Resthaven, was my visit with Doris Jones in the spring of 1988.

Along with the funeral home, the second dominant event of the first year of operation was my acquiring the 30 percent of stock owned by Rushing, Meadows, and Campbell, each of whom had 10 percent. Rushing, in particular, I had been interested in having an original interest in Resthaven because of his locally peerless experience in commercial real estate and related construction. Meadows headed up Briercroft, which had real estate connections. Campbell was perhaps brought in because of his financial interest some way in the commission we were splitting. Without Rushing, in particular, the planning of the funeral home and working with the architect would have been much more of a challenge. But we had hit the ground running on the funeral home objective so were well along on it before I acquired the stock of these three. It happened, however, before the end of 1965, for my financial statement at that date reflected 74.21 percent of the stock of RMP (the balance being held by Norton).

Not too long after the organization of Briercroft, Rushing bought the control of Security National Bank, located near the intersection of Slide Road and 34th Street in west Lubbock. As part of his group, I bought $15,000 worth of the bank stock. Since Rushing had more long-term interest in the bank, and I in Resthaven, we merely swapped stock, with me conveying my stock in Security for his in Resthaven. My December 31, 1965, statement indicates that I had bought Meadow's stock for the same $15,000 on a note payable in 120 months. It appears I had made five or six monthly payments as of the end of 1965. It also appears that Campbell surrendered his 10 percent of RMP stock to RMP in exchange for its recognizing Campbell as the sole payee on its long-term $50,000 "commission" note set up in the purchase from Brown. Doubtless this treasury stock transaction accounts for my odd 74.21 percent and Norton's 25.79 percent interest in the outstanding RMP stock. These percentages would remain in effect until Norton sold his RMP stock to me, for reasons explained later.

Formation of Resthaven Funeral Home, Inc. (RFH)

Resthaven Funeral Home, Inc. (RFH) was formed as a separate corporation in 1965 and was licensed to operate as a funeral home in about December of that year. From the standpoint of the public, the two corporations operated as a single business known as Resthaven of Lubbock (ROL), though the ownership of the two was different. Norton did not want to participate in RFH. From the first I held 52.5 percent and Bob Brown the other 47.5 percent of the RFH stock.

Two things created a financial problem right off the bat.

First, for a long time, at least several weeks, we got no business, I mean zilch. Bob Brown called me at my law office one day, sounding excited. He said, "We have a body in the house." That was exciting. I could see the cash register beginning to roll. As it turned out, it was a pick up and embalm trade case; a case indeed, but produced virtually no revenue. "Pick up and embalm" was a phrase used within the industry to describe the common practice where one funeral home, to accommodate the need of another funeral home, usually non-local, picks up and embalms a decedent's remains on behalf of the funeral home hired by the family—done as a courtesy for a nominal charge.

The common practice today, as it has been for decades, is that emergency ambulance service is provided by independent companies formed for that purpose. Such was not the case until a few years after RFH was formed. Until then it behooved each funeral home to offer ambulance service. So when RFH built its funeral home, it added a spacious second floor that included dormitory space for ambulance drivers. In addition to the employment costs, at least one efficient, well-maintained ambulance had always to be available. These services were a substantial net expense. The competitive necessity of providing such service is illustrated by the morally questionable, but realistic, description of what happens, for instance, in the case of an automobile accident. NASCAR operators would have done well to recruit funeral home ambulance drivers for its races, for race is what funeral home drivers did when called by the highway patrol to come to the scene of an accident. The first one to get there would pick up the dead body or bodies, leaving those still living to the drivers hot on his tail. The winner got the funeral service(s), the others got paid far less for ambulance service, if they could collect it.

I was losing money big time, $55,000 the first year in RFH (it was also operated as a Subchapter S corporation). The well-documented 1966 credit crunch gave me a scare. Lenders quit lending. The cemetery continued profitable, but the funeral home was a financial sump-hole. Bob Brown found Singleton and his associates who bought Brown's interest. In time, seeing the 1969 credit crunch coming, I succumbed to the same temptation and sold my RFH stock to that group. But I did so with a right of first refusal if they should later sell. Due to deterioration in the general level of cooperation over that decade as well as Singleton's advancing age and declining health, I was able to buy all of the RFH stock back in 1979. By that time, RFH was getting a decent amount of funeral business. But that reacquisition is the point from which real progress in the overall combined operation commenced. By that time I was the sole owner of both RMP and RFH, which were merged into the single corporation Resthaven of Lubbock, Inc. (ROL), and all signals were on "Go"—but on this I jump ahead, for significant events occurred in RMP in the 1970s.

Operations of ROL (1964–1968)

From the first, the operation of RMP was very successful, providing cash flow abundantly, at least as well as I had projected. Upon the formation of RMP, Norton and I had opted to have it treated as a Subchapter S corporation, meaning that its operating results would be passed down to us essentially as though it were a partnership. By virtue of our allocation of our total $900,000 purchase price to the assets acquired from TMP upon its liquidation, a substantial part of which was allocated to the accounts receivable, we were able to pass down substantial tax losses to ourselves even though we realized that it was very profitable economically. Between those tax benefits and the income I recognized from the law practice, the far less favorable results from the operation of RFH could be maintained until I sold my RFH stock in 1968. The cemetery continued profitable beyond this 1968 period.

The Events of 1973/1974

Aside from the ongoing national trauma of Watergate that eventually led to Nixon's resignation from the Presidency on August 8, 1974, two significant events regarding RMP occurred in 1973/1974. The first was Norton's sale of his RMP stock to me. The second was the refinancing of RMP's long-term note to Brown.

Norton's Sale to Me

Norton and I were running into tax problems. Together we owned all of the stock of two corporations, Smith & Baker, Inc. and RMP. The law firm was taxed as a regular corporation, and the time had come that RMP had written off so much of its original cost basis allocations that it was no longer producing losses to carry down to its stockholders. We thus needed for it to terminate its Subchapter S status and be taxed as a regular Subchapter C corporation. The problem was that when two corporations had the same controlling ownership within a closely affiliated group, they could have only one corporate surtax exemption between them. This exemption provided that the first $25,000 of corporate income would be taxed at 22 percent while everything above that would be taxed at 48 percent. We planned to talk about what to do about that situation over lunch.

Well do I remember walking the three blocks east to the great barbeque sandwich shop in the 1300 block of Texas Avenue. We had started talking about the problem as we walked. About half way there Norton said to me, "Why don't you just buy my stock?" I asked how much he wanted for it and he quickly gave me an amount, which I believe was approximately its book value, but in any event the amount was $90,000, which I agreed to and arranged to immediately pay him in cash, on March 31, 1973. Aside from solving the tax problem from his standpoint, the trade made sense for him. He was an equal partner in the law firm and only had a 25.79 percent stock interest in RMP. Moreover, he was never enthusiastic about dealing with the deceased, aside from representing their estates as a lawyer. He had shown no interest in owning any part of RFH when it was formed, and in our board meetings matters relating to RFH and the cemetery's relationship to it took up an appreciable amount of time.

Refinancing the Brown Note

This event was a signally important financial transaction for me. Bob was beginning to hurt when the Arab oil embargo hit in 1973 and interest rates jumped up to 9 or 10 percent. He asked me if I would raise the rate. We worked out a deal where I would raise the rate to 6 percent if he would forego any principal payments until the end of the note payment period, September 1994. Also, he agreed to my request to subordinate his mortgage to a $300,000 bank loan that I would use to purchase securities that I would also pledge to him on the note. My plan was to buy convertible bonds, which were then selling at 50 cents on the dollar and paying a 12 percent yield (on the 50 percent) which would just meet the 6 percent level of payments on the revised note to Brown. These bonds came due right around 1994. They had good balance sheets behind them. The principal was then at about $600,000, so the bonds would mature at that level and pay off the balloon at the end. However, before actually closing the deal, I did some figuring with convertible preferred stocks. They were paying about 10 percent dividends, of which 85 percent was not taxable if owned by a corporation. My calculations showed I would be way ahead that way as compared to the bonds, so that is what I did. Then good fortune beamed on me, for that was done just about the time of the 1974 stock market bottom (Watergate era). From there those convertibles did nothing but go up in value, so I doubled my money in very short order.

The Complex of Other Middle Ownership Period Operations

Upon acquisition of the cemetery in 1964 I inherited, as office manager, a college boy named Gary Cathey. Not too long after that Tom Weaver joined me, right out of college as I recall. Tom was a good and loyal employee. It was in 1975, under his leadership, that the kneeling Christ in Gethsemane feature was added, sculpted by a New York City artist named Zuckerman, who brought the marble base for it from Cortina, Italy. This project will be included in later discussion of features. In 1977 a headhunter organization, working for a national funeral home/cemetery company, hired Tom away from me to manage the large Crown Hill cemetery in Denver. The loss of Tom was a real blow, but I got sore at him when he promptly hired some of my key employees, including sales manager, and tried to hire still more away from me. Fortunately, the years healed those ruffled feelings, but his departure set in motion a series of events that did not work out well.

A former ministerial staff member in our church, Roy L. Ward, was hired to replace Tom. In an effort to keep our operation competitive for our other key employees, I conceived the idea of expanding by acquiring other cemetery or combination operations. At an earlier time, the new Peaceful Gardens cemetery south of Lubbock was apparently facing some financial difficulties. The bank to which it owed money called me to ask if Resthaven might be interested in purchasing it. I was very interested. However, I was even more concerned about the possibility that RMP's acquisition of the only other memorial park serving the community would violate the antitrust laws and subject RMP not only to possible governmental penalties but also to substantial damages in a civil restraint of trade class action suit. I hired the Crenshaw, Dupre & Milam law firm to give me an opinion on the matter, and they confirmed the dangers involved. In the long run, that cemetery would become more of a factor, but in those days that was minimal.

However, I looked for acquisition possibilities in Denver and in Little Rock, neither of which was feasible. What was available were two cemeteries in Longview, Texas, the west one of which was a memorial park with a new funeral home on it. RMP purchased these. They turned out to be a real headache and a costly diversion. This acquisition was either in 1977 or 1978, and the operation was continued until 1986 when we were able to sell it to Gibraltar Mausoleum Corporation based in Indianapolis, which owned and operated cemeteries and funeral homes around the country. Longview is in East Texas, 474 long and boring miles from Lubbock. The cultures of East Texas and West Texas are also miles apart. It was a management headache from first to last. Had I had any idea that I would be able to reacquire our own funeral home in 1979, I would have passed up the idea of expanding elsewhere. I do not recall that we lost a lot of money on the eventual sale, but operationally it cost me over the years, and was the source of much worry and concern.

Contemporaneously with this effort to expand, I tried to provide my key employees with incentive to stay by selling 25 percent of my ROL stock in 1978 to the four who were most critical, Roy L. Ward, President; Phillip Welch, Comptroller; Sam R. McWhorter, Park Superintendent; and Larry Vaughn, Sales Manager. No down payment was required, and their interest-bearing notes were payable over a period of years, with certain obviously necessary restrictions. All this effort probably had no significant beneficial effect either. Ward's employment was terminated on August 15, 1983, and McWhorter's on September 15, 1983. Ward's stock was purchased by RMP as treasury stock, and McWhorter's was purchased by Welch and Vaughn. However, by the end of 1985 all the stock of Welch and Vaughn was purchased by ROL as treasury stock. ROL made payments to me on the notes the final balances of which were paid at or before closing of the sale of ROL in 1993.

Upon the termination of Ward as president, Phillip Welch was promoted to president and served until replaced by our son Mark in 1984, Phillip returning to his family's similar operation in Big Spring about that time.

As the relationship between the funeral home's Singleton group and my cemetery group seemed to diverge in operation and philosophy, the cemetery offices were moved into rented office space on the south Loop 289 near the Franklin-Bartley Funeral Home. Because of the limited space available in the funeral home building, that rented office space was continued even after my reacquisition of the funeral home until Phillip Welch led us in constructing, in about 1983, the office and sales building near the northwest angular corner of the ninety acres, bringing everything back onto the ROL premises.

When I acquired Resthaven in 1964, the NE 30 acres was under agricultural lease to a cotton-farming tenant. It kept down the weeds and produced a small amount of revenue. So gradual was the platting of additional cemetery space that the actual use of that NE

Investment and Business

acreage for cemetery purposes was seen as being decades away, if even during my lifetime. In order to convert it to a more profitable use for the foreseeable future, I conceived of developing an upscale mobile home park on it, with spaced concrete platforms. I personally did a survey of all existing mobile home parks in and around Lubbock, and considered the need. It looked feasible and I applied for proper zoning to proceed on it. As required by Lubbock's zoning ordinance, notice of a change of zoning had to be given to every property owner within a certain distance of the proposed zone. A good client of Norton's lived near there. Norton understandably called her attention to the upcoming hearing and a large opposing crowd showed up. My application was denied.

Still wanting to make the land more productive over the long term, I noticed the attention being given to the development of pecan orchards. Texas has a USDA sponsored pecan orchard operation, and the State of Texas has one. Sam McWhorter and I, and probably Tom Weaver, visited both operations and garnered advice from the personnel there. Together we planned and put in a sub-irrigated pecan orchard with great hopes and expectations. There was one problem we had not given adequate consideration to. Pecan orchards and cemeteries need massive attention during the same growing period in the year. Our first priority was the cemetery. The pecan orchard was an untended stepchild. The effort was not a total waste, however. When I had acquired Resthaven it was loaded with evergreen trees that were increasingly undesirable. About the time the young pecan trees were taking hold, the evergreens were gradually removed and other deciduous trees, including oak, pecan and various other, replaced them but with improved spacing. Most importantly, the cemetery's beautiful entry mall was immensely enhanced by lining it with pecan trees that in time made a most impressive sight upon those entering the premises. And they provided a very desirable quantity of shade for the annual Memorial Day program put on by the park in cooperation with one of the veteran's organizations.

During the operation of Resthaven there were two situations where I found it necessary to discharge an employee that was especially painful to both me and the employee. One of these was a Mexican park employee, a fine man named Jimmy Guerrero, who had worked for Resthaven for several years. The problem that had been observed was his accident-prone tendencies. This danger was serious where there is operation of machinery and possibility of serious injury to people or damage to property. Letting Jimmy go was made especially difficult because of the fact that he had no other income than Social Security to look forward to, even if he was old enough to begin drawing it. While it could be of no help to Jimmy, it was that event that caused me to put in a generous defined benefit pension plan for all employees so that I would not have to go through this difficult situation in future years. While my motivation for creating the plan was for the other employees, as the highest paid employee, it also sheltered a fairly significant retirement benefit for me. Jo Anne also drew a small amount of pay for her service on the board and ended up with a small retirement account. When the plan terminated, in favor of the plan of the purchaser, and all employee accounts became fully vested in the employees upon our sale in 1993, I opted to merge my own plan benefits into the IRA from the law practice.

The other painful situation was the discharge of Sam McWhorter. Sam had been with me from just months after my 1964 purchase of TMP. He was a lovable creature that would not hurt a fly, but just was not getting the job done. Things were deteriorating in the park very badly. Not all of it was Sam's fault, but I had to have a manager who could turn things around. It was a very hard decision to make just out of personal feelings. It hurt Sam and it hurt me inside. But it had to be done. Ron Hillis was a godsend.

The problem was that the original cemetery water lines, installed in 1948, of cast iron, were beginning to leak like sieves. Not only were the mains going out, but we did not know where they were located. We had no maps. Our sod no longer existed. We had goat head and other weeds and tons of legitimate complaints. After Ron came on board, we bowed our backs and went after the problem. We plowed well over $100,000 into a new water system installed by our own people and with our own, or rented, equipment. Ron located the lines, trenched and replaced the original water lines with a good PVC system. We built from there with great emphasis upon good grass, higher quality trees, and regular edging of markers and other maintenance. The turnaround in this area over this time period was absolutely astounding. What had been countless loud and legitimate complaints turned into the most wonderful community chorus of compliments and expressions of appreciation and gratitude, not only from property owners but also from other citizens of the community. Beautiful grass, flowers, and trees were everywhere visible. Ron Hillis, a former marine who had owned his own landscaping business, did an incredible job. He was crushed when his wife left him not long after that to marry a relative of his. His mother, who lived next door to him, took over as mother for their five young children. We were a support to him through these times, as he was a lifesaver to us. The mutual warmth between us has remained to this day. It was hard for me to see the buyer of ROL in 1993 soon let him go. But he has come back each year to head up or be significantly involved in the Memorial Day program.

Reacquisition of the Funeral Home

The year 1979 was very significant for me in more ways than one, but certainly it was one of the most significant in my Resthaven years. From 1968 till then the Resthaven operation was fragmented. I had no control over when it might again become unified, only that if and when the Singleton group decided to sell, I would have the right of first refusal. That time came in 1979 and there was not the slightest question but that I would exercise the opportunity. It did not really come in the form of a right of refusal. Singleton was not foolish on the matter. Soliciting a different buyer without first approaching me would not only expose our inner workings to public display but almost certainly be a futile undertaking in the end. My recollection is that there was not the slightest bit of haggling over price. I believe C. V. Singleton had reached an age and stage of health where he did not want to have to market it to someone else and did not want to scare me off with a price that would force him to do so. And he probably sensed that it was in my interest to reacquire the funeral home operation and that I would not resist any reasonable offer. I also think that his minority stockholders as they then stood, funeral directors from some of his other locations, were probably eager to liquidate their minority interests, particularly with Singleton's age and health in mind. Happily, as I remember, it was a pleasant and smooth transition that accomplished the needs of each side.

As happy as 1979 turned out to be for me, the national and worldwide economy was a nightmare. It is likely that this stark fact was the most significant motivator, insofar as timing was concerned, for the decision of the Singleton group to sell. The first energy crisis had occurred in 1973, and the second was in 1979. The Shah of Iran left his country in early 1979. Oil prices were going through the roof, and interest rates were on their steepest rise for at least a century. A severe recession was forming in the United States that began in July 1981 and lasted through November 1982, stemming from a contractionary monetary policy adopted by the Federal Reserve under Paul Volcker's chairmanship to control the rising inflation. The U. S. was hit by what became known as "stagflation."

During a particular period, whose precise time parameters I do not have, on behalf of both my own funds and the Resthaven trust accounts I then managed, I played the government bond market with such a degree of success that I was told that the Lubbock National Bank's trust department, trustee of the Resthaven-related funds, watched my transactions and placed orders on their account that tracked what I was doing. The movement in these markets was dramatic in the seventies and eighties. My bond trading would have been within the time frame of the last half of the seventies and the early part of the eighties. Investing in equities in those years was tough, which probably accounts for my emphasis upon the treasury bond market. Since all the bonds were purchased through the Federal Reserve Bank of Dallas and were held there for our account, I placed all buy and sell orders through the trust department at Lubbock National Bank, which served as trustee for all Resthaven trust funds. Access to that market otherwise would have been more difficult for me. Some sage said that as between skill and luck, one should take luck every time. While I felt there was some reason behind all my moves, I have to accept that I also was lucky on them. As I recall my King Midas touch finally came to an end, but not in a very costly way. The truth is that following 1982 the equity markets began to command my attention, and the quantity of funds I was managing was expanding rapidly.

It seemed to me that there was a palpable coming together of the personnel and the overall operation within the entire Resthaven organization once the ownership was consolidated and overall planning could be coordinated. Critical to the success in the industry is the ability to do well in pre-need selling of both cemetery inventory and funeral services. Both were subject to regulation by the state of Texas. A certain amount of each cemetery lot sale had to be put into a perpetual care (PC) trust account. We call this trust our "Statutory PC." However, Resthaven always contributed more than the law required, these extra amounts going into what we called "Voluntary PC" accounts, of which some developed over time for specific maintenance purposes. Resthaven was entitled to distribute the income from these funds to provide its care of the cemetery. In truth, the cost of maintaining the cemetery at the level we desired exceeded the income from these funds. But, when our son Mark became president in 1984 and we did a financial analysis on the matter, we came to the recognition that there were both operating and income tax benefits from contributing to these voluntary PC accounts as much as we could reasonably justify, for the contributions could be deducted as operating costs even though the income from the accounts would continue to be perpetually available to help defray cemetery maintenance expenses.

It should be borne in mind that it was not until 1984 that I moved my office to Resthaven. So all of my investment activity and much of my involvement on behalf of Resthaven was conducted from my law office, with clerical assistance from my legal secretary.

From this point forward till the sale in 1993, the operational and investment aspects, though complementary and equally essential to the success of Resthaven, will be discussed separately.

Operational Aspects:
Aspects Affecting both Funeral Home and Cemetery

1. Previously I had mentioned in the segment on *The Smith Firm Years* that the greatest factor motivating me to retire from law practice and move my office to Resthaven was our son Mark's coming back to assume the presidency of Resthaven. The prospect of being able to work with a child in the running of the family business was powerfully alluring, but I could hardly have imagined how effective and meaningful those years of working together would actually be. Mark had wonderful people skills. He related warmly and productively with everyone in all departments. He quickly grasped the operation, and his experience in working while in college, his business degree, and his experiences in Colorado, all served him and Resthaven well. Things were accomplished together that probably could not have come about without the product of our two heads working together.

2. In all my years of professional life I had a legal secretary. Word processors were wonderful enhancers of productivity, but they were a far cry from the mechanical typewriter I had developed great proficiency on in high school and college years. Electrical typewriters threw me, running away when I left my hands on the keys. But they were nothing compared with computers and word processors. When I first moved my office to Resthaven, one of the work force there filled what secretarial needs I had, letters and other documents or

files. But in considering the effective use of our work force, it did not make a lot of sense for me to have a secretary at my beck and call. One day Mark said to me, "Dad, you are just going to have to learn how to use the word processor." Everything about the computer and word processor was maddening to me to the point that I sometimes wished I could slam it against the wall. He was exactly right, of course, and over the years I have come to wonder how I could do anything these days without it. In fact, as the years have rolled by, my steadiness of hand and the legibility of writing have slipped and I avoid writing anything by hand when I can get to my word processor and write it there, even on simple notes to Jo Anne.

3. Our laws require the proper disposition of the remains of every deceased human being. There are many options, but the health and well-being of society necessitate disposition in one of these lawful ways. Licensed funeral homes and cemeteries are essentials in most all of these instances. Aside from the legal requirements and the customs of civilized societies, human beings have a natural tendency to respect the remains of their deceased. That is true even though most everyone knows that the body is no longer the habitation of that human being, for that body served that being through that one's earthly life. It is moving to realize the extent to which our nation, from its combat zones, has spared no effort to find, identify, and return those remains to the next of kin of the deceased. The disposition may be of the simplest option available, including donation as cadaver to schools training those to care for living human bodies.

Those of us serving this need of society must be committed to doing so with the fullest respect to every family, and the remains of its loved one, regardless of how simple the family's choices are.

4. Selling. Selling is essential to a successful operation. While it is perhaps not the most important ingredient for success, no other is more important. Operationally, it is of two types. The first is in "at need" cases, those that have done no pre-need planning. This is normally handled by staff members other than pre-need counselors. But successful operation demands a vigorous pre-need counseling staff,

a sales force, that reaches out to members of the public to plan these difficult things in advance. Most people naturally tend to put it off. It is a service that makes the process far less trying at time of need when all the decisions, including related paperwork, otherwise have to be made. It is far simpler when that has been done in advance. Ideally the pre-need package will include whatever cemetery product (burial, crypt, or niche space, marker, or cremation urn) is desired as well as the selection of funeral product (casket and other itemized options). The price is pegged and the difficult decisions made in advance, especially when it is a choice to be made between mates.

No aspect of a combination funeral home/cemetery operation is more challenging than recruiting, training, and retaining effective pre-need counselors. Not everyone is capable of doing this job, and those who are become priceless employees. Over the years, several names come to me as among our more outstanding counselors: in the early years Lorena Holleyman, then Lillie Elder, Rita Grisham, Troy Myers, and Carroll Jones, a former pastor of ours.

5. For many reasons, cremation has represented a growing mode for disposition of human remains, not always simply because it is a less expensive alternative. It is a highly personal matter. Obviously, the choice of this mode affects both funeral home and cemetery by lowering sales volume, but must and should be offered free from any effort to influence the customer's choice. With the passage of time, more and more funeral homes have installed their own cremation facility. Resthaven was the first to do so in Lubbock.

6. In Texas both funeral home and cemetery sales have aspects that are governed by state law and are subject to periodic reporting and auditing by a particular section of the Texas Banking Commission. In general, Resthaven complied with all requirements and had no problems with that commission. A significant problem was developing near the end of our ownership of Resthaven having to do with my involvement in the investment of trust funds subject to that Commission's governance.

7. In both pre-need and at-need cases, in both funeral home and cemetery, overselling was bad policy and we tried to avoid it. This policy had its greatest application on funerals because of their relatively higher portion of total cost. One case we had pointed up the importance of this policy and the chance to stress it with our personnel. It actually involved two violations of good judgment on the part of the at-need funeral counselor who took care of the family in question. The contract for service was completed and funeral and burial service were completed. But either the insurance policy the family had provided turned out not to be in effect or some other factor caused the cost of service not to be fully paid in advance. The family was simply unable to pay anything more. I instructed that the account be written off, but I also admonished all counselors to avoid trying to sell more costly services without securing full payment (including confirming validity of any life insurance policy where proceeds are assigned). I prepared a form that counselors were required not only to deliver to each family making such final at-need arrangements but that their family representative sign as having received it. The form in effect said, "You do not honor the deceased by spending what is needed by the living." The ministers in town loved this policy also.

The greatest practical guard against such overspending was that we required full payment in advance of the service that was to be performed. Contrary to many types of sales in normal commerce, there is a unique loss of collectability after a funeral service has been completed and the body buried. Disinterment and disposition of the remains is both unthinkable and essentially unlawful since some type of lawful disposition of a body must be made. Of course, funeral and burial expenses have a high priority among claimants in the administration of a decedent's estate, but in most all cases where it would be necessary to file such a claim there are not sufficient non-exempt assets to provide any recovery, especially after attorney's fees.

Requiring full payment before services are provided helps to assure that a family does not spend more than it can reasonably afford. Even in many cases where the family could scrape together the necessary funds, sensitive observation by the counselor, especially after emphasizing the contents of the above-mentioned form, should help to keep a family's selections in a range proper for that family and its circumstances.

8.A memorable trip occurred in about June of 1978 that bore significantly upon each of four of my independent post-1957 activities starting with this death-services section, but also meaningfully a part of the sections on travel, distance running, and music activities still to be covered. The trip was occasioned by an international cemetery convention to be held in Vienna, Austria. So far as I am aware this is the only such international convention held during my involvement in the business, but it was very special. The group visited Vienna's Central Cemetery, "the biggest of almost 50 cemeteries in the city." It was opened in 1874 and is Europe's largest in number of interred. "No cemetery in the world boasts more graves of great classical composers and other famous musicians." These include many who were interred elsewhere prior to 1874 but whose remains were then disinterred and then re-interred here in honorary graves impressively memorialized. Among the famous interred here are Beethoven, Brahms, Schubert, Johann Strauss II, Gluck, Salieri, and Schoenberg. While "Mozart's body is irretrievably lost, buried in an unmarked grave in Vienna's St. Marx Cemetery," perhaps the most impressive marker of all the listed musicians commemorates him in this cemetery. Pictures and descriptions of all these burial sites can be found in an article captioned "Where the Great Composers Go to Decompose," in the footnote below.[1]

In addition to seeing these famous burial sites, while in Vienna we toured both a mortuary and other regular burial sites in this or another of Vienna's more prominent cemeteries. At the mortuary we were fascinated by the location of the crematorium directly under the place where the casket lay briefly in state. After the service,

---

1   See http://www.freerepublic.com/focus/f-chat/1993333/posts.

somehow the floor was opened and the casket lowered directly down for cremation. Cremation had become a predominant mode of disposition of remains. But even burials in these cemeteries were for a period of time only, not permanent. Spaces were not sold but were rented for a term, ten years in most cases. Failure to make all the payments on the ten-year rental would occasion removal. Moreover, failure to maintain the appearance of the grave, which was the responsibility of the family or its friends, also occasioned removal. The rental period could be extended beyond the ten-year period, but as soon as either the extended rental payments or the proper maintenance ended, the remains of the decedent were dug up and disposed of more unceremoniously and the space was prepared for the remains of the next decedent. Obviously, in virtually every case, the time would come, at least within a few generations, when no one would come forward to discharge the dual requirement for extending the period of the interment.

Aspects Primarily Affecting the Funeral Home

9. When I was able to reacquire the funeral home, I disseminated my intent that on funeral services we strive for a level of merchandise and service where we provided the best in town for the lowest cost. It was not feasible to apply the goal to the cemetery since it seemed obvious that, except for those families already tied to the City Cemetery or simply unable to afford the cost, there was no comparison between the quality of our cemetery product with that available elsewhere in Lubbock. Of course, what is the "best in town" is, to a great extent, a subjective matter. But that was to be our goal and we had to feel that we were meeting it or that steps were being taken to meet it. It was always my feeling that across the board this goal was accomplished. We did surveys to determine the cost of all the services provided by other funeral homes, and if the collective cost of the most generally ordered services was lower in any other qualified funeral home, we adjusted our cost levels downward to accomplish this goal. Some judgement had to be made, of

course, because there might be such great disparity in the quality of an item of service in a particular funeral home that it could not be considered the same service. Still, the total dollar level was generally such as to meet this goal.

10. The funding of pre-need funerals is basically of two types, life insurance policy or funeral trust contract, in each case being for the dollar amount of the contract. The contract fixes the price of the service and the schedule of payments to be made. The larger operations normally seem to have owned and operated their own insurance company. I was not interested in owning a life insurance company for that purpose, so we only sold funeral trusts. In each case the shorter the pay period, the greater the benefit to the funeral home because the funding of the policy or the trust was completed earlier and all the earnings therefrom accrued eventually to the funeral home (or its insurance company). These earnings could only be drawn out when the service was rendered or upon the customer's optional cancellation of the contract and withdrawal of the amounts paid in; in the case of insurance contracts, perhaps only the cash surrender value could be withdrawn at customer's option. In the case of our pre-need trust contracts, the principal amounts sans earnings could be withdrawn by the customer. The amounts paid in had to be deposited with the bank trustee by the tenth of the month following payment by the customer. These accounts were carefully audited by the Texas Banking Commissioner's auditors. The investment of the funds by the trustee was governed by the investment provisions of the Texas Trust Act which was couched in normal language about prudence but otherwise not specifically restricted. As it applied to us, I applied the limitations liberally which, as earlier indicated, became an issue with the Commission.

During the period after I had reacquired the funeral home, the dollar amount of our sales of pre-need funeral trusts was impressive to me. While I do not have the records now, my recollection is that it fluctuated around $1,000,000 a year. Over time, this became quite an enhancement to the value of the funeral home operation.

11. Consistent with the growing volume of funeral trust sales, I kept my own records of the reported death notices and obituaries in the local paper, showing the number of cases each month for each of the funeral homes. During the late 1980s and early 1990s, Resthaven reached the point that it was getting over 40% of the total local funerals. The other funeral homes consisted of Rix, Sanders, Franklin-Bartley, Henderson, and two each of Latin and Black funeral homes. In spite of the Latin funeral homes available, many Mexican families seemed to like to use our funeral home because these people were very family oriented and we had space for them to assemble, but most important we permitted their decedent to lie in state in the chapel, especially during Rosary services. We did not get many Black services. But in my record keeping I only kept track of the services rendered by Resthaven and the four other listed funeral homes, including their Latin or Black funeral services.

To show the dramatic change from my early days in the funeral home business, Rix Funeral Home told the dominant Batesville Casket Company that if it sold to us, Rix would not buy from their company. Batesville's sales people apologized for them, but toed the Rix line. In time we buried Rix, figuratively speaking, and Batesville came rushing back with open arms. In my earlier days, the percentage of Lubbock services that were of minority races was relatively small. That is no longer the case today, especially with the growth of the Latin community. Both Latin and Black cases have represented increasing portions of the total deaths in Lubbock. Of course, things have changed very significantly in this respect and in the competition from other funeral homes and the cemetery south of Lubbock from what they were while I still owned the company. In spite of that Resthaven is still one of the leading providers in both funeral and cemetery services, and the population of Lubbock has continued to increase steadily over the years. I follow the obituary page in the paper every day, a holdover habit I will probably never drop.

12. In addition to her participation with me in all events for Resthaven involving travel, and her participation in weekly board

meetings, there were four activities in which Jo Anne was meaningfully involved, three of which she handled without my participation. Beginning with my reacquisition of the funeral home in 1979 the company began to do a good bit of advertising in the various media but particularly on the local network channels. Jo Anne had served in the 1960s as the president of the active Lubbock Women's Club, the youngest president it has had to this day. She had also served as president of the Lubbock County Bar Auxiliary and the Haynes Elementary School PTA, and was active in the CPA auxiliary as well as church and other activities. In short, she was as well known in the community as I had become through my practice and activities. We appeared together in most all of the television advertising.

She alone selected the bronze statuary for the newer Babyland section. This section has personal meaning for us since two of our twelve grandchildren, neither of whose parents lived near Lubbock at the time, died within their first six months and are interred in that section.

During the 1980s Resthaven expanded, revised both interior and exterior layout, and re-decorated and re-furnished the funeral home building. An interior design friend was employed for the decorating and furnishing functions. Jo Anne was fully involved with the decorator in all of that process in which I had little input, other than perhaps on some financial aspects.

Each patron Resthaven served was given or sent a questionnaire for evaluating our service. Jo Anne responded to any and all complaints on these.

13. In 1984 the Federal Trade Commission promulgated rules whereby funeral homes were required to prepare and deliver to anyone requesting it an itemized list of every service they provide and the cost of that service, and to offer to its customers the services selected by the customer at the price set for each such service. It was a healthy rule and did not give us any problem in administering once we had done the necessary cost analyses and prepared our list. It served us well in being able to accomplish our goal of offering

the lowest cost in town. Of course, because of the different mix of items selected that make up the most typical funeral service, and the different prices each funeral home allocated to items on their list, determination of the lowest cost for every family was not something that had a fully scientific answer. But it helped us in making the effort.

14. Far more ominous was something that threw every funeral home that sold pre-need funeral trusts into an absolute funk in 1987. It was the issuance by the IRS of Revenue Ruling 87-127 having to do with the income tax treatment of both customer and funeral home on income earned while the funds were held in trust and at the time of its distribution when the services were rendered. Essentially it provided that the trust was to be treated as a "grantor trust," meaning that the income in the trust attributable to that customer's paid-in funds was to be taxed to the customer each year as it was earned. The funeral home was to be taxed only as distributions were made to it, but it would be taxed on the full distribution of accumulated earnings. I do not remember if there were any advance administrative communications with the industry or whether the ruling just dropped on us like a bomb. My recollection is that we were aware that it was coming down the pike. When it came out, or soon thereafter, the Service made it clear that it would not be applied to funeral trust contracts entered into prior to 1988. This was a huge relief, insofar as it did away with the nightmare of having to communicate these ill tidings to all then existing contract holders. It left in place the sizeable problem of how to handle the allocation of income to contracts sold in the future, when new funds were pooled for investment purposes with those of contracts sold before 1988, and a host of other administrative headaches for the future.

For perspective, when one buys a life insurance policy, the premium payments earn income for the insurance company and none of that income is ever taxed to the holder of the policy (unless surrendered for cash in excess of all premiums paid), nor is there any income to the beneficiary upon the death of the insured. Thus, the customers of funeral homes that had operated using insurance policies, whether issued by their own in-house insurance company or otherwise, were not faced with any threat of taxation on the income from moneys earned on the policy reserve. But probably most funeral homes that did not own their own life insurance company tended to sell funeral trusts under the provisions of state law. All of these funeral homes, including Resthaven, were thrown into a tizzy by the prospect of having to determine how much of the earnings each year were attributable to post-1987 contracts, how that portion should be allocated to post-1987 customers, and what a drag it would be going forward on the marketing of new funeral trusts where the tax burden would have to be disclosed.

In February 1988, the National Funeral Directors Association (NFDA) sent to its members a copyrighted, lengthy analysis of the ruling and its countless aspects, that had been "prepared for the members" by NFDA's tax counsel Bob Wellen, of the law firm Fulbright & Jaworski, in Houston.

Frankly, I do not remember what the ruling's eventual consequence was. As related later, we made gifts of Resthaven's stock in 1987 and in that year's gift tax return stated, in regard to the revenue ruling, "The change was so adverse that commencing January 29, 1988, the corporation ceased indefinitely the sale of such trusts."

Aspects Primarily Affecting the Cemetery

15. Resthaven was a member of the Texas Cemetery Association (TCA), probably the largest and most active cemetery association in the United States. At least after the earliest years, if not also even in them, several of us from Resthaven attended the annual TCA convention, always held in one of the larger Texas cities. Jo Anne and I, along with the president and park superintendent, would regularly attend, and because sales were such an important aspect for all member cemeteries, the manager of the sales force would almost always be there. On occasion our park superintendent or sales manager would be on the part of the program that focused

upon that officer's area of responsibility. These conventions were serious business affairs. They provided a sharing of knowledge and experience, but also established camaraderie between the various institutions and their officers and staff members. The social element was an important part, and along with the gravity of our business there was an offsetting levity in these gatherings. While Resthaven maintained a staff of highly professional funeral directors and morticians, I have no remembrance of their participation in any comparable state association. Certainly I would not have been a member, nor did I ever attend a meeting of such a group. Consequently, even though eventually the revenue from funerals exceeded that from cemetery sales, I always considered myself more of a cemeterian. A signal honor within the TCA came to me, unquestionably through the very considerable influence of the grateful purchaser of our business. I was made a life member of the association, but this was at the end of my involvement. While there may have been one or two others, I only know of one other person who received such an honor who was not in one of the major city operations, being Dallas, Fort Worth, Houston, and San Antonio. It is my understanding that the granting of life memberships was discontinued a few years later.

16. It was perhaps as late as in the 1980s, but certainly well before the end of that decade that a major change was made in the marketing of ground burial spaces. All sections that had been platted and dedicated for ground burial up to that time were for the burial of the remains of one and only one deceased human being. These involved the traditional digging and filling of the space, always done by backhoe. Resthaven would continue with such burials in the sections that had been opened up till then. However, generally all new regular sections that were to be developed were to be for double depth burial. These were in what are called "lawn crypts." The entire burial area in these new developments would be excavated to a depth sufficient to put down a gravel-type drainage of several inches at the bottom. A double-depth concrete crypt would be placed on top of this and then covered with several inches

of dirt that would be sodded over and be sufficient in depth for a healthy root system for the grass. Each double-depth space was to be sold with a standard size bronze marker, which would be ordered and installed after the first interment. The first interment would, of course, go in the lower half, with a concrete shelf placed above it on side ledges to support the interment of the second occupant, normally husband and wife. These spaces proved to be popular with our customers.

17. Not long after Ron Hillis and the park crew finished installing the new water system and reestablishing a healthy sod everywhere, as well as impressive and colorful natural flower areas, we entered upon a new type of undertaking. Outer burial containers were required by our park rules and regulations for all ground burial. This was essential for proper surface management, as well as providing extra protection for the casket and remains. Up until then we had purchased from third-party suppliers all such outer burial containers, which were either vaults or concrete box-shaped casket containers. The latter of these was less expensive and were of a standard reinforced concrete of specific dimensions. Vaults were domed on top and made of more expensive material, either reinforced concrete, metal or ceramic. More of the box-type were sold, but each family made its own selection.

At the point of time in question we began to manufacture our own box-type concrete outer burial containers. Ron Hillis and our son Mark planned and carried out the addition of necessary building modification and equipment acquisition. The maintenance area was enclosed by a wall that closed it off from the open space of the cemetery itself. It was on the east side, well up into the cemetery from 19th Street and over from Frankford Avenue, adjacent to the residential area beyond it to the east. A large variety of substantial vehicular and other equipment was parked in the open area within the wall. But a modern metal building provided both an office for Hillis, a coffee break area for park crew members, and work space out on the concrete floor. In order to manufacture our own concrete containers, the building was extended a good distance on the north end and its ceiling and roof were several feet higher than the rest of the building in order to install an overhead crane system for movement of materials into the molding forms and to move the finished containers for stacking elsewhere. The equipment necessary for this operation would have been quite expensive, but Ron Hillis found a bankruptcy sale in the Oklahoma City area where virtually the complete set of equipment we needed was purchased for a small fraction, like ten cents on the dollar, of what it would have cost new. The operation proved successful and was continued so long as I owned the company. After my sale in 1993, the buyer discontinued such operation since it had its own sources of supply and chose to consolidate its needs rather than have multiple production facilities.

18. In 1975 Tom Weaver led us in establishing the Kneeling Christ in Gethsemane feature in the northernmost section then in development. He commissioned for the project the New York City sculptor, Zuckerman. With the exception of the attractive smaller bronze feature in our newer Babyland section, which Jo Anne selected, all subsequent sculpting art was performed by the young Terrence O'Brien. Our pre-need counselor, Troy Myers, had told us about him. When we asked O'Brien to give us a preliminary presentation he was still farming near Lamesa, a town 55 miles south of Lubbock. We hired him for the first project and that led to the next. He soon gave up farming and did such things as the bronze statue for the Ronald McDonald House in Lubbock, which has been used in many of such charity's locations through the United States.

The first O'Brien sculptures were of the four prophets for the Garden of Prophets section, which was our first lawn crypt section. It was located on the west side of the cemetery next to Frankford Avenue. As that section was being sold out, the circumstances were developing that led to the development of the large circular section just east of it and immediately north of the circular section in which the Kneeling Christ feature was centered. Central to this newer circular section was the most impressive of all Resthaven's cemetery features, the Empty Tomb topped by its descending angel. The bronze statue of the Kneeling Christ stood six feet in height from his knee level. Consistent with that, the descending Angel on the Empty Tomb stood 9½ feet in height without any upper extension of its impressive wings.

The Empty Tomb section and feature might never have come about absent the necessity to dispose of excess dirt generated from the hundreds of ground burials taking place each year. A few years earlier we had begun to deposit all of this in open land on the east boundary just north of the walled maintenance area. A painted concrete block wall about six feet high extended from the maintenance area north along the east boundary separating the cemetery from the adjoining residential area. The time came when the first acre or two north of the maintenance area had dirt piled on the level up as high as the top of the fence. West Texas is not short of west winds which are famously capable of transferring real estate through the air. We were getting an increasing cacophony of understandable complaints from those neighbors under this frequent siege of flying dirt. Something had to be done.

I've always loved the mountains, so I suggested that we needed to create our own mountain in a functional way. And thus came the idea to move all this dirt into this new circular section, an area of about five acres, to create that mountain and put an empty tomb feature on its summit. It was felt that such feature would be most theologically fitting just to the north of the Christ figure in Gethsemane.

We began moving dirt into a mound ascending up to about forty feet above the flat surrounding area, with the empty tomb to go on its summit opening to the east. I wanted a bronze angel to be landing on top of the tomb. For this we commissioned O'Brien to create a small-scale model as a starting point. To begin with, the idea was for its wings to be extending upward as it landed. Simultaneously we were working with an engineering firm on the structural aspects of mounting it. It would be atop a steel pillar buried about forty feet in the ground. The hollow inner core of the angel would house a framework upon which the angel would be mounted. The engineers nixed the idea of wings extending upward, saying that it would be nearly impossible for a structure of the contemplated size with wings extended upward to survive for long in the strong winds that would bear upon it from the west. O'Brien created the impression of an angel that had just landed, doing so by putting a clockwise swirl into the lower part of the wings.

Once O'Brien's small scale model showing this effect was approved, he was commissioned to proceed. It was completed expeditiously and sent to the foundry for casting. It was completed and stored while we tried to solve the question of how to accommodate the Americans with Disabilities Act of 1990 (ADA) requiring ease of access to the disabled. The hill was too steep for direct ascent, the anticipated cost of long circular walkway ramp was daunting, and the ramp would consume hillside that might otherwise be developed into crypt-like entombment sites.

In the midst of these considerations, we were having difficulty contemplating how to construct the tomb. The indicated cost of having it built by artisans out of concrete was about $250,000. So we conceived of the idea of building it out of very large stones of the type used for the base of the Kneeling Christ feature. We bought a flat bed truck and crane and sent Ron Hillis and some of his crew to the Texas hill country to acquire, load, and transport these large stones to Lubbock. Each stone weighed several tons, so several trips were necessary but all were finally accomplished. The only thing was, having all of the stones there, we still could not figure out how we were going to construct the tomb from them. Fortunately, it was about this time when we were contracting for the sale of Resthaven, a subject coming up shortly. One of the conditions to the sale I insisted upon was being involved in the consummation of the feature and completion of the layout of the surrounding section and I had to approve of all of it. The buyer was a large company with a national presence. It had a landscape architect in charge of planning cemetery developments. He made wonderful suggestions with which I completely concurred, including lowering the mountain so that it sloped up gradually starting from the circle's outer perimeter. Converging ramps from the edge to the tomb were in full compliance with the ADA requirements. The buyer had access to concrete artisans who built the empty tomb. The angel, which we had completed earlier was installed. The entire section is an artistic masterpiece and has been accepted by the community with gratitude. Many Easter sunrise services have been held at the tomb.

All of these bronze features represented a considerable enhancement in comparison to the otherwise meaningful two or three molded concrete features developed by the cemetery organizers in the original sections near 19th Street. Pictures and descriptions of all of these new bronze features are available via the Internet.[1]

Low Turnover of Personnel

From the time in 1979 when I reacquired the funeral home, and even before that insofar as the cemetery was concerned, we did not have a problem of high employee turnover; quite the contrary, for it was a stable work environment. Except for the two employees mentioned earlier who had to be let go for operational reasons, Tom

---

1 See my website at bibleandanthroposophy.com, or more fully: http://www.bibleandanthroposophy.com/Smith/main/anthroposophy.html then click "About Edward R. Smith" which brings up http://www.bibleandanthroposophy.com/Smith/main/smith1.html. Then at bottom of page, click "Smith's collaboration on the artistic recreation of Christ's Resurrection" which brings up http://www.bibleandanthroposophy.com/Smith/main/smith3.html. The highlighted links to each of the four sets of photos are as follows:
   1. "See the Prophets" which brings up http://www.bibleandanthroposophy.com/Smith/main/smith3picturesofstatues.html.
   2. "Christ figure kneeling in prayer" which brings up http://www.bibleandanthroposophy.com/Smith/main/smith3jesuskneeling.html.
   3. "See the Angel" (Opens labeled "The Angel at the Tomb") which brings up http://www.bibleandanthroposophy.com/Smith/main/smith3angel.html.
   4. "See the Empty Tomb" (Opens labeled "The Open Tomb") which brings up http://www.bibleandanthroposophy.com/Smith/main/smith3opentomb.html.

Weaver and sales manager John Petree whom Tom took with him to Crown Hill, and our outstanding funeral director Chris Adams who left for a coveted funeral-supply distributorship, there was almost no turnover of personnel. This seemed especially true during the six years that Mark served as president, years that seemed to have a special glow in the cohesiveness of the entire staff. Our year-round staff probably averaged around 33 to 35 employees. Except in later years when we contracted with third parties to provide such workers as their own employees, we always hired more employees, probably eight or ten, in the park during growing season.

Gifts of Resthaven Stock to Children

By 1987 I was becoming concerned about the impact of the Federal estate tax in the case of one or both of us dying. I decided that we should make gifts to our children using our annual gift tax exclusion amounts ($10,000 for 1987 from each of us to each of them) and beyond that a substantial portion of our estate tax exemption. The amount of the latter had been moving up for several years before that and had moved from $500,000 each in 1986 to $600,000 each in 1987. We made gifts on May 18, 1987, December 18, 1987, and again on January 26, 1988.

Before making any gifts we reorganized the stock structure of the company, surrendering all of our shares of common stock for 2,280 shares of the new stock, of which 228 shares were voting common stock and the remaining 2,052 shares were non-voting common stock. While tax law precedent recognized that non-voting shares were worth less than voting shares, in all other respects, as on dividends or liquidation, non-voting common shares were treated the same as voting common shares.

On May 18, 1987, each of us gave our one-half community interest in 207.328 shares of non-voting common stock to each of our three children. On December 18, 1987, the same procedure was followed except a total of 103.664 shares were given to each child. Again, on January 26, 1988, we gave 20.9428 shares of non-voting common stock to them. On the basis of case law precedent, we claimed a 25% reduction in the value of each share given to the children on the grounds that it was non-voting stock. And we claimed a 10% reduction in the value of all common shares for the gifts in December 1987 and January 1988, since two significant negative events had occurred after the May 1987 gifts, namely, the October stock market crash and the issuance of Revenue Ruling 87-127. The full annual gift tax exclusion was claimed on both the 1987 and 1988 gift tax returns, and 74.75% of our $600,000 each estate tax exemption was claimed in 1987. No taxes were reported on the returns, nor were the returns audited.

There was not, in 1987 or 1988, the slightest thought that we would sell Resthaven at any time. With Mark having returned and seemingly solid in the position, we anticipated family ownership and operation for the indefinite future.

Mark Pursues MBA Degree at Tech in Evenings

In the fall of 1997, Mark enrolled in evening school at the Texas Tech Business School, in pursuit of an MBA degree. His daughter Emily had been born on November 15, 1984, and his son Jeremy on March 31, 1986. While it would keep him busy, it is something that he and his wife Jill felt was the thing to do. If that was what they desired, it appeared to me to be of benefit to Resthaven in the long run. Indeed, even during the period of his study, applications of his additional schooling benefitted Resthaven's operations, and seemed to further enhance his capabilities as president and chief operating officer.

In the long run his MBA degree considerably changed the trajectory of our family's ownership and operation of Resthaven. Mark had a perfect 4.0 GPA and was selected to be the student speaker at the Business School's graduation ceremony in the spring of 1990 when he was awarded his degree. I was more than a little bit concerned when Mark told me during that last semester that he wanted to "do the interviews." It came as quite a two-pronged jolt to Jo

Anne and me when Mark and Jill visited with us at home one evening and told us that he had decided to take an offer from Conoco. One jolt was that our only two grandchildren born in Lubbock would be leaving. Emily would be approaching five years of age and Jeremy would be four when they left before 1990 was over. The other was what a loss his great leadership would be for Resthaven. Moreover, it meant that family ownership would soon come to an end, for by then it was obvious that neither of the other two children would choose to come back and make their career here, and Jo Anne was concerned about the ever-present possibility of me dying or becoming incapacitated and the responsibility of the company falling on her shoulders.

As so often happens, what appears to be a dark cloud ends up with a silver lining. In the long run, Mark's move prompted me to move more meaningfully into the next phase of my life, a phase that was even then in its early stages.

The End of Family Ownership of Resthaven

During our years of participation in TCA activities, we had become friends with so many in the larger Texas operations. Among those were the owners and operators of Restland in Richardson (Dallas). George Young, its former owner who had visited with us when we were in the organizational phase of the funeral home, had sold that operation to Stewart Enterprises Inc. (Stewart), of Jefferson, LA (New Orleans). We had established a warm relationship with all the top personnel at Restland, and Jo Anne and I had been in the New Orleans home of Frank Stewart, principal shareholder, whose family I believe had started the Stewart Enterprises operation. By 1990 Stewart had a sizeable national presence in the funeral home/cemetery business.

As soon as Mark's plans to leave Resthaven became known, realizing that I would need to make the earliest favorable disposition of the company I could, our most obvious route to start with was a visit with the top officers of the company in New Orleans to discuss the possibility of negotiating the sale of Resthaven to Stewart. In the time window between Mark's announcement to us of his plans and his departure for Conoco, we were able to promptly schedule a visit with those top personnel. Jo Anne and I, along with Mark, flew to New Orleans. Of course, we took with us our recent financial statements and reports on the various trust funds and our market share of Lubbock funeral services. After leaving this with them to mull over, their executives treated us to the most delightful tour of their New Orleans facilities and we socialized warmly. We were lodged well overnight and then met with these executives the next morning. While we had been with Frank Stewart some the previous day, I believe he was not present when we met to hear what kind of an offer they would make to us.

When I first looked at the sheet upon which the amount was written, I knew that we would not be negotiating further. But the warmth of our friendship was such that I did not want to expressly state my disappointment or say anything that would clearly disparage their offer or seem inappropriate after such warm hospitality—which, of course, was normal treatment of us under the circumstances. Within these limitations I did say, in some manner or other, that we were good friends and that I did not feel we should negotiate further on the matter at this time. Not an unfriendly, and certainly not a hostile, word was spoken by anyone. We parted on that level and returned to Lubbock. As Mark left Resthaven, we had no other specific plan for disposition, nor would time have permitted his participating in any further effort to sell.

The amount Stewart had offered was $3,000,000. While that was 20% higher than the $2,500,000 we had put on the value of Resthaven's stock at the time of the gifts in 1987, having come through the ordeals of that earlier time period, and Resthaven having continued to dramatically rise in its operations, and hence, in my judgement, in its value, I had expected something closer to $5,000,000, and at least $4,000,000.

We continued to operate, but for two reasons I felt the need to try to determine what the business was really worth on the market. A combination funeral home/cemetery operation in a city the size of Lubbock and with comparable economic and competitive factors—it was difficult for me to even imagine finding any comparable sales to go by. Because the operation was increasingly profitable, I was not burning up with the desire to sell it, in spite of Jo Anne's concerns if something happened to me. I was in rather excellent health and physical condition, only about 59 years of age, and had arranged for Katy Pendergrass, a CPA and our comptroller for a few years, to move into the presidency, which she did and was performing well.

Of critical importance to me was to gather some idea of what the value would be for estate tax purposes in the event either of us died. Our share of the stock had been reduced by the 1987 gifts, but what we retained would considerably exceed the two $600,000 estate tax exemptions, and we needed to know how to plan things going forward.

As this concern was percolating, Larry Garrigan, as though prompted by a god friendly to my need, made his exquisitely timed appearance at Resthaven. Larry was a regional marketing representative for a company in Tallahassee, Florida, by the name of Thomas Pierce & Company (TPC). Larry was an effective, but also a warm, welcome, and most helpful presence with Jo Anne and me throughout the rest of our ownership of Resthaven. From Larry's presentation, TPC's credentials for appraisal of our type of business seemed especially fitted to my need for a meaningful evaluation. I related to Larry my need for an appraisal and my probable interest in hiring them, pointing out that it appeared I would need to be selling at some point in the future and that when that time came, if TPC was hired and did a good appraisal job for me at a reasonable fee, it would be well positioned when the time came for me to choose a sales agent.

Jo Anne and I went to Tallahassee to meet the people Larry had told us about. According to Larry, Jon Thomas was not only a licensed funeral director with many connections, but had also been a senator in Florida. Larry also told us the other name partner was Bob Pierce, a CPA with excellent analytical skills. Their staff also included lawyers, agents who bought and sold such properties, and others. They represented both buyers and sellers of operations in this industry.

At the TPC offices, I met privately with Jon and Bob. They offered to do the appraisal for a fee of $3,000. I agreed. In retrospect it was an unbelievably low fee. Surely several times that amount of work went into its preparation.

Once the fee had been agreed upon, Bob advised that they would need to secure detailed operating and other information from our records and our appropriate personnel. Thereupon I made arrangements through Katy to make available to Larry or their other people the information they requested. This was done.

In due course TPC informed me that its work was complete and that Bob Pierce would like to come to Lubbock to present the appraisal to me. He did. In order to absent ourselves from the Resthaven premises for a meeting that was confidential, we met together in the sunroom of our house. Present were just Bob, Larry, Jo Anne and me.

If Bob left any of what their staff had compiled with us, which I doubt, it has been disposed of, although later items they prepared are retained. What they had done is to present every significant purchase and sale of a funeral home/cemetery operation in the United States within a very recent time frame. And there had been several inasmuch as the market was heating up in this industry. National operators were increasingly in competition for the acquisition of the dwindling supply of those still owned in private hands or in hands otherwise offering for sale. On the basis of their analysis I was convinced that they knew what they were talking about. Their appraisal set the value of my operation at $7,000,000. I immediately told them that if they could get that price for it they could proceed as my agent to find a buyer for it.

Investment and Business

Accordingly, TPC proceeded to prepare extensive brochures to send out to prospective purchasers after such purchasers had signed "Confidentiality Letters" with respect to the information sent them. I still have the two brochures they prepared for such purpose, one for the cemetery and one for the funeral home, each about an inch thick. The brochure for the funeral home contains a date at the bottom of certain opening pages stating "11/6/92.9:50am" followed by "Copyright 1992 Thomas, Pierce & Company." The one for the cemetery is identical except the stated time of day is 10:30 a.m. From the fact that two different times of day are given, I judge that these dates and times refer to when the brochures were completed in TPC's office rather than when Bob and Larry met with us in Lubbock to present the appraisal.

These brochures were then sent out, TPC advising each recipient who had signed the confidentiality letter to submit its proposed purchase price and its willingness to send representatives to Lubbock who had the authority to negotiate for the sale. TPC may have suggested a minimum bid. Nine national companies responded sending their proposals as well as expressing their willingness to send such authorized personnel. TPC advised us that nine was too many to invite to Lubbock for such negotiations and that I should select three that I was most interested in coming for that purpose. Even though Stewart Enterprises signed the letter and submitted a proposed bid doubling what it had offered us on our visit in 1990, I felt it had its chance earlier. I did not include it among the three. I chose Service Corporation International (SCI), the largest of all operators, listed on the New York Stock Exchange, The Loewen Group, from Vancouver, British Columbia, then the second largest such operator in North America, and an entrepreneurial company from Indiana.

My best recollection is that both Bob and Larry were present with us when we met with the representatives of these three companies in the sunroom at our house. The four of us (Bob, Larry, Jo Anne and I) met with each company's representative(s) privately (apart from the other representatives) in sequence, each making a pitch for their company and stating what they were offering to pay.

It appeared from its representative that the Indiana company was primarily interested in buying businesses and preparing them for ultimate resale at a profit. I did not like that, and made the decision to pass on it. I do recall that both the SCI and Loewen bids were in the general range of what TPC had told me its market value should be. However, the bid of Loewen was $500,000 less than the SCI bid. My funeral directors had expressed their view that they were not favorably disposed toward SCI, largely because of its acquisition and operation of some funeral supply businesses, including its own casket company. So, in spite of the fact that Loewen's bid was appreciably lower, out of consideration for the views and feelings of Resthaven's funeral directors, I opted to accept the Loewen bid.

Larry went with Jo Anne and me to Vancouver to meet with Ray Loewen and his group the week before Christmas, 1992. As we met, Ray Loewen, the founder of the company, did two things that were alarming to me. First, he attempted to renegotiate the price that his "authorized representatives" had given me in our Lubbock meeting. Second, he asked Jo Anne and me to come with him into his office, obviously for the purpose of getting us away from Larry. This latter is the type of thing that seemed unethical to me coming from my legal background and experience where it is seriously unethical to talk to your opposing counsel's client out of that counsel's presence.

We had indicated to Loewen that we were coming to Vancouver to wrap up the deal according to what had been basically negotiated by his representative in Lubbock. He wanted to wrap it up, but I told him that we would not be doing so during our time up there. In fact, I wanted to go back to my funeral directors and SCI. I told SCI what had happened and said to them that I wanted to assemble every employee in our chapel with SCI sending some of their higher officers in SCI to speak to them. I said if they could convince my employees that they were a worthy company for us to sell to, then I would deal with them. They sent three, one of whom was Bill

Truscott, who was a friend I had known from TCA for a long while. I believe that the second or third top officer in the company was also there. It was a good meeting and my employees were convinced by it.

So, while the SCI officers were all there, Larry went off with them to privately hammer out the details. He came and went a few times. Each time it seemed to me that things were moving my way favorably. Finally, Larry came in with a figure 28.57% higher than the $7,000,000 appraisal figure TPC had given me at the outset. The deal was struck. There was a lot of document preparation, the contract with exhibits being seven or eight inches thick, which I still have.

My recollection was that the sale was closed on February 1, 1993. Both Bob and Larry were there with Jo Anne and me. I think something very important to the sale occurred on that date, causing me to hold it in memory. My thought is that it was probably the date we had all set for closing, which had to be pushed forward because of the amount of document preparation not yet completed by then. That date was also otherwise a very significant one for me, as it would have been the third of three to occur on that date, making it the most memorable day in the year for me: my dad died February 1, 1954 and I started law practice in Lubbock on February 1, 1959. In fact the sale was closed on February 18, 1993.

After the closing, Bob Pierce told me that he had never seen a closing go so smoothly. The contract provided for reductions in the price under certain conditions. I actually anticipated some such reductions. Never were these even checked into by SCI. I think SCI wanted our operation so badly that it did not want to rock the boat by raising any of these before closing. SCI's Bill Truscott told me the day that we reached the agreement at the funeral home in Lubbock that I had made him "the happiest man on earth."

As stated earlier, Resthaven was reorganized prior to any 1987 gifts. I surrendered all of its outstanding common stock in exchange for 2,280 shares of new stock, 228 being voting common and 2052 being non-voting common. The gifts to the children were of non-voting, each child ending up with 331.934 shares, leaving me with 1,056.198 non-voting shares. In December 1992, before all conditions to the contract were in place making it mutually binding, I gave 153.805 non-voting shares to various charities. My intent was to give approximately ten percent of the shares we had left to these charities. That was done and the corporation redeemed these shares immediately prior to the closing of the contract. The amount paid by the corporation in that redemption was exactly $500,000.[1] Jo Anne and I claimed a charitable deduction in our 1992 joint income tax return in the amount of these gifts, and we did not have to include the proceeds of that stock in our reported capital gains on the sale.

The tax basis of my shares was minimal because of the write-downs taken while the Subchapter S corporation election was in effect. That minimal basis carried over to the children on the gifted stock also. The top marginal capital gains tax rate for 1993 was 39.6%, the highest at least since WWII. Collectively between the children and Jo Anne and me, the family's capital gains tax for 1993 was about $2,000,000 of which Jo Anne and I paid about 60%. But each child ended up, after taxes, with approximately $1,000,000 cash. On our joint return, Jo Anne and I paid well over $1,000,000 in capital gain taxes for that year. On my letter to IRS transmitting our check for over $1,000,000, I requested that they kindly return the extra enclosed copy of my letter acknowledging receipt, for which I thanked them in advance. The lady who returned the copy had written on it, "You are very welcome!"

One aspect of my deal with SCI is that it offered me the choice of taking the payment in cash or SCI stock. I chose cash for myself and the children. The closing price of SCI stock on February 1, 1993, was $16.93 per share. Adjusting for stock dividends, that price rose to a high of $45.43 by February 1, 1996. As so adjusted,

---

[1] The $500,000 comprised endowment gifts in the designated amount to the following charities: First United Methodist Church, Lubbock, $200,000; Community Presbyterian Church, Lake City, CO, $100,000; Texas Tech University, $100,000; Anthroposophic Press, Inc., $100,000.

it eventually rose to a high of $88.09 on March 2, 1998. It collapsed significantly between December 31, 1998, and January 4, 1999, and continued thereafter to slide to a comparable price of $3.87 on December 1, 2000. On August 1, 2013, that comparable price was back up to 48.17. At one point in the years after the sale, I told Jo Anne that I did not think she had married much of a genius. But in those years when it became obvious that the industry had paid such high prices in its acquisitions that it found itself in a credit bind and share prices dropped dramatically I told her that I was feeling smarter all the time. At least I think Bernard Baruch might have approved of my choice.

Many interesting anecdotal events occurred during my years of Resthaven's ownership, such as when the Hell's Angels shot holes in the plastic top of our burial set up, or when, in an Asian family's service, the strap on the lowering device under grandma's head broke sending her unceremoniously into the grave head first. The family's post-chapel grave side ritual itself took two hours and the entire litany was preserved by them on video camera. I told our director to tell them there would be no charge for our services and that we would pay them $5,000, thinking we would likely never see them again, including at the court house. It was only a couple of months later when one of grandma's sons came in smiling and said he had another family member to bury. I shamefully wondered if, by chance, they had partially cut through that strap before the service and then caught it all on video. In truth I imagine the video was to send to family back in Asia.

Epilogue on Larry

Larry Garrigan called us a couple of times in the years after our last dealings with TPC. We felt that our transaction had a special place in his heart, as it did in ours. It behooves me to relate the painful last word we received on Larry. During our times together we learned that he was then in his second marriage. He had one child from the first marriage living with its mother in New Jersey, and two children with his then current wife. As we flew from the Vancouver meeting he was anxious to get home to Houston because the very threshold of Christmas was upon us and he wanted to be with his family.

Some time had passed since we had last heard from or of Larry. Desiring to know how things were with him I made a phone call to TPC in Tallahassee. I talked with Bob Pierce who said that Larry had divorced his second wife and married again but had become depressed and taken his own life.

David Horton is a retired Methodist minister of Tallahassee who, like us, has summered in Lake City, Colorado, for many years and while there attends its Presbyterian church. In 2010 or thereabouts, I learned from David that he had known both Jon Thomas and Bob Pierce well. He said that both of them had died. TPC is still doing business in Tallahassee, headed by Jon Thomas II, but now describes its service as "business brokers," especially for small business owners.

Fund Investment Activity During the Resthaven Years

The investment income from the various funds associated with Resthaven's operation, from the time of my acquisition in 1964 until sold in 1993, was extremely important over the years. The modest size of funds in the earliest years not only reduced its significance in those years relative to later but meant that I did not do active investment management of them in that time frame. Only perpetual care funds existed until the sale of funeral trusts began, and then those funeral funds were not under my management from the 1968 sale of the funeral home till it was reacquired in 1979. The modification of the Brown note in 1974 was a highly profitable move from an investment standpoint, as related earlier. Also related earlier is the success I had in trading Treasury bonds from the late 1970s through the early 1980s. Other than in these areas, I do not recall much personal involvement in fund investment activity for Resthaven. What I do remember is that in the rise of the S&P 500 index from the weekly

Investment and Business

low of 62.34 in 1974 till its high of 140.52 in late 1980, a rise of 125.41%, I was getting high investment returns in my law firm IRA, noted by other members of the firm, and I'm sure similar results were being secured in the funds I was managing for Resthaven.[1] So obviously we were doing well with the Resthaven funds, but until the early contributions to the pension plan commenced, only perpetual care funds were involved. These were increasing, but the real explosion of funds began when the funeral home was brought back to me in 1979.

At some point in the early 1980s my emphasis shifted from Treasury bonds to equities. All of our trust funds were held in the trust department of Lubbock National Bank(LNB), which acted as trustee under the Texas Trust Act and the requirements of the Texas laws relating to the types of funds related to Resthaven's operations. LNB had established a relationship with the trust department of Republic National Bank in Dallas (RNB), and through RNB had Discount Brokerage Service (DBS) offering very competitive commissions and expeditious service. However, I did not move Resthaven's business to DBS until sometime probably in or about 1982. For some time prior to that I had used the services of my friend, Curtis Sterling, then with Rauscher Pierce & Co. Years earlier Curtis had hired me to represent him on the sale of his newspaper publishing business in Brownfield, Texas. Curtis gave good service. We (Resthaven and I) were a big account for Curtis. But I was attracted to the lower rates available through DBS and did go ahead and move. Curtis understood, for the difference in rates was substantial. LNB told me that we were the most active client at DBS through these years.

In these years I was "managing" several different Resthaven, personal, and family investment funds. The term "managing" as it related to the Resthaven accounts meant advising LNB as trustee

---

1 To see the weekly S&P 500 index chart from 1960 through the present, see stockcharts.com, at http://stockcharts.com/freecharts/historical/spx1960.html?st=sp+chart+1980+to+present.

what investments to make. It, of course, had the legal right to resist my advice, and an obligation to do so if prudence required it, but our results were rather generally positive, often substantially so, and it never resisted any move I recommended. The funds I was managing consisted of the following:

Resthaven Funds:
    Perpetual care (statutory and voluntary)
    Funeral Trusts
    Pension Plan
Family Funds:
    Our community
    My law firm IRA
    Jo Anne's parents
    Uncle Frost and Aunt Ruth Myers (a double relationship; Frost was a brother to Jo Anne's father and Ruth a sister to Jo Anne's mother; they had no children)

What became obvious was that it was a real headache to invest separately for all these different accounts. My solution was to operate out of a single in-house fund called "Resthaven Associates," at least for Resthaven, our community account and my IRA account. I think the two Myers accounts were handled separately. The details of how I handled that system cannot be recalled, but it seemed to work out quite well for all of the group. It, as well as the fact that I was placing orders, with the trustee's approval, was looked upon with increasing disfavor by the Banking Commission as the years went by, but this did not fester into a serious head until the threshold of our sale in 1993. I was then given a cease and desist order with loss of operating approval if I did not comply by a stated date. But the nature of my investment activity changed significantly after the crash on October 19, 1987, an event about which more appears below.

From the S&P bottom of 103.71 in the fall of 1982 to its August 1987 peak of 335.89, a five-year period, the rise was 223.87%. These were my all-time most fruitful years of market activity. During these years I came to the conclusion that any year that I did not accomplish at least a 25% return was not a good year. For purposes of comparative market activity, the rise of the S&P index from the October 1987 bottom at 223.91 to its high at 1527.46 early in 2000, a twelve plus-year period, was 583.18%. The rise from its bottom of 800.58 in late 2002 to its high at 1561.80 in late 2007, a five-year period, was 95.08%; and its rise from 683.38 in early 2009 to its then high of 1729.86 in August 2013, a four and a half-year period, was 153.13% (this high was eclipsed later that year).

The corrections at the end of each of these three periods of advance were generally swift and steep, but the steepest was in 1987 and the one-day drop on October 19, 1987 was the most severe in S&P index history. I was most fortunate on that day. But first a look at the various advisories or managers I had at various times during the first three of these periods. They included the Value Line Investment Survey, Robert Prechter and his Elliott Wave publication, Ray Dalio, Michael Marsh, the Bank Credit Analyst, and Ira Greenspon. A word about each of these is in order.

1. Value Line Investment Survey—this was a substantial service that gave extensive financial information, commentary, and rankings on the sixteen hundred largest capitalized public companies. They were treated by industry, but each industry and company it comprised was updated each calendar quarter through thirteen weekly issues. I may have started this service during the 1970s. It was not cheap but was very valuable and led to many profitable selections.

2. Robert Prechter and his Elliott Wave publications—in the period between 1982 and 1984 Prechter was becoming the buzz in the industry. He had called the bottom in 1982 and turned very bullish. It was doubtless in either late 1982 or sometime in 1983 that I went to Fort Lauderdale to a one-day or weekend presentation he was giving. I subscribed to his advisory service and studied his book on the Elliott Wave, becoming somewhat proficient in its use through my own charting and telephone advice from them. The

Investment Seminars, Inc. (ISI) was sponsoring investment seminars in various locations in these years, putting together top market advisors. I attended several of these during the 1980s. One of the first of these was two-pronged, the first of which was in NYC, then adjourned to Bermuda. Prechter was in the Bermuda portion. Again I was impressed.

3. Ray Dalio—Yes, this is the same man who, continuing to operate as Bridgewater Associates, many years later became the hottest hedge-fund manager in the industry, amassing a fund that brought his own net worth into the multiple billions, and one of the world's mega-rich persons.[1] ISI soon held another two-pronged investment seminar, first in London and then Lausanne, Switzerland, on the shores of Lake Geneva. As a subscriber to his advisory publication, Jo Anne and I arranged, while on our way to London to go by the offices of Dalio in Westport, Connecticut for a personal meeting with him. He arranged for us to stay in a scenic historical lodging near the water and on a beautiful golf course, and then he met with me in personal conference on our investment activity. He was most down to earth and cordial, but I could tell that his penetration into the technicalities of the markets was immense—way over my head. It was a memorable visit. I continued with him for a while, but eventually, after coming onto Prechter's bandwagon, de-emphasized the Dalio connection. Though my mid-1980s experience with Prechter was very profitable, more so than with Dalio, this obviously turned out to be a major long-term wrong turn in the road. While I've had no further connection with Dalio, or with any hedge fund, my impression of him as a market technician, hedge-fund manager, and as a person, is very high. Having been with him on a most personal and congenial level at one time, I am dazzled by what he has accomplished in the financial world, while still admiring him as a person.

4. Michael Marsh—my memory of how I first met Michael is fuzzy. He may have been a speaker at one of the ISI seminars, or

---

1 See http://en.wikipedia.org/wiki/Ray_Dalio.

Investment and Business

perhaps I found him through some other connection. He was a money manager, living in Geneva, Switzerland. In the mid-1980s I turned a portion of our funds over to him to manage. He moved funds around on an international basis. It was either at the conclusion of the ISI seminar in Lausanne, or after another one at another time in Zurich, but while Marsh was managing some funds for us, that Jo Anne and I went by for a conference with him in Geneva. I well recall staying at a nice hotel on the lake where the rate was $300 per night. I do not think I went to sleep that night, thinking about how much every minute there was costing me. Michael's fee for his services was 20% of his net annual gains, but he did not participate in any net annual losses. He earned some pretty nice fees in 1985 and/or 1986, and it looked like he was heading for a good year in 1987, and then came October 19, 1987. As I will relate, I actually made about $250,000 on the day of the crash, but Michael lost almost the same amount for me that day, having just that day or the day before switched funds between Hong Kong and Japan—I do not remember which direction, but the switch was most unfortunate, probably from Japan to Hong Kong. That year was the end of my relationship with Michael. His fee arrangement worked for him like the house's odds at the casinos in Las Vegas.

5. Bank Credit Analyst (BCA)—I started taking BCA's monthly market analysis during the 1980s. It was well done. I do not remember that I necessarily made or lost a significant amount based on it during those years, but it seemed to be a stable and sound financial analytical service, so I stuck with it. Sticking with it turned out over the very long haul, into current times as I write, to have worked out well.

6. Ira Greenspon—part-owner of a Chicago Commodities brokerage house, formerly a floor trader on the Chicago Mercantile Exchange (Merc). I traded almost feverishly with him from probably about 1985–1986 until at least the crash in 1987, and probably for a short time thereafter. Main trading was done in S&P futures, on which I was heavily short at the time of the crash. I visited in his

home; went running with his attractive wife (he did not run but she did—she wanted to go with me, and she was a good runner); put on a colored trader's jacket he procured for me, and I was on the floor of the Merc with him when one of my orders was placed and executed. Not much later, his wife left him, taking his children, crushing him, and the conditions in commodities trading generally went south. He, and perhaps his firm, ended activity and I lost all contact with him. He told me that I was the only person he knew who, within one trading day, sold an S&P futures contract at the high tick of the day and bought it back at the low tick of the day. It was only on one contract, but that illustrates the superiority of luck over skill.

As mentioned briefly earlier, all of my investment activity prior to September 1, 1984, was conducted from my law office. My time involvement was gradually shifting from practicing law to the affairs of Resthaven, and my secretary's work followed mine on these matters. This was one of the several factors that figured into my retirement from law practice on that date in 1984.

The last of ISI's seminars for which I registered was, again, two-fold. At least that was its structure at the time I registered. The first prong was a week in Sydney, Australia. The second was a week in Hong Kong. Not too long before the date for the Sydney portion, ISI cancelled that week's session because of inadequate registration. These conferences were during the cooler part of the year, since the Sydney part was in the southern hemisphere. Two things probably contributed to the relatively greater interest in Hong Kong. First, it was in the thick of the investment world, and Sydney was not quite at that level of perceived importance at that time. Second, both the cost of the Sydney travel and its distance travel-wise probably influenced many of ISI's clientele.

While it will be mentioned again later in the Travel section, it is also relevant here. Having already blocked out the time for the travel to both destinations, and probably paid for air travel to both, we decided to pass on traveling to Sydney, opting instead to spend that week in Singapore. ISI had offered an optional ten-day, four-city tour of China following the Hong Kong portion. We had signed up for that, so on that full trip we went to Singapore, Hong Kong, and China. Japan had been the powerhouse in the Pacific region up to then. In relation to the rest of the Pacific, things were on the threshold of a massive shift of emphasis. Although as I write this there is some hope and early indication that two decades of deflation and economic stagnation in Japan may be ending, from the time of this ISI undertaking until the present, powerful changes have been made in the relative economic circumstances of Japan in relation to Australia and the emerging nations of Southeast Asia, China, Taiwan, India, Malaysia, Indonesia, and others. Except within the activities of Michael Marsh for our account, the influence of these massive shifts did not enter into my investment activity until after the 20th century ended.

As the period from 1982 through 1987 was coming to an end, more and more funds were coming into the total investment pool that I was handling. At one point, probably in 1987, the actual dollar amount of the investment pool was $14,000,000. While my personal holdings were not insignificant, and on a lesser scale that would be true of the two Myers families' accounts, most of this value was in the various Resthaven accounts, virtually all, if not all, of which was held in trust for various purposes (funerals, perpetual care, or pension). Still, in a sense, with the qualified exception of the pension plan funds, all of the investment income would come down into the ownership of Resthaven at some point, and even the principal of the large funeral trust balance would largely get to the corporation's pockets as it provided the services in later years.

This was a most sobering realization to me during those times, making my trading positions necessarily considerably larger. But what then was taking place was a dramatic leveraging of these amounts into significantly higher levels. I had become fairly adept at trading based upon my hourly charting of the market under the principles of Prechter's Elliott Wave publications. These worked like a charm for me during this period up to and through the crash on October 19, 1987. So substantial was the leverage I had reached that at one point, probably in 1987, it rose to a level of over $100,000,000. To put that in perspective, however, it was composed of three different levels of leverage. To the extent of the basic $14,000,000, there was no leverage. But I was involved in futures contracts, predominantly on the S&P 500 index, though sometimes minimally including Treasury bond or precious metals futures. In retrospect, my fairly informed guess is that these futures contracts leveraged that $14,000,000 exposure to between $40,000,000 and $50,000,000. The rest would have been leverage through options, primarily on the futures contracts. On these, one can lose only the cost of the option, so while the probability of loss is substantial, the amount of it is a small part of the potential leverage. I was generally successful on the futures trading, but not on the options part. I think the gains on the former substantially outweighed the loss on the latter.

During and after the middle days of the 1980s through the period of the 1987 crash, I had subscribed to a service on which I could follow the various markets around the world, and especially the stock and stock futures markets, right down to the detail on how things stood at that moment. It took four seconds from the time of a trade on these exchanges for it to appear on my computer screen. When not otherwise preempted or sensing quietude in the market, I spent the market portion of each day glued to that highly intense activity. I updated my Elliott Wave chart of the S&P every hour, interpreting its likely upcoming direction and keeping the phone close by for a call to either Greenspon or DBS for placement of buy and sell orders. During these times, it was not at all unusual for the immediate net market value of the pooled portfolio to fluctuate as much as $250,000 over a fifteen-minute time frame. That was until October 19, 1987.

The market had actually topped and started down in August 1987, but not yet massively.

By August 1987 Prechter had been getting cautious, admonishing his clientele that a historic high was in the process of occurring and that the fall from that point would be long and often precipitous. He was right on the latter, not the former. The formation that was taking place was what he called a fifth-wave ascending diagonal triangle—or more accurately the fifth of a fifth of a fifth, etc. dating back for at least two centuries, based upon records also from England. From being the raging bull during most of the 1980s, he was a prophet of horrible doom once that triangle had reached its upper apex. For those not familiar with the Elliott Wave, which will be most of my readers, it was heavily based upon the Golden Mean, or more precisely the famous Fibonacci ratio (1.618/1.00). That ratio is reflected not only in the creative spiral of our galaxies but manifests pervasively throughout the physical world's phenomena. It was Prechter's publications that instilled the significance of that creative spiral into the rest of my life's activities.

It may have been that the triangle was completed in August, but if so, that would have been only the very first move down, preliminary to the more precipitous ones that would play out on the wave before long.

Going into October 19, 1987 I was on the edge of my seat observing that the apex of the bounce from that first down move seemed to be playing out in the market's action. When I judged that it was then happening, I sucked up my gut and dramatically increased the number of short S&P futures positions I was holding. My judgment was right on. I had reached that decision a short time before word came from Prechter's offices that the critical point had been reached, and to sell long positions and go 200% short. What happened on October 19, 1987 can hardly be related to anyone who did not live through it. Being so heavily short, the down move was most welcome. However, then it got scary even for me in my heavy short position. The fall was not like anything I had ever had any inkling could happen. Buyers disappeared. If one had been brave enough to step in and buy during that drop, it would have been like trying to catch a speedily accelerating and dropping knife, namely, one would have been crushed. I sat there stunned, one part of me in glee about the explosion upward in value my positions were experiencing. But there was a human element in me realizing that blood was running on the streets in the larger investment community, with doubtless impact upon society.

The market did not close that day at its lowest point, but still the percentage loss for that day was the largest in history in our stock markets. It was 20.47%, the next closest being on October 15, 2008 at 9.03%. But at one point during the day, the drop was, I believe, closer to about 24%.

When the dust of the trading day settled, my net position for the day, on futures contracts and other non-Marsh investment portfolio, was a gain of about $250,000. As mentioned earlier, the funds Michael Marsh was managing took a loss of approximately that same net amount that day. And his funds were at a net loss for me for the year. I relieved him when the calculus of his position dawned on me. Having been generally involved in market enhancement, I had not adequately considered that calculus till then.

But while I was heavily beholden to Prechter for my good results in the 1980s, that ended as the days moved past the crash. While Prechter realized that there would be bounces along the way, he was still totally committed to the idea that October 19, 1987 was just the first salvo in what would be a long and totally destructive decline in our stock markets. Having had good luck following him, I followed him on this in the sense that I became a bear going forward. While it was nothing so dramatic as the decade had been for me up to then, I probably lost a bit of money trying to play the downs and ups for a while.

However, I was in the process of withdrawing my main interests in life from active market activity, opting for what I recall as being a money-market mentality that lasted for years. Not only was it influenced at least well into the nineties by my still paying some attention to Prechter's periodic publications—I had stopped charting myself—but I was in the process of making a life-changing change of direction, one that involved many years of intensive study and eventual publishing on the works of Rudolf Steiner which I first discovered in 1988. This will be the topic of the concluding segment of this autobiography.

Investment and Business

Most notable over the longer run, from an investment standpoint, was the advice that BCA was giving. At the start of the 1990s it began to point to technology and how its rapid development would positively affect the equity markets going forward. BCA was right on the mark, and it stayed that way through most of the 1990s before becoming cautious as the market in the dot.coms became more and more insanely priced.

While Prechter had been good for me in the 1980s, he was a major, probably *the* major, cause of my entirely missing the technology boom and market's upward explosion in the 1990s. It was something of a silver lining, however, that I also missed the crash in that market early in the year 2000. My hesitation to attribute my having missed the technology boom in the 1990s entirely to Prechter's influence is due to the fact that my value structure was changing in a way that required heavy commitment in a different direction.

Fortune had generally smiled on my economic situation, but the time had come for me to step aside from that aspect being more than a maintenance function. Going for further gains was not that important. Preserving what was there, both for me and my family and for the support of charitable endeavors became my focus. Our livelihood since 1993 has depended upon our investments and occasioned my continued involvement in investment activity. But since 1988 it has never been my top focus.

I continued my subscription to Prechter's publication for some years after 1987, but eventually realized that he had been wrong in his projections from that time on, save for short-term moves. At one point I discontinued it, re-subscribing a few years later after the turn of the century, and then later terminating it probably for good.

BCA, on the other hand, has continued to be a helpful advisory. Its available investment services have literally exploded in both number and depth over the years. It is largely now for institutional investors and each of its services is far more pricey than what I had started out with. Finally, within the last couple of years, I subscribed to its Global Investment Survey (GIS) while continuing the monthly reports I had gotten for over two decades. Because I was one of their early customers who had remained faithful, and because I was just an individual investor, and an older one at that, BCA gives me their services that I select at half price. That is still a costly figure, but I have found it worthwhile in relation to the size of our investment portfolio. Except for the time just before the market topped out in late 2007 when the portfolio value approached eight figures, the value has remained pretty constant, modestly higher than the middle seven-figure range. While we do not live lavishly in relation to what we could afford, we do live in comfort relative to the earlier years of our lives and are not deprived of anything we really want. But our wants have remained far below our capacity to provide, and it has been meaningful to contribute a significant portion of our income over the last couple of decades to charities that are important in our minds. Jo Anne and I have essentially the same philosophy on all of this.

The time period during the 1980s when I was so heavily leveraged in the markets was too intense. Because of the tensions it created, not among the most noble, often I've characterized it as the nearest thing to hell on earth that I've experienced.

Previously I've adverted to the increasing admonishments coming from the Banking Commission in regard to my directing the investments within Resthaven's trust funds. The hectic nature of that investment pretty much ended in 1987, becoming more placid in 1988 and beyond. But the practice, such as it was, continued. It was, I think, the more frenetic years that got the Commission's attention and started its requests to desist. The more passive involvement in the last four years of my ownership of Resthaven may have reduced the decibel levels of its constant audit findings on the matter. But the matter did not end. The Commission was becoming more insistent by 1992. Finally, in about the late fall of 1992 it issued the cease and desist order requiring that I cease all investment advice to the trustee, and placing of its trades, on penalty of loss of our license to do business as a cemetery and funeral home.

Whether I was in violation of the governing Texas Trust Act or not would have been an issue for litigation. While not entirely clear one way or the other, I probably stood a good chance to lose on the issue had it come down to the point of challenging the administrative findings, on which the burden of proof might well have been on me. Fortunately, that was a battle I would never have to engage. We were in the process of closing our sale to SCI, one that was very timely in so many different ways.

Charity, Civic Work, Politics, and Travel

These four activities are grouped together in a single section because, while each was present to some degree over the course of my adult years, by my assessment none rose to the level of a major activity like those allotted individual treatment herein. Each was simply incidental to the more dominant spheres of activity. While the charitable element, at least in absolute terms, increased in step with our capability to give, my civic and political involvement was heavier in our earlier days in Lubbock, diminishing in the later years.

Charity

There is no virtue in touting one's charity. One who enjoys any degree of wealth should not feel proud of charitable gifts made, no matter the size or amount. Jo Anne and I have both felt that charitable giving is an essential element of our lives, but we recognize that giving at any level which is not sacrificial and free of fanfare is not spiritually constructive. Public charities happily accept anonymous gifts and usually publicize them as such. But, human nature being what it is, typically these charities find it advantageous to give public recognition to their donors. The Sermon on the Mount sheds light on the spiritual aspect of such giving:

> When you give alms, sound no trumpet before you, as the hypocrites do in the synagogues and in the streets, that they may be praised by men. Truly, I say to you, they have received their reward. But when you give alms, do not let your left hand know what your right had is doing, so that your alms may be in secret; and your Father who sees in secret will reward you. (Matt. 6:3)

Except for occasional help for individuals in need, rarely, if ever, have we risen to that level. But we have felt the need to share our good fortune for many causes of a charitable nature.

In the early days of our marriage and starting our family, when we had to be frugal to stretch my limited earnings to cover our living costs, we gave less than ten percent of our income to charity, and the bigger part of our giving at that time would have been to our church. As our income increased from my law practice and the operations of Resthaven, our giving has gone well above the ten percent, typically a multiple of that, and the portion going to the church has become a smaller percentage of the total. Countless minor gifts ($100.00 or less), including memorials, would always be made throughout the year, but the major gifts would be made toward the end of each year.

After discovering the esoteric Christianity of Rudolf Steiner in 1988, gifts to the Anthroposophic Press (a.k.a. SteinerBooks), for the translation, publication, and dissemination of his works, have been by far the largest single annual gift. Somewhat in order below that have been our gifts in the field of music, specifically to the Lubbock Symphony Orchestra and additions to our endowment at Texas Tech for scholarships in the music department; from there to our churches (mainly in Lubbock, but some also in Colorado); next would be World Vision, followed by Lubbock's South Plains Food Bank, then the Salvation Army and the Lubbock Women's Club Historical Foundation. Jo Anne served as president of the LWC many decades ago, having served at a younger age than any other president to date. She remains an active member there.

Endowment gifts we have made over the years include the following:

1. By far the earliest was to the SMU Law School, in an amount that I estimated would provide a student scholarship about equivalent to the one it granted me.
2. A few years after opening my own law office in Lubbock, we began to create, by annual gifts, an endowment fund at Texas

Tech University, the use of which was originally at the discretion of the University.

3. As mentioned in the previous section dealing with my law practice and business activities, specifically in connection with the sale of Resthaven, we made gifts of Resthaven stock immediately prior to its sale that generated endowment gifts as follows:

   a. First Uni.ted Methodist Church Everliving Trust (for building maintenance), $200,000
   b. The Edward R. & Jo Anne M. Smith Endowment Fund at Texas Tech University, $100,000 as an addition to the endowment fund we had previously started
   c. Community Presbyterian Church, Lake City, Colorado, $100,000
   d. Anthroposophic Press, $100,000

At some time in the 1980s, probably soon after my study of classical piano performance there with Dr. William Westney, we changed the undesignated character of our endowment fund at Tech to be primarily for the music department, after providing a law scholarship in the amount of $1,000 per year. Finally, early in 2012, at the suggestion of the School of Visual and Performing Arts (which includes music), our endowment fund was split into one for the music school and one for the law school, with the larger part (89.05%) going to the music school and the smaller part (10.95%) to the law school. The music school seems to require each of each year's scholarship recipients to write a letter to Jo Anne and me telling something about themselves and thanking us for the scholarship. In recent years there have been about fourteen or fifteen such letters each year, but for the 2013/2014 school year, there were twenty-one such letters.

Texas Tech pools its endowment funds, and the professional management it has used has produced rather consistently good results. The school's policy has been to distribute each year, for its designated purposes, four and one half percent (4½ percent) of the value of the fund at the start of the year. Experience has shown that this policy has permitted its funds to grow in value so as to maintain, or even enhance, their relative benefits over the years.

Civic Work

Becoming involved in his community can be important to a young man beginning a law career. One of my early efforts along that line was in the Optimist Club. An older local downtown club was sponsoring the formation of a new club of "young Optimists." The Midtown Optimist Club was its offspring. I was elected its first president. In order not to interfere with daily work schedules, we chose to make it a breakfast club. Our weekly meetings were at 6:30 a.m. The club survived that first year, but the early morning hours began to take their toll. As our burst of early enthusiasm spent itself, attendance dwindled. The Midtown Optimist Club died a slow death after two or three years, though a small handful of us continued to meet for a while as friends rather than "Optimists." Never again did I join a service club. I was doing okay professionally without it and did not want to make the time commitment.

For a few years in the 1960s, and possibly into the early 1970s, I was involved in some way in the annual United Way drive, not in any high capacity but in making phone solicitations on a list of prospects. And then at one point I served on its budget division, which considered and acted upon the annual requests from the various public-interest organizations the United Way supported.

Not long after Briercroft Savings & Loan Association began operation in the early 1960s, Max Tidmore filed to run for election as Lubbock's mayor. He won the election, and he soon appointed me to serve a three-year term on Lubbock's Planning and Zoning commission. The commission met in the city council chamber one evening a month to take up all planning and zoning requests. Unlike in later years when a more humane procedure was adopted, we met till we had heard and acted upon all requests. Often we would not adjourn until the wee hours of the morning. During the last year of my term, I served as chairman. Roy Grimes, a neighbor across the alley from us, was on the commission during the same time frame. We would drive to and from the monthly meetings together. Roy, several years my senior, held a high office in the naval reserve from which he later retired, but he was preeminent in public education circles in Lubbock, both as a school principal and in the administration of the school district, and later on the school board.

Texas Technological College, as it was known in our earliest years in Lubbock, soon thereafter became Texas Tech University. A major centerpiece of life in Lubbock, to which anyone working for a livelihood here was beholden to offer considerable allegiance, quickly appealed to me as an area of worthwhile activity. I do not actually remember how I became involved, except that I know it was at an early stage of my professional life. We had perhaps already begun to contribute modest amounts toward an endowment fund in the development office there. It was probably in the last half of the 1960s and into the 1970s that I began to serve on the Texas Tech University Foundation board, soon becoming its secretary, and then its chairman, in both capacities also serving on its executive committee. When, later, the Texas Tech University Medical School Foundation was organized, I served as chairman of its board. By some stroke of fate, I am the only person who has served as chairman of both such foundations. Since the medical school foundation has gone through transitions associated with the immense growth of the medical school and its health sciences branch (county hospital), no one else will have the chance to serve in both such chairmanships.

In addition to our endowments at Tech, I (or Jo Anne and I) have had membership in what was first the President's Council and later the Chancellor's Council at Tech. Basically that is a group which anyone can join by making annual gifts at a certain level that go toward student scholarships.

Masonic work is not really a civic activity in the normal sense, but mention is made of it in passing. Jo Anne's father, T. H. Myers ("Doc"), of Wichita Falls, and his brother, Frost O. Myers, of

Charity, Civic Work, Politics, and Travel

Waxahachie, Texas were both thirty-second-degree masons and had also gone the York Route in masonry. Frost had risen to the level of KCCH during his life and was then posthumously awarded the honorary thirty-third degree. Both of these brothers wanted me to take the Masonic work. Respecting their wishes I applied to the Yellowhouse Lodge in Lubbock and attained the Master Mason degree, the so-called "Blue Lodge." It was interesting work, but I had no time to pursue it and never attended meetings or engaged in the lodge's activities after that. In later years, while studying Steiner's work on the subject, I was glad to have had the experience of going through that first degree and gaining some idea of what it was all about.

For some years in the 1960s and '70s, I served on the official board of First United Methodist Church, neither seeking nor wanting a leadership position in it, but by a point in the 1970s I was serving as chairman of the Worship Committee. My main accomplishment in that position, which I often say is "my claim to fame," was the hiring of Gordon McMillan as the combined head organist and choir director. Our former choir director was wanting to resign. Our search for replacement narrowed the list down to one we really wanted to interview and hopefully hire. He was the organist-choir director for a church in Tucson, Arizona. We paid his way to come to Lubbock for a visit. We ended up hiring Gordon, but it was not a simple matter. Gordon is a person with a lively and charismatic personality. He volunteered candidly, almost eagerly, that he was gay, distinguishing himself from his "straight" brother and only sibling, who was a Methodist minister in California. Gordon completely convinced us that we must offer him the job. I often kidded Gordon over the years about his saying in our initial interview, "I cannot imagine why anyone would not want to hire me." Rather than being taken aback by the statement, we thought he had read our minds. We did offer him the job and were a bit concerned when he said he wanted to give it some thought and would be back in touch with us.

Not knowing how gregarious he was, we had made arrangements to lodge him in a downtown motel at a time when the downtown was going the way of so many central cities as action moved outward to new areas, leaving the downtown in a state of virtual desertion, especially at night. While Jo Anne and I were not members of the Lubbock Club, some choir member was and Jo Anne and I, with another member of the Worship Committee, arranged to take Gordon to that club for an elegant dinner atop the First National Bank Building, with its panoramic windows overlooking the city. Unfortunately, and very atypically, there was only one other couple eating there that evening.

When Gordon got back to Tucson, he called saying that he very much appreciated the offer but had decided to stay where he was. Being very disappointed, but not surprised, I told him that we had not put our best foot forward for his visit and insisted that we pay his way back for another visit. He agreed. We had the whole choir, duly prepped for the occasion, at our house for a rousing evening of lively visitation with him, and we put him up with nice lodging in a more active part of town. On the basis of this visit, he accepted the job.

Over the course of the next three decades Gordon McMillan became "Mr. Music" in Lubbock. Not only did he develop a choir program at FUMC that pulled in high quality singers from all over town and from those involved in the music school at Tech, but he put on numerous well attended, high quality Broadway musicals, with auditioned talent, in the civic center. He was a live wire in the music community and the music program at FUMC was one of the city's bragging points.

A few years after the turn of the century he began to think of retirement, targeting his thirtieth year in the position. Unfortunately, he left after his twenty-ninth year as one of the many casualties of an unfortunate period of clerical leadership.

While it will be more fully covered in the spiritual section later, I taught a married couples' class, the Cornerstone Class, at FUMC from the Sunday after Easter in 1963 until Easter Sunday, 1988.

By the middle to late 1970s, as other activities squeezed out time for involvement in civic activities, I avoided, to the extent possible, civic type commitments that would take time away from the demands of my other pressing and personally important projects. The one position that I welcomed in later years was serving on the board of the Lubbock Symphony Orchestra. It commenced as a major project was nearing completion in the year 1997, the year my first book was published. LSO board members were appointed for a three-year term. That could be followed by another three-year term, at the end of which the member's board service must end for at least one year, after which the appointment cycle could be repeated as often as it was mutually acceptable. Accordingly, I served two such six-year stints starting in the 1997/1998 season and ending with the 2008/2009 season. I was invited to serve again in the 2010/2011 season, but declined in view of my age and other continuing personally important involvements. Our substantial financial support of the LSO has, however, continued.

During the years Jo Anne and I spent so much of each summer in Lake City, Colorado, we were associate members of its Community Presbyterian Church (we still are). The church was one of the recipients of Resthaven stock in late 1992 from the sale of which it received $100,000. The gift was designated as an endowment. It more than doubled the amount of the church's existing endowment funds. Such funds were more urgently needed by that church than most, since it employed a full-time pastor and had only a small local membership, thus counting on its summer visitors for much of its financial support. A few years after the gift, I inquired how the endowment funds were invested. To my chagrin, I learned that they were in a CD at the local bank, earning a quite modest income. Hearing that, I expressed concern, if not displeasure. The next thing I knew the session asked me to serve as chairman of a newly formed endowment fund committee. This I did for about fifteen years until after we had transferred our house there to our children and began spending less and less time there each year.

One who thinks about civic involvement per se normally and naturally relates it to the community where the citizen resides. But community can mean one's residential neighborhood or extend to the farthest reaches of the earth. The term community can describe an enormous variety of cross-sections of the planet's peoples, requiring only that the group have some commonality of interest. Accordingly, one of my "communities" has been, is, and will continue to be, the membership and teachers of my Flora, Illinois high school class of 1950. An earlier section covered my high school years. Obviously there was a community during that period. But that period ended over sixty-three years ago as I write, and in some ways the sense of community has grown even stronger as we have advanced in years. Awareness of community doubtless receded from our minds as we headed out into the world from high school. Thanks to the members of the class who remained in Flora, the first efforts to reconnect were taken by many of them. Specifically it had to do with all that is necessary to bring about class reunions. I have no record of just what anniversaries were honored by a reunion. I had nothing to do with this undertaking in those years. Several locals, most notably Bonny Holland Morris, took responsibility and carried these off. Probably the first one was on the tenth anniversary, though possibly the fifth. That local group continued for several decades. Just when Bonnie and her group began to feel overburdened by all the organizational effort required I do not remember. However, some of us far-flung class members became aware of this situation, and with gratitude for all the locals had done, undertook to relieve them from most of these burdens. The locals continued to be active, and on some things it was only they who could do certain tasks. But the responsibility eventually shifted to several of us who had left Flora right out of high school. I'm going to estimate that it was somewhere between the thirty-fifth and forty-fifth anniversary when we took that responsibility off of their shoulders. There were several of us who formed a committee to make decisions. But it was up to someone to chair all of this. That is when

I stepped into the breach and began, in the absence of someone else volunteering, to serve as chairman of our reunion committee and of the reunions themselves, the responsibility that Bonnie had theretofore shouldered.

For a while I believe we met every five years, but as the years passed and we became aware that some were dying, we began to meet twice within each five-year stretch of anniversaries. Eventually, it became obvious to me that we needed a more complete roster of names of members and spouses, addresses, phone numbers, and email addresses. I made up my mind to undertake finding every class member. With the help of computers, white page searches, and the help of class members, I was eventually successful in locating every last member. There were 125 in our graduating class, though in more recent years we have expanded that number to include any student who was in our class during any one of our four high school years, if that member wanted to be counted as a member. I assigned the abbreviation FHS50. The first complete roster was dated October 30, 2003, and it is updated each time there is a change of information. As I write, the total number of class members stands at 154, of whom 87 are still living and 67 are deceased. I am the one who maintains the roster and sends out messages to all those who have email addresses. Tommy Harrell also often sends out messages, and he has a group of classmates who each take responsibility for staying in touch and communicating with certain of those non-email classmates.

While I have retained the responsibility for maintaining the roster and sending out communications to the email membership, after our 60th anniversary reunion in 2010 I advised that I was resigning from chairmanship of the reunion committee and of the reunion itself. Tommy Harrell stepped into that breach for the sixty-second reunion in 2012, but only for that year's reunion. Even though a reunion committee was appointed at that sixty-second reunion, no one has stepped forward to assume the chairmanship, nor has there been any indication that there will be any further reunions. Whether or not there are, our lines of communication remain open. It has been mentioned by some members that a lot of credit for keeping the class together and its spirit so alive is the work I took over from Bonnie and the maintenance of the roster and the communication of information as it comes to me. I have the feeling that there is a special karmic community of those of us in FHS50 and that a great, unifying spirit exists between us, living and dead.

Politics

It was quite natural, I suppose, that coming from a southern Illinois Republican family I should carry that political leaning into my young adult life. Illinois was a two-party state, so it was something of a challenge when we moved to Texas in 1950 to begin trying to adapt myself to existence in a one-party state, one opposite from my own background and leanings. In reality, Texas had two parties, both within the framework of the Democratic Party, one branch being conservative and one liberal. That worked fine so long as it dealt only with Texas, but it created unnatural alignments at the national level where Texas had a voice only in the Democratic Party. The Civil War and its aftermath left powerful embitterment through the South toward the Republican Party that would take generations to overcome.

An interesting polarity presented itself in the second of my three years at Midwestern (1951–1952). Two government courses, one each semester, one American and one Texas, were required. Texas Government was taught by Professor A. F. Edwards and American Government by Associate Professor John G. Tower. It was Tower's only year to teach. He was in the process of a philosophical move from the Democratic to the Republican party and that very year (1952) met and married Joza Lou (Honey) Bullington, daughter of Grover Bullington, of a powerful family within the sparsely populated Republican Party of Texas.[1]

---

1   See http://en.wikipedia.org/wiki/John_Tower.

Professor Edwards, or "Prof" as he was called, was lively and much older. A lifelong Democrat, who made no secret of it, he was well liked and respected by all. He used to say that the Republican Party was the natural place for rich people, a seed planted in my mind that germinated over the following decades. Prof Edwards had taught a Sunday School Class in the First Methodist Church for years.

John Tower, stood a towering 5 feet 3 inches in height. His father, Joe Z. Tower, was a Methodist preacher who had been a pastor at the First Methodist Church in Wichita Falls before our move to Texas. I am told that he was so short that a platform was built for him to stand on so he could see, and be seen by, his congregation.

Tower became politically active after his year of teaching. He was chosen by the state convention to run against Lyndon Johnson for U. S. Senate in 1960. Johnson, of course, won, but having at that time been running for both Vice President and Senator, his senate seat was open and a special election was held in an off year. Five Democrats of various persuasions were in the free-for-all election. Tower, the only Republican, got far more votes than his nearest opponent, William A. Blakley. The two top vote getters were then paired in the runoff. The Democratic electorate was not unified behind Blakley. Tower won. John knew me (as "Eddie") and we were friendly. Jo Anne and I made plans for me to go to DC for his swearing-in ceremony. I had been able to schedule a conference with the appellate division of the IRS in Dallas that meshed nicely with my flight schedule to DC. While in that conference, the previously-mentioned call came that Jo Anne's water had broken and that I should immediately head back to Lubbock for she would deliver our baby before the day was out. Our daughter Jill, now Jillian, was born that evening. I missed the swearing in, but got the better end of that deal.

Over the next nine years I would be Lubbock County chairman for the following four different Republican candidates: Robert

Morris for governor, 1962; Bill Hayes for Lieutenant Governor, 1966; Eddie Paxton for the Texas legislature, 1968; Congressman George H. W. Bush for U. S. Senate, 1970. Morris and Hayes lost both statewide and Lubbock County. Paxton lost in his legislative district. Bush lost statewide but carried Lubbock County.

Memorable experiences as Bush's Lubbock County chairman included telephone conversations with his Harris County (Houston) campaign chairman, James Baker, whose active political life in the national arena would later gain prominence.[1] From the first, I was impressed with Baker's simple and friendly directness. Also notable in hindsight is that I brought Bush to our house briefly in the course of one of his campaign rallies in Lubbock. Bush's capabilities were obvious to me as he spoke responsively to groups here in Lubbock.

During the 1960s and at least into the 1970s I regularly attended our Republican precinct and county conventions and on at least one or two conventions was chosen as a delegate to the state convention. I remained supportive of Republican candidates at the ballot box through both of Ronald Reagan's campaigns, and my personal affection for Reagan never waned. However, it was during his time in office that a combination of circumstances both within the Republican Party and within my own inner convictions led me to part ways with the party of my ancestral family. It is ironic, in some ways sadly so, that the year of my first change at the ballot box was 1988, the year my former candidate, George H. W. Bush, was elected President. The sad aspect is that my change had nothing to do with any lessening of high personal respect for the man himself, a respect that I have retained to this day. With this change, aside from supporting Democratic candidates at the ballot box, I have become totally inactive in politics, devoting my efforts in areas that have become far more important to me. But that is for a later section of my life's account.

---

1 See http://en.wikipedia.org/wiki/James_Baker.

Travel

For those fortunate enough to be able to do it, travel is a condiment of life, not one of its major activities. At least such has it been for me. My temperament would never permit it to be more than that. By our early thirties, our circumstances were improving to the point that travel was increasingly an option that we exercised with great satisfaction, within such limits, on a fairly regular basis for several decades. We traveled by car, plane, and ship, and fortunately are old enough to remember when flying, even in coach seats, was a pleasant experience. In recent years, the latter has ceased to be the case. While flying remains an occasional necessity, it is seldom comfortable or stress free. Advancing years have magnified its negatives. Even other modes of travel have suffered in removing, for their term, the increasingly attractive comforts of home.

But in those years when both our family and financial situation opened wide our travel options, we did experience many memorable trips and experiences. Those we remember will be given with little elaboration beyond simply listing them. As it became apparent that we were approaching this time around thirty years of age, we realized that we would be offered so many more opportunities for travel than our parents had been able to enjoy. As mentioned in an earlier section, before we began to travel, we borrowed enough money to give our parents, Jo Anne's parents and my mother, adequate funds for them to go on a European travel tour. This they did together with seemingly great appreciation and enjoyment.

When Jo Anne and I reflect back through our now almost sixty years of marriage, we made a lot of trips, so many that if all were given mention it might belie their mere "condiment" status. But in reality, when those that were only incidental to some major activities of my life are excluded, the balance, spread over the time period involved, do not constitute a major separate life activity, at least not in my mind.

Most all of our travel will fit into one or more of the following categories:

> Incidental travel related to:
> Military Service
> Investment and Business
> Writing
> Raising Young Family
> Family affairs
> Other travel purely for diversion,
> pleasure, and/or personal discovery

Military Service

The "Army" section described these travels. Aside from experiences normal from living in Southern California for a year and a half, and three prior weeks in San Francisco, the explorations of northern Arizona's many natural wonders, while on army audit assignments at the significant Navajo Ordnance Depot west of Flagstaff, stood out and are warmly remembered. These include the Grand Canyon, especially the Labor Day weekend with the other Ed Smith hiking into the Havasupai Indian reservation in the western canyon area; climbing Humphreys Peak (12,637 feet elevation), the highest point in Arizona, in the San Francisco Peaks Range just north of Flagstaff; hiking down to the river from the Grand Canyon's south rim; Jo Anne and I riding a mule to the river and back from the south rim; romping in Oak Creek Canyon south of Flagstaff; the Painted Desert east of Flagstaff, Navajo Indian pole dancing in Prescott; Sedona before its later expansion; Flagstaff itself while it was still a simple, small community; and various other regional attractions.

Investment and Business

These included the delightfully arranged ISI (Investment Seminars, Inc.) conferences in the mid-1980s. Specifically described were those to New York City, Bermuda, London, Lausanne (Switzerland), Sydney (Australia; canceled), Singapore, Hong Kong (with optional ten-day tour of China in 1986 to the cities of Beijing, Xian, Guangzhou, and Shanghai). A separate conference was held in Zurich (Switzerland), from which we traveled on our own over to Geneva to meet Michael Marsh there as previously described. The couple that organized these ISI seminars were canny in combining impressive investment speakers with nice accommodations in appealing locations. Their meetings were highly informative and very valuable as investment was becoming an increasingly demanding activity in my life in that time frame. These trips were delightful travel experiences, and the associations while there were both pleasant and informative.

Also described in the Investment and Business section was the visit to Vienna, Austria for the international cemetery meeting, and the travel following that, which included the visit with Hermann and Dorothea Schlumbaum in Wennigsen, Germany, near Hanover.

Following the visit to Bermuda, where I first heard Robert Prechter, of Elliott Wave fame, speak, I attended, without Jo Anne, a weekend lecture series he gave in Fort Lauderdale, Florida.

Writing

We enjoyed a great variety of travel to major cities in the United States and Canada after I joined the AAR/SBL (American Association of Religion/Society of Biblical Literature) and began to attend their annual conventions. The AAR and SBL were separate entities, but sufficiently related in common interests that they held their conventions together except for a few years when the AAR chose to meet separately. When that happened, I discontinued membership in the AAR and attended only the SBL convention. Happily AAR realized its mistake after a few years and the two began holding joint conventions again. I discontinued my active membership in the SBL in 2012, but am still listed as a retired, inactive member. The size of their joint membership rosters, as well as their convention attendance, was so substantial that they could only meet in large cities where the central convention center and all the major hotels around it could be blocked out several years in advance. During the fourteen years (1998 through 2011) of my SBL membership, the annual convention was held in the following cities (always all day Saturday through Monday and half day on Tuesday): Orlando (1998), Boston (1999), Nashville (2000), Denver (2001), Toronto (2002), Atlanta (2003), San Antonio (2004), Philadelphia (2005), Washington, DC (2006), San Diego(2007), Boston (2008), New Orleans (2009), Atlanta (2010), and San Francisco (2011).

Jo Anne attended all of these with me except the one in Nashville. Typically she could explore more than I since the convention occupied a fair portion of my time. My publisher had a booth in the exhibit hall, and when I was not attending one from the enormous menu of papers, I would spend some time in its booth, as well as exploring the numerous other exhibit booths.

Also associated with my writing was attending the annual SteinerBooks Seminar held each year, starting in 2004 in mid-March in the spacious top floor meeting room of the student union building at NYU. The floor to ceiling windows gave a spectacular view looking north over Manhattan. I was a speaker on the program in 2004 and 2012, and have made all of them to date through 2013. Since two of our three children live, with their families, near Philadelphia, this annual meeting was an opportunity to visit them during the trip. New York City has a special mystique that made this annual visit special.

Raising Young Family

All of the memorable travel done as part of the process of raising our young family comprised the following four distinct categories of trip: auto-camper; Lake City, Colorado camping and hiking in the San Juan Mountains; skiing; and three that were special while the boys were in high school.

The Auto Camper

The year our daughter Jill (now Jillian) turned five, in 1966, we bought a tent-top camper trailer. We rented it for a week, with an option to apply the rental on its purchase price at the end of the week. Our immediate objective was a trip to Big Bend National Park on the Rio Grande, across from Mexico. A huge storm hit us our first night there. I said to myself as I watched the top bend and sway in the furious wind and rain, "Baby, if you hold, you are mine." It held, and it became mine at the end of the week. We kept it for probably eight or nine years, when, it having served us well, we donated it to a local charity. A lot of fun trips were made in it, some right here in the state of Texas, to both the easternmost and western-most points of the state. But the most memorable were the two three-week trips we made in it in the summers of 1967 and 1968. The 1967 trip, which was the best one of all we were to make, was up through Colorado. We've seen so much of Colorado that I cannot be entirely sure, but I believe that is the trip when we visited the Dinosaur National Monument in the NW corner of Colorado before proceeding up through Jackson Hole, Wyoming. We camped there in Teton Village, where Jillian went off exploring on a trail by herself and was incensed when a Park Service Ranger, whose help we had sought, saw her strolling nonchalantly by herself and brought her back to us. From Grand Teton, we drove observingly through Yellowstone National Park before exiting the west side into SW Montana, then north to Glacier National Park. By tragic coincidence, just as we were nearing Glacier, the news reported that two girls who were tent camping in different locations in west Glacier had been mauled and killed during the night by a Grizzly bear or bears.[1] We stopped at a ranger station and inquired about what precautions to take in hiking, since the kids and I planned to hike to the Grinnell Glacier. We were advised to make a good bit

---

1 These incidents appear to be covered in Jack Olsen's book, *Night of the Grizzlies* (see http://en.wikipedia.org/wiki/Night_of_the_Grizzlies).

of noise so that we would not surprise a bear. We bought bells for our belts, carried tin cans with rocks in them to shake, and had a rule that someone in the group had to be talking or singing all the time. We made so much racket that hikers approaching us always seemed to be laughing. It was a beautiful hike. We did make it to the glacier area. Not only was Glacier our favorite national park to visit, but the campsite there was the best we ever had. From Glacier we crossed over into Canada, going north to Calgary then west to Banff and the beautiful, nearby Lake Louise, visiting its lodge, then north on the Banff–Jasper highway to a campsite just shy of Jasper before retracing back down that breathtakingly scenic route. We went out on the Columbian Ice Field, stopped at the Athabasca Falls where the ground beneath our feet shook from the mighty force of the falls, which seemed to me more powerful than Niagara Falls, though perhaps not so wide. From the Lake Louise–Banff area we crossed over to the west side of the divide dropping down through Kootenay National Park (Canadian) and made our return trip home.

Our route for the 1968 trip took us first to an area of the west coast by way of Yosemite National Park where we camped and explored. Detailed memory fails us on just where we got to the coast, but doubtless we started our coastal drive north not too far north of San Francisco, perhaps moving inland for brief stretches. The most distinct memory we have of that drive north was discovering our first Shakey's Pizza. It was in Coos Bay, Oregon. Shakey's Pizza parlors were, for us, a delightful comet that inflamed our pizza appetites for a short while and then disappeared. But that event has not disappeared from the memory of a single member of our family. Ironically, with all that we experienced in those three weeks, it has remained the single most immediately identifying event of that vacation. Our trip took us to Vancouver, BC, whence we boarded our car and camper on a ferry to Vancouver Island, exploring its southern area, especially beautiful Victoria at the south end. We probably took a different ferry back to the mainland. Our return trip took us back through Lake City, Colorado, where we set up the trailer for a night, then on home.

We made many other family trips in the camper, including many national parks or monuments, primarily in the West or Midwest. In the early years, I had to be responsible, with a bit of help from Jo Anne and/or the boys, for getting the camper leveled and stabilized before we could occupy it. However, the boys were growing and learning, and in short order they had picked up the essentials and before our camper days were over, they did the setting up by themselves with little, if any, help from me. A rule was instituted that no one, at least not the boys, could go to the toilet before the camper had been duly and properly set up. That made for a fast, if not always the best, set up. But their efficiency was good.

Lake City, Colorado, and the San Juan Mountains

No other location has been our travel destination as much as Lake City, Colorado, which will be described more fully later, but during the years that we had the camper, it went with us every year to Lake City. We were familiar with all the campgrounds there. We did not need, and could not use, camper hook-ups, like those in town, required by more elaborate trailers or recreational vehicles. We used only rustic sites in the mountains. The most frequently used were those on the east side of Lake San Cristobal, the large naturally formed lake for which the town is named. The water level of the lake is at nine thousand feet. The elevation of the campsites overlooking the lake from its east side was considerably higher. The memories of those wonderful family days together are deeply etched into the being of each of our children and ours as well. The children and I hiked the mountain trails a lot. Jo Anne, never an athletic individual, found other ways to enjoy the area and its beautiful outdoors, including visiting the little shops in town or just sitting at the campsite reading in peace.

Mark and Michael were active in the Boy Scout troop sponsored by our church. I was not a scout leader or assistant, but I did lead the "mountain men" backpacking trip for three years. The first year would have been in 1971. The troop went to the scout camp at Tres Ritos, New Mexico. I merely assisted that year as another father was the leader. However, in the summers of 1972 and 1973 I led the backpacking group. But I said that if I was going to lead it, it would have to be in the higher mountains of Colorado, which it was. The base camp for all the boys was located at the ghost town called Capitol City, located ten miles or so up Henson Creek west of Lake City. The mountain men group (mostly ages fourteen and fifteen) left from there and packed over the higher ranges and back, climbing Uncompahgre Peak (14,305") on the way. We were only out on the trail three or four days and intervening nights, but covered quite a distance on foot.

During each child's college days, I made it a point to go on a backpacking trip with that child—just the two of us. As I recall, each trip was for three days and two nights. The trip with Michael was in mid-August 1979, the one with Mark was in late July 1980, and the one with Jill (Jillian) was in mid-August 1982. For a number of years I owned a half interest with the late Bill Hall, of Lake City, in 550 acres where the Fourth of July Creek enters the Lake Fork of the Gunnison River. The trip with each boy went up the trail by that Creek and then on up over the ridge far above it and down to Powderhorn Lakes on the far side. We caught trout for our breakfast in a little stream that ran out of the lake and not far from our campsite. In the evening we roasted marshmallows over the embers of the campfire. Michael had a mustache above his upper lip at that time. He got his first marshmallow tangled up in the mustache and found that getting it out in the frigid stream water was too much of a challenge. He roasted no more marshmallows. Mark and I descended into the wrong canyon and had to climb back up and make our way south to the next one over. On the way between the canyons, a Mexican shepherd saw us coming toward his tent and came over to greet us. He could not speak English nor we Spanish. However, he invited us into his tent and offered to heat up some coffee, which we accepted. It was old and strong, but we toughed it out, and I gave him two dollars for the courtesy and we were off again. At least it was out of the wind and warmer in the tent.

Jillian opted for a different trail, on the other side of the Lake Fork valley. We climbed up to the camp below Crystal Peak, then north to where we could go over that ridge and down the Ridge Stock Driveway to the edge of the forest near the headwaters of Big Blue Creek where we camped for the second night. Both water and wood were available, but we were both so tired that we ate something cold for supper and got in our sleeping bags for the night. Jillian had cut her foot badly at a swimming pool shortly before our trip, and it became difficult for her to carry her pack back down from that campsite to the North Henson Creek road that led back to the main road along Henson Creek toward Lake City. I ended up carrying both of our packs some of the way and then leaving her at a decent resting place and going on down to where I could catch a ride into town and bring a vehicle back up for her.

These one-on-one backpacking trips were special for me, and I believe also for each child.

Skiing

Skiing is an athletic activity that was completely foreign to me in my youth. For those in the vicinity of mountains, especially in Colorado, it doubtless was an activity even then available to some. However, the increasing, general popularity of skiing seemed to be a phenomenon focused very much on the very years when our children were exposed to it among their peers. It is a winter sport, and my love of the mountains was summer oriented. But by the time the boys were in junior high, or what is now often called middle school, they were mounting a serious request that we get into skiing. Jo Anne was not at all inclined to it herself, and probably would not have been even without having then recently had disc surgery on her back. But take up skiing we did, as it could be worked into our schedules, especially during school holidays or breaks. They were always family trips, but only the children and I participated while Jo Anne would have hot chocolate or other good things ready for us when we returned. Our first exposure was at the ski resort at Ruidoso, New Mexico. The four of us took a day of lessons, and we were off and running, so to speak. We purchased the necessary skis, boots, poles, and essential ski wear for everyone, and made one or two ski trips to New Mexico or Colorado ski areas each season. None of us became skilled to the point of "paralleling," that pretty form where the skier seems to move so fluidly with skis together and legs, hips, and torso swaying seemingly so effortlessly down the run, or through the fresh snow where available. But we could get down most of the runs, even those with moguls, without doing too much damage to ourselves or others, and on a big part of the runs we could go from top to bottom at a pretty good clip without stopping. So long as the children were still at home, or came home from college, I continued to ski with them. But when they had moved on, it was not a sport that I cared for enough to continue it alone, hence my skiing days came to an end.

The Three Special Trips

For me, high school was four years, the ninth through the twelfth grades, called the freshman, sophomore, junior and senior years. But for Jo Anne and our children, here in Texas, high school was only the last three years, tenth through twelfth, or sophomore through senior. It was during spring break in March in the boys' three high school years, 1974 through 1976, that we all did a special family trip together. For the first of these, we flew to Washington, DC, to expose the children to our nation's capital and several of its institutions, monuments, and other attractions. We visited our Congressman George Mahon's office. He was chairman of the powerful House Appropriations Committee, and was also a genial and attentive host for our brief visit. For the second trip we flew to Mexico City, and after some sight-seeing there boarded a bus for a trip to Cuernavaca, thence to Acapulco for sunning and swimming on the beach and getting our first taste of Mexico beyond the border towns. Our third and last of these trips was to Hawaii, where we toured three of the islands, Oahu, Hawaii, and Maui, in that order. We flew between the islands and rented a car on each of them. It was a very full week. We drove almost completely around the big island. It was a long drive and there were many sights to see and places to explore. Our main time on the beach was at Maui, but there were also interesting things to see and explore on that island as well. Decades later Jo Anne and I would travel to and explore the fourth island, Kauai, but our earlier week with the children could not be stretched to include that one.

Family Affairs

When a couple makes their home, and pursues their livelihood, hundreds of miles from the families of their youth, it makes for a lot of simply mundane travel for special events, such as holidays, funerals, and weddings, as well as trips just to stay connected. We have lived in Lubbock, Texas since early 1959. Jo Anne's family lived in Wichita Falls, some 220 miles east of Lubbock, and my mother and living relatives were primarily in Flora, Illinois, approximately 1,000 miles NE of Lubbock. Once Eisenhower's interstate highways were essentially in place, travel to Illinois became much easier, especially with the toll roads through Oklahoma. We drove on countless trips to each of these birthplaces. There was nothing exotic about these stretches, so much so that it is to a great extent a misnomer to characterize them as "travel." As trips to these ancestral homes became less frequent with the deaths of our parents, trips to the homes of our children took their place. Son Michael is the only one whose career has been in Texas, in the Dallas-Fort Worth metropolitan area, while son Mark has largely been in Wilmington, Delaware and daughter Jillian in Bucks County, Pennsylvania, mainly in Newtown. We have made quite a few trips to these respective areas, but as we advance in years travel to these areas may become less frequent or even come to an end. In the late years of her life, mother often said that she just could not travel from Flora to Lubbock any more. We understood then, and have even greater understanding now.

Other Travel Purely for Diversion, Pleasure, and/or Personal Discovery

Except as is otherwise obvious in the telling, these are travels that Jo Anne and I did by and for ourselves. Except for the first two sections, each of which spanned many years, they are mentioned in the chronological order in which they occurred.

The Lake City Years (1960–2012)

Lake City, Colorado, is in a category all by itself. In a sense it was not "travel," but rather a place special in our lives and those of our children. The first summer we were in Lubbock, 1959, we took our vacation on the Conejas River just inside Colorado's southern border, west of Antonito. It only whetted my appetite. I got a good map of Colorado that fall and studied it to find the place with the highest mountains and the fewest people. It sort of stood out like a sore thumb. It was the surrounds of Lake City. Its Hinsdale County has five "fourteeners" within its borders. The county is the least populated of the sixty-four counties in the state. Here is its official population count for the years we have spent there: 1960 (208), 1970 (202), 1980 (408), 1990 (467), 2000 (790), 2010 (843), 2012 est. (810).[1] Of course, due to summer residents, such as we were, and vacationers, these numbers swell in the summer months. Jo Anne and I failed to visit Lake City in only one year between 1960 and 2012, and that was because our camper trip simply did not take us by there or allow enough vacation time to go otherwise. Typically we would spend our vacation, normally two weeks, there. As departure time neared, and as we drove away, I was always seized with a deep melancholy, thinking that it would be another year before we could get back. I always said that I did not want to own a second home until I could

---

1 See http://en.wikipedia.org/wiki/Hinsdale_County,_Colorado.

afford to spend a major portion of the year there. For twenty years (1987–2007) we owned our dream home there, spending four to five of the warmer months in it. Not only were those years when affording it was not a problem, but they were years in which I could do the work I needed to do from my office in our house.

In the earlier years I did a lot of trout fishing in the streams, but as the years went by I gave that up in favor of hiking the trails and climbing the mountains. For many years I organized a weekly hike and could transport myself and four other hikers to trailhead in our 1988 Toyota Land Cruiser. Jo Anne had less to look forward to and do there than I did. Realizing that my own high country abilities were receding and that she was less and less desirous of spending so much time there, I said to her one day, "I think the time has probably come to sell our place." It was a hard decision for me to come to, but I knew it was the right one, and certainly one that she appreciated. The decision to list it for sale was made rather immediately and our children, who had been raised going there every summer, were informed. Mark and Jillian and their families lived near Philadelphia and were not able to utilize the house as much as Michael's family, who lived in Colleyville, Texas. He moaned at our decision. While we did not encourage him to acquire the house, it was his desire to do so. Consequently we worked out a complicated arrangement to convey the property to the children equally by gift, but in such a way that he ended up with the house, encumbered by a third party loan, and the other two children with cash equal in value to the house equity that Michael got. The gifts were spread over a period of six years to avoid gift taxes. Unfortunately, the arrangement in 2007 was right at the peak of the market, and in the long run has not worked out well for him or us financially (we still own an adjoining lot that has also fallen in value and failed thus far to sell). Up through 2012, by agreeing to pay him a proportionate amount of his annual tax, dues, and upkeep expenses, we have spent some time in the house.

It is hard for me to express the depth of feeling I have as I remember all the years and all the trails and mountains that I hiked and climbed. It is like a deep ache, yet one for the experiencing and memories of which I am so grateful.

The Puerto Vallarta Years (1983–1997)

The only other place we traveled for personal relaxation and enjoyment over a stretch of several consecutive years was Puerto Vallarta (PV)—fifteen years, starting in 1983 and ending in 1997. These were winter travels that were a seasonal counterbalance to the summers in Lake City. Our first trip to PV was for a week starting on Christmas, 1983. It was not long before we increased our stay to two weeks. We actually made more than one trip in one or both of the first two years, including one in June. We stayed at the Sheraton, a bit less than a mile north of downtown, on our first three trips. On these, we walked to and from town, and kept noticing a Mexican hotel, the Rosita, at the north end of the Malacon, the wide and scenic walkway that was open to the sea but raised a few feet above the beach. Shops and restaurants lined the other side of the street from the Malacon. During our last stay at the Sheraton, we became curious about this Rosita hotel. We went in to inquire and inspect. It was perfectly located to enjoy the Malacon and the downtown. The room prices were a small fraction of those at the Sheraton—like $20 a night versus over $100. They increased over the years, but were always priced well below the hotels north of town, and the rooms were clean and nice. We made a reservation there for the year ahead and followed that practice over the years, quickly learning that room 8 (ocho) was the most desired. Three rooms on the ground floor had patios facing the sea, and room 8's patio was the largest. Reserving it a year in advance, with deposit, worked out well. To elaborate all the things that were so enjoyable and memorable to us in those years would take more space than I should use. It is perhaps enough to say that many years later Jo Anne and I were eating in a booth in a restaurant somewhere. She looked at me and asked, "If you could choose to go to anyplace in the world right now, where would it be?" I replied, "I'll bet you know—Puerto Vallarta," to which she responded, "Yes, me too."

The sad thing is that all of these wonderful years, so full of happy memories, ended because of a bad experience on our last trip, the one in 1997. Times were generally prosperous in the U.S. and Canada, and Canadians were flocking to the warmer extremes in midwinter. A group of Canadians from the eastern province of Ontario or Quebec came to PV together and rented enough rooms to accommodate all of them. Our deck was the northernmost of the three that had decks. The room with the deck immediately south of ours was rented by one of the Canadians, but it was used by all. They were a vulgar, mean, and hateful lot that drank, partied, and caroused, using the room for purposes that were offensive to us to say the least. Our complaints to the management did no good. We decided that we would not return if we were going to run the risk of such exposure in future years. After a decade or so, we began to consider returning, but by that time Mexico was beginning to be ravaged by drug lords. We perceived there to be dangers for us that we opted to avoid. But the many wonderful years that we stayed at the Rosita will forever abide warmly in our hearts and memories.

Our Cruises

The cruises we have made are listed below. On each is included the date of the cruise, the area, and some of the places visited, duration, friends who were with us (if any), and cruise line (if remembered or recorded).

1. March 1969—We were able to fix the year and approximate month of this cruise by the fact that two songs were new and popular; the first, published in 1967, was "Spanish Eyes" and the second, published in 1968, was "Those Were the Days." Both remain favorites of ours and bring back pleasant memories of that first cruise. It was in the Caribbean, including San Juan, Puerto Rico, and St. Thomas in the Virgin Islands. The duration was

probably seven to ten days. We were alone, and do not remember what cruise line it was.

2. June 1972—Norway, its fiords being the most breathtakingly beautiful to us from all of our travels. We flew first to Amsterdam, from which we sailed to a port north of the Norwegian fiords whence we stopped at ports all the way around to Hammerfest, which claimed to be the northernmost city in the world, though there are smaller communities further north. From there we sailed out into the open sea to the north end of the fiord country, thence south through that great beauty, touring Grieg's home in Bergen. It was a two-week cruise, touted as a "medical-legal lecture cruise." The late Charles Galvan, tax professor at, and then dean of, the SMU Law School was the legal lecturer. Perhaps it was suggestively promoted as a business trip for tax purposes, but I did not claim a deduction for it because it would have been highly questionable morally and proving that these lectures were the principal reason for the trip would have been virtually impossible. But the Galvans were good friends and we had a lot of good visiting with them. We do not remember the cruise line, but think the ship was the Bremen. It had a German crew.

3. September 1979—Amsterdam to Athens, for two weeks, in a ship called the Danae. This cruise included September 10, our silver wedding anniversary. The Miles, Richard and Karen were married on September 19, nine days after we were. He was my law school roommate. He and I were each other's best man. They were delighted to join us, for the trip encompassed both anniversary dates. It was a dream cruise, probably our best. The crew was Greek, but we do not remember the cruise line.

4. Mid-February 1983—Seven-day Caribbean cruise with the Miles. It included Kingston, Jamaica, and Cancun, Mexico, but the planned stop in the Grand Caymans was prevented by weather. We do not remember the cruise line.

5. August 1994—Alaska and Inland Waterway trip, for at least two weeks. We planned this trip for our fortieth wedding

anniversary. Inasmuch as we would be leaving during our summer stay in Colorado, several of our neighbor couples from there went with us. We flew from Seattle to Fairbanks, traveling from there by train and bus, with two nights in Denali National Park. It was hotter the day we toured there than it was in Lubbock and the entirety of the Denali mountain was fully visible. In Anchorage we boarded a Princess ship for a seven-day cruise on the inland waterway back to Seattle, stopping at several ports, including the memorable Skagway.

6. Christmas 1998—Panama Canal, Costa Rica, Ochoa Rio (Jamaica) on the Regal Princess for seven days.

7. February 2000—Australia, Tasmania, and New Zealand, on Princess Lines' Sky Ship for fourteen days. Ironically an additional optional three-day side trip to Ayers Rock was scrubbed because of flooding, affording us ample and rewarding extra time to enjoy Sydney, a real favorite. We also first visited Cairns and later Melbourne. The cruise circled and visited the southern island of New Zealand, then Wellington and Auckland on the northern island.

8. Holiday Cruise Christmas 2004 through New Year's Day for belated 50th wedding anniversary trip—seven days on Royal Caribbean Line's Rhapsody of the Seas. We left Galveston, Texas, in historic four-inch snow. Points visited included Key West, Playa del Mexico, and Cancun. For this celebration we took our three children and their families (sixteen of us at that time). It was a festive time, enjoyed by all. Bad weather delayed our arrival back in Galveston, but as we were departing from the terminal to fly our separate ways, Michael's then five-year-old son Nathan waved back and yelled, memorably, "See you on the next cruise."

9. October 2007—Seven-day cruise down the western Coast of Mexico from Los Angeles on Royal Caribbean's ship Vision of the Sea. Ports included Cabo San Lucas, Mazatlan, and Puerto Vallarta.

10. April 2008—Sixteen-day cruise London to Venice, with stops in Le Havre, Lisbon, Gibraltar, Barcelona, St. Tropez, Livorno (Tuscany), Civitavecchia (Rome), Capri, the Amalfi Coast (Italy),

Sarande (Albania), Dubrovnik (Croatia), and Venice. This trip was planned by three couples (the Bakers, Borens, and Hollingsworths) who remain close since the men served years ago on a bank board together and continue, with wives, to meet monthly for a dinner party rotating among their respective homes. All are friends of ours, and they collectively invited us to join them.

11. December/January 2008–2009—Fourteen-day Caribbean cruise, on the Grand Princess, from Miami, to Aruba/Bonaire/Curacao, St. Vincent, Antigua, St. Thomas, and Princess Cays (Bahamas).

12. December/January 2012–2013—Fourteen-day cruise covering both Christmas and New Year's Day, on the Golden Princess, from Los Angeles to Hawaii and back. Hawaiian stops included Hilo (Hawaii), Lahaina (Maui), Nawiliwili (Kauai), and Honolulu (Oahu).

13. May/June 2013—Sixteen-day cruise on Oceana ship Marina, from NYC to London, but we disembarked at Dublin for a seven-day Brendan tour of Ireland. Sailing from NYC we stopped at Bar Harbor (Maine), Halifax and Sydney (Nova Scotia), Quebec City (Quebec), Corner Brook (Newfoundland), Cork and Dublin (Ireland). It was a wonderful tour with a superb guide. We especially loved western Ireland.

14. August 2014, when we will celebrate Jo Anne's eightieth birthday (July 2, 2014) and our sixtieth wedding anniversary (September 10, 2014) by repeating the same Alaskan trip and inland waterway cruise that we did for our fortieth wedding anniversary. None of our children had made that trip, and all were desirous of doing it. Since our descending family has increased in size through marriages and births over the twenty-year interval, we will take on this trip our three children, their spouses, and their three live-at-home grandchildren.

Charity, Civic Work, Politics, and Travel

Trips with Jo Anne

Except for a few occasions when we joined, either in the planning stage or later, or were joined by, personal friends, it was just Jo Anne and I traveling together in what follows, and the listing below is in no way exhaustive. We remember trips to the River Walk in San Antonio, and a year we spent Christmas in Las Vegas, to see how much it had changed in the more than fifty years since the one trip we made there while I was in the service.

Purposely, I must jump ahead to my running career in order to give credit where it belongs for the chronology of these trips. While the origin of my running career goes back to 1961, it was on December 30, 1967, that I made my first handwritten entry into what is now, in December 2013, approaching forty-six years of meticulous recording of daily exercise. Insertion of pertinent trip information, such as in describing where it occurred, or the time lapse when none occurred, has made it possible to give chronological dates far more precisely than could otherwise have been done by either of us, or by both together.

1. Mid-September to early October 1983—Toronto, Niagara Falls, Montreal, Quebec, Barre (Vermont), by car. This is the first of two long car trips from Lubbock to the eastern provinces of Canada. Almost certainly we would have passed on each through my home town of Flora, Illinois either going or returning home. The trip was prompted by a passing friendship with a man we had met on our Caribbean cruise, no. 4 above, in February 1983. He and I met while participating in talent night on the ship. He sang "Return to Sorrento" and I played, rather poorly I thought, a Chopin polonaise. We went first to visit him in Toronto, and he took us to Niagara Falls for a day of sightseeing there.

In Montreal, I went for a run from our hotel up to the top of the mountain implicit in the city's name. Not a difficult ascent. In Quebec City, we stayed at the famous Frontenac Hotel. It was a memorable night. A severe pain developed in my lower abdomen, later diagnosed by Dr. Victor Igal in Lubbock as prostatitis, for which he prescribed an antibiotic cure. The night is memorable to me because it is the first time I entertained the idea that I might have a terminal condition, which led me to think about what I would need to do to get my affairs in order. Jo Anne had to pay a king's ransom for a small bottle of Pepto-Bismal for me in the hotel shop.

2. Late July 1996—Mount Rushmore National Memorial, Chief Crazy Horse Memorial, and Badlands National Park; we drove up from Lake City, Colorado. I was oblivious of the existence of the Chief Crazy Horse Memorial, and questioned whether we should pay the $12.00 parking lot fee. Jo Anne insisted. It was the high point of the trip for me, awesome in scale and sheer undertaking. I bought James R. Walker's 1983 *Lakota Myth* in the visitor's center, listing it in the bibliography of my first two books and citing it in the text of the second.

3. Nova Scotia, Prince Edward Island, October 7–28, 1998—These were the ultimate destinations. We drove up through Flora, Illinois and London, Ontario, through Quebec to Nova Scotia. High points of our visit to these islands were Fort Royal National Historic Park, Peggy's Cove, the Alexander Graham Bell Museum in Baddeck, on Cape Breton Island. But the two highest points for us were Peggy's Cove, lying southwest of Halifax near the mouth of Saint Margaret's Bay, and the NNE drive up the west coast of Cape Breton Island. The lighthouse at Peggy's Cove was picturesque, and the visit there was contemplative inasmuch as the Swissair Flight 111 crashed five miles offshore from there on September 2 of that year, killing all 229 on board. But the highest reward of all was the long drive up that west coastline of Cape Breton, so much like the picturesque austerity of Scotland itself, all the way to the Cape Breton Highlands National Park.

From Nova Scotia we drove the new bridge across to PEI (Prince Edward Island), where Jo Anne wanted us to go by the points associated with the book *Anne of Green Gables*, which we did. PEI was quaintly interesting, but its features were not as uniquely rewarding as the high points experienced on Nova Scotia.

Driving home, we stopped in Bar Harbor, Maine, arriving the day after the tourist season there ended, the delightful result of which was a drastic reduction in the cost of the lovely shoreline accommodations where we stayed two nights. We greatly enjoyed our visit in Bar Harbor. Heading south, we drove to Great Barrington, Massachusetts, location of my publisher, where we visited with dear friends and associates. The long drive home took us through Tennessee at a time when the fall colors were brilliant. But a horrible traffic delay on the Interstate for a NASCAR race greatly inconvenienced us and increased my disdain for that "sport." The stop was so long people were getting out of their cars. I was among them, and found my way into the woods to relieve certain pressures already substantial before the situation exacerbated them.

4. Utah scenic sights in the 1990s and 2000s—Jo Anne and I made several trips into Utah during this time frame. The state has scenic drives that are breathtaking and canyons, national parks and national monuments that must be seen in their colorful majesty to be appreciated. With the exception of a serendipitous discovery on a drive from Colorado over to Green River, Utah, namely, Sego Canyon north out of Thompson just north of I-70, virtually all of our memorable travel experiences have been in the southern third of the state, south of I-70 and east of I-15, but extending also into northern Arizona. The discovery of these places is now easy for anyone with Internet access. To attempt to list or describe them all would carry us too far afield.

5. My Sophia Tour, May 19–June 11, 2000—The first week of this Sophia tour, led by my friend, Robert Powell, was devoted to tours in, and lectures about, the gothic cathedral in Chartres, France. For the following two weeks, the tour was to ancient spiritual sites in England, Wales, and Scotland. This tour relates more to the final activity of my life set out herein, and will not be detailed here other than to say that my roommate was Kevin Dann, then of Vermont,

with whom my friendship continues. To cover all of this tour would add too much to accommodate in this writing. Suffice it to say that it prompted me to want to take Jo Anne back and retrace it, which I did as to the part in Great Britain the next year.

6. Great Britain tour, June 6–26, 2001—Tour with Jo Anne to retrace the Great Britain part of Sophia tour of 2000. Attracted to this travel were our close friends, the Bakers and the Mitchells. Norton Baker was my longtime law partner, and Diane Mitchell was our travel agent. Jane Baker and Horace Mitchell were both close friends of Jo Anne and me before they married, respectively, Norton and Diane, and the three couples did other traveling together. This journey was a classic memory that afforded us many hilariously funny incidents to remember. In both the 2000 and 2001 trips, the tiny, but historic, Isle of Iona was perhaps the most special place of the many that we experienced. It lay west of the Isle of Mull in Western Scotland. Iona is in the Hebrides chain of islands. We visited Fingal's cave, open to the ocean, on a small basaltic rock island, a modest motor boat ride from Iona. It was this trip and cave experience that inspired Mendelssohn's "Hebrides Overture."

7. Sierra Vista, Arizona, December 23–31, 2001—Jo Anne and I wanted to drive somewhere accessible in roughly a day from Lubbock to spend a week together over the holidays. Desiring somewhere enticing that we had not been to before, essentially meant studying our Atlas in points west. Sierra Vista, on the map, looked inviting. It was a wonderful, relaxing holiday time together in a simple setting. To my surprise, it was the entryway into the U. S. Army base called Fort Huachuca, which we drove and walked through during our stay. Ironically, during my days in the Army Audit Agency at the tail end of the Korean War, there were two military base audits to which assignment was more or less equated to being sent to Siberia, except they were in the dessert rather than the Arctic. One of these was Fort Huachuca, and the other was Yuma in the SW corner of Arizona. Times have changed the general outlook toward these.

8. Florida, all the way to Key West, April 5–22, 2002—We planned this driving trip in order to visit with a number of friends and former high school classmates, and to visit several places. We drove first to New Orleans, then across Mississippi and Alabama on I-10 to the Florida panhandle, then south on I-75 through the Tampa/St. Petersburg area to Sarasota, where we looked at the condo my childhood friend, Charles Younger, has there for winter occupancy, then on through the Fort Myers area to Naples to visit Ninette Peterson, whom I met on my Sophia Tour in Chartres and Great Britain in 2000. From there we headed to the Keys and drove that slow and tedious route all the way to Key West and back. Returning, we headed up I-95 to Plantation (Ft. Lauderdale) to visit with my high school classmate, Tommy Harrell (renamed, as usual, by the military, George T.), on north to Epcot (Orlando) before going over to visit with my relative and high school classmate, Dale Edward Smith and wife Sina, in Palm Coast. Driving north we visited Jekyll Island because of its connection to the history of Methodism, walking the beach before continuing our journey north to Savannah for an overnight stay and to experience driving through the elegant area of its historic homes. Thence to Ashville, North Carolina to visit our retired Barre, Vermont friend Ed Comolli (from days in Vienna in 1978 and Boston in 1979) who lived nearby, and to walk the Biltmore Estate grounds. Blairsville, Georgia, to visit Jo Anne's high school friend, Judy Beal Rogers, was our next, and final, destination before the long drive home (through Monroe, Louisiana and brief greeting to Jo Anne's cousin Virginia Vincent). While visiting Judy in Blairsville, I walked the nearby lake and a short portion of the Appalachian Trail.

9. Texas Valley, Christmas 2003—As a child Jo Anne had been in the south Texas valley with her family, but I had never been farther south than Corpus Christi. We took a week covering Christmas and drove down to that popular "snowbird" destination. Specifically, we covered the more populous Brownsville/Harlingen/McAllen area, but my notes suggest that on our return we swung along the Rio

Grande as far as Nuevo Laredo before heading homeward up I-35 for part of the way before angling northwesterly toward Lubbock.

10. Chicago, Detroit, and Mackinac Island, May 23–June 2, 2004—A trip jointly planned by the Bakers, Mitchell's and us. We all agreed that Chicago was a good place to start, and I wanted to hear the Chicago Symphony Orchestra and to attend my first baseball game at Wrigley Field, having been a stoic Cub fan since they won their last pennant in 1945 (and I'm still waiting for another). Mitch, having been a Ford dealer in Littlefield, Texas for many years, as had his father-in-law before him, desired to have us all tour the Ford plant in Dearborn (Detroit), Michigan. We flew to Chicago to start all of this, flying thence to Dearborn, whence we rented a car for the rest of the journey. From Dearborn we drove NW to Grand Rapids to tour the Gerald Ford Presidential Library, thence north to Mackinac Island where we had reservations at the famous Grand Hotel, for the pricey Memorial Day weekend. The hotel's front porch is claimed to be the longest in the world at 660 feet—two football fields laid end to end. From here we left our friends and traveled to Wilmington, Delaware for the high school graduation of our grandson, Jeremy Smith. Our friends continued on, traveling through Wisconsin and reported enjoying several notable places before they got to Chicago for their flight home.

11. Globus Tour of Germany, with ending Visit to Basel, July 2005—This trip, which for us covered July 1–18, was planned together with the Bakers. It was a two-week bus tour, except for a first-class train ride on the fast Eurocity train from Düsseldorf to Berlin. The route was clockwise, starting and ending in Frankfurt. The first stop was for a short but scenic Rhine River boat ride through castle country, proceeding on from there by bus through Cologne, Dusseldorf, Berlin, Leipzig (where we visited Bach's Thomaskirche), Nuremberg, Rothenburg, Munich, Oberammergau, King Ludwig's fairytale Neuschwanstein Castle, Lindau on the eastern side of Lake Constance, the Birnau church on Lake Constance, the Black Forest, Heidelberg, and back to

Frankfort. But Jo Anne and I departed our friends at Heidelberg to travel back south to Basel, Switzerland. There we took Angela Schlumbaum, daughter of Jo Anne's post-WWII friend Dorothea Schlumbaum, and Angela's fellow Jose out for dinner and a nice visit. But my main objective in going to Basel was to go out to its suburb, Dornach, location of the Goetheanum, worldwide home of the Anthroposophic Society, and visit its surrounds. Jo Anne and I took the public transportation out to Dornach and went through the Goetheanum together, as best we could. Then the next day I had an appointment to see Sergei O. Prokofieff, grandson of the Russian composer and prominent anthroposophist writer and lecturer on the work of Rudolf Steiner. He pulled a copy of my first book out of his bookshelf, and we had a picture made together. It was a meaningful visit in his office, after which he gave me a personalized tour of the massive Goetheanum. Whether it was that same day, as I believe, or the next, I then went for a substantial hike across to the valley to the ancient caves of the Hermitage, a place with a rich history to anthroposophists, and where Saint Odilia of Alsace[1] (662–c. 820) is said to have found solace, where I spent some contemplative time alone, and then walked on down to the Arlesheim Clinic originally founded by Steiner's close medical associate Ita Wegman. The walk was made longer by my dead reckoning, trial and error, mode of locating it, but I found it and then using the same mode of reckoning eventually found my way back to the bus to return to Basel. The day's experiences were most meaningful for me.

Changed Nature of Travels

Jillian's twins, Micayla and Myers, were born prematurely July 24, 2005, forty-six days before her targeted delivery date on September 7. We left Lake City on July 29 driving to Yardley (Bucks County), Pennsylvania to help her and Donald with the babies till September 2, when we drove down to Mark and Jill's house in Wilmington,

---

1 See http://en.wikipedia.org/wiki/Odile_of_Alsace.

Delaware to recuperate before starting our drive back to Lake City on September 6. Since we were the twins' only living grandparents, our year-end holiday travels (Christmas and/or Thanksgiving) were spent with them through their first six plus years. What travel we have done simply for our own enjoyment since their birth has been cruises discussed earlier.

As stated at the outset, travel for the sake of personal relaxation, diversion, or enjoyment is a condiment of life, one that Jo Anne and I have enjoyed. It is essentially an activity for pleasurable satisfaction rather than sacrifice, hence cannot, in my estimation, be counted as one of life's more noble activities nor one that advances the spirit or serves humanity. For that reason, such travel cannot rise to the level of what I consider my life's primary, and important, activities, as I have attempted to set them out in this work. Thus, I have included it in this section along with other activities that, whether or not worthwhile, were merely incidental to the main course of my life.

The Threefold Denouement

The vantage point from which I now, in these early years of my ninth decade, survey my life, permits me to draw, with a fair amount of confidence, a certain satisfying conclusion. By the last half of the 1970s my immediate family had attained a certain maturity and its economic needs had been provided for. In retrospect, it can be seen that these circumstances presented options for other commitments. My assessment now is that those options led me successively into a triptych of new and increasingly satisfying involvements. It is hard for me to imagine that the last of these will end before the expiration of my own life span, though one can never know what disabilities and experiences one's last years might bring.

The first two of these involvements came to be called, by Jo Anne and me, my "two irrational dreams." Both of these were fulfilled before the third, with increasingly irresistible attraction, revealed itself.

Running

The first of my two "irrational dreams" was to run the Boston Marathon, but that dream was nowhere on my horizon until many years after the origin of my running activity. As with most beginnings, it was unrecognizable as such at the time. The stage for it was described by the following paragraph from the "Law Practice" section above, where I discuss the end of my days with the Nelson, McCleskey and Harriger law firm:

As the end of 1960 drew near I had high expectation that I was about to become a partner in this firm where my two years had been such a happy and successful experience. Never during that time did it occur to me that I might not become a partner. As it turned out, I never did. The first two months of 1961 were among the most draining and stressful periods I have lived through. While light finally appeared at the end of that tunnel, it was dark in the passage through. An evening routine began for me that helped burn off adrenalin and alleviate stressful anxiety. It was the seed that grew into my distance running career, but that is a story for a separate section to follow.

In short, it all began as a simple stress-relieving effort. In the evening of most every work day, after eating and giving Mark and Michael their bath, it being dark at that time of the year, I would go for a walk. My steps were aggressive, but more was needed. So every little while I would break into a run for maybe a hundred yards or more. With each outing, the running distance increased at the expense of the walking portion. Aside from tennis shoes, as they then existed, running gear outside of athletic departments did not exist. I may have had an old pair of tennis shoes, but my feet are wide (size 8, triple E in the army) and tennis shoes were not. It would be a while before I found a poor substitute, but the running increased until my separation from that law firm and the opening of my own office. But it did not stop. Stress relief was still needed,

The Threefold Denouement: Running

but another element was entering the picture—the idea that running was good for health. I was twenty-eight years old and had been away from organized athletic activity since football in my first year of college.

I began to develop a running "wardrobe" consisting of sweat clothes in cold weather or whatever shorts, blue jean or otherwise, I had in warmer days. The footwear options were few, with none satisfactory. I settled upon black leather coaching shoes, as I called them. They were the type that football coaches wore, or so I thought. They had thick rubber soles that were ribbed transversely on the bottom for traction. They were heavy and would have been a nightmare as racing shoes when that time came later. But I could get more width in them, with better foot protection, and these were the more important things.

Running gear in those days either did not exist or was beyond access to a rank beginner like me.[1] A young friend named Jim McWhirter opened a running shoe store in the Security State Bank Shopping Center several years later, perhaps not until the 1970s. He also sponsored foot races on weekends for a few years. In time stores selling not only running shoes but running clothing of all sorts appeared. These things were somewhat contemporaneous with my own increasing involvement in the sport. In other words, my running career was part of the avant garde of what eventually became overwhelmingly popular. Judging by the running gear available for amateurs out in the boondocks in the 1960s, the new sport was still in its dark ages.

My running for stress relief began in the fall/winter of 1960–1961. It would be exactly seven years, 1967 to 1968, before I made the first entry, on December 30, 1967, in what is now, as I write in December 2013, a hand-written daily exercise record of forty-six years. Its oldest sheets are a bit fragile and tending to fade but are still legible. Not only do they give my running history, they also

---

1   See http://www.runnersworld.com/print/63182?page=single.

provide something of a chronological history of our lives—at least as to those events that affected my running schedule or location.

But the primitive nature of equipment back then did not suppress the significance of the activity for me. As earlier stated, our first visit to Lake City, Colorado, was on our summer vacation in 1960. I had discovered Lake City by inspecting a Colorado map to find the place with the highest mountains and the fewest people. On that map, one peak, Uncompahgre, elevation 14,305 feet, near Lake City, drew my attention. In those days, every mountain I looked at challenged me to climb it. In July 1963, I promoted a climbing expedition with a foursome, myself included, to tackle Uncompahgre Peak. Joining me were Briercroft Savings & Loan associate Henry Huneke, who worked for W. B. Rushing, Broadus Spivey, attorney and my substitute teacher of the Cornerstone Sunday School Class, and Elven W. Watkins III, one of my clients in regard to his father's estate. All were young and vigorous enough to make the climb, which we did from the west up a steep draw, without knowing that there was a trail all the way up starting from the east (which I did not know about until my fourth climb). Nevertheless, I suggested to each of them that some extra training in order to handle a climb to that elevation was very advisable. Probably I took that advice more seriously than the other three—I had seen that mountain, they had not. My objective was to get to the point that I could run three miles without stopping. In that early day, running that far seemed like quite an accomplishment—and it probably was. I did get there. Reaching that level of conditioning may shortly thereafter have saved my life, or so it was speculated by the doctors who got me through the near death experience in August 1963, discussed at the first of the Resthaven segment above.

That first sheet of my exercise record was on white, lined, notebook paper, perhaps like the boys would have been using in school. It was entitled "Mile Time," and thus may not have listed all the running we did. Each entry showed the stopwatch time it took each of us on that day to run a mile, except that on seven consecutive running days in the middle of the sheet no time is given for our boys. There were twenty-six days listed starting December 30 and going through February 15. My fastest mile then was 5:50. The boys had just turned ten years old on New Years day, and I was thirty-six. Mark's fastest time was 8:03; Michael's was 7:56.

No record was kept of any running between February 15, 1968, and its resumption on April 26. From the latter date, the record was just of my runs, but from April 26, 1968, through March 27, 1969, almost a year, with very few days missed, the only listing is my timed one-mile run. My fastest mile recorded during that period was 5:07 on February 2, 1969. Certainly I ran more than one mile a day, for at the very least, the one-mile course did not start for a quarter of a mile from our house and I ran it both ways. On March 28, 1969, I ran two miles, and thereafter my distances varied, always more than a mile, and I recorded the distance and total time. On April 20, 1969, I ran four miles, and progressed upward from there until in my mid-sixties when I regressed from running to a run-walk and then to simply walking. There were days that I swam at the YMCA before the sad day in the 1980s when it closed. On these swimming days, distance and time were also recorded.

Over the next several years the monotonous pattern developed of running the same set distance every day. For significant stretches it would be three miles, then four, then five. By 1973 the distance generally became six miles, but that was frequently rotated with days when I would swim an equivalent time period, typically a six-mile run alternated with a one-mile swim (later, in marathoning days, the swim would be two miles). The swimming was a good balance, and had the advantage of relieving stress that can take a toll on the body's running mechanism.

The infection that had nearly killed me in the summer of 1963 had reached so far up into the peritoneal cavity that it invaded my gall bladder. The doctors had tried to remove the gall bladder then, but it hemorrhaged so heavily that they sewed me back up and told Jo Anne that I probably would not get through the night.

But I lived, and was the proud owner of only part of my gall bladder. I was told in 1963 that it would soon have to come out. But it continued, rather miraculously they thought, to function somewhat. Finally, on August 12, 1976, it was removed. Gall bladder surgery was not so tidy then as it is today, when the surface incision is minimal. This was the second trip the surgeons had made into that part of my anatomy, so the upper part of long scar that stretched from my lower abdomen to my gall bladder was reopened a considerable length. Because of my high level of conditioning, my stomach muscles were strong and lean. To minimize the risk of tearing the wound open when I coughed or sneezed, the doctors implanted on the incision a circular framework a few inches in diameter, having parallel wires extending from one edge across to the opposite side, somewhat like strings in a harp. The frame opened on one side, like the jaws of a shark. Of course, I was sedated when this was done, but those wires went into my skin on one side of the incision and came out on the other side of it. They were stretched taught so that I could not pull that incision open. The frame with its cruel wires held it shut. But when I coughed or sneezed, I felt the pain from each one of those wires. That pain was the best cough medicine that could be imagined. And one should also be advised to refrain from laughing. Smiling was fine, laughing was not.

The latter was a problem. Inasmuch as I was into running by then, a friend gave me the book *Dr. Sheehan on Running*, published in 1975.[1] It was the perfect gift. But immediately inside the front cover was the following Mark Twain saying: "Anyone who has had a bull by the tail knows five or six more things than someone who hasn't."[2] Spontaneously I roared with laughter. Ouch! Ohh! Ohh! Ohhhh....!

The six-mile run interspersed by the one-mile swim continued on into 1976, but it appears that I soon began to experiment with

---

1 See http://en.wikipedia.org/wiki/George_A._Sheehan.

2 See http://www.evula.com/quotes/twain.php.

different running and swimming times, often less distance running, but not less swimming. Then in and around February 1977 the distance would often be increased above six miles and the swimming distance above one mile. On February 19, the run went to nine miles, then back to six, rotating with swimming at 1.2 miles and then 1.4 miles.

Late on the Saturday afternoon of February 26, 1977, a memorable run occurred. I had gone over to the quarter-mile track at Evans Junior High School and planned to run five or six miles on it. The day was mild, humid, and overcast, sort of dreary in appearance. But it was comfortable running and I felt so good that a crazy thought entered my head. I would run a marathon distance without stopping that evening. One problem, I had to get word to Jo Anne so that she would not worry about why I was not home in a more regular time period. Fortunately, at about mile five or six, a man came walking by on 58th Street, near the north end of the track as I was in that vicinity. I hailed him over, gave him our phone number, and asked if he would please call Jo Anne and explain why I would be delayed getting home. He agreed, and she later confirmed that he called.

At mile twelve, I was feeling like it was going to be no sweat to do the 26.2 miles. That was the last time I had that thought. Over the next two or three miles I began to think it might be a bit of a problem, and by mile eighteen I stopped and walked home. Any experienced runner would know that running that distance in humid weather without drinking any fluids was insane. Obviously, I was not yet an experienced distance runner. I was not feeling too good that evening, and went to bed not long after I got home. My head was swimming so bad that I felt I was going to fall off my side of our king-size bed. To go to the bathroom, I crawled.

At eighteen miles, I had "hit the wall," in the lingo of endurance sports. The conventional wisdom in distance running at that time was that this occurs at three times the average daily mileage one has run over the last thirty days. Since I had been doing about six miles a day, in retrospect it made sense that this was about the maximum I could go—it was. I had not yet gotten to the point at that time of knowing any "conventional wisdom" of distance running. But as I came into that wisdom from "Runner's World" and other sources, I would obviously increase my average daily running distance before attempting a marathon race—nine miles would be about the minimum.

My distance did begin to average up over the next few months. I was making noises about preparing to run a marathon. Jo Anne, having seen what eighteen miles did to me, would not hear of it. She insisted that I go to Dr. Kenneth Cooper's clinic in Dallas, well known as the "Cooper Clinic," and do all the testing to see if I should run marathons. She seemed to have confidence that they would put the quietus on any such undertaking. To that end, we went to Dallas. I ran 9.5 miles at Whiterock Lake on both June 19 and 20, and then on June 21, 1977, I subjected myself to that clinic's very thorough physical exam with the specific purpose of determining whether I should hazard marathoning. The results of my exam were announced to Jo Anne and me, being that I should definitely go in for marathoning as I was quite fit to begin training for it and do the race. Jo Anne appeared ready to assault the man right there on the spot. She was aghast! "But, but..." But she lost that argument, and I got into my training. In the end, she was a good sport and supporting mate. As time went on and my condition kept improving, I expect she felt there really was no serious risk involved.

The first steps on the slippery slope to the Boston Marathon had been taken. We are now at the point to leave my daily exercise notes. We have entered the time frame that is best accounted by my file document, "Memoirs of Our Boston Trip—April 12–21, 1979. These memoirs still carry the excitement of the race, for they were written immediately after it. The details are those of a runner actually in the race. I could not possibly write such a report now, almost thirty-five years after the event. In that ecstatic frame of mind, I began writing them by hand on a legal pad while we were still in

Boston, then on the plane trip home, and then wrapped them up in final typescript form around midnight on Sunday, April 22nd, six days after the race. What follows is just as it was handwritten and then typed out upon arriving back home.

I did not give up running after Boston, but running then surrendered its primacy to the second of my "irrational dreams," as shall be seen in what was to follow.

Memoirs of Our Boston Trip—April 12-21, 1979

The journey to Boston actually began in the fall of 1976 when Mother sent clippings of the first Labor Day marathon in Flora, Illinois, my home town. I'd been running for years—but never before with a defined goal. Subconsciously at first, then secretly, I began to test myself toward the thought of marathoning. Could one, then 44 years old, roll back the clock so many years, or was the thought madness? It was not really safe to discuss the matter openly. But *Runners World,* Sheehan, and other publications, said "Yes" and, what's more, told one how to prepare. (I had gall bladder surgery in August 1976. Fourteen days after surgery, I ran two miles. My friend Pat Hildreth, who had run my tail off for six miles one day, had sent me a copy of Sheehan's book on running to read in the hospital.)

Certainly Boston was not in the picture in those days. Rather the question, "Could I run continuously for 26 miles 385 yards?" And if so, my goal was to do it in Flora. (A year earlier my high school class had held its 25th reunion, and I savored the thought of showing them I had not changed physically during those years—evidence my psychologist was right in labeling me narcissistic.)

From then until now, I have registered for five marathons and run three. Those other two were in Flora on Labor Day weekend, 1977 and 1978. In the summer of 1977, not yet being educated on muscle stretching, I pulled a gluteus muscle (rear end), and in August 1978, I had hernia surgery. Since Boston presently represents the end of my marathoning ambitions, my original motivations may well go unsatisfied.

I do not feel that I have run as fast a marathon as I am capable. Palo Duro Canyon, scene of the first one, simply is a difficult course. My 3:24:38 there, for a first one on January 14, 1978, was merely acceptable. At Dallas, on December 2, 1978, my training period was short (due to hernia surgery in late August) and the weather extremely difficult (100% humidity, 75–85 degrees) temperature, and 30-mile-per-hour winds, which were headwinds 60% of the time). Actually I walked eight times the last nine miles. Whether it was from too fast a pace the first 16 miles, or the weather, or both, my time of 3:26:45 was disappointing. My actual running time at Boston was faster than either of these, but still short of my desires. I blame training difficulties.

Many of you have seen the clipping in the Lubbock paper which followed my first marathon. The matters there described about our family discussions on my running will not be recounted. Ever since we went to Flora for the 1977 event Jo Anne has been understanding, helpful and cooperative in dealing with my running madness.

One learns early, in serious running, that racing of all sorts, from two miles to 26 miles, is essential for development. Reading is also a must for the masses who have no personal coach. And in this running and reading, the sights of the serious distance runner will eventually and inevitably be drawn toward Boston. It is Mecca. It is the birthplace of the salmon. Boston, New York, and Fukuosa (Japan) are the triple crown of marathoning. Fukuosa is by invitation only, to the world's elite. New York is magnificent, in the style of the nouveau riche, open to all without qualifying standards. It is Boston, with its 83 years of tradition, its devoted and supportive spectators, and its qualifying entrance standards, that is the most prestigious of all in marathoning.

The increasing numbers of recent years caused Boston to set qualifying entrance standards. In 1971, it established standard qualifying times as follows: 3 hours for males under 40; 3½ hours for females and males over 40; within the preceding 12 months. The exploding, geometric rate of growth in qualifying entrants (as with marathoning in general), if continued, makes one thing perfectly obvious. Either these qualifying times must be substantially lowered, or those with the slower times will be chugging it out in close order drill for 26 miles.

The desire to avoid either of these alternatives put special urgency into my staying healthy for, and competing in this year's Boston Marathon. Moreover, there has been another area in which I desire to try rolling back the clock. As a school boy, I was a classical pianist. As between law and music for a career, the former prevailed. But the latter discipline never lost its appeal. Running and racing 35 to 40 miles a week, from now on, appeals to me. The much greater hours and energy required for marathoning simply preclude any possible renaissance in music. Particularly would this be so in trying to meet substantially lower qualifying times for Boston.

With these preliminaries in mind, I return to the days immediately after Dallas on December 2, 1978. My plan was to relax and enjoy myself through the holidays maintaining only 40 to 50 miles a week and getting psychologically ready to begin the build up again in January. Three months is typically considered a good training schedule from this level—and with Boston being on April 16, the plan looked perfect. Generally the idea was to accelerate rapidly after mid-January to a level of about 84 miles a week including hill work at Buffalo Springs Lake; maintain that for about six weeks; drop off mileage somewhat with emphasis upon intervals (sprints of shorter distances up to one-fourth mile) and shorter mileage races; then taper down about two weeks before the race.

Training problems commenced immediately. The weather in January spawned paranoia. Thus crazed, I started out in freezing drizzle about 7:15 a.m. on Monday, January 29—heading south on Memphis Avenue. South of 98th Street the pavement ended. A half mile or so south on the dirt road I encountered dogs and a turn in the road. I was having terrible problems keeping my glasses from glazing over, and I was apprehensive about footing. I decided to turn around and head for home and settle for a six or seven mile run (having intended a longer one). One of the dogs, a minute rascal, kept barking and nipping at my heels. I endeavored a backward kick with my right foot while still running and in doing so twisted my weak left ankle (originally sprained in a baseball game at Carlisle, Illinois) and went down with a sprain. The month of February was virtually a total loss. Only into March was I able, with great pain and discomfort in the ankle, to approach the 84 mile a week level. My log shows only ten days in March where the ankle was free from pain and discomfort, being listed even then as sensitive. On only three occasions in March (including April 1) did I do a 20-mile run. Only two or three times in late March and early April did I endeavor any short races, and my speed training time was too abbreviated to be of great help.

Always though, I was driven by the considerations outlined above. My motto became, "Boston, even if I have to walk!" On one cold, windy Saturday in early March I ran alone for 16 miles at Maxey Park. The ankle was hurting all the way. I did the last mile by imagining myself running at Boston to the cheering of the legendary crowds. Between the pain and the emotion of that last mile I found the tears streaming down my cheeks for the last one-fourth mile.

Finally on Sunday, April 1, I did three laps around Buffalo (19.65 miles and hills), and began the two week tapering. It is customary among many marathoners to do "carbohydrate overloading" just before the race. The procedure is to do an exhausting run seven days before the race—referred to as a "depletion run," to exhaust the muscle cells of their supply of glycogen. In my understanding, glycogen is that which converts to energy during the race, and is to be stored by this loading process. It helps to prevent hitting the proverbial "wall" at 20 miles or so. After the depletion run, for the 6th, 5th and 4th days before the race carbohydrates are avoided as totally as possible. For the final three days, the diet is primarily carbohydrate. This time I followed the suggestion of getting my carbohydrates primarily (though not exclusively) from fresh fruit and juices to avoid feeling sluggish. I also followed the suggestion, even then, of taking enemas the evening before the race, going almost

The Threefold Denouement: Running

entirely on juices for 24 hours before the race, and taking nothing except three small glasses of juice early (4:30–6:30) the day of the race. I believe this diet was beneficial.

Back, however, to more problems. During my depletion run at Buffalo (13.6 miles on Monday, April 9), I began to feel as if I had lead in my arms. That was the beginning of a stomach virus which lasted virtually up to and through the race. To taper off is one thing. To stop running is another. Extreme dizziness and weakness stayed with me on the 9th. On Tuesday the 10th I felt the same but went out to run. After a block I quit. Gravity tugged at every muscle in my body. I felt terrible. On Wednesday the 11th I struggled four miles, and felt bad the rest of the day. Our plane left for Boston (via Durham, North Carolina) at 10:40 a.m. on Thursday the 12th. I got up early that day, ran four miles, and felt weak and dizzy the rest of the day. On Friday, the 13th, in Durham, I thought it wise not to try to run, and did not.

But now the trip itself begins to weave into the fabric. From the beginning, there was a certain amount of bargaining in Jo Anne's acceptance of my marathoning. She has, as I do, a weakness for travel. I convinced her that marathons were held in many exotic spots and that if she would stick with me on this she would see the world. She did not have to be convinced that I needed a nurse on these trips. This was obvious on my first two marathons. Since neither of us had ever been in Boston, she eagerly joined me in planning and preparing for the trip. It was understood that we would stay over for several days after the race. Through the race, the time was mine—afterwards it was hers. We had some personal matters we desired to take care of in Durham, North Carolina, so it worked out well for us to be able to include a stop there in our plans.

We arrived Durham Thursday late evening the 12th, after several hours of anxious traveling. Weather and holiday crowds ever threatened unexpected delays. With great difficulty we finally found the Hilton Inn (in our rented car with no adequate map). During the day Friday we did find time, and I the energy, to enjoy driving around town. We were impressed with the beauty of the area; and by two things in particular. One was the Duke Chapel. It is a magnificent gothic structure. I could not believe its height. Something about the fact it was Good Friday made the visit more appropriate. An organist and musicians were practicing. On the lighter side, a pigeon was loose in the nave, and we chuckled thinking what a unique challenge all those Easter bonnets would present.

The other attraction mentioned is the Sarah P. Duke Memorial Garden on the West Campus of Duke University. A stroll through this peaceful, wooded, and flowered area was soulful. It is maintained by the botany department at Duke (which has no horticulture department). Durham is a newer city than we had suspected. Evidently this guy Duke was a plantation owner in this area, near Raleigh, and the university, as well as the city itself, sets pretty well on his site.

Something happened back at the motel Friday evening, the 13th, which activated a little adrenalin and nudged me into the chute of final psychological preparation. Actually I desperately needed a good dose of this. My intestinal area still knotted in discomfort and I had little stamina. Even as late as Friday I calculated that there was at least a 50% chance of not feeling well enough to complete the race, if I could even start. My morale was very low. Everything which had gone before now seemed perched on the precipice of the awful canyon of waste. I had made up my mind to go out and start, even if I was sick. At least I could say that I had run in the Boston. I was taking a bath when the phone rang. Jo Anne took the call. It was Chuck McDonald from the *Avalanche Journal* (Lubbock's paper), who asked that I call him back collect. I was not totally surprised. During the training period, on days when my ankle was particularly troubling me, I resorted to distance swimming at the YMCA in an effort to keep aerobic capacity from ebbing too much. On these occasions, locker room conversation got around to the point that about April 5 or 6, Roy, who works for the paper said he was going to talk to the sports boys about it. I told him about Don Andress, local orthodontist who had also registered. I told Roy

The Threefold Denouement: Running

when we were leaving. Having heard nothing before departure, the matter was forgotten. However, it was a most welcome shot in the arm Friday night before the race.

My newspaper coverage after my first marathon (in Palo Duro) and the press coverage both before and after Boston flatters me to the point of embarrassment. The later coverage should be attributed almost entirely to timing, in relation to the recent phenomenal rise in interest in running in general, and marathoning in particular. I simply was at the right place at the right time. Merit had little to do with it. As a matter of fact, my failure to acknowledge many superior runners would be shameful. Our West Texas Running Club has several superior runners in the masters division (over 40). From San Angelo, there is Tom Mayfield, then 39, who won the 36-40 category in Dallas with an incredible 2:32, and then turned 40 and won his division in Houston in January. Tom richly deserves recognition and to represent this area in races such as Boston. However, Tom is not financially capable of doing so. Then there is Dale Thompson from Amarillo and Norman Smith from Midland, both Masters runners from our area who hoped to run as fast as in the two-forties at Boston. They were there for the race (but not perhaps of great interest to the Lubbock paper). One Masters runner in Lubbock who is superior to me is Jack Shropshire, 43. We ran together at Palo Duro, each in our first marathon. I beat Jack by two minutes, but he trained only about four miles a day. In his second marathon—at Houston in January—he did a 3:05, and aspires to break three hours. Jack was phenomenal in college, barely missing an Olympic berth as a sprinter. I've never beaten Jack in any other race and do not expect to. Jack planned to come to Boston this year. Unfortunately he waited too late to run his qualifying race. He was a late entry at Houston, missing out on pre-registration and consequently receiving certification too late to register at Boston by the March 19 deadline. John Trompler, 30, is a local runner who has come on strong, running a 2:54 in the tough Dallas weather. Undoubtedly financial considerations kept him from Boston. Michael (J. J.) Jenkins, of Lubbock Christian College, ran a 2:42 in 1978 in the tough Palo Duro Canyon marathon. These and others truly merit recognition, yet I ended up with the publicity. Failure to so acknowledge would be gross immodesty.

Along this same line is another circumstance. My accomplishment would not be newsworthy in the New England area, nor even in many other metropolitan areas trending northeasterly. Persons such as Tom Mayfield, John Trompler and J. J. Jenkins would enter Boston as easily as they do Clovis, Dallas, Houston or Palo Duro. It is a local race. No expense is involved. Registrations at Boston are predominantly either from New England or from runners primarily older who are financially able to travel. Consequently, the big mass of runners at Boston come from nearby.

Before leaving Durham for Boston, two other lines of acknowledgment are in order. First are the New England friends we met a year ago in Vienna. Next is my good friend Herb Beattie from Tulsa. Among the former are Ed and Tip Comolli, Barre, Vermont; Jim and Peggy McDermott, Hastings on the Hudson, New York; and George and Joyce Kilbourn, Newton, Massachusetts. We had a wonderful time with all these folks in Austria at the International Cemetery convention last year. Most of you have read Jo Anne's report of that trip. For several months, even before my qualifying race, we've been writing these friends about our plan for Boston. As the date approached, Ed Comolli sent us a map of Boston with the race course marked. The Kilbourns were to be away at a cemetery convention in Hawaii, but to our advantage United Airlines went on strike and the convention was delayed. More later on all these, but they (particularly Ed) helped us lay our travel plans—and it was agreed that I would see them first as I went by the Newton Cemetery (which George Kilbourn manages) right on the course. I called their attention by mail to the following statement from page 215 of Jim Fixx's famous book: "... the race's most drama-conscious spectators—a silent and attentive throng with a finely honed taste for the sight of suffering. Why else would they choose to do their watching on Heartbreak Hill?"

The Threefold Denouement: Running

No one has more inspired me in marathoning than Herb Beattie, 44. Not only was the January 1978 Palo Duro Marathon the first for Jack Shropshire and me, but also for Herb. Before that race I sized Herb up as a contemporary, about my speed whom I could probably beat. Not so, he beat me by seven minutes with a 3:17 (7½ minutes per mile average). He went on to Boston last year where he ran a 3:10. Shortly thereafter he set a two-mile record in Oklahoma for his age bracket in 11 minutes. He helped me in the summer of 1978 by advising how to get registered at Boston, getting an A.A.U. number, etc. His WATS line lets us shoot the bull at leisure. I next saw Herb at Dallas in December. Actually, I did not anticipate seeing him in the 2400 person crowd, with his improving speed. To my surprise I caught up with him at about 14 miles and we exchanged the lead several times as one or the other would walk. His effervescence, even in all our agony that day, was inspiring, and he showed constant concern for all his running companions. We ran together for the last couple of miles, but he beat me by ten seconds as we made our final kick the last few hundred yards (uphill).

No one thing did more to cement my goal on Boston than the WATS line conversation I had with Herb on his return in 1978. He was simply beatific. He said it was a love affair between 5,000 runners and 1,000,000 spectators. His body was nothing but adrenaline. He had no pain, and hurt nowhere. The girls at Wellesley were unreal. He became "depressed at 15 miles" because he thought "in 11 more miles it will all be over." He was nearly incoherent as he chattered on ecstatically. In summary, he said, "You've just *got* to run Boston."

So, early Saturday morning, April 14, we boarded at Durham for Boston. We arrived on time shortly after noon and picked up a Datsun rental car, which jumped badly in need of a tune-up. Herb Beattie had reserved four rooms at Holiday Inn—Government Center. He early advised me to stay near the finish line (which we were by subway). He recognized his ambition in March by running a sub 3-hour marathon in 2:56 at Tulsa, and decided at the last minute not to make Boston this year (to my surprise and regret). But the reservations were another way in which Herb was helpful. The hotel was within walking distance of Quincy Market, a prime attraction.

    Typically, Jo Anne had gathered an arsenal of information in advance, particularly on eating places. It was understood, though, that no eating would be done until after the race, other than my Spartan menu. The first thing after settling into our room was to go out for a walk to Prudential Center. The Boston race could be not unfairly designated by a series of location names, e.g., Hopkinton, Wellesley, Heartbreak Hill, Beacon Street, Kenmore Square, Prudential Center. On a downhill ramp, squarely in front of Prudential, on the Boylston Street side, the mob thickens, and the race ends. At Prudential, the sponsoring Boston Athletic Association (B.A.A.) offices, on Easter Sunday between 11:00 a.m. and 5:00 p.m., all registered entrants first learn (and pick up) their computerized numbers. Underneath Prudential, after the race, runners are herded for necessary care and articles. It is at Prudential that runners board busses at 7:30 to 8:30 on race morning to ride to Hopkinton (traffic being generally too bad to get there otherwise). Thus, we sought the Center. Herb had said, I understood, that it was only a couple of blocks away. The cruel truth dawned on us after we had set out on foot never reaching it. We finally got up to Beacon Street where we could see it. (Prudential is one of the most imposing structures on the Boston skyline.)

    From there we retreated back to the hotel to get the car. Our first objective was to reach Prudential, and our next was to drive the course. A picture is worth a thousand words—in knowing the course—particularly the fabled hills of Newton. Frustration abounded. Excluding only Washington, DC, downtown Boston is incomparably difficult—we were mice in a maze. When we finally got to Commonwealth Avenue for the drive west out of town, we relaxed, but prematurely. Unknown terrain and congestion maintained the challenge. One writer said that the scenery of the Boston

The Threefold Denouement: Running

Marathon was not inspiring unless one enjoys "urban sprawl." Only for brief distances between the start at Hopkinton and the early communities of Ashland and Framingham was there any hint of a rural setting. Nevertheless, my eyes were hungry for every feature of the course, and studied it intently as we struggled westward on roadways to be miraculously cleared and lined with people in less than 48 hours. When we got to Hopkinton we found the starting line area and studied it. The legendary high school where last minute preparations take place was the next attraction. Nearby was a school which we mistakenly assumed to be the high school and drove around it. By now, its smallness did not surprise me. Hopkinton was truly a rural community in appearance. Having surveyed this, we headed back to see the course from the same direction we runners soon would.

The events were making me feel a little better. I had missed running entirely on Friday. Typically, one runs for only a couple of easy miles the last two days. When we reached the hotel I was eager to try a little run—anxious to see if my limbs still felt leaded and my stomach tight. The bowel signs continued to say the problem was not over, but now I wondered how much of that was attributable to the event itself. I headed up Charles Street to "The Commons" and ran about 20 minutes. It was after dark, but the run felt fairly good, and that alone buoyed my spirits. I knew then I would finish the race, and I once again began to think about finishing times and lack of training. We had been advised that official certificates would be sent only to those who finished within their respective qualifying times. With the mass at the starting line, this could be difficult. Runners were lined up in groups of a few hundred, according to their numbers issued by computer according to their qualifying time. I rightly anticipated that I would be far back in the pack. Other runners, betraying last minute jitters, were out in abundance all that day, even as I ran well into the evening. After the run, my spirit was expectant and happy, and I slept peacefully and well.

It gets light early in Boston, and our room faced east. It was Easter, the most glorious day of our faith. I hope many of you prayed for me that day, for my religious awareness was inundated by a flood of other concerns. We rose early. We could not pick up our number (and buy the $2.00 bus ticket for Monday morning) until 11:00 a.m. Only one big thing had to be done before that. We had to find a way for me to conveniently get to Prudential at an early hour on Monday. The time allowed for this mission greatly exceeded that needed. Subways considered, Herb was right. Our hotel was only a few blocks from Prudential. We ended up milling aimlessly around the Prudential and Sheraton lobbies in a sea of runners (and their entourages) similarly engaged, for well over two hours. Actually, Jock Semple, of the B.A.A., was plastering the computer sheets of names and numbers on the marble walls soon after we got there. Laid end to end, these probably would have been longer than a football field. At long last, he reached the Smiths, and I got mine—X332. All runners qualifying under three hours simply had numbers. All others were preceded by a letter T, V, W or X. The W's were women. The T's, V's and X'S were men over 40, and were in order of qualifying time. The booklet our kits contained showed 4403 regular qualifiers, 999 each of T's and V's, 517 W's and 941 X's. These excluded over 800 doctors of the AMA who get a different type number without qualifying. And, of course, there are a few thousand who gather at the rear, uncontrollably, and run without numbers. So you can see that I had a few souls in front of me. Incidentally, Jim Fixx, author of a famous book on running, had number X7. If he showed up, I never saw him, but he would have been in the group just ahead of me, and may well have stayed ahead of me.

One oversight I regretted. In the excitement of the moment I failed to look up Don Andress' number. It seemed insignificant at the time. He had made reservations at the Copley, and I was certain I would see him. On the way back to our hotel it dawned on us that we had not seen him—and wished then we had looked for his number. Mysteriously, his number was not in the booklets in our kits. When the numbers were posted Monday morning inside the Hopkinton high school it would have taken an idiot to fight his

The Threefold Denouement: Running

way to any number but his own. I was not to learn until later that a last minute emergency prevented Don from coming. Having learned our numbers from the computer sheets, we located the station from which all X packets would be dispensed, and continued milling until 11:00 when everyone queued up at some station. It was the better part of another hour before they actually started giving out X packets. Eventually we got ours, then bought our bus ticket and cleared the area for the subway and hotel—anxious to go out to Newton for another look at the hills and to loosen up by running a couple of miles on them.

We drove over the hills a couple of times. Runners were in fair abundance, many obviously not concerned about the morrow's race. I chose an area of hills and instructed Jo Anne where to drop me and where to wait. The third of the four hills seemed the worst to me, so I chose to cover at least part of it. It was apparent that by late in the race one would have to negotiate these intelligently or pay for it. They started at 16-1/2 miles and ended at 21-1/2 miles. It was their location and close proximity that earned them collectively the term Heartbreak Hill (though the last of them is, for that ultimate reason, sometimes so described). Two miles on these was quite ample in view of the admonition to avoid strain and preserve energy.

On Saturday afternoon we had spotted the Newton Cemetery. Only a small back portion of it was visible from Commonwealth Avenue through a chain-link fence. Newton represents a traditionally nice part of Boston. Cemeteries in New England are very different, from a legal, organizational standpoint, than most progressive cemeteries in other parts of the country. However, from the physical standpoint, we always try to see the leading cemeteries which are close by. Our friend, George Kilbourn was sufficient reason alone to see this one. After my run, we found the main entrance (following George's telephone instructions) and were impressed by its quiet and well maintained beauty and dignity. It is the principal cemetery for Newton. It was at some point between the cemetery (up on Commonwealth Avenue) and the Newton City Hall to the east where our friends, the three couples, were to be on the morrow. The Comollis were driving in on Monday, as were the McDermotts, and would be staying in a motel south of Newton. We would see none of them before the race, logistical and rest problems considered.

Shortly after the word got out in Lubbock that I planned to go to Boston I got a call from Tom Griffith, a fellow lawyer there, who said his daughter, Sarah, was working in the Boston area and would welcome the opportunity to be of assistance if she could. In most marathons, the race organizers have aid stations with water, E.R.G. and other amenities spaced every two or three miles along the course. These are particularly vital if the weather is warm or humid, to prevent dehydration. Boston has been an exception for the reason that the wonderful people along the way have always taken it upon themselves to care for the runners in this respect. Warm weather in some recent years, together with ballooning registration, led to a change in policy. This year, aid stations were provided at approximately five mile intervals. I did not know this long in advance, so was most happy for Sarah to volunteer her assistance. The necessity having passed, we nevertheless were pleased to have our own personal supporter stationed along the way. To implement recognition, we called her, and had a visit in our motel room on Sunday afternoon after returning from Newton. She was a charming girl, and we enjoyed hearing of her work of an apprenticeship nature in filming. We discussed a location where she might situate, and chose the fire station area early in Newton.

One problem had plagued Jo Anne and me from the very first. We knew of the crowds and the traffic problems. We knew from my prior two marathons that I would need help in navigating after the race, if not more. Therefore, her presence at the finish was a must. Yet loved ones were to be prohibited in the nurture area under Prudential. This was a matter of concern. We both wanted her to see me at other points. This had been possible at both prior marathons which had involved circular courses. Boston was from point to point—no repetitions—and virtually no chance to move from spot to spot. Boston vibrates with this event. Patriot's Day itself is almost like the 4th of July there. News media is immersed in it. Coverage is incredible. The event of the day, and of the days before and after, is the race. We finally decided that she would remain in the hotel watching it on TV until the winners had finished (which we knew would be around 2:10 p.m.), then head for the subway and the finish line to see me come in (hopefully before 3: 30 p.m.). This was to work out fine, though our meticulous efforts to meet near the Prudential Center afterwards aborted, and we made our separate ways back to the motel.

All runners going by bus were told to be at Prudential no later than 8:30 Monday morning. Busses would leave from 7:30 through until 9:00. All runners were to be at Hopkinton by 10:00 though the race would start at 12:00 noon. So often when a major event looms I sleep well, while lesser excitements leave me tossing. With the passing years, my sound sleep ends by 3:00 or 4:00 a.m. This important day I slept until 4:15, having retired restfully at 9:00. I got up for a small cup of orange juice at 4:30, then back to bed until 6:30, and up for good. Two more small cans of orange juice—no more nourishment until evening. I felt lean and good, with only a slight hint of discomfort in the intestines. All possible precautions had been taken.

Cloudy, cold, and wet weather was with us in Durham and escorted us up the coast to Boston. Forecasts were watched by all runners. The final ones were accurate. High for the day in the low forties (actual high was 42 degrees), light rain, very slight wind in our faces from the east. Miserable day for the crowds. We could shed any worries about the dreaded devastations of a warm, humid day.

Already we had experienced the penetrating chill of this current Boston weather. Anticipating a long wait outdoors in Hopkinton, I dressed as warmly as possible. Vans were to be provided for runners to send back their top clothing in bags to be picked up underneath Prudential at the end. Each kit contained a tag with the runner's number and a particular color. All bags were both collected and dispensed by color, a tribute to organizational ingenuity.

I was at Prudential by 7:40 a.m. I've never seen more busses, almost all being of the austere yellow school bus variety. I boarded immediately and found a seat. There was almost total silence. I've ridden these leviathans to many an athletic event. Only for the most crucial games did the depth of silence ever approach that on this bus. At first every man was an island alone, bottled up with the realization that soon the road would challenge every fiber of his being, physical, emotional, and intellectual and bleed it of every ounce of preparation so laboriously stored. No women were on this bus, except the volunteer driver.

Mercifully, the ineptness of our driver eased some tensions, if it created others. I did not know much about getting around in downtown Boston. However, after 8 or 10 minutes, I told the fellow next to me that we were going the wrong way in relation to the Prudential Center. At 15 minutes we were back at the starting point, the driver admitting that she did not know how to get to the turnpike. Somebody from the back of the bus went up to help her, and we followed another bus from there. She apparently did not know bus procedures at the turnpike pay station. She brought the bus to a stop with the middle of the bus opposite the attendant's booth, realized she had to speak to him, and started to back up. A horn and several shouts from the rear of the bus brought her to a halt, so the attendant got out of the booth and went forward. The head shaking in the bus had really begun. When she was finally ready to go, she started out, but had forgotten to change from reverse to forward gear. More horns—more yells—both more urgent. A voice, "There's a car back there." Another voice, "There was!" The driver had already succeeded. No one was thinking about the race now. There was nervous laughter and head shaking. At the clover leaf exit from the turnpike, the voice from the back spoke for all, "Easy on the Curve." As if on a listing ship, all leaned far to the right. Many must have been the thought, "This is the end of it all." By that time, happiness would have been arriving safely. We saw a sign "Hopkinton 2 miles," then made a turn, and in a little while a sign "Hopkinton 3 miles." Shortly, however, we were there, and the original set of tensions resurfaced. "There?" This was not the school I had surveyed on Saturday. The bus had driven past the starting line a great distance, but this was the high school. We were one of the early busses to arrive at the school.

Soon after we had gotten onto the turnpike I had struck up a conversation with my seat mate. He seemed a decent, quiet sort. He looked too heavy—he was 190 pounds (down from 215), but had qualified with a 3:10. He was from Pennsylvania coal country and had driven up Sunday evening. His first marathon had been Boston in 1978. I asked him how that could be. He had come up unqualified and run from the back of the pack. He insisted that one would run well in Boston because of crowd enthusiasm and support. He said that he would not make one mistake he made last year. This time he would control his pace and not foolishly spend his energy pouring it on for the screaming girls of Wellesley College half way through the race. Good advice I was to remember. Near Hopkinton I asked him what work he did. He was a Catholic priest. His name was Frank McNellis, and I later caught up with him near midway, recognizing him by the "Father McNellis" on the back of his shirt. He moved slowly on ahead though, and I hope and trust he did well. One fine fellow, I thought. My observation is that if the non-running talents of the participants were surveyed, a very able, responsible segment of society would be discovered there. Outside the school I saw and visited with Dale Thompson, Amarillo, and Norman Smith, Midland, and all wished all well. Entry into the gym was easy. Some were already sprawled there or napping. I chose the line for the john instead. It was approximately 9:00, give or take a little. A half hour or so later I was through the john line. By that time not only was the gym packed, but the hall was so crowded it took about 10 or 15 minutes of struggling to get outside. I did not relish killing time in the chilling cold, but staying inside was out of the question.

At least the rain had not started. I was clad in my running shorts and T-shirt, thermal long handles, running suit, rain jacket with hood, wool ear band and blue dress sox over my low cut running sox. Eventually I found an incline to the south of the practice field and lay down on this, relaxing in the pervading chill as best I could. Across the field to the east and north was a wooded area. In view of the crowded conditions in the building, a more convenient woods was never known. Ten thousand sighs of relief could be heard there, the greater depth of the woods being for the girls who passed by hundreds of unconcerned males en route. On a more relaxed occasion, one could truly enjoy watching the variety of response to these moments of anxiety. Some could not help burning up energy; others stretched, and one of these was a fascinating performance itself; and the variety was endless; but the most impressive thing was the seething parade back and forth across the field with the fully staffed firing squad on the periphery in the traditional stance. Sometime between 10:30 and 10:45 I made my own way over, but modesty demanded a few steps into the woods, a precaution not possible later near the starting gate and time.

From the woods I returned to begin stretching muscles, particularly hamstrings, on the grass of the practice field. Then back to the parking lot behind the school, now filled with busses. The busses in turn were filled with runners trying to stay warm. I had not realized these were available. The best I could do was get inside a door and stand up. At last a fellow exited and I sat down on the steps. Time was drawing close. The vans for our bags closed at 11:30. We had to walk to town which was variously reported as being from one-half to one and a half miles, the uncertainty of which was a problem since that walk had to be made in final racing gear. (I later measured the distance by car and it was .6 mile to the nearest end of the line.) All were ordered to be at the starting line by 11:40. Allowing 22-1/2 minutes to walk at a four m.p.h. pace, I planned to doff all extra clothes at 11:15. Before leaving the bus, I spread Vaseline under arm and on nipples, then removed everything but the running suit and headband.

Then I headed out into the chill for the van. A final decision was what to wear on my head. There were four choices, namely, nothing, a terry cloth sweat band, the wool band, and a sock cap. Eventually I chose the sweat band. I needed some warmth, little as it was, but wanted something disposable if the need ceased. Between 5 and 10 miles into the race, I took it off and tucked it partially in shorts, anticipating possible need for other purposes. One of my friends, running the Clovis marathon, had found a headband helpful in dealing with the manifestations of diarrhea in the absence of anything better.

Many runners were waiting until the last to shed their outer garments. The ones with experience had worn old, holey or cheap sweat clothes which could be worn to the last minute and thrown away. If I had one word of advice to other first-timers, it would be to go so prepared.

But by 11:15, I was stripped to shorts, T-shirt, and terry cloth sweat band. The rain had begun to fall lightly. I headed toward town in the line going that way. Rumor had it that 1,000 runners still had not left Prudential. I doubt that, but truly the late arrivals were just getting to the high school and were expending precious energy running to get there and change. Printed instructions said portable johns would be available downtown. I never saw one, and I needed it —more from the virus than nerves. Modesty did not prevent many runners, including me, from the use of backyard tree trunks in town. Finally I hit the ground for more stretching and then headed to my starting gate by 11:40. Between the chill, the drizzle, and nerves I was shaking uncontrollably. My biceps had knotted so that I could not straighten my arms, and I bobbed constantly so people could not see the uncontrollable movement in my jawbone. Mercifully, the assembling mass of bodies itself both broke the slight east wind and gave off its own warmth. The countdown had begun. TV reports said 13 helicopters would be overhead. I silently prayed they would all stay in the air.

Most had stop watches, set very close to correct time. By 11:58 there was a general readiness. We were probably a quarter of a mile from the starting line and down a hill. We could neither hear nor see what was taking place. The elite runners with single and low double digits had their own dressing room and transportation and were brought in at the last minute—properly so. When all were in place, and within the last two minutes, all separating ropes were dropped, and the various segments closed ranks forward. But back where we were, one could only hope the starting gun could be heard so as to activate watches. Unfortunately this was not to be. Zero second came and went with no action, then a roar from the starting area and we activated our watches by educated guess only. Later in the race, I compared mine with official splits, and it appeared the gun was seven seconds into history when I clocked in.

The race was on! But we stood still. In a moment there was slow forward movement and we walked haltingly. Four minutes into the race (or 4:07 more precisely), I walked past the starting line. The walk turned into a slow jog at 5:30 (or 5:37). For the better part of a mile the course was downhill, but in this crowd that helped none. Nevertheless, we were on the run, assured that soon the aching chill would be past, and be gradually replaced by another type of ache.

But with all the problems, I was filled with joy. For over three hours I was to feel a spiritual dialogue with those crowds along the way. For the first five miles, an unselfish runner stayed in my vicinity and ran at the same pace. I suspect he may have been planted by the B.A.A. He clowned and expended great energy in whooping up the crowd. He took a swig of every proffered beer and shouted incessantly, "All right folks, let's hear it for the runners!" or "Let's hear noise for the runners." And he got it, even from those otherwise chilled and still. I asked him how long he could goon like that, and he gave a cheerful reply, but faded from my awareness shortly thereafter.

The course itself starts at Hopkinton and proceeds easterly, in order, through Ashland, Framingham, Natick, Wellesley, Wellesley Hills, Newton, and onto the final streets of Boston, namely, Commonwealth Avenue, Chestnut Hill Avenue, Beacon Street, back to Commonwealth Avenue, across Kenmore Square

The Threefold Denouement: Running

and later across Mass. Avenue, then right onto Hereford Street two blocks to Boylston, turning left onto the lengthy finishing ramp at Prudential Center.

Most of you have seen pictures of the mob of runners. If 10,000 people were spread evenly over 26 miles, it would be one person about every 13 feet. Considering that all started together, and the vast majority finished within a 1-1/2 hour time span of each other, the event had some similarity to an infantry division double timing it for 26 miles down a two-lane highway. One cannot see down the road as far in New England as in West Texas. However, at a curve to the right by a body of water I judge to have been Fisk Pond at 9-1/2 miles, I expect we could see for 3,000 feet, and it was like a column intact. A fellow near me remarked, "It's got to be depressing to see that many runners out in front of you."

Spectators were abundant. The weather doubtless reduced their number, but there must have been a million anyhow. Few places were without any, and each little town was lined, with the main crossings being mob scenes.

Experienced runners are advised to wear shirts or something identifying themselves. I had two West Texas Running Club shirts along. I had not decided on the bus whether to put a running singlet on top for extra warmth. Frank McNellis said, "You have no choice. By all means display that West Texas." Which I did, to my great satisfaction. Countless times I heard it from the lips of the crowd. "Good going, West Texas, you're looking strong!" "West Texas, okay!" One shouted, "Yea, Texas—Longview." Another, "Hey, Texas, Lubbock"—I wanted to stop but did not. Two or three yelled, "Hook-em horns," and I grimaced slightly. Always I tried to wave or smile or yell, or some combination thereof—with greater energy at first, but always with deepest sincerity and sometimes with a lump in my throat. At one point, a fellow who had been trailing me for some time came abreast and said, "You must be from West Texas."

A TV announcer quoted Bill Rodgers later as saying he had a personal problem, "He had to go to the bathroom for the last ten miles. I, too, had a 10-mile problem. By Framingham, at five miles it had started. At every filling station and natural cove thereafter until the foot of the Newton Hills, I agonized over the decision of whether to waste precious time by stopping or to tough it out with assurance of an excruciating finish. Happily, I chose the latter. By some miracle, the problem ended with the first hill of Newton. The crowds originally throttled me. Then it was my bowels. Perhaps, unwittingly, Providence was making me preserve strength to be able to enjoy the thrill of a strong finish in the heaviest crowds of all.

Boston is such a fantastic event. The organizational task is now herculean. My gratitude and respect are immense. Thus, one criticism may be allowed. I saw almost no mileage markers along the way. If they were there, they were not generally visible. The ones I saw did not look official. And most, in a misguided effort to be helpful, told the remaining distance rather than that already traversed. The arithmetic of calculating pace from this, while on the move, is practically impossible. I had read of this shortcoming. Its existence in this particular event is simply surprising. I mean no sour grapes when I remark that possibly those phenomenal runners of the Greater Boston Track Club (who captured spots 1, 3, 7 and 10 in the mens, and 2nd in the women's division) might not need these signs. However, the streets of the Boston Marathon, by and large, are not adaptable to training on—they are congested with city traffic.

A runner simply cannot escape being thankful to these Boston crowds. All along the way, individuals staked themselves out as good Samaritans dispatching water, E.R.G., ice, orange slices, beer, soft drinks, band aids, and you name it. Actually, these sources were better than the formal aid stations because runners could stop individually rather than fight the crowds at the official stations. All this aid was less critical in this weather than if the weather had been warm. Nevertheless, it was necessary, and the loving concern of those people in providing it generated a lump or two in my throat. I always thanked these individuals pointedly.

The Threefold Denouement: Running

One of those people was our friend, Sarah Griffith, Tom's daughter. I can still picture her standing alone on the outside of a curve as I came along. She gave me water and wished me well. I do not remember the exact location, but I think it was generally in the early stages of Newton.

There were three areas in which the crowd support was simply and uniquely magnificent. The first of these was at fabled Wellesley College. This stands at about 13 miles. At least a quarter of a mile before, runners can detect this special distaff roar—like a grandstand filled with women. The approach is one crescendo, and the narrow path through this feminine crowd is like the pounding culmination of a vibrant concerto. No red-blooded man could be unaffected. When we were past it, all in my vicinity joked about finding a route back around to run through there again. Father McNellis was right. One might control his speed there, but he would not lag.

And speaking of women, one of the finer diversions of a place like Boston is that a runner of my abilities will often find it quite comfortable to follow a lady runner. At least it provides a pleasant change of scenery, if one is willing to swallow his chauvinism long enough. Sooner or later, however, these dames either had to run off from me or be challenged. Both occurred frequently.

In my two previous marathons, one experience was common. At 16 or 17 miles, I faded noticeably in stamina. The last ten miles was a psychological battle, based on physical exhaustion or agony or both. No other aspect more preoccupied my mind for this race. Especially in this race, where the hills commenced at that point. So from Wellesley to the Charles River, largely downhill, I kept myself well in control, alert for any sign of exhaustion.

The first clear indication of distance covered (which I can remember seeing) was near the Charles River, just before the hills of Newton. The indicator, official or not, said ten miles to go (as I recall). My watch said 2:05 plus. Subtracting five minutes, more or less, for delay at start, this meant about eight miles per hour, or

7-1/2 minutes per mile. In spite of all earlier problems, a finish time under 3:30 seemed possible if only the hills did not slow me unduly and my stamina lasted. I felt the last six miles would be fast if the glycogen held out.

Obviously, at 2:05 the winner was nearly in. Before the race I had said to Jo Anne that I hoped a new record would be set—a world record if possible. I wanted to be able to say I ran in the race where a record was set. As you probably know, Bill Rodgers set a new American record at 2:09:27, taking 28 seconds off the record he set at Boston in 1975. The world record of 2:08:33 was set by Derek Clayton of Australia in 1968. Rodgers took the lead in the hills of Newton. Radios and spectators all along the route got this news to us virtually as it was happening. We all shared some of the thrill of knowing Bill was out there going for broke. I heard radios along the way announce his time as he finished, and I knew he had his record. That alone was a good omen.

At that very time I was entering the hills of Newton. Thankful was I for the days of training on the steeper hills at Buffalo. Without strain I leaned into these hills, determined to be steady but not over exert. I seemed to at least hold my own on the first two hills. I have no recollection of pain on them. It was almost as if they did not exist. I just kept moving, seemingly slowly. Perhaps I was resting up for my rendevous at about 19 miles, in the middle of these four hills, with our group of cemeterian friends. (I had laughed at the irony of having a convenient cemetery at the 19 mile point in these hills.)

Later on our friends mentioned that they had met before the race for a sharing of the pictures of our Vienna trip. It had been a year since we had met, and then only for a week. They did not say, and we politely did not inquire, but it seems obvious they were concerned about missing me through lack of recognition in that crowd. One of them told me, "You know, the last we saw you in Salzburg, you were running away from the bus as we left for the airport; and today you came running toward us." They laughed about how I got across the Atlantic, and I laughingly replied that I was a pretty good guy. Actually, it was sort of funny. I had told them roughly how I would be dressed. The only problem was that there were four or five possibilities for my top part. Only my number and the color of my shorts and shoes were actually known. I chuckle to think about Comolli trying to pick out all the approaching yellow shoes.

Fortunately I knew about where they would be and kept to the right side of the road with an eye out for them. All of a sudden, there was a mutual sighting, and I threw my arms up in approaching and they snapped pictures. Bless them—I had sent a packet of E.R.G. and three of them had glasses full enough to drown a horse. I got the best of one down, shouted—welcome at this reunion, and said, "I'll see you all later" as I scrambled on, with the clock still in my mind. It was an emotional refresher just before the last two hills.

Again these hills seemed to come with relative ease. I could not believe it. Without a doubt, the crowds were a factor. It was here, on the upward grade of each of these four long hills, that collectively the second of the magnificent crowds assembled. The farther up the hills, the more intent this spectator support. There must have been 50,000 or 100,000 cheerleaders in the group. Everyone seemed to reach out an encouraging hand of support and cheer you on. They were like angels—simply fantastic. Then on Heartbreak Hill, the last of the four, those on the top shouted jubilantly that "It's all downhill from here"—a figurative, if not literal, truth.

I had "cased the joint" and knew that at the top of the final hill was a slight dip then back up to the same level—and there was the gothic structure of Boston College looming up. That was my irrefutable landmark of the top of the Newton Hills. Rounding this, a magnificent sight came into view—Prudential Tower something less than five miles away.

About halfway up this last hill, it dawned on me that I did not have the faintest indication of a loss of stamina. In the light of my two prior experiences, the realization was like the glorious blast of color at sunrise. I began ever so slightly to pick up my speed. It was here I began to pass group after group. Each time I would size up my own feelings and the pace of those ahead. At this stage it is a good idea to challenge only when you are satisfied you can do so decisively. Time and again it worked. While occasionally some runner would do the same to me, not many did. Thousands of better runners were ahead, but at this particular location I began to feel the aura of a hero coming in. It was as if I were running only a three or four mile race where one knows he will hurt but that his muscles will hold in there strongly to the finish if he endures the pain. I could feel the taste of blood. I knew the 3:30 was well within reach, and I was becoming increasingly confident of staying strong all the way in.

Somewhere along here a couple of miles out, on Beacon Street, or at Kenmore Square, the great crowd again became, for the third and last time, the magnificent throng. From here on it was crescendo all the way.

I have three breathing cycles. The fully aerobic cycle is one full breathing cycle (in and out) every four steps. As pace quickens, I go to a partially aerobic cycle of one every three steps. At top speed, or heavy aerobic, I breathe a full cycle each two steps (breath in on one foot and out on the other). In Dallas I was on the middle or fast breathing cycle most of the race. I do not believe I was ever on anything but the slow cycle at Boston excepting only the middle cycle on the upper hill stretches, and the middle and fast cycles during the last five miles. I did not want much left at the end.

The Prudential Building disappeared from sight somewhere within the last two or three miles to reappear only sporadically. But the crowds kept us informed—or tried. Actually as the final mile approached, the shout ceased to be how much further it was. Instead the pervading chant was, "You've got it made! Keep going!" It was almost 30 years ago since I was a high school athlete. Yet here I am in the avenues of Boston, heart pounding madly and joyfully, muscles responding beautifully, and spirit soaring like an eagle. No one can ever know the ecstacy who has not been there.

Later I contemplated the experience of Bill Rodgers. There must have been a deafening roar as he approached for the full 26 miles. I seriously doubt if any time in the history of the world any athlete has ever been exposed to greater encouragement for so continuous a period as was he on this date. I saw a replay on TV and heard the finish line announcer shout to all as he came down the ramp, arms waving, that "Here comes Bill Rodgers, the greatest long distance runner in the history of the world."

Before concluding, a word on my cold feet is in order. I eventually got sufficiently warm to survive. The east wind in our face was light, but always chilling, even on the run. My cotton work gloves kept my hands passably comfortable. My last conscious thought about my feet was sometime shortly before the Newton Hills. I could not believe they were still so icy. Somehow my sox and shoes had gotten wet. I have run in wet weather before, but never with my feet being that cold. Actually I do not know how they got that way.

Water under foot seldom penetrates above the high platforms of the Nike LD 1000s I was wearing, and the rain did not seem heavy enough to have soaked through to the bottom of my feet. But they were wet and cold all the way. Maybe it was well. I finished without a single blister and no newly blackened toes—incredible for the world's tenderest feet. With lighter shoes (Nike Elite Racers), blood came through my sox at Dallas, with ample blisters and black toenails.

A word about crowd control is appropriate. Last year, with a field less than two-thirds the size of this, but with ideal spectator weather of about 50 degrees, the crowds pressed in to create problems for the runners trying to pass. It got publicity. The police this year were effective. The crowds everywhere were controlled. In the most enthusiastic spots, passage room was adequate given the number of runners. This police control worked a hardship on *our* picture-taking plans.

One of the casualties of Jo Anne's being so limited in seeing me was her inability to get pictures along the way. Ed Comolli got some shots. Hopefully they'll turn out well. Our plan was for Jo Anne to get me at the finish, and then get pictures of the crowd and general setting. She stationed herself, with the greatest difficulty, out in Boylston Street on the fire station side of Hereford Avenue. She could get only a glimpse of me. A policeman kept telling the people to get behind the barricade. She ignored him. Finally he zeroed in on her, and as she was crawling back I went by, turned the corner into the final chute and disappeared from her sight before the finish line. She did see me and was happy to know I was under the time limit and looked strong. But she missed a picture, and in her frustration failed to take others. Herb Beattie said last year the official photographers (a source of revenue to the race itself) got some good shots of him. With the crowds this year, I'm wondering if that was possible with me, and hoping so. They did in Dallas.

I went back out two different days later in the week, when the sun was out and took pictures along the course. It was like a sentimental revisiting of bygone battle scenes. Things had changed. It was business and traffic again as usual, and the sun was out (instead of clouds and drizzle). The comparison reminds me of the poignant milieu of the musical *Brigadoon*, the town which existed only one day every 200 years where an outside fellow fell in love with one of the town girls on that one day. The next day it was all gone for 200 years. The setting at Boston returns each Patriot's Day. Still these pictures will be meaningful to me as my mind fills in the rest—and they may be helpful to some of you who aspire to Boston.

Finally came the parting tears. Several times on the course my emotions almost overcame me. Too many discouraging things had happened. Too many painful miles had been put in in the determination to be there this time. Sometimes when a spectator yelled out to me and I waved back and smiled, my face would contort as if I were going to bawl at the same time. In the final few miles, when everything was working so well, I could scarcely keep the tears back. I was a ball of pent-up emotion. Back in March in Maxey Park I thought of Boston to get through pain, and the tears came. Today, at

Boston, the crowds and cheers were there, in spades. Gone were the pains of Maxey, but there in Boston my mind went back to Maxey, and only with effort could I defer the tears.

I entered the final chute and poured it on still more. The crowd of runners there required lateral movement, and some hesitation, but my final time was well under the 3:30 limit. My clock said 3:26:38. Add seven seconds, then subtract something (at least 5 minutes) and you have my best marathon time. Of the time in the abstract I am not proud, but under the circumstances it is all right.

And of the endeavor, I say that if I live to be 100 I expect to remember few things with greater satisfaction and joy.

The few remaining mob discomforts and the onset of chill were soon things of the past. In any event, they were swallowed up in victory. While tired, I was not exhausted as after the other marathons. Eagerly I looked forward to the evening of reunion and celebration with our friends.

I tried locating Jo Anne after the race at the spot suggested in the printed instructions. The spot she and I had earlier prearranged was too far away through the mob and the plan was abandoned. However, we were poorly coordinated as to the suggested spot. I had managed with considerable effort to locate and don all my warmer gear. (Tentatively each runner was given a foil blanket until his clothes could be located—from which one local writer dubbed all finishers as "baked potatoes"). In spite of buoyant spirits and warmer gear, when I emerged from the building the chilliness was obvious. After only a short look, I decided to head for the subway. Considerable time had lapsed and I suspected that Jo Anne might already have done the same. Not so, however, for having been through these with me before, she stayed around for a good while thinking I might still be below and needing her when I came out.

In picking up a room key at the hotel desk, I noticed messages—one telegram and two phone calls. The phone calls had both come in at 4:20 p.m. E.S.T. The telegram was datelined April 15 (Sunday) 3:12 p.m. E.S.T. Why it had not been brought to our attention on

Sunday I do not understand. It read, "We hope Monday is a super day for you. Good luck from all the Hamiltons. Owen and Lucy." It did me as much good after the race as it would have before, and these dear friends were so thoughtful to remember us at this time. Of the calls, one was from Jill saying, "Call as soon as possible." The other was from Doug Rains, with Channel 28 in Lubbock. Jill's sounded ominous, and with foreboding I returned her call first. Her message was simply that Doug was trying to reach me in regard to the race. Later, as I was finishing my bath, Chuck McDonald at the *Avalanche Journal* (Lubbock paper) called. My state of euphoria came through somewhat in his write-up. Jill called us Tuesday morning saying that we'd had coverage on all three TV channels, some radio, and the newspaper. She laughed and read where the paper quoted me as saying, ". . . as I was going up Heartbreak (mistakenly quoted Parkway) Hill, at the 21 mile mark, I suddenly realized that—hell, I'm not even tired." With respect to the "hell," I said to Jo Anne, "I did not say that, did I?" She said that I sure had. Our cemetery manager, Roy Ward, called me later from Longview and said he was going to have to give me some lessons on press interviews. That language did not bother our son Mark. His friends ribbed him about what his old man had said about the girls at Wellesley. Actually McDonald was remarkably thorough and accurate for a fast interview.

The conversations with Jill and Doug Rains were completed before Jo Anne got back. After we related the more urgent news to each other, one thing remained. The emotion which had started in Maxey Park on the 16 mile run, and had welled to the surface many times during the race only to be repressed, was still there and the time had come to let it out. I hugged Jo Anne and thanked her for her understanding and support through all these weeks, and in the process the sobs came and I cried like a baby for awhile. But it was a happy cry.

We communicated with our New England friends by phone between 5:00 and 6:00 p.m. to confirm, since I had expressed misgivings before the race about being available that soon. By 6:30 they

The Threefold Denouement: Running

all came by and we headed to Jimmy's Harborside, a famous seafood restaurant. We had the pleasure of meeting and visiting with Duncan and Ruth Munro who had also been in Vienna but whom we did not meet there. Duncan is manager of the impressive Mount Auburn Cemetery in Cambridge, Mass. and is a past president of the American Cemetery Association. The evening was great. It was good for us to eat with abandon for a change (though running does bring about some change in eating habits and desires).

I did not sleep well that night. No particular aches or pains --just too tired.

We were fortunate that the Comollis were able to stay in the area until forenoon Wednesday and the McDermotts until mid-afternoon Tuesday. Of course the Kilbourns lived near. On Tuesday morning the Comollis and McDermotts picked us up for a delightful day of sightseeing. We went first to the U.S.S. Constitution (Old Iron Sides) moored there in the harbor. The U.S. Navy still mans and maintains the ship, and its sailors give tours. We went aboard and schooled ourselves on its vitals and other information. It was quite a warship. At one time it stayed out for two and a half years, surviving on provisions from other captured ships. Once below the deck, we could not stand straight. Fortunately sailors then averaged only 5'7" (with 5'6" being the minimum. Comolli is a tall fellow—he really had troubles. I got tired bending over and sat down on an object and watched people. I watched one tall and handsome young fellow (whom I later learned was a marathoner from California) bump his head and then quite decently mouth an inaudible but appropriate epithet about a dog's offspring.

In this vicinity we went in to see the photographic presentation of the Bunker Hill battle (and some on Lexington and Concord) put on by Raytheon Corp. It helped one re-orient. Regrettably we had not reviewed our early Revolutionary history before going up.

Nearby we visited the Bunker Hill site and monument. Actually it is Breed's Hill, but the British label stuck when they reported it as Bunker. The colonial commander said he wished we could sell them more real estate at the price they paid for that one. Comolli, representing Barre Granite Association and knowing stone well, remarked that the monument was made of Quincy granite, and, as I recall, he said John Adams owned those quarries so the monument was a good deal for him. (Do not hold me to this if it is not historical.) Other old structures nearby seemed to be of the same stone.

Actually Bunker Hill is in Charlestown across the mouth of the Charles River from Boston. Jo Anne got ahold of a map showing the current land mass overlaid by the land mass in 1775. It is hard to appreciate the significance of certain strategies the colonists used, if we look only at today's maps. Most of the neck of the land mass which now expands off from Beacon Street is fill which did not exist then. The neck of the peninsula was narrow—which presented greatly different military possibilities or problems than a larger land mass would have. It was the events associated with this that brought about the ride of Paul Revere from this area out to Lexington and Concord.

From here we drove over to the Quincy Market Area for a light snack at the old Union Oyster House—what else but oyster stew. Parking was almost impossible. Fortunately, this was within walking distance of our hotel, but this time our friends had a car. Before going into the Oyster House we went by Faneuil Hall nearby. This was sort of the town hall in Boston where many patriotic meetings occurred. It is still a meeting place. It is a central part of the renowned Freedom Trail.

After lunch, we made our first tour of Quincy Market. One can hardly say too much for that. It is a restored market area of old and is sort of an amalgam of mall type and street type shops. Actually shops do not generally open onto any street, but in between each of the three long structures is a walkway with lighted trees, benches and other amenities. One could survive a long time on the sumptuous eating in the area. We could not begin to try it all. There are tasty specialty counters with everything from Chinese food to lobster. Then there are restaurants ranging from French to more casual. Of course, there are also many other retail shops. In fact,

The Threefold Denouement: Running

Bill Rodgers has a newly opened running goods shop there, where I bought a Boston Marathon T-shirt for myself and a Bill Rogers singlet (top) for Mark and Michael. We would later frequent this area several times—and for good reason.

Soon it was time for the McDermotts to leave. Our memories with them from Europe are fond. Perhaps best of all was the evening when the four of us went to Grinsing, several miles out from Vienna in the wine growing district. We had a delightful dinner—and the legendary new wine, served in a unique sort of contraption, was as good as I've had. The saying is that if you go to Grinsing and remember the ride back, you have not really been to Grinsing. Our tour from Salzburg included Berchtesgaden (Hitler's resort area). Jim was there three days after the war ended, and we enjoyed dubbing him "General McDermott." Farewell for now, McDermotts. See you later.

For a little rest, the Comollis returned to their motel and we to ours. I went out for a 20-minute run. It was, of course, somewhat painful with the stiffness and all.

That evening the Kilbournes came in (Joyce had been in town with a niece during the day) along with the Comollis, and we had dinner at Lilly's, the exquisite French restaurant in the Quincy Market. These flucy places, with their tra-de-da French accented, entirely proper waiters are fine if one can establish that through all this seeming veneer they are just ordinary people. Ed Comolli took care of that. With sort of a bull-in-a-china-closet approach he asked the prim waiter if there was anything good on that menu that was cheap. That brought everything down to earth, and just to prove that the delicacies were not for him, he ordered a 14 ounce steak. He was not pleased when Tip suggested to him that that was almost a pound. That's Comolli. We all enjoyed the meal more because he was along, and not just because he and George were paying.

At Vienna, we got acquainted with the Comollis and McDermotts first, and only later with the Kilbourns. However, George and Joyce come on strong. I mentioned earlier their getting together to go over pictures before the race. Now it was our turn. We saw the Kilbourn pictures before dinner (the Kilbourns having arrived earlier) and the Comolli's after dinner, all in our room. It was good to see all these scenes again. Of particular interest were the pictures made by the Kilbourns before they joined our group. George had started in Luxembourg in the infantry in 1943 and gone into Germany. He and Joyce went a couple of weeks early and retraced the path he had followed as a foot soldier. We found this fascinating.

When the evening was over, we were all dead tired. Jo Anne and I had the advantage of being able to tumble in bed. The others had a sleepy drive.

By agreement, we met the Comollis at Mt. Auburn Cemetery in Cambridge at 9:30 Wednesday morning. Jo Anne and I drove by M.I.T. and Harvard for a quick look en route, since they were convenient. The trees and shrubs at Mt. Auburn are botanically labeled, and the traditional style cemetery is a showplace. It is 170 acres, but only about 12 remain for interment. They bury fewer casketed remains than we do at Resthaven, but have about 150% of that number of cremations, a practice understandable where land is so scarce. The personages buried there would represent a respectable portion of American history and literature; Oliver Wendell Holmes, Henry W. Longfellow, and that sort. I happened by chance to see the name Felix Frankfurter in the columbarium. A tower was built in the cemetery so that families across the river in Boston could see the burial situs of their loved ones. This tower probably provides as good a side view of the Boston skyline as is available. I took pictures of the skyline. From here, I could see contoured the hills of Newton and the sweep inward to the Prudential Tower. I must say that Duncan Munro, a licensed engineer having served this cemetery 14 years, is a most knowledgeable and capable manager. He was kind enough to discuss and show me pertinent financial records on the operation. We have given limited consideration to establishing a crematorium, a project whose time probably has not come in Lubbock. However, I was given an in-depth view of the cremation facilities and process—something our manager, but not

The Threefold Denouement: Running

I, had previously experienced. Duncan was a genial host and tour guide, and we like now to think of him and Ruth as among our New England cemeterian friends.

By 11:00 a.m. we bid adieu to Duncan, Ed and Tip. We drove inland to Lexington, Concord, and the North Bridge (site of "The Shot Heard Round the World"). It was not our purpose to take time with any stops in Lexington or Concord, but we did get out and study the terrain and encounter which occurred April 19, 1775 at North Bridge where the rustic colonists steeled up their nerve, attacked the British, and put them to rout, thus providing the inevitable spark for the waiting powder keg—and the Revolution was underway.

Jo Anne had been told by Joyce Kilbourn to visit, and if possible eat at, the Wayside Inn. This is to the southwest of Lexington and Concord, near Sudbury. The Inn was on the Boston Post Road and served as a hostelry in the early day. Longfellow evidently served to catapult many things to fame. Paul Revere was one. Wayside Inn another. His poem immortalized it. En route to Lexington and Concord we had seen the homes of Louisa May Alcott and Ralph Waldo Emerson. En route to Wayside Inn we went by Thoreau's Walden Pond. Fortunately it is a state park now, because otherwise it is not remote any longer. We arrived mid-afternoonish at Wayside Inn and had a delightful lunch in one of its antiquated rooms. The tables and chairs were not comfortable, which convinced me of their general authenticity. I still squirmed with a recovering body.

Contrary to the earlier Boston weather, Tuesday brought gradually improving conditions with increasing sunshine. While still much chillier than we had anticipated, the weather became more accommodating for tourism. From Wayside Inn we dropped down to Hopkinton. The sun was out, and I wanted to take pictures of some of the meaningful scenes along the marathon route—both for my own future reminiscing and to help other runners who might want early concepts of what to expect. The sun was great for the pictures—but, of course, when I reminisce I'll have to supply clouds, rain, and crowds. With all our stopping on the way back, we got to downtown Boston too late to have enough light. I shot pictures, but decided to go back later, if possible, and get others. Furthermore, there was something wrong. I was simply unable to trace the exact course from Boston College to Commonwealth Avenue (at Mass Ave.). Somehow or other, I felt my retracing of the route here may have been inaccurate, but only later was I to ascertain this. On race day, of course, any idiot could have found the way—but would not have paid much attention to road signs.

Speaking of road signs, they were scarce in the Boston area. Signs generally existed only for roads you were crossing. They assumed if you were on a principal artery that you knew what it was. This was maddening to us newcomers.

Back at the motel, Jo Anne rested. I donned my gear and went out for a 30-minute run along the Embankment. This is a very pleasant parkway area between Storrow Memorial Drive and the Charles River Basin. Runners and cyclists abound there. For that reason it was not rare to see girls running alone even after dark. It was dark by the time I got there. The lights from across the River Basin were mirrored in the wide body of water. It was beautiful to run there in the evening. We later had a simple meal at the Harvard Club restaurant nearby and Jo Anne accompanied me for a rather lengthy walk out the Embankment, then up Commonwealth and back down Charles Street, a big triangle, which I estimated to be at least three miles. The Embankment is a part of the fill which did not exist in colonial days.

We set Thursday aside to go down to Cape Cod. Our New England friends cautioned us against expecting too much—for which I'm grateful. We stopped at Plymouth Rock on the way down and went on board the assumed replica of the Mayflower. I was impressed by its small size. It was manned by people in colonial dress. One man in particular had on his blousy shirt, all the trappings, and a full beard and mustache. A tiny lad of probably two years and not over 24 inches tall walked by him with his parents and said, "Hello,

The Threefold Denouement: Running

Jesus." One of the ladies nearby told him he should have responded, "Bless you, my child."

We did not go all the way out on the Cape. In fact, we only went to Hyannis Port. Jo Anne wanted to see the Kennedy resort area. The traffic was choked up on what would seem to be archaic street design. The weather was still cold. We hated to think what traffic would be like in warmer days. The difficulty of getting around was tiresome. I was not favorably impressed, nor was Jo Anne I believe. The actual Kennedy compound itself was, of course, elaborate and impressive. What else could you expect? We parked in the nearest private pull-off along the beach. Jo Anne read and walked in the area. I went out for a 40-minute run. It was midday, brisk and sunny. The run was good, though not in view of the beach unfortunately. That evening Jo Anne and I went back to Quincy Market to eat. We were dying to try the individual food stalls, and we did. But Jo Anne ended her evening with a praline pecan crepe at the Magic Pan—probably her all-time favorite dessert.

Friday was set aside, agreeably, to go our separate ways and do our separate thing. Jo Anne's day included more of the Freedom Trail, specifically, Paul Revere's house, Old North Church (Episcopalian), Old West Church (Methodist), and the Boston Tea Party site, as well as shopping in the main downtown shopping area to which neither of us had been. Minus the shopping I would like to have seen all these, but time ran out and more urgent desires prevailed. The one thing she learned which interested me most was that Paul Revere was a good citizen and respected, but not particularly famous or "revered," during his life. Others of his day performed equal feats, even on the same occasion. But information about him was sufficiently preserved to fill Longfellow's needs. From the day of "The Midnight Ride of Paul Revere," this sleeping patriot would never again be obscure.

My day Friday was to commence early with my starting these memoirs. Thereafter I wanted to get Bill Rodgers' signature on my race number, and return to ascertain the exact route of the course about which I was still confused, and then shoot pictures of this final area in better daylight. I worked on these memoirs until 10:45, then left for Quincy Market. Personnel at Bill's store in the market had told us that Bill was to be honored at Faneuil Hall at noon on Friday. They had said he was good about signing things, and that maybe I could catch him at these ceremonies, or at the store beforehand (he normally spent more time at the Brookline store). I finally did get his signature after the program. The mayor, Kevin White, was there, as were all the Greater Boston Running Club members finishing in the top ten (as well as Patti Lyons who finished second among women). So was Will Cloney, director of the B.A.A. News coverage was extensive. A band was out from Boston College. The day had been proclaimed "Bill Rodgers Day" in Boston. The mayor said that with all our team sports, we were really short on heroes, persons whose victory was entirely personal. In my judgment he rightly said that, to millions of people in our land, Bill Rodgers, this unpretentious little fellow with four marathons faster than any other American has ever run, as well as other world and American records, was a hero. White aptly defined a hero as "One whom you're not embarrassed when you're caught staring at."

From there I caught the subway to Cleveland Circle. That name came up the first day I arrived, the race went right by it, but I simply could not find it on a map. This day that was a project and was accomplished. Not far after dropping downhill at Boston College, the race course veered off to the right from Commonwealth Avenue onto Chestnut Hill Street. This was one long downhill block, and near the bottom happened to pass right in front of Rodgers' main store. It ended at Cleveland Circle, a subway terminus, where it turned left on Beacon Street and stayed until rejoining Commonwealth much nearer in. It is here at the Circle that Prudential comes finally into view to remain until the brownstones themselves obscure it in the final blocks. I was happy to recognize that portion of the course where I had known such elation on Monday. I shot a few pictures at the Circle area, then hopped on the subway back on Beacon Street, getting one shot through the window. I got off the subway just before it went back underground, probably a couple of miles from the Center. I walked these happily, shooting up the balance of the roll by the time I reached Prudential.

Back at the hotel I went for a 40-minute run on the Embankment. My memoirs were not touched again that day. Jo Anne had selected, with my total approval, a restaurant called the Chart House for our final evening meal. It was on Long Wharf, just beyond Quincy Market from our hotel. During the day she had located it and, typically, sized up how to get there. The fourth subway stop was practically at the front door. This was a delightful and relaxed place. Jo Anne had never had "a" lobster. She had eaten lobster, but not "a" lobster. These were available at one of the stalls in Quincy Market for as little as $6.50, ala carte. We both agreed that none of the "dignity" of eating "a" lobster was available there. The atmosphere just was not right. So she ordered a plate with a lobster and a steak. At the other end of the spectrum, neither of us had eaten New England scrod, a type of fish. So I ordered that, the plan being that we would split the steak and scrod. She almost quailed when the lobster got there. Reminded me of the slave girl, Prissy, in *Gone with the Wind*, who knew everything about delivering babies until the time came. The long and the short of it was that we ended up splitting the lobster too. It was all good. We got away with everything but a little of the scrod. It, too, was good, but not our favorite.

We checked in well ahead of schedule at the airport Saturday morning, and I got back to these memoirs. From then until we arrived in Lubbock at 6:30 in the evening, I was scratching on them. No plane trip ever passed faster and still I did not finish. Cecil Mackey, president of Texas Tech, boarded our plane at LaGuardia. It was good to visit with him, but I later apologized to him. This writing made me almost antisocial. Back on it Sunday afternoon and evening, I finally finished the draft. I knew that once I started in on the matters waiting for me, this wonderful trip, and these memoirs, would be finished.

Some trips and experiences are so wonderful that we just hate to see them end. So it is with Boston and me. It is midnight Sunday and I am still floating. There is a slowly engrossing melancholy. Boston, from conception to completion, has been both painful and richly rewarding. A major goal—now accomplished. There is the happy, yet profoundly sad, feeling that a major phase of my life has come to an end. Most assuredly, I will always watch the Boston through a mist, even when the sun is shining.

Postlude to Boston

My time as reported in the "'Racer's Recordbook' 1979 Boston Marathon Official Computer Results," a copy of which is in my files, was 3:26:12. The B. A. A. Marathon's President was Will Cloney. His letter transmitting such "Recordbook" had, on its back, a listing of the "Finish Time Allowance," or handicap, based upon one's location back of the starting line. My number was X332. The allowance for runners with numbers X234 to X652 was six minutes. So, my recognized time, with such allowance, was 3:20:12.

Some interesting statistics pertaining to qualified runners:

> Runners entered, 7,927
> Runners started, 7,910
> Runners finished, 5,958

The pre-race bulletin listed 7,855 registrants, including 517 women and 7,338 men. My number X332 represented the 6,729th qualifying number among such 7,338 men pre-registered. 5,151 men and 203 women finished faster than 3:26:12.

Running Boston was a dream-worthy experience. That said, the above statistics show that it provided me with plenty to be humble about.

Music

While well under ten percent of my years have been primarily devoted to it, I consider music one of my most meaningful involvements. It provided the second of my "irrational dreams," and the middle of the three significant activities of my adult years outside of the economically focused realms of law, business, and investments. These latter dominated my fourth through eighth septenaries (seven-year segments), that is, from age twenty-one (1953) to fifty-six (1988). In successive order, the three non-economic activities, running, music, and anthroposophic study and writing, began almost imperceptibly to encroach upon the economic realms during my later thirties and then to seriously and increasingly compete with those realms for time and energy commitment with each passing year until, possibly excepting the interlude of the investment activity of the mid-1980s, they moved clearly into dominance as the 1970s blended into the 1980s.

My own sense is that I was not born with a natural aptitude for music. I am not aware of having had any early musical leanings, nor have any been mentioned as noticeable by any family member. Aside from my love of what I call "the great music," that produced by the masters of the 18th and 19th centuries, as well as some of the late 19th and early 20th, never has the popular music of my time been particularly meaningful to me, though the "easy listening" variety has been pleasant. Playing popular music and church hymns has not interested me. I strongly dislike so much of what has developed starting with the 1960s, especially rock and the heavy, steady, pounding beat, such as one hears while stopped at traffic signals. So much of what is popularly called "music" is amplified electronically to such an ear-splitting decibel level that it must surely result in loss of hearing. Viscerally, I perceive it to be spiritually degrading. I am just a cranky old man, but on such sound pollution I have considerable company in my generation.

Never have I had any aptitude for playing by ear or creating original song or musical score. But playing by the notes as written, as demanding as it can be, challenged me in my youth, and having taken up that challenge, over the years it has created in me a deep love for, and appreciation of, "the great music."

My own instrument was, and is, the piano. In my youth, for a while I played the pipe organ at church and the cornet in grade and high school band, but developed no interest in them beyond some early basics, happily dropping them without accomplishing much.

In the earlier sections entitled "Other Childhood Memories" and "High School," my own musical beginnings and involvements are described and need not be repeated here. The end of piano lessons during my senior year in high school was like the wistful end to tender teenage romance, the sacrifice of one dream for another.

My family retained its piano, but relinquished the house it was renting in Wichita Falls in 1951. Mother, dad and Mary Anne had moved back to Flora soon after dad's 1950 brain surgery. From then until around the end of the 1950s, I had no piano available, nor would I have played it much during that decade anyhow. Jo Anne and I acquired a used black upright in 1959 or 1960, followed a few years later by a Baldwin Acrosonic. The children each started taking piano lessons at around age seven. I do not have a memory of playing very much during the 1960s. However, at some point as the years went by I began to pull out some of my music and practice a bit. During the 1970s, the seed from my youthful dream, having lain fallow for years, put forth shoots that prompted me to wonder if I could ever go back and get to the point where I would be able to play one of the great piano concertos with an orchestra. It was a ridiculous idea, of course, but it would not go away. Running was taking all my extra time and energy, but financially we were doing much better and I managed to squeeze out some time to dig out some of the more challenging compositions that I had played in high school, adding another or two, like Chopin's enchanting "Fantasie Impromptu."

The Threefold Denouement: Music

The shoot from that youthful seed, the ridiculous idea of playing such a concerto, poked its head above the ground at least some time between 1976 and 1979. Cecil Mackey was president of Texas Tech during that three-year period, and I remember standing at the front door of his residence for some reason, and my idea of giving Tech a new concert grand piano and playing such a concerto on it came out during the conversation. He seemed highly receptive to that idea. Mackey became president of Michigan State University following his three years at Tech. I wrote to him following the concert, referring to his early support of my pursuing this dream, and enclosing a copy of the program and a cassette tape recording. He responded warmly, on behalf of both himself and his wife, Clare, congratulating me, writing in closing, "We think of you often and send our best regards to you, Jo Anne and the family."

During the occasions when Jo Anne and I had been in Germany, I had been impressed by how good restaurants would so often have a violinist strolling through the dining area playing to the accompaniment of a lovely grand piano. The piano seemed always to be a Bosendorfer. The Bosendorfer piano is an elegant instrument. Before our trip to Vienna, I had determined that the factory where these pianos are made is in Vienna. From some source the information, whether true or not, came to me that Bosendorfer began to build these sturdy pianos to withstand the punishment the brilliant young pianist, Franz Liszt, was giving the pianos of his day. Indeed, there seems to be at least some credibility to the story, as I infer from available material on the matter.[1]

Our visit to Vienna in 1978 to attend the International Cemetery convention has previously been mentioned in several connections. Discussion of one unique experience there has been deferred till now. Whether the Vienna trip was before or after my casual visit with Cecil Mackey, I cannot now be sure, but that it was essentially contemporaneous I'm certain. In any event, having learned

---

1 See http://www.boesendorfer.com/en/history.html.

that the Bosendorfer factory was in Vienna, and having found its location, lacking any better approach on the matter I walked cold turkey into its factory and, upon my request, was ushered into the office of the plant manager. I introduced myself, said where I was from, and told him that I had in mind donating a new concert grand piano to Texas Tech University in Lubbock, Texas. He was understandably interested. I explained that I was considering the Bosendorfer piano for such gift, subject to the wishes of the university's piano faculty and music department leadership. With that introduction I asked if they had any pianos available for me to play while we were in Vienna. He explained that at that very moment they were in the process of shutting down the plant for a long weekend of vacation. However, he said that if I would return the next day at a certain time, which was either at noon or 1:00 p.m., there would be a custodian there who would let me in, then he would leave and lock me in the plant for two hours before coming back to let me out. No one else would be in the plant during those two hours. It was hard for me to believe such good luck. As I picture it in my mind, it seems that there were four or five pianos in the plant's showroom—certainly there were at least three. I appeared at the designated time and, with only mild misgiving that the custodian might overlook returning to let me out, I luxuriated in playing each of those lovely instruments.

We did end up giving a new concert grand piano to Texas Tech for its Hemmle Recital Hall. But it was not a Bosendorfer. It was a Steinway & Sons piano manufactured in New York rather than a Bosendorfer from Vienna. At least in this country, if not in Europe, at that time, and probably still, the Steinway is the preferred instrument of concert artists, and it was the Steinway that was the unanimous choice of the piano faculty.[1] Possibly some influence upon the

---

[1] For a comparison of the musical qualities of the Bosendorfer as against the Steinway, and for the fact and reason for general preference of artists for Steinway, see http://en.wikipedia.org/wiki/B%C3%B6sendorfer and http://en.wikipedia.org/wiki/Imperial_B%C3%B6sendorfer_%28piano%29.

faculty choice was its experience with the German-made Bechstein concert grand piano that had been at the Tech recital hall for a time. Liszt is noted as having favorably mentioned both the Bosendorfer and Bechstein as the only two pianos that could withstand his performances. The Bechstein that was at Tech was, for a time, on the floor of the Baldwin piano dealership in Lubbock where I once played upon it. I thought the notes in the upper range had a wonderfully crisp sound like silver dollars dropping on cold steel. Possibly the dry West Texas climate had not agreed with the instrument. In any event, Steinway it was to be. Piano faculty members Drs. William Westney and Richard Redinger, went to the factory in New York to select the instrument, which was delivered either in late 1981 or early 1982, as a gift from Jo Anne and me.

Even though I was doing a lot of distance running in the last half of the 1970s, somehow I found the time and energy to seriously practice several classical piano pieces prior to the 1978 Vienna trip. Consequently I had by then memorized a sufficient repertoire to give me a pretty good feel for the keyboard's action and the quality of the sound produced. But my piano practicing in the build-up toward marathoning was not done with Vienna and Bosendorfer in mind. Rather the "irrational dream" was taking hold of me.

While I have no tangible record of it to fall back on, a certain visit with Harold Luce, then head of the music department at Texas Tech, surely occurred in the latter part of 1978. It occurred as a result of a phone call I made to him from my law office. We were on friendly terms simply by reason of my various involvements with Texas Tech and its development office. In the call, I said to him that I had something I would like to talk to him about. Might I either come to his office or he come to mine? His immediate response was that he would come by mine on his way home. He lived just off of Indiana Avenue a couple of miles to the south, and our offices at that time were at the corner of Indiana Avenue and 22nd Street, three blocks south of 19th Street that defined Tech's southern boundary. It was, for him, a straight shot.

He showed up at the appointed late afternoon time and I shared with him my life history insofar as it involved playing the piano. More importantly, I told him of my "dream" of playing one of the great classical piano concertos with an orchestra. He listened with keen interest, and I put the question to him, "Do you think I am out of my mind in trying to do this?" His answer, "By all means I think you should pursue your dream," was such a finely honed prevarication that I later thought he must surely have thought it through in advance—though he could hardly have anticipated my question—unless Cecil Mackey had mentioned it to him or somehow or other I had said something about it that had gotten back to him. He would, in time, confess to me what would have been a more truthful answer.

Our discussion did not end with my question and his answer. We launched into a "Where do I go from here?" discussion. He said that it would be impossible, or essentially so, for me to accomplish such a thing without first studying music theory. But since we were not talking about me becoming a student at Tech, he said that he would be happy to meet with me in his office one afternoon a week and teach music theory to me. We started that shortly after the beginning of the year 1979, as I was zeroing in on the April 16, 1979 date for the Boston Marathon. These sessions with him were fun and, for me, educational. They went on through the year, including, as I recall, most of the summer. In the fall he told me that I now had the equivalent of a year's course in music theory. He said that he was enjoying our sessions, but wanted to know where I would like to go from this point. I told him that I would really like to get to the keyboard, and I think I indicated that it would be very special to me if I could study with Dr. William Westney, who, since my days of studying with him, is now "Bill" to me. Of course, it would be as a private, paying student, not as a registered Tech student. My recollection is that he did not give an immediate approval of that arrangement, but it soon worked out that I was permitted to audition with Dr. Westney.

The Threefold Denouement: Music

The tentative response of Dr. Luce to my expressed desire to study with Westney was understandable. Westney was born in 1947 and was only thirty-one years of age in 1978, the year he had joined the Tech faculty. I had seen and heard him perform during the 1978/1979 school year and was completely captivated by his keyboard skill. That first impression and judgment proved to be extremely well vindicated.[1]

So, when Luce informed me, early in Westney's second school year, that I could schedule an audition in the latter's studio, I was thrilled, and intensified my practice prior to that event. My initial visit with, and audition before, Westney occurred in November 1979. I do not recall having met Westney in person prior to that. Whatever anxiety I may have had going into his studio was quickly dispelled by his warm and calm manner. Without show he exudes intelligence in a simple, calm, and pleasant way. After a brief visit he inquired if I would like to play something for him. Of course, my answer had to be, and was, that I would like to do that. I told him that I had committed to memory some nine numbers by classical composers. I do not recall that I listed any of them. Very well I remember, however, his next remark that it was hard to imagine that I could play that many very well. Certainly he was not speaking about the capability of a professional pianist, but rather one who was neither a music major, nor involved in public performance in any way, and who had not studied with anyone for thirty years, and even then only in a small Illinois town. He was, of course, absolutely correct, but the extent to which he was correct was beyond my ability to understand at that point—a lack that was rather quickly overcome. I chose to play for him Chopin's "Fantasie Impromptu," as mentioned earlier

---

1   A simple Internet search under "William Westney" amply rewards. His own website is widely informative. A search under "William Westney Curriculum Vitae" provides an impressive and extensive picture of his accomplishments. Perhaps not overly visible is the fact that each of his three academic degrees, all from Yale University, garnered *summa cum laude* honors.

a piece that I had never formally studied or ever performed in front of even a small audience.

My performance was, I thought, without any major baubles, at the conclusion of which I awaited his remarks. He said, without hesitation, "You have good finger facility, but you do not play like an artist." A compound sentence of thirteen words that both compliments and criticizes. A jewel of simplicity, spoken directly and in low-key. Free of any hint of flattery, it was a judgment easy to accept, especially since it seemed to imply that he was ready and willing to be my teacher. Without a lot of discussion, we quickly agreed upon his fees and scheduled the first of my weekly lessons to start in the upcoming week. It was the beginning of a relationship that has progressed from teacher and student to warm and personal friendship, one that has spanned thirty-four years as I write in late 2013.

Westney's studio comfortably accommodated two Baldwin studio concert grand pianos, sitting side by side, teacher on the left and student on the right. The studio was spacious enough for class sessions where each student would perform before his other students, their peers in piano study, after which these other students would comment critically on the performance. Normally, only a few students would perform during a given class session. Inasmuch as I was not a regular student, I only appeared in sessions when I was to perform. In a sense I was a guest of the class, and I was at least twice as old as their norm. I did not appear more than two times, and I'm not sure that I appeared more than once—which time I remember because my playing was disastrous—but a priceless experience in the learning process, and the students were gracious in regard to my performance. In any event, I was nervous being subjected to this new type of experience. In the end, I would redeem myself very publicly to the happy awareness of all of them.

Bill started my instruction at ground zero on technique and simple fundamentals, critically important but an entirely new element to me. What I was striving for now, was to rise to a level that met the approval of a high professional, such as Bill Westney clearly was. It would turn into the most demanding discipline I would have encountered, including all that was involved up to and including the culmination of the Boston Marathon experience itself.

To have a person of his immense professional competence sitting to my left illustrating technique or illustratively performing passages that I was expected to master was stimulating to the highest degree. Of course, I was not expected to attain that level of perfection, but great inspiration flowed from it into my being in the four and a third years that I studied with him. He was charitable in his instruction, complimentary when deserved and helpfully corrective when needed. There was no equivocation. You came to trust his guidance without the least hesitation. He had been there and done that, and done it to a high level of perfection. What a priceless privilege those years were.

I studied with Bill from that beginning in November 1979 until I had recorded, on April 24, 1984, my 1984 recital numbers.

To put some things in perspective, my original goal, expressed to Dr. Luce and understood by Bill Westney, was to play one of the great classical piano concertos with an orchestra. Obviously, since I did not expect to be on the professional circuit, such as would be required to perform with the Lubbock Symphony Orchestra, my prospects for an orchestra were pretty well limited to the Texas Tech Symphony Orchestra, performing in its Hemmle Recital Hall on the new piano to be provided there. It is fairly obvious that not every amateur who might otherwise dare to undertake such an accomplishment had the standing or wherewithal to bring it about as I did. While the price is much higher today, and was arrived at in a way that did not involve any dealership profit, the cost of the piano in 1981 was $25,000. Those who might be able to afford it might not be able to convince those who could approve them doing so. However immodest it may sound, I had for many years developed something of a reputation as a local lawyer and businessman who was involved in the community, and that probably had a good bit to do with me ever getting the door open in the first place to make the try for it. At least the scenario, as unlikely as it might have seemed, must have had some sort of appeal to those who helped bring it about. As indicated in the section on charitable activities earlier, I emerged with a profound gratitude to Tech, and to its music department and Bill Westney in particular.

But to further put the matter in perspective, such things as working such a program into the music department's schedule at Tech, including reserving the recital hall, had to be set down months in advance. The recital season is essentially in the late winter or in the spring. If it is not scheduled in time for one season, it would need to be delayed till the next. The music department's calendar had to be pretty much in place well before the end of a calendar year. So, in the early or middle fall months of 1981, the date of Tuesday, March 23, 1982 was set aside on the recital hall calendar for me to play the concerto. From November 1979 to March 1982 is a total of twenty-eight months, starting from my beginning with basic keyboard technique that I had never really had before. There was an immense amount of ground to cover in that short time frame. Bill chose for me Beethoven's 3rd piano concerto. Just when that selection and my early work on it began I cannot say for sure, but it must have been no later than early in 1981, perhaps even late 1980. To this I will return, but much needs to be covered before getting to that.

In working with Bill, there was no study or playing of scales, as such, that I can recall. Supposedly I came into his study with the knowledge of scales gained in my music theory study with Dr. Luce. Not having been involved as one both educated and regularly involved in musical performance or pedagogy, when the name of a particular scale, such, for instance, as F♯ minor, was mentioned, it put me into a time-out to think it through. While there were different types of scales, they were always identified to some key on the keyboard in either its major or minor mode. The note upon which the scale started was that for which it was named, and it, in any octave, was known as the "tonic." A major scale started on the tonic and progressed upward seven notes to the tonic one octave higher. The notes in any scale are assigned a number, such as second, third, fifth, or seventh, but that number is arrived at by including the lower tonic note so that the "second" is only one note higher than the tonic and the "seventh" is only six notes above the tonic and one note below the tonic octave. Thus, any scale has only seven notes in it, except that it becomes eight when the tonic octave note is added, the tonic being counted twice. Counting the tonic only once, there are twelve notes in the chromatic scale, which includes every white and black note on the keyboard within one octave. Interestingly, the numbers seven and twelve figure into our music much as they do in our colors (the twelve in color being more esoterically revealed), reflecting a profound relationship between sight and sound. The five black keys introduce the concept of a half step, as do the intervals between the keys of E–F and B–C. Thus, in a major scale all steps from tonic up to the tonic octave are whole steps except between the third and fourth and between the seventh and tonic octave. In the normal minor key, the steps are all the same except the first of the two half steps is between the second and third rather than between the third and fourth as in the major. There are more refined variations, such as the melodic minor or the harmonic minor, but these need not be gone into here.

Without regard, for now, to the selections I worked on during my study with Bill, certain things stand out, even now, in my memory having to do with how one performs a piece of music.

One of the most important of these was playing notes (or chords) in "legato." *Legato* is an Italian term meaning smooth. Musically, it means to let the movement from one note to the next flow smoothly without sound interruption, as in staccato or other detachment of sound between notes. Strangely, I do not remember ever having dealt with that concept in all my years of playing as a youth. Perhaps I may have sometimes played that way, but it was different, at least for me, from playing that way consciously.

A certain minimal acquaintance with the meaning of musical terminology was important. The more obscure or infrequently encountered terms were not so critical, but terms found in almost all major works are important. Major examples would include *allegro* (lively, fast); *vivace* (livelier, faster); *presto* (very fast); *adagio* (slow); *largo* (expansively slow); *andante* (Italian word meaning "walking," thus a walking pace or tempo). *Forte* or *fortissimo,* indicated respectively by an "*f*" or "*ff,*" are indications of loudness, to which the addition of more *f*'s increases the loudness. The opposite of *forte* is *piano* (soft) or *pianissimo* (very soft), indicated respectively by a "*p*" or "*pp,*" again with the addition of more *p*'s increasing the softness. There are also various markings, one of the most common of which is expanding or contracting lines, *crescendo* or *decrescendo* (increasing or decreasing loudness). It is important to pay attention to the phrasing marks, those sweeping lines that define musical statements, just as in grammar there are phrases, clauses, and sentences, whereby words are connected to give meaning more than they would by being just a collection of words. A musical score is a series of musical statements put together to tell a musical story. All of the above are some of the more frequently encountered and basic terminology or symbology. Dictionaries or glossaries of musical terms are readily available, including online.

One should feel the music, for it will get across to the ear of those who listen. Some head or body engagement is normal, but it should not be very demonstrative, for it tends to be distractive or even distasteful to those who watch as well as listen. It is more important for one's feeling to come through in the sound that is produced than in the visible head or body movement of the pianist.

One of the most helpful suggestions on technique came, I believe, from Dr. Luce, although possibly also from Bill. It had to do with the next to last note or chord in any phrase, most especially when it was a seventh that was about to resolve into the tonic on the last note. That penultimate note should be played clearly and be held a bit longer to build anticipation for the concluding note of the phrase.

The Threefold Denouement: Music

This was especially true when it was a seventh note or chord resolving into the tonic to end the phrase. This pause creates a natural longing in the listening soul to hear that last note, an anticipation that is then satisfied when the phrase concludes with the final note, tenderly rendered.

At the outset of my lessons, Bill would select pieces for me to work on. Most of these were of modest length and involved various types of playing, all working to the end in sight. I do not have a record of many of these early ones. It could not have been too long into my studies however, when, while driving I happened to hear on the classical music station, broadcast from a Texas Tech affiliate station, a Beethoven sonata that I was unfamiliar with. It was long enough that I had to sit at my destination to hear the last of it and get its number. It was his sonata number eighteen (there are thirty-two Beethoven sonatas published). It comprises a usual three movements, the first in allegro, the second a "scherzo" marked "allegro vivace," and the third a *"menuett"* in a *"moderato e grazioso"* (moderately with grace) tempo followed by a *"presto con fuoco"* (Italian *"con fuoco"* means "with fire," thus with great vigor and speed). I loved the whole thing, but the most memorable aspect of it is that it is the first, perhaps the only, time I ever laughed at a Beethoven number, and it was not because it was not brilliant but rather that it actually seemed funny. The movement that made me laugh was the scherzo, which means playful or light-hearted. But it was the way the artist played it, with pauses for emphasis before the raging, playful passage would begin. I simply broke out laughing as I drove, and had to wait through both segments of the Menuett movement to find out what this piece was. Immediately it was on my list of pieces I wanted to learn. Bill went along with it and I had a great time playing it.

Brilliant pianists who have attained high levels of technical perfection frequently play with great precision at blazing speed. While I marvel at, and admire, their accomplishment, I must confess that, for me, so often this very speed destroys the musicality of what they are playing. It is their accomplishment, and not the beauty of the music, that thus stands out.

Many times Bill emphasized that speed is relative and is subservient to the meaningful musical expression the pianist brings to it. Bill himself often plays very fast, sometimes a bit faster than I would really like, but his music is always done in taste and with a high degree of perfection, and I always enjoy seeing and hearing him play and attend all his performances if I am in town. In time, my own CD recordings were shared with a professional musician I knew when he was in high school in Wichita Falls—in Jo Anne's class. After listening to them, he wrote saying that I played amazingly well as a "lyrical pianist." In short, I think he meant that a lot of expression came through in my playing. I believe that became more and more true. My playing never rose to the level of technical perfection that is regularly demonstrated by professional pianists. But those who have listened to it, including professional musicians and pianists, have commented on just this expressive quality along with surprising capability for an amateur.

I learned to play that sonata no. 18 to the point where Bill seemed pleased with it and I had great enjoyment with it. Otherwise, however, it is like the flower born to blush unseen, for I have no recollection of ever having played it in public performance and it preceded the time when my playing was recorded.

In retrospect, I have to wonder if Bill's selection of a Beethoven concerto for me to perform may have taken into account his evaluation of that early work I did on sonata no. 18. A Beethoven concerto is essentially a Beethoven sonata that merges pianist and orchestra into one.

Probably our work on the concerto started soon after that. It would have taken me some months to complete work on that sonata, and there was much to cover between starting on the concerto and performing it on the grand night of March 23, 1982.

The Threefold Denouement: Music

During the four plus years of my study, aside from the concerto performance, I prepared the following three different annual recital programs:

November 1981 Recital Series:
    Chopin, Ballade, in G minor
    Debussy, Reflections in the Water
    Debussy, Dance
    Schumann, Soaring
    Schumann, Why
    Liszt, Hungarian Rhapsody no. 2

Spring 1983 Series:
    Mozart, Sonata, in C, K no. 330
    Chopin, Waltz, in G♯ minor, Op 64, no. 2
    Chopin, Polonaise, in C minor, Op 40, no. 2
    Rachmaninoff, Prelude, in D, Op 63, no. 4
    Debussy, Isle of Joy, in A
    Rachmaninoff, Humoreske, in G, Op 10, no. 5

1984 Recital Series (recorded 4-24-84):
    Chopin, Scherzo, B♭ minor
    Rachmaninoff, Prelude, Op 23, no. 6, E♭
    Chopin, Ballade no. 4, Op 52, in C

Over the course of these years and recital programs, I played solo numbers before various audiences that invited me. All of this music was recorded by Dick Burt (Dorian Systems) as I played it, without audience, in our living room on my Baldwin studio concert grand piano. These were reel to reel tape recordings. Compact disk (CD) recordings had not yet come into general circulation. The CD prototypes were being developed somewhat contemporaneously with my musical study. For years, I gave these recordings on audio cassettes to family and close friends. The sound quality of the cassettes was so-so to begin with and deteriorated over the years. My relationship with the music department at Tech was such that I was contacted by the technician in the Tech music department who proposed to work from the original reel to reel recordings to make master compact discs, which he did very professionally. From these master copies, Crystal Clear Sound recordings in Dallas, a commercial operation, has made for me over the years hundreds of copies which we have given away to countless friends or, in fact, to most anyone who shows an interest in having a set. The set includes, on one CD, the entire Steinway Dedication concert program, and on the other CD, the following selections from my various recitals:

> Chopin, Ballade no. 1, in G minor (1981)
> Debussy, Reflections in the Water (1981)
> Rachmaninoff, Prelude, in D, Op 63, no. 4 (1983)
> Chopin, Scherzo, B♭ minor (1984)
> Schumann, Why (1981)
> Chopin, Ballade no. 4, Op 52, in C (1984)
> Rachmaninoff, Prelude, Op 23, no. 6, E♭ (1984)
> Chopin, Waltz, in G♯ minor, Op 64, no. 2 (1983)
> Liszt, Hungarian Rhapsody no. 2 (1981)

Those to whom they have been given have generally, after listening to them, commented with most gracious admiration, and often with amazement.

Ironically, my local reputation as a pianist had reached a certain fairly high level among those who knew me or knew of me, but all of this flowered about the time I was giving up such study and performance. The entirety of my adult musical study period took place while I was still actively engaged in both the law practice and as owner and top management person of Resthaven. My piano had been demanding up to six hours a day within that overall schedule of activity. While it was a magical time, when music was the most jealous of these three mistresses, so to speak, it was a schedule I could not continue to maintain. Having recorded my 1984 recital series on May 24, 1984, I put all music away and have not played anything seriously from that day to this. But those four plus years were another Camelot era for me, and music has been a significant part of our lives since that time—all magnified by what could be carried away from those wonderful experiences.

But alas, again I jump far ahead of the most demanding and exciting times leading up to the 1982 concerto program. I cannot remember in just what order all of these things came together. One thing is clear, however, by some point in 1981, I had worked through the three movements of the concerto to the point that I could put it aside while I completed the pieces in my 1981 recital series to the point I could play them before an audience. If I were to try to play, with an orchestra, in front of a recital hall filled with live people, and had done no public playing for over thirty years, I must get ready to do some playing in front of audiences. There is an immense difference between playing in the privacy of one's own studio or living room, and playing in front of a live audience, all from memory and without the presence of any musical score. To that end, work on the concerto was shelved and I dove into preparing to perform the entire 1981 recital series before four different audiences of long-suffering friends in our living room. All four of these were done in November 1981, and not a single one of them was done without my messing up at least one of the numbers, mostly by a failure of memory.

At one point in my work on the concerto, Bill asked me to play the first movement in one of his class sessions before his other students as critics. In all my piano lessons on the concerto, Bill played the orchestral part on the other piano, and this he did in the class session also. The performance was a disaster. I could not get through it. Rachet up the level of pressure, if I could not play it before the relatively small audience of piano students—albeit they would be the more critical. As critics, though, they were merciful, for they understood something of what I, or anyone facing the same plan, would be going through, although I do not know if any of them were privy to my plan. At some point I had to save face with them, and with myself. The clock was ticking and the calendar was moving on. My thinking now is that this breakdown was in the late spring of 1981. I probably resuscitated my standing with Bill enough, though, to lay the concerto aside in order to work up the recital program that I was to begin performing that fall. Once those performances were over, and recorded for future use, I got back to the concerto with a vengeance. One problem—Bill said I needed to start over on it. We were then in December 1981, and we were then on the Hemmle Recital Hall calendar for March 23, 1982, a mere four months away. Our family went to Illinois for Christmas with my folks. But I was in panic mode by then and made arrangements with the large piano store in downtown St. Louis to get into its premises to practice while it was shut down for the holidays—and that I did.

In the days that followed, I was making good progress, through devoting virtually all my time and energy to this project. It was in this time frame that Bill told me that if I expected to be able to get through all these movements on the evening of the performance, I must get to the point that I could move entirely away from the piano and play every note in my mind consciously from memory. This was the most difficult thing to accomplish in the training phase. I was able, at last, to do it, lying on the sofa in our living room. Bill also said that I must then take that ability with me to the concert hall and that I must not let anything or any occurrence during that evening take my concentration off of the memorized content of that concerto. If for even an instant something drew my attention away, or if it just drifted away, I would wake up in shock not knowing where I was and full scale panic would set in. He even told me of such an experience he went through momentarily while playing before an audience of three thousand in NYC's Queens borough in a performance he had won the right to give through competition. He recovered, but spoke of how terrifying it was for an instant. I can now state for a fact that if I had not stuck strictly to his advice on this, I would have gone down at a certain point in the first statement of the first movement on concert night.

As the critical date approached, he began giving me helpful advice that only a performing artist could give from experience. He taught me how to bow. Knowing that drugs were a problem with some performing musicians, he said that the excitement of the event was all the stimulant I would need and that it was not wise to take any other. This came as a surprise, for performance enhancing drugs were nothing I had ever touched or even considered—probably had not heard much of in those days. I had, however, since first prescribed, used a considerable amount of the headache medication that my doctor had recommended for my severe headaches, Fiorinal (aspirin, caffeine, and butalbital [a barbiturate]), the only medication that had ever given me significant headache relief, especially tension-related headaches. I do recall taking my usual headache dose (two tablets) before leaving for the recital hall, for I had plenty to give me tension.

To put the matter of tension in perspective, consider that Jo Anne and I had arranged for a large catered post-performance reception at the elegant University City Club. It was located across 19th Avenue from the southeastern part of the campus, near the music building. We had mailed out five hundred personalized invitations to friends and other members of the community we knew. Each of the 500 invitation cards read as follows:

> Your Are Invited To Hear
> EDWARD REAUGH SMITH
> PERFORM BEETHOVEN'S CONCERTO NO. 3
> FOR PIANO AND ORCHESTRA
> in dedication of the
> STEINWAY CONCERT GRAND
> provided by
> THE EDWARD R. AND JO ANNE M. SMITH
> ENDOWMENT FUND
> of the Texas Tech University Foundation
> Tuesday, March 23, 1982, at 8:15 p.m.
> HEMMLE RECITAL HALL
> and afterwards at the reception
> UNIVERSITY CITY CLUB
> LUBBOCK, TEXAS

Inside the folded invitation was printed the following:

> Seating capacity of Hemmle Recital Hall is 600. For the benefit of those who desire to be assured in advance of seating, admission will be reserved until 8:00 p.m. for those holding tickets. After 8:00 p.m., seats will not be held for ticket holders. Tickets are free. If you desire tickets you may reserve them by calling 742-2270.

Accordingly, formal tickets were printed and widely distributed to those requesting them in advance. The recital hall was full and substantially all were comfortably seated before the 8:15 starting time.

Moreover, several close relatives and other special out-of-town guests had accepted our special invitations to attend. We had made arrangements for a separate local couple to greet each guest upon arrival and host them through the course of their stay, providing transportation to all events. We had reserved, as our guests, rooms for all of these visitors at the largest motel on South Loop 289 for the course of their visit. All three of our children, including spouses of those married, were here from out of town, but none of these needed hosts. All understood that I was not to be disturbed prior to the performance but surely wanted to visit with them afterward.

The list of these guests and their host couples was as follows:

Out-of-Town Guests

Relatives
    Frances R. Smith & Mary Anne Ayers, Illinois[1]
    T. H. & Jewel Myers, Wichita Falls, Texas[2]
    Jean & Johnie Tucker, Wichita Falls, Texas[3]
    Frost & Ruth Myers, Waxahachie, Texas[4]

---

1 My mother and sister.
2 Jo Anne's father and mother.
3 Jo Anne's sister and her husband.
4 Jo Anne's double uncle and aunt. Frost is T. H. Myers' brother and Ruth is Jewel Myers' sister, a second marriage for each with neither having children.

Bryce & Judy Colclasure, California[5]

Other Special Guests

Fred Tewell, Oklahoma[6]

Myra Robinson, Big Spring, Texas[7]

Richard & Karen Miles, Fort Worth, Texas[8]

Dean & Mary Ellen Carlton, Dallas[9]

Broadus & Ruth Ann Spivey, Austin[10]

Ken & Sammie Ford, Perryton[11]

Local Hosts

Duane & Pat Jordan

Norton & Joan Baker

Morris & Pat Nunley

Barry & Chris Squyres

Bob & Holly Schuster

Roy & Mary Ann Ward

---

5 Bryce is my older cousin; Judy is his wife.

6 Fred Tewell was my debate coach at Midwestern University, but then currently teaching at Oklahoma State University.

7 Head of Robinson Drilling Company in Big Spring, a client, and a very special friend.

8 My law school roommate, and we each served as the other's best man nine days apart in September 1954.

9 Dean was an attorney in Dallas with whom I worked together on a number of legal cases.

10 Broadus was a trial attorney who started in Lubbock but moved his widespread practice to Austin. He filled in for me as Sunday School teacher when I could not be present in the early days of my teaching the Cornerstone Class. He was one of the four of us who did our first climb of Uncompahgre Peak (14,305") in Colorado, in July 1963. Later, when our daughter had a terrible automobile accident between Austin and College Station and was transferred to a hospital in Austin, Broadus and Ruth Ann insisted that we stay with them while we were there to be with our daughter.

11 Ken was president of Ford Tool Company, oil-field related, in Perryton, Texas, a client of mine referred to me by Bob Schuster. Ken had his own private jet, so could move about easily.

George & Beverly Babcock
Victor & Judy Igal
Ben & Norma Robinson
H. A. & Darlene Anderson (Standby)

The piano had arrived in or near December 1981, and it may actually have been used for some performances prior to mine. With it in the recital hall, I was eager to begin getting scheduled opportunities to play on it. This was not easy to do as the demands for both the instrument and the recital hall were constant. A handwritten note dated January 25, 1982, from Cathy Crist Talcott, who was in charge of scheduling all usage of the recital hall, read as follows:

> Hello Mr. Smith—Enclosed is your confirmation for the practice times you requested. I can't wait to hear the concert! Happy practicing! Sincerely (signed)

I remember that on the few occasions when I was able to practice there, I frequently looked up to the landing above the storage area that surrounded three sides of the parquet floor of the hall. Mentally I pictured Beethoven sitting up there, as in the famous "The Thinker" pose, pondering the music as I played. It was an emotional inspiration.

The event sparked a relatively major flow of local and other media attention, both before and after. Among these items are the following:

1. Article in March 21, 1982, Lubbock paper topped by shoulder and head shot of me, entitled "Lifetime Dream Comes True for Lubbock Lawyer," reading:

> Lubbock lawyer Edward Reaugh Smith will offer a recital at 8:15 p.m. Tuesday at Texas Tech University's Hemmle Recital Hall, backed by a faculty orchestra under the direction of Phillip Lehrman. There is no admission charge.
>
> He will perform Beethoven's "Piano Concerto No. 3" on the new Steinway Concert Grand Piano that he and his wife, Jo Anne M. Smith, have recently given to the Tech music

The Threefold Denouement: Music

department. The performance will be preluded by a dedication ceremony, in which Mrs. Smith will formally present the $25,000 instrument.

Smith studied piano for 10 years while growing up in Flora, Ill, competing in piano competitions during that time. He always wanted to play a major piano concerto with an orchestra. From his high school days until 1979, Smith had had no further musical education. But in 1979, he resumed his study with William Westney, Browning Artist-in-Residence at Tech.

The Steinway Concert Grand Piano, on which Smith will perform, is the result of a gift made in December 1980 by the Edward R. and Jo Anne M. Smith Endowment Fund of the Texas Tech University Foundation. In the summer of that same year, a specially formulated committee from the piano faculty of Tech traveled to the Steinway & Sons factory in New York City to personally choose the piano that was to find its new home in Hemmle Recital Hall. [Our gift may have been made early, in December 1980, but the faculty trip to select it would not have been prior to the summer of 1981, with the piano delivery in or about December 1981. While the gift went through our endowment fund at the foundation, we actually wrote an extra check at the time of the gift as an additional contribution to that fund.]

2. A sixteen-page fold-out brochure published for the Texas Tech University Department of Music, edited by David Payne, dated March 1983, gave the entire front page to a report of the dedication concert. It contained a picture of Jo Anne and me sitting on the bench at the piano on the floor of the recital hall, and read:

> A Steinway Concert Grand, gift of the Edward R. and Jo Anne M. Smith Foundation, was dedicated in a Hemmle Recital Hall concert on March 23. An orchestra of music faculty and students under University Symphony conductor Philip Lehrman accompanied Mr. Smith in his performance of Beethoven's *Piano Concerto no. 3*.
>
> Edward Smith is a member of the Lubbock law firm of Smith, Baker, Field & Clifford. He is also a licensed CPA, active in

business, political and community service in Lubbock. A schoolboy athlete and musician, he has continued those interests. In April 1979, he ran the Boston Marathon in well under qualifying time. That November, he resumed piano study, working with Browning Artist-in-Residence Dr. William Westney. His performance of the Beethoven concerto would mark a major achievement in any concert pianist's career.

Mr. & Mrs. Smith's gift included funds for Dr. Westney and music colleague Richard Redinger to travel to New York to select the new piano. Additional funds provided for care and storage of the new instrument backstage in Hemmle Recital Hall. The Music Department is indeed grateful to the Smiths, and to our other benefactors, for their support!

3. The March 24, 1982, issue of Lubbock's *Avalanche Journal* (Lubbock's newspaper) displayed as the top left item on page D-3 (social section) a 6 x 4 inch version of the same picture that was featured on the front of the 16-page March brochure of the Tech Music Department. The following account was immediately below the picture:

> RECEPTION GIVEN—Edward R. And Jo Anne M. Smith were honored Tuesday at a reception at the University City Club for their gift of a Steinway and Sons concert grand piano to the Texas Tech University department of music. The reception followed a dedication piano concert at which Smith performed with an orchestra of Tech music faculty members. (Staff Photo By John Chadwick)

4. The April 19, 1982 issue of my hometown paper, *The Daily Clay County Advocate Press,* Flora, Illinois, using an entirely different head and shoulders 4 ½" x 3 1/4" picture, presented a lengthy write-up entitled "Recital realization of long-time goal." In addition to two paragraphs devoted to the dedication program itself, it gave something of a biographical update on me since I had graduated from high school and left town thirty-two years earlier.

The Threefold Denouement: Music

5. A letter in my music file, dated November 22, 1982, is addressed to Dr. William Westney at Tech and reads:

> Dear Bill:
>
> Thanks so much for bringing by the Summer 1982 issue of Steinway News. Sorry we were not here when you came. Some friends of my wife's family in Wichita Falls knew the people from Olney, Texas who were on the same page and, of course, knew Jo Anne. Her folks sent it to us and we got several extra copies from C. A. Rodgers after that. Nevertheless, I very much appreciate your thinking of me and dropping it by.
>
> The little finger on my left hand still bothers me when I practice even after nine days so maybe this week in Colorado will be a good rest for it (I am dictating this on Saturday). I look forward to another lesson when we can get it scheduled.

The *Steinway News* was Steinway's "Summer 1982" edition, eight pages in length, with pictures relating to the placement of Steinway pianos during that period. The C. A. Rodgers mentioned owned the local piano store that handled our purchase for Tech. The picture of Jo Anne and me on the bench in front of the piano that was made by John Chadwick of the Lubbock *Avalanche Journal* appeared in the upper left corner of page five. There were a total of twenty-five pictures, of which ours was the eleventh. The following was below our picture:

> Edward R. And Jo Anne Smith are shown at the keyboard of a Steinway concert grand presented by them to Texas Tech University for the new Hemmle Recital Hall. The instrument was dedicated at a special concert at which Mr. Smith performed with an orchestra composed of members of the Texas Tech Music Faculty. The piano was delivered by Lubbock Music Center, Steinway representatives in Lubbock, Texas.

But let us return to the countdown and the program itself. Often I have commented facetiously that for once in my life I wanted to be able to sit down at the piano and "flip my tails." Prior to this concert event, I had never worn, or even had on, a formal tuxedo jacket with tails, nor have I since. But I had often observed pianists take their seat before the concert grand and "flip their tails" in the process of sitting down. Naturally I had to do that. Today this tradition seems not so strong as it was, though most highly formal events seem to honor it. I rented the outfit and Jo Anne made a picture of me in it standing on our driveway.

One of the most elegant productions that graced the occasion was the program that the music department prepared for hand out to attendees at the door. It was on a stable, high grade of white printing material nine inches in height and eighteen inches in width, with two folds so that, until opened, its dimensions were nine inches in height and six inches in width, comprising six pages. The front page contained essentially the same material as the 500 formal invitations that had been mailed out. Inside the cover page, page two contained a biographical sketch of me. When thus opened, the middle of the three inner pages, page 3, contained both the program for the dedication, and then the formal listing of the concerto and its three movements—Allegro con brio, Largo, and Rondo Allegro. Page four, the last of the three inner pages, gave the name of the conductor, Philip Lehrman, and then all members of the orchestra.[1] Page five, the last page with content, was on the back of the program, but in a way that when the front cover was opened, this one is the first thing seen. It was a picture of me seated with Jo Anne standing off my left shoulder—perhaps made by someone at Tech.

One of my greatest concerns and causes for anxiety was the lack of opportunity to practice the concerto with the orchestra. While as a youth I had occasionally played accompaniment for a singer or some instrumental performer, never as a youth or adult had I ever so much as played with an ensemble, let alone an orchestra.

---

1 There were six first violins, five second violins, four violas, three celli, one bass—(comprising nineteen strings), two flutes, two oboes, two clarinets, two bassoons, two horns, two trumpets, and one timpani—(thirty two in all). The principal on each instrument was a faculty member, as were several of the others, and the rest were advanced students of their instrument.

Granted, I had played in Bill's studio while he played the orchestra part. But I yearned for time to get accustomed to playing this piece with the orchestra. Such opportunity was distressingly scant. We rehearsed together one time, on the night of March 22, the night before the dedication concert. And we went through all three movements *only one time*! Conductor Lehrman wanted to go through the slow, middle Largo movement a second time. My preference was for the two faster allegro movements, but that was not to be. While, as I recall, my performance at the rehearsal came off fairly well, *it was only one time!* While this doubtless fit better with the logistics of the music department and its faculty, I was screaming in my mind for more, but it was not to be.

On the day of the concert, I mixed private resting time with private practice time. Out-of-town family and other guests were advised in advance that, while I looked forward to visiting with them after the program, they should not try to greet or visit with me beforehand. Instead of coming to our house they should go with their hosts directly to the motel.

In the final countdown, Dr. Luce, who was to preside over the dedication, had handed out to each of the platform guests a precisely timed schedule of the program. The copy marked for "Mrs. Smith" (Jo Anne) read as follows:

Steinway Piano Dedication

Platform guests

Mrs. Jo Anne Smith
Dr. John Bradford
Mr. W. B. Rushing
Dr. Harold Luce

Platform guests will meet at 8:10 p.m. in the back-stage area on the West side of Hemmle Recital Hall.
House lights down at 8:15 p.m.

Platform guests go to front of stage (orchestra members already in place)

Dedication Ceremony

1. Introduction of Mrs. Smith.
2. Mrs. Smith makes formal presentation of the piano.
3. Introduction of Dr. John Bradford, Vice President for Development at Texas Tech University.
4. Vice President Bradford accepts the piano on behalf of Texas Tech.
5. Introduction of Mr. "Dub" Rushing, Chairman of the Board of Directors of the University Foundation.
6. Mr. "Dub" Rushing reads the Resolution of Appreciation from the Foundation.
7. Response from Harold Luce.

House lights up after applause.
Platform guests leave stage and find seats.
Chairs and lectern removed.
Performance of Beethoven piano concerto begins.

The recording of the entire program and performance captures all the remarks made by each of these. My files contain a copy of only Jo Anne's formal presentation and the final response by Harold Luce, both of which, for the benefit of those who do not have the recording, are brief and given below. Bear in mind that I was not present in the hall for any of the dedication program prior to my own appearance to play. When I first listened to the recording of the program, I lit up with appreciative delight at the last thing that Dr. Bradford said as he turned away from the microphone and talked to Jo Anne, but audible to all, "Finally, to you, Jo Anne, and to Ed, wherever he may be—probably on his knees somewhere praying," the audience got a good laugh. Our longtime friend Betty Doris LaRoe, never to be squelched, was sitting on the front row, and I had no trouble detecting her hilarious laugh.

The Threefold Denouement: Music

When Dr. Luce introduced Jo Anne, the audience stood and gave her an enormous and continued outpouring of thunderous applause. It was so impressive that, before she began to speak, she uttered to all, "Thank you, my goodness!" And then she gave her dedication speech:

> In the summer of 1950, a not yet 18 year old high school graduate from Flora, Illinois moved to my home town of Wichita Falls. I was 16 that summer. We met casually at the youth activities of the Methodist Church.
>
> There was something unusual about that boy then, at least in my eyes. In September we had our first date; four Septembers later we married; and now, almost 32 years later, I still see the unusual in my husband. (A considerable wave of laughter erupted from the audience)
>
> Time does not permit that I should try to catalogue, for better or worse, all of his characteristics (more laughter), but one of them is his methodical, logical, objective mind. You might find it strange in one who can lose himself in classical melody, and at times I have found it maddening to cope with, since I am of a somewhat different nature.
>
> But many years ago, long before he had much to give away, this methodical, logical, objective mind determined that it was good for everyone when someone made a helpful, meaningful gift. That it helps the recipient, at least in most cases, is obvious. But he was totally convinced that it helped the giver even more. Of course, being a tax lawyer, it makes you very happy when it is time to pay your taxes. (Laughter) But more important, it makes you happy inside.
>
> Ed and I have come to see that helpful gifts bring to the giver an asset of far greater value than he parts with. He and I both want to say that the piano setting before you tonight is an asset of this great university. But the honor of having been able to give it is an asset of ours of far greater value.
>
> We want to thank each of you for sharing this exciting night with us.

Again, for Jo Anne, the audience stood and gave her a further enormous and lengthy round of applause. I think they all knew how she had put up with me, but her activity in the community had itself been substantial, so she was very well known and loved by many.

Concluding the pre-concert dedication program were these words from Dr. Harold Luce:

> On behalf of the faculty and students in the Texas Tech University Department of Music, I want to express our deep appreciation to Mr. And Mrs. Smith for their thoughtful generosity in giving us this magnificent new Steinway Concert Grand Piano. I also want to take this opportunity to say a word regarding my personal admiration for Mr. Smith in what he is doing here tonight. To dare to appear in public as a soloist with an orchestra in a major concerto requires considerable skill, long hours of preparation, and a bit of courage even on the part of professional musicians. For an amateur musician, even a highly talented one such as Ed is, to attempt such a feat requires even greater courage and more preparation. As an attorney, I'm sure Mr. Smith has never faced a larger jury that he does tonight. (Laughter)
>
> I would also like to comment on the orchestra we are using this evening, which includes members of our faculty as well as several advanced students. The orchestra is about the same size that would have been used in a performance of this concerto in Beethoven's own time.
>
> Finally, may I express again our most heartfelt thanks to Ed and Jo Anne Smith for the gift of the piano.
>
> Will you please join me in expressing our gratitude. (Applause)

Shortly the concert mistress came out to applause, struck the A on the keyboard and all strings tuned up. A short period of silence followed, after which I came onto the floor of the hall, to the standing ovation of the crowd. Arriving at the corner of the piano, I bowed, stepped to the bench, flipped my tails, sat down, tested the bench height making any needed adjustments, fit my hands upon the keys, then to my lap, and, after a moment, raised my face to the conductor and nodded for him to begin.

The Threefold Denouement: Music

Beethoven published five piano concertos. Each of the five begins with an extensive stretch where the orchestra plays alone before the piano makes any significant entrance. On the first three, the pianist plays no note until the conclusion of this lengthy orchestral introduction, a thorough presentation of the theme of the first movement. On the fourth, the piano opens with a simple, five-measure statement of a main theme in the first movement, then sits back for the long orchestral introduction. On the last, the fifth, the "Emperor," the orchestra plays its first ponderous note, but on the second beat while that note is held the piano enters and plays a considerable statement, and then exchanges the early flourishes with the orchestra until the piano finally relinquishes this stirring entrance to the orchestra for the usual Beethoven orchestral introduction.

As I nodded to the conductor, I was preparing to listen to the orchestra perform the first 110 measures of the concerto as a thorough statement of the first movement. The tempo was set and I entered on measure 111 and played pretty well, in tempo, with the orchestra through measure 181. The orchestra took the exchange alone from measure 172 through 180. The next two measures were mine alone, consisting of four soft half notes that were intended to introduce the first statement of a new theme that descended in a stirring rondo-like Beethoven cadence into the base clef. The approach to the statement began with a series of sixteenth-notes at measure 182. Perhaps here I missed the advantage of having gone over this with the orchestra more than once, but at this point, in the excitement of approaching this statement that I wanted so much to do boldly and well, on nervous impulse I blasted into an accelerated tempo. The abrupt change was noticeable on the recording, particularly in the disconnect, tempo-wise, with orchestra that was trying to keep up. I nevertheless maintained the faster tempo through the completion of that full statement that ran through measure 227. But in measures 205 through 208 I was in trouble, having lost the left hand that was to have taken over the running sixteenth notes. I maintained the rapid echoing octave in the right hand so that those who have neither played this music nor listened to it enough to pick up on all of its finer aspects do not usually realize what I am leaving out—this was the first time through this statement; but probably some in the audience sensed that I was having trouble at this point. Our son Mark told me later that he thought I was in trouble in this passage, and he was right. Fortunately, again perhaps thanks to Bill's advice to memorize everything in my head, I picked up the left hand again in measure 209 and got through the end of that statement. The orchestra took over, reestablishing the correct tempo, and I settled down. I had survived and there would not be another such incident. During the orchestral interval, I resolved to get hold of myself and not make that nervous tempo error again. Indeed, that determination worked out for when the repeat of that statement, specifically where the left hand broke down in measures 205–208, I got every note in there and it felt great. The first passage (in 205–208) was in c minor, but the restatement of it (in 381–384) was in C major and the wholesomeness of the major key surged through triumphantly.

There were many passages through the rest of the concerto where I was not happy with the way I played, but when, after the evening was over and I was with Bill at my next lesson, I said to him, wanting his honest opinion, "I did not think I did very well." He replied with much emphasis, "It was a rousing success!" I felt better, and, in fact, considering the event in its entirety and the responses, I believe his evaluation was more accurate than mine. Of course, in listening to the performance I still notice every spot where I could, and should, have done better. But I got through the entirety of it, with an increasing confidence with each passing measure. There were several places where to maintain the tempo I simply had to get to a certain point on the proper beat and when I was unable to play it up to my full capability I nevertheless held on to that tempo. The orchestra and I were in sync after that one nervous dalliance when I played too fast, rushing the tempo. I was beginning to feel the thrill of playing fairly well and to sense that

The Threefold Denouement: Music

the audience was very much into it with me, and that I was not going to embarrass anyone by breaking down.

Harold Luce, commenting later on the problem area of measures 182 through the end of the statement at 227, said that from that point on I settled down and it went very musically. Emilia Westney, Bill's wife, was sitting with him in an upper row of the hall. Either from her or someone, I got the word that when I had been settled down for a while she turned to Bill and remarked, "Ed is playing very well." Evidently Bill, though probably agreeing up to that point, was not ready to fully relax and enjoy it. As I understand, he did not reply other than by a barely perceptible nod of the head while continuing his intense focus upon the situation.

When the last notes of the third movement died down, there was an immediate standing ovation. I rose, bowed, and immediately exited the stage. Bill had prompted me on the normal protocol. Do not wait very long before returning to bow further, pausing, and exiting again. I do not remember if I did that one time or two, but the applause continued. So, having anticipated that possibility, I went back out, sat down on the bench, without having said a word about what I would play. For encore, I played Debussy's "Reflections in the Water." Probably it was the best I had ever played it anywhere, including in my own private living room. Dick Tolley, prinicpal trumpet for the concert, told me later that the concerto was very good and that he was then floored by that encore.

The imagination in the "Reflections..." was of one sitting by the side of a totally still pond of water, then throwing a pebble into it. The piece, in D flat major, begins softly with the haunting three-note theme—A♭, F, E♭—and that theme recurs throughout. At first it depicts the wave beginning from the spot the pebble enters the water. As the circle of the wave enlarges in area it rises in intensity till it climaxes in majestic sound before waning as the wave expands further until the pond is again totally still. The soft final note mesmerizes in stillness till it fades slowly, ever so slowly, into a calm, silent quietude. I raise my head and the standing applause is tumultuous. I bow and exit, repeating this a time or two until the applause dies away.

The dream long awaited and anxiously approached is now history, and the celebration can begin—which it did forthwith at the University City Club.

The reception was a true celebration, very well attended, and, insofar as I could tell, deeply felt by everyone; perhaps, if their words and expressions were true, with a combination of marvel at the performance, on one hand, and relief that a disaster was avoided, on the other hand. Jo Anne and I stood in the receiving line. It was long and our guests' comments to us were effusive. Finally, we got to the last person in the line. It was Dr. Harold Luce. Never could I forget his remark to me, "Now I will answer your question. I did think you were out of your mind!"

On April 12, 1982, he wrote to me at my law office:

> It was a red-letter day for anyone in the non-profit sector when one can enjoy the gift of a concert grand piano and then enjoy a gala after-concert reception, also paid for by the artist!
>
> Many thanks for the gift which made possible one of the most pleasant evenings we have had in a long time.
>
> Sincerely, (signed) Harold (Harold Luce, Chairman, Department of Music)

Jo Anne had prepared, in advance, a nice brunch at our house on the morning following the concert for all of our out-of-town guests. This was a priceless time of visiting with family and those close friends who had traveled to Lubbock for the concert. Over half of those from out of town are no longer living as I write. Particularly touching for me was the presence of Fred Tewell from Stillwater, Oklahoma, and my cousin Bryce Colclasure and wife Judy from Alameda, California. All three of these died within only a few years of the concert.

Countless letters, both laudatory and appreciative, came through the mail in the days following. As I write, I've just looked

The Threefold Denouement: Music

back through them, and find it impossible to select any sample as adequately representative of all. Each was unique and immensely gratifying. So many of them expressed great respect and appreciation for Jo Anne and for her elegance and eloquence on the occasion, and many also expressed their respect and affection for her in general.

In an effort to do justice to everyone who contributed in any way, I wrote the following form thank-you letter dated April 6, 1982:

> Dear _____:
>
> The anticipation and excitement scale will probably never hereafter have measured higher, in my life, than on the evening of Tuesday, March 23, 1982! In preparation and consummation, I probably experienced every catalogued emotion. And I very much felt in that wonderful audience a great outpouring of love, concern and friendship, for both Jo Anne and me, and for our loved ones.
>
> To each of you who was so gracious in serving on the program or in the orchestra, recording, videotaping, publicizing, serving as a host couple to our out-of-town guests, attending from a great distance, sending flowers, food or gifts, or telephoning or telegraphing long distance, we cannot adequately express our thanks. It is not practical for us to respond in writing to that other multitude of wonderful letters and cards, local telephone calls and personal visits, both before and after the event, from friends and loved ones.
>
> The total response was overwhelming—and our feelings about it and the event, ineffable.
>
> Please accept the foregoing remarks as being applicable to each of you. More personally, be assured that your _____ is and will always be treasured.
>
> Gratefully yours, (signed) Edward R. Smith

Ninety-four of these letters were sent out, the blanks in each case being filled, first with the recipient's name(s), and then with what the person(s) contributed to the event.

The concert was a watershed event. It marked the successful conclusion of that "irrational dream." But what was the future to hold? It seemed that all of a sudden I was catapulted by the event to the point of having a local reputation as a pianist. While many who were there, or who later listened to the recordings, seem to rank the performances as being on a professional level, by no means was I even close to that accomplished stratosphere. In my own mind, I still had a long way to go to reach a point of personal satisfaction. Moreover, it would be hard for me to turn down requests to perform. To continue studying would require fitting the practice time into a schedule that was otherwise already sufficiently full. My decision was to continue studying with Bill and trying to develop pieces to the point worthy of public performance. There were not that many requests, but there were invitations and opportunities to perform part or all of the recital program that I prepared for each of the remaining two years that I would study. In the course of these additional two years, while pressed to reach a level of perfection, I was not under the extreme pressure that I had subjected myself to in playing the Beethoven concerto in that ceremonious Steinway dedication concert.

My pianistic capabilities continued to enhance through those next two years. The period from my first lesson with Bill in November 1979 till the concerto in March 1982, comprised twenty-eight months. From March 1982 till I recorded my 1984 recital program on April 24, 1984, comprised twenty-three months.

Shortly before the end of that last time period, Bill and I were together in his studio, and the question on my mind, and doubtless his, was, "Where do we go from here?" It seemed that a level of competence had been attained from which I would either have to continue working higher, or recognize that I had come as far as was feasible for one with my other involvements. Whether this was said in precisely those terms in that last lesson, that was its substance. In this light, Bill asked me what I wanted to do. It was a poignant moment for me, and probably also for him. I told him that, when I had finished recording the 1984 recital program, I did not think I would undertake anything further. It was my decision. Probably sensing the inevitability, and advisability, of this decision, he accepted it calmly. He acknowledged that I had accomplished what I had set out to do, and more.

When I concluded the recording on April 24, 1984, I put my music up. I have not returned to the piano in any serious way since then. Countless people have moaned when I tell them this. They seem to think that I could continue to play. But early on, Bill said to me, in answer to my inquiry, that if I was not ready to perform a number in a proper way, I should courteously shy from any attempt to play it before them. It was good advice. When Jo Anne and I moved onto the Carillon Senior Living Campus on April 9, 2004, and for many months thereafter, I was besieged by the residents to play for them. Not once have I done so. One quickly loses the capability of performing unless relentless practice continues, and that was out of the question. We have hosted numerous recitals in our fairly commodious living room, including visiting pianists of the Lubbock Symphony Orchestra and many of Bill's advanced piano students needing to perform before an audience in advance of their own upcoming formal program recital.

While my days of study and performance ended in 1984, those fifty-three months I studied and performed deepened my love for the "great music" and my appreciation for those who rise to the level of performing it publicly. The CDs that capture what I was able to play in those months have continued to generate words of astonishment and appreciation from new friends to whom it remains our pleasure to give them.

The Appearance of Destiny

Prologue

In this section, when contextually appropriate and helpful, I refer to my own writings. They, with their acronymic abbreviations, are as follows (in the order of their publication by Steinerbooks, Great Barrington, MA):

Abbreviation	Title
BB	*The Burning Bush* (orig. ed. 1997, rev. ed. 2001)
IBJ	*The Incredible Births of Jesus* (1998)
DWJL	*The Disciple Whom Jesus Loved* (2000)
DQWIM	*David's Question "What Is Man?"* (2001)
SLJ	*The Soul's Long Journey* (2003)
TSRYR	*The Temple Sleep of the Rich Young Ruler* (2011)

IBJ and *DWJL* are small books. Each was written in a simpler mode than the others and focused upon a single important essay in *BB*. The focus of *IBJ* was upon *BB*'s "The Nativity," and the focus of *DWJL* was upon *BB*'s "Peter, James and John."

Preface

Human and other creature relationships reveal the divine and stand at the pinnacle of life's purpose and meaning. These aside, though intertwined, the most meaningful aspect of my life, and that for which all of the foregoing has been preparation, was the emergence of my primary destiny as I concluded my fifty-sixth year. It was in 1988 when I first came across, in my studies, the name of Rudolf Steiner. By my estimation, my life's work and meaning, including in its relationships, has been defined from that moment on.

In ancient Sanscrit, the word meaning fate, or its synonym destiny, was "karma." There it always coexisted with the concept of reincarnation. Karma and reincarnation (K&R) are not only

The Threefold Denouement: The Appearance of Destiny

connascent, born together, but one implies the other. They are opposite sides of the same coin. For the first two millennia of the Christian era, certainly at least since the fourth century, Western theologians have disdained these concepts. Steiner proposed early in the twentieth century that the time had come to recognize K&R as primal spiritual reality. Based upon my substantial contemplation of his extensive ouevre, both his writings and transcribed lectures, and my own years of studying and teaching the Bible, the spiritual reality of karma and reincarnation is, *for me*, moral certainty. I have argued cogently that the law and the prophets that Christ came to fulfill, according to his Sermon on the Mount (Matt 5:17–18), is the law of karma.[1] While K&R inheres all my writings, *BB*'s essays "Karma and Reincarnation" and "Lord of Karma" deal specifically with it, as does the entire volume *SLJ*, which is subtitled *How the Bible Reveals Reincarnation.*

In the foregoing, it is not my purpose to urge my convictions upon any reader, but only to substantiate the way in which I have used the term destiny, and to give a basis for understanding much that I will be saying about it in concluding this writing on my own life.

Preliminarily, I should also explain why I emphasize my discovery of Steiner as concluding my fifty-sixth year. The complexities of K&R are extensive and are detailed in my writings and cannot be condensed for inclusion in this preliminary statement. Suffice it for now to say that the karmic debt that an incarnating soul is born to deal with, in one way or another, is inscribed into it in the womb in nine successive stages. They play out in nine seven-year segments, that I call "septenaries," constituting the first sixty-three years of life. The septenaries of life are a matter of ancient wisdom.[2] The first three are more easily detectable, being the second dentition at seven, puberty at fourteen, and adulthood

---

1 See "Karma as the Law Christ Came to Fulfill" in SLJ (8–17).

2 See my introduction to Rudolf Steiner, *Turning Points in Spiritual History: Zarathustra, Hermes, Moses, Elijah, Buddha, Christ.*

at twenty-one. These relate to the "body." The next three relate to the "soul," and the last three relate to the "spirit," the "body, soul, and spirit" that Paul speaks of (1 Thess 5,23). The "spirit" is one's "burning bush" that never dies but in its long journey reincarnates ever and again toward perfection (cf. Matt 5:48). After age sixty-three, each person (soul) has addressed, in some manner, the small portion of its spirit's (or burning bush's) accumulated karmic debt that it (as descending spirit), with the aid of the spiritual hierarchies, set for itself, its "soul," to address in this life. It is after the first fifty-six years that one begins to address the karma inscribed into the highest of its nine septenaries. After age sixty-three, the soul serves and creates what lives in its spirit in future lives and ages. Each of us has been on the long human journey from the beginning and will be till the end when all becomes one again (Eph 1:9–10).

This is why, as I looked back upon it in later years, I marveled that it was only after fifty-six years that I discovered Steiner. His works preempted my life activity for that last seven years, and have ever since. In 1994, when I was sixty-two, I began to write *BB* which was published in 1997.

The Journey in My Destiny

Given what I recognize as my life's primary destiny, my journey toward it started well before my birth. There is nothing unusual in this. To constitute one's primary destiny, it would have to be formed before birth. Jeremiah and Paul each explicitly considered it so in his own case (Jer 1:5; Gal 1:15). I've already elaborated the details of the earthly aspects of my life thus far. What I look for now is what led me to find my way to Steiner, my inner experiences while engaging with his works, and the developments that eventually led me to recognize those works in my life as being my primary destiny.

The Threefold Denouement: The Appearance of Destiny

How I Found My Way to Steiner

No effort will be made to penetrate to subconscious levels of influence, though such influences are by no means denied. Only events within my conscious experience as they occurred and which, in retrospect, I am convinced were significant in my life's path to Steiner's works, will be mentioned. Chronological sequence will be applied, where possible, and for ready identification I attempt to so number them below, with commentary to follow:

1. My dad was employed as a land man by the J. J. Lynn Oil Division, of Kansas City, Missouri, in 1946, the year I entered high school in Flora, Illinois.

2. In the summer of 1948, my family drove from Flora to the San Fernando Valley, in the larger Los Angeles area, to visit my mother's sister and her family. By this time, the immense stature of J. J. Lynn, in our family psyche, was firmly established. Dad made arrangements for us, as we drove through Kansas City, to have a brief visit with Mr. Lynn in his office. We knew that Lynn had strong spiritual leanings, though I did not discover the depth and nature of them until recent years. Nevertheless, meeting the man in person was an experience for which I have always been grateful. The Lynn connection was providential and was a critical element in my journey in so many ways, but specifically on the matter presently addressed.

3. Dad worked over a large geographical area, as needed. During, or shortly before, my senior year in high school, the Lynn organization wanted dad to move to Wichita Falls, Texas. At dad's request, they agreed that he could travel from Flora and defer moving to Wichita Falls until after my high school graduation.

4. While riding with the father of one of my teammates to a basketball game we were playing in Mt. Carmel, Illinois, probably in January 1950, dad had a seizure, the first visible symptom of the brain tumor that was not diagnosed as such until about November of 1950. He continued to work, but had mini-seizures from time to time.

5. Upon returning from our trip to Washington, DC, and Gettysburg, following my graduation, we left my homeplace at 152 Meyer Street forever, headed for Wichita Falls, Texas.

6. Dad liked both the preacher, Al Freeman, and the men's Sunday School teacher, Pat Morrison (an Irishman) at First Methodist Church, where we began attending not long after our arrival and, I believe, soon joined as a family.[1]

7. I was too busy during my high school years in Flora to "date around," nor was that my inclination. For the first two years I had a steady girlfriend from church activities. That ended and I had a few isolated dates my junior year. Then the second of my "steady" relationships began. The girl was the stepdaughter of our minister. Her name was Sara. That did not start until my senior year, and it was a relationship that had probably grown out of being together so much at church and all of a sudden she entered my awareness in a deeper way. This was my most serious dating relationship right up to the time we left Flora in 1950. My close friend, the late Charlie Rankin, and his wife Betty, came to Wichita Falls to visit us fairly soon after we got settled down there, and at my request they brought Sara with them. It was a poignant time together. We were in an impossible situation, and I think the reality of that hit us both during these days though it was not said at that time. She had graduated a year before I did and gotten a job. It was obvious that she was not going to college, and perhaps did not have either the financial or family support to do so. In looking back over those few days together while the Rankins were there, I realize that Sara was very much ready to get married. And we both knew that I had a long way to go to get through college and law school and could not soon marry. All of this was unspoken, but lay barely below the surface. The parting from that time together was both difficult and sobering.

---

1 The Methodist Church had various predecessors before the Evangelical United Brethren and the Methodist Church merged on Apr. 23, 1968, to become the United Methodist Church.

The Threefold Denouement: The Appearance of Destiny

The exact sequence of events is blurry, but it is clear that Jo Anne came into my life for the first time that summer. She had turned sixteen on July 2, 1950, and it was probably after that and after Sara had left that I put my eyes on Jo Anne during the youth square dancing and singing in the enclosed outdoor courtyard of the church after Sunday evening services. I was rather immediately attracted to her, but a bit shy. As she drew my more than considerable interest, the relationship with Sara faded and I remember dreading having to bring up to her that I had found another girl to be interested in. The friendly gods relieved me from having to do so. While trying to bring myself to write to her, I received a letter from her saying that she was seriously dating a man, Harold, a farmer and a few years older, the son of our next-door neighbor and good friend on Meyer Street. She married Harold quite soon after that and lived on the farm with him until his death. I remember seeing her at a softball game in Flora a few years after she married. She never looked my way and we never spoke. I suspect that she was aware I was there. To this day, I still hold Sara warmly in my memory. Our relationship had the elements of a Greek tragedy in a way, doomed from the start. I deemed her a very good person. But Jo Anne was soon to help me get over Sara. My sister, Mary Anne Ayers, is registrar of Flora's DAR chapter. From its records she tells me that Sara died two years ago, on February 21, 2012.

I have gone to a bit of length to relate the Sara romance because I think there were forces behind these events, including the roadblock in that relationship and its happy conclusion for both of us, that account for the immediacy with which my focus turned to Jo Anne.

An event that is one of the type that one always remembers occurred during the short period when mother and dad were back with Mary Anne and me in the house on Hayes Street. By then, our parents had gotten to know each other pretty well, and cordially. Mother said to me one day, clearly speaking for dad as well as herself, "We sure do like Jo Anne." More lay in that statement than might normally be inferred from such few words. Neither of my parents had ever spoken to me, either favorably or unfavorably, about any of the girls I had dated before Jo Anne. She is the one and only girl to whom they ever gave their wholehearted approval for me. And Jo Anne's folks also made very clear to me by their many warm hospitalities and accommodations that they felt the same way about me for their Jo Anne.

8. Dad appeared to be recovering from the brain surgery he had in November 1950, enough so that he and mother returned to Wichita Falls for a short while before Lynn moved them to Abilene, Texas. But dad was beginning to go back downhill by then and their stay in the Abilene apartment did not last long. When they moved from Wichita Falls to Abilene, Mary Anne went back to Flora to stay with Grandma Reaugh and get back in school there. My parents soon returned to Flora, and moved back into the house on Meyer Street, never to return again to live in Texas. Dad died on February 1, 1954. At twenty-one years of age I became the son of a widow.

9. In early 1963, Glenn Chambers, the minister of education at First Methodist Church in Lubbock came to my law office and talked to me about the need for the formation of a new young married couples' class. As happens with the passage of time, the prior class of that nature was by then no longer "young married couples," and there was quite a number of young couples with no proper class home. He wanted Jo Anne and me to take over the formation and nurturing of a new class. We did. Jo Anne worked a lot with the group, especially administratively, and I became its regular teacher. The first class met on the Sunday after Easter that year, and the name it chose for itself was the Cornerstone Class. I served as its regular teacher for twenty-five years to the week in the sense that I taught through Easter Sunday, 1988. A high proportion of our class sessions were on specific books of the Bible, which we went through, in one manner or another, three times during the course of that quarter century. I estimate that I spent approximately 25,000 hours in those studies over that period. Those twenty-five years occupy a special place in my heart and

memories, and were immensely preparatory for what was to follow that period almost immediately.

10. During the night of August 19/20 (Monday/Tuesday), 1963, I had a near death experience (NDE). My appendix had apparently ruptured by early Saturday morning, August 17, but I sought no medical help until late Monday afternoon. By then my abdomen was greatly distended and the pain was intense and I needed something for the pain. Jo Anne drove me to an osteopath's office. I was in my bathrobe and walked at nearly a 90° angle at the hips. I lay down on his examination table. He looked at my abdomen, touched it lightly and told us to get to a surgeon. We had as yet no family doctor in Lubbock, but had recently met Dr. Victor S. Igal at a function at Horace and Diane Mitchell's house in Littlefield. He had just moved to Lubbock and gone into partnership with Dr. Clifford Payne, and the two of them had the Taylor Hospital across from their offices near University Avenue and 6th Street (which is now Mac Davis Lane). Dr. Payne assisted Dr. Igal in the surgery. Gangrenous infection encompassed my entire peritoneal cavity.

Dr. Igal remained with Jo Anne all night, telling her that I had only a small chance of living through the night. I did survive that night and progressed up to a point when my fever became a constant and led to further exploratory surgery on Friday, August 30, when I was in a much weakened condition. My hemorrhaging in the infected gall bladder area caused them to seal that off as best they could and close me up, essentially to die. Dr. Igal told Jo Anne that my chances of surviving the night were nil. But I did and left the hospital after three weeks.

The NDE was a signal event for me, suggesting that I should never fear the event of death itself. It was so wonderful that my return to consciousness, with the accompanying pain and discomfort was a crude shock. During the periods when I was unconscious or at least only semi-conscious, between the surgeries I kept hearing the old hymn "There is a Fountain Filled With Blood." Its several verses are given near the first of the "Blood" essay in my second volume, *"David's Question, 'What Is Man?'"* Jo Anne said that during these periods I kept pointing to the door and referring to the angels there. She said that this was a disturbing sign to Dr. Igal.

11. My nearly dying that summer led to our purchase of Resthaven, as described in the section on Resthaven. It was this venture that provided the financial base that gave me greater freedom not only to devote myself more substantially to Steiner's works but also to support the publication of those and related works in a material way.

12. While I had, in one way or another, from an early age, gained an exposure to the Bible's contents up to the time I began to study and teach it in 1963, from early in that twenty-five-year span, its contents, history, inter-relationships, and challenging passages came increasingly into my focus. While never did I feel that they were devoid of a vitally important message, as my study and contemplation of them progressed, my dissatisfaction and frustration with prevailing Christian theology and biblical interpretation (hermeneutics) and dogma increased to a critical point. For many, this route has led to the agnostic.[1] But with me it served a different purpose which, I believe, came from the influence of Jo Anne and her parents. From early in our four years of dating and thirty-two years (at that time) of marriage, I was very much aware of their firm belief in the reality of reincarnation. During that thirty-six years, I did not accept it as reality, but neither did I reject its possibility. My position was that we could not know so long as we were alive. But as my dissatisfactions arose, the thought began to grow in my own thinking that if reincarnation were a reality, it might indeed solve

---

1 That this is a not uncommon experience of those engaged in in-depth academic study of the Bible, including among many who are professors in religious history in our higher universities, see Charles Hedrick, *When Faith Meets Reason*; also my keynote address to the ninth annual SteinerBooks Seminar in New York City in March 2012, to be found on my website *bibleandanthroposophy.com*.

some of what I called "biblical knots" that were becoming increasingly difficult for me to overlook.

The net result of this is that I began to study everything I could find that dealt with the subject of reincarnation, to which I will shortly return below.

13. At least two major factors came together to cause me to resign as teacher of the Cornerstone Class at the completion of a full twenty-five years measured from Easter 1963 to Easter 1988.

First, during the last two years of this teaching period, I began to explore the possibilities of reincarnation in some of the lessons. News of this got back to the then head of my church's education department, who expressed concern to me in a way suggesting her judgment that it was not appropriate for me to be bringing that type of thing into the class sessions. To continue teaching without following this thread presented to me a sterile future from which I wanted to spare both the class and myself.

Second, we bought our home in the Lake City area of Colorado in the fall of 1987 with the plan of spending four to five of the warmer months of the year up there, which we did for twenty years. This was incompatible with my continuing as the class's regular teacher.

14. By 1986 I was deeply engaged in investment activity, related largely to the increasingly sizeable trust and other funds associated with the Resthaven operation. Additionally, with son Mark on site in Lubbock as president of the company, I could handle the various administrative affairs that fell to me, as well as investment activities, by telephone, fax, or regular mail. These occupied a fair amount of my daily time, but we were only spending, in 1986, two weeks of vacation time up there. We were in a commodious condominium on the north shore of Lake San Cristobal from which came the name of the town Lake City. The lake's northern end is five miles upstream from town. It is a beautiful lake formed over the centuries by the damming effect of the Slumgullion (meaning mud slide) from a major section of a distant ridge breaking

off and beginning a multi-century journey down to the river (the Lake Fork of the Gunnison River).[1]

Jo Anne brought two books with her that summer, which she read. After she finished them, I picked them up and read them in sequence. The first was *Holy Blood, Holy Grail*, stimulating for me even though ultimately problematical. The second, Dr. Leslie D. Weatherhead's *The Christian Agnostic*, was the more significant in my journey. Weatherhead is probably the most prominent Methodist of the 20th century, occupying at that time the pulpit in London from which John Wesley had ministered. J. J. Perkins, for whom the theology school at Southern Methodist University is named, was a member of First Methodist Church in Wichita Falls and had endowed the Perkins Lectures.[2] Weatherhead was its lecturer in 1954. Jo Anne and I attended all his lectures, and to this day, for many he seems to stand out among the numerous prominent lecturers through the decades.

The big double whammy in Weatherhead's book was his explicit, well-reasoned, and substantially documented suggestion in the last third of his book that we need to take a new look at reincarnation, and he makes a strong argument for it. To me, this was a full license to proceed, as a member of the Methodist Church or otherwise, to delve as deeply as I could into this subject matter. I began to read everything I could get my hands on that dealt with it.

15. My focus upon pursuing the reincarnation study is doubtless the reason that from the time of reading Weatherhead's book, I started back with *Holy Blood...*, then Weatherhead's book, and kept a written list, in sequential order, of all the books read up till I discovered Steiner, and then even beyond until around the time I started writing *BB*.

The list contained 29 books between Weatherhead's book and Edouard Schuré's *The Great Initiates*. The first ten of these were

---

1 See http://en.wikipedia.org/wiki/Lake_San_Cristobal.
2 See http://www.fumcwf.org/ministries/perkins-lectures.

The Threefold Denouement: The Appearance of Destiny

by Ruth Montgomery, the authenticity of at least some of which I became increasingly doubtful. However, immediately following her books, I took up Edgar Cayce and his work, joining the Cayce organization's Association for Research and Enlightenment (A. R. E.) and attending some programs it offered.

As part of my A. R. E. studies, I read what was identified as its "Recommended Reading List," comprising ten or twelve books, which included Weatherhead's *The Christian Agnostic* that I had read earlier; and one of the last on the list was *The Great Initiates*. This book was published by Harper San Francisco in 1961, the publication page indicating the book was under 1961 copyright held by Rudolf Steiner Publications, Inc. It was in the Introduction of the book that I first came across the name Rudolf Steiner, some time in 1988. There it said that Schuré identified the three most significant friendships of his life, Richard Wagner, Margherita Albana Mignaty, and Rudolf Steiner. It appeared that Steiner was the most powerful of the influences, giving instances of why. It was these instances that burned their way into my soul and had, eventually, to be pursued, though I knew not then how.

The Introduction to the edition of Schuré's book that I read was written by Paul M. Allen, from South Egremont, Massachusetts. Allen was an anthroposophist, a Scot, but by the time I read the book and had written *BB*, he had moved back to Scotland. Shortly before Allen's death, but after my *BB* was published, Gene Gollogly, of the Anthroposophic Press (now also d/b/a SteinerBooks), suggested that I call Allen, as he was a big gruff-sounding Scot with a great personality who would be delighted to hear from me. I did call and had a marvelous visit with him. Sadly, it was not long before the news came of his death. In the years that followed, I have had the happy opportunity of meeting and visiting with his surviving wife, Joan Allen, who either stayed in, or returned after his death to, the United States to continue her anthroposophic work here.

However, while the name Rudolf Steiner stuck in my mind, I did not get around to checking him out and finding my first book of his until I had read some 32 other books related to my search. Finally, it occurred to me that the librarian at the Texas Tech Bookstore, on the Tech campus, had been helpful to me in the past in finding books. I called her and asked if she had ever heard the name of Rudolf Steiner. Saying that she had not, she volunteered to check him out in her library sources. A day or two later she called saying, "You are not going to believe this. My source material has two pages, in fine print, with two columns per page, listing Steiner's works, a big part of them being German titles." By handwritten note she mailed a copy of those pages to me, postmarked February 3, 1989. I told her, when she called, that the *Encyclopedia Britannica* account of Steiner gave the titles of three books. One of those three was Steiner's autobiography *The Course of My Life* (later editions being simply his *Autobiography*), which he died before completing beyond the year 1906. She ordered it for me, and with it came a catalogue from the Anthroposophic Press, both of which I picked up at her office as soon as they arrived in 1989. With that book and catalogue I was off and running in my study of Steiner. But now it is time to summarize this first leg.

Summary of First Leg of Journey

One thing stands out in this first leg like a lofty peak soaring far above its surrounding foothills. All else is watershed from that. Shorn of all else, from my perspective my family's move to Texas accomplished little, if anything, other than to lead me to Jo Anne. No sooner had we gotten down there than dad's increasing attacks led to their return to Illinois after only short stints of trying to work in Texas. The time they actually spent in Texas was minimal. But they got me there, I met and married Jo Anne, and from her and her family the seed was planted in me that led, in due time, to my own serious study of reincarnation and Rudolf Steiner's works.

The Threefold Denouement: The Appearance of Destiny

The starkness of this picture became clear to me only in more recent years. There was much suffering and heartache on the way, but the net result, in my mind, is crystal clear.

What I've often pondered to my depths is what this might indicate dad's purpose was in this life. His adult life was short. Born June 4, 1905, he was only twenty-four when the stock market crashed in October 1929. He lived through the great depression and the second world war, then had a happy few years of employment from 1946 till his first seizure in early 1950. He managed to barely get me to Wichita Falls, where Jo Anne lived, and into the church where she belonged, before his days there were essentially over. He was the best father one could ever want, and without ever having said so to my remembrance, his words and actions told me his love for me was of immeasurable depth. Mother lived as a widow from early 1954 until late 1998, feeling no desire to have any other man than dad. She told me she felt "Frank" was the best man who ever lived.

It is impossible for me not to ponder that his purpose may also have been to lead me to Rudolf Steiner, and, to that end, to help lay for me a sound foundation in my early years. Dad was born as Steiner was beginning to bring into modern thinking his teachings on Anthroposophy and the scriptures, and I was born in 1932, one year before the Nazis took over power in Germany and Christ, its antithesis, reappeared (his "second coming") in the earth's etheric (life) realm.

Dad lived in hard times and suffered mightily his last years, but I have to think that his life was very well lived and that he lives and journeys in the spiritual realms in service to all.

My Inner Experiences while Engaging Steiner's Works

The Joy of Finding

Usually inner experiences, as I use the term here, arose for me in conjunction with outer experiences. The most intense of these inner experiences was the sensation of cold chills running up and down my spine as I contemplated something of Steiner's I had just read. Typically in my early days of reading, I would arise and start at 4:00 a.m. It was a dark, still, and silent time, when my thoughts could soar without worldly distraction. A significant part of my days of studying Steiner took place during the warmer months of the year when we were in our Colorado home. Usually, during these productive years, they started sometime in May and ended sometime in October. The seasons played themselves out as the aspen and cottonwood leaves burgeoned forth in late spring, displayed their changing array of color, and fell in golden flurries in the early fall, while the pine, spruce, and fur trees kept their full green dress throughout the year. While it was cold outside at night, sometimes I would step out on our deck and simply ponder the massive vault of stars in the heavens above, especially on moonless nights. When the moon was bright, it was almost like day, but haunting in stillness. My study of Steiner made these times all the more special.

Even though we were much further east in the time zone at Lake City than we were in Lubbock, it did not get light early there, even in the summer, for our house was on the lower western slope of a mountainous ridge rising nearly three thousand feet behind us. Via a long S curved gravel road, the Lake Fork of the Gunnison River flowed northward some 250 feet below us through the floor of the valley between two high, parallel mountain ridges. The ridge on the west side of the valley rose at least as high as that to our east.

Daylight came ever so gently. From my recliner in the windowed living room, the blackness of night gave way almost imperceptibly in the sky above the sloped western wall, the top of which was miles away, but the light could only be detected when the height of the far ridge caught the first ray of the sun, whence the light progressed downward to the river valley and then exploded all around us as if in one fell swoop it encompassed our slope.

This descent of the light was metaphor, as I rose from my deeper reverie of study and shifted the zone of consciousness to daylight.

The Threefold Denouement: The Appearance of Destiny

Almost always, those most intense inner experiences first mentioned came about when what I had just read and contemplated threw brilliant light upon biblical passages, an enlightened comprehension that simply had not been a part of common biblical dialogue, either theological or hermeneutic. Inevitably these passages began to form an important part of the big picture of the long human journey and its "mystery of Golgotha." The Bible had been growing increasingly frustrating for me. Now, each new revelation plumbed wonderful new depths of insight. An integrated picture of our human journey, and its substantial reflection in scripture, was forming in my mind. A more powerful eye seemed to be helping me along. It is as though an angel was helping me convert Steiner's words, even when they did not specifically refer to scripture, into seeing them reflected within, and adding a higher meaning to, the scripture itself.

I wanted to "shout it from the housetops" (Matt 10:27; Luke 12:3), and it would soon fall upon me as spiritual necessity that I should write, joyously but methodically, so that others of serious mind could enter into the same comprehending light that I was feeling deep in my own soul. But to write, the more mundane "methodically" had to prevail over any sort of impulsive "joyously." First came the inspiration, and then the longer and more painstaking perspiration.

Essential Methodology

Perhaps instinctively at first, whenever a Steiner passage seemed to throw light on a specific scripture, I would find and note that scripture in the margin of the book I was reading. Very quickly, the methodical necessities, if I were to shout these things from the rooftops, so to speak, became obvious. In looking at just that first catalogue, it was immediately obvious that the first few books that I read were just the tip of the iceberg. Clearly an immense amount of reading lay ahead of me. This material was a stream that was neither narrow nor shallow but wide and deep. Some method had to be devised so that I could find my way back to all these marginal notes when their subject matter became relevant to my writings on specific parts or ideas in the Bible. I was going to need to have some method of collating all of these notations into a meaningful system that I could use when writing. The system seemed to make itself known right off the bat. It would revolve around an assembly of "words and phrases." These I began to assemble. It was not at all hard to come up with some of the most obvious ones. But as the work progressed, new words and phrases appeared on the list.

In the earliest days of compiling these references, I simply looked up the specific biblical passages and noted them in the margin without identifying them to a word or phrase. Since this method generally prevailed through some of the most basic early books, when these references were later found in the collations under a specific verse or passage of scripture, they were usually the best and quickest avenue to exactly what I wanted. However, as my catalogue of words and phrases grew, and it seemed to do so exponentially, I soon came to the point that if a specific biblical passage fit into one of those words and phrases, I simply put that word or phrase in the margin without noting the precise biblical chapter and verse. As a word or phrase would be added, I would do a side study to find as many passages of scripture on my own that could be seen to have some relevance to that word or phrase. In all of this, I kept a concordance right with me all the time as I read. When some Steiner passage seemed to ring true to some particular scripture, I would run the word and all its synonyms I could think of through the concordance and put those scriptures down, in canonical order, under that word or phrase. This system greatly multiplied the scriptures from the marginal notations, because a whole array of scriptures would be thrown up as having some relevance to what was said on that page of that book I was reading. I developed a system of abbreviations for each book I was reading, derived as much as could be on a more or less acronymic basis using the first letter of each major word in the book's title, but done in a way so that no book would end up with the same abbreviation as any other.

The Threefold Denouement: The Appearance of Destiny

Every so often I would print out these collations, numbering the printings, and going through each one when I got around to writing on a particular word or phrase. By the time I started writing, the collations consisted of approximately 700 pages. They were in canonical order from the first of Genesis to the end of Revelation. These were priceless, for they led me to book and page, where a quick scan down the margin would show me precisely the place on the page of the book in question (mostly Steiner's) that was relevant to the word or phrase (or scripture itself, when separately identified). My first two volumes identify themselves on the front cover as a biblical commentary in "Terms and Phrases." Eventually, it was clear that I would only be able to write on a very limited number of the most important terms and phrases in my collations. But even on those not specifically written on, I often needed to go to them for some specific purpose.

When I have mentioned these collations to others, they have urged me to make them more widely available. I have tried to make arrangement so that, upon my death, they will be carefully secured and taken possession of by a person whose mission is related and very supportive of my own. But there is a Herculean obstacle to their being of equal utility for others to what they have been for me. The bibliography at the end of *BB* lists all of Steiner's works that were at my fingertips as I began to write, as well as their abbreviation, date, and publication data. But the availability of these publications, as they have changed over the years in so many ways, will make finding the lecture or writing that I have collated a considerable problem, and the page reference may be different there, and there will be no marginal notation to call attention to precisely where on the page my collation refers. Unless my own library is kept with these collations, it will be difficult for them, in their present form to be of much value to others. The fact that over time my method of collating changed from putting specific scriptures in the margins to putting the term or phrase there, and thus throwing up a large array of somewhat related scriptures and somewhat related Steiner passages, will pose an immense problem. Add then the likelihood that over time the publication of all Steiner's works will be encompassed within the *CW* collection (Collected Works), so that the lecture or writing in question would have to be traced into a *CW* volume, and the user might well by then, if not before, have thrown up the hands and given up. I have briefly given thought to updating all the bibliography in *BB* to indicate the *CW* reference pertinent to each part of the book from *BB's* bibliography. Since the publication of the *CW series* is in its early stages, completion of an adequate cross referencing from *BB's* bibliography to *CW* volume and page is very premature, and almost surely will continue to be so during the balance of my life.

While still on the "methodical" and more mundane aspects necessary to give effect, in writing, to my "inner experiences," I felt compelled to acquire for my personal working library all of Steiner lectures and writings that had, at any time, been published in English translation, in any manner, including by unpublished typescript, or at least to do so to the best of my ability. As a practical matter, this meant I should get everything of this description the Rudolf Steiner Library, in Ghent, New York, had in its files. The librarian and staff were diligent in getting out to me such as I requested. Their only requirement was that I pay postage both ways and get the items back to them within the time allowed in the same condition as received. I was always scrupulous in doing so. Already, by then, I had ordered, received, copied, and returned to the library a good many such books, or machine reproduced copies that had become essential for me to read. But as I drew ever closer to the time when I would begin to write, I felt the necessity of completing the assembly of all these works. I had no thought that I would ever be able to read all of them. The library cooperated to the fullest degree, helping me to identify the works available (they had lists that were most helpful, which they supplemented), and shipping to me in boxes large chunks of the material. I went through the mind-numbing process of running every page of every item through my copier, assigning an abbreviation to it within my system, and arranging all such machine-reproduced copies in chronological order in red rope file jackets and into my files. Approximately two thirds of the titles in the bibliography in *BB* are works copied and processed in this manner.

Swimming in the Ocean

I have, on occasion, referred to Steiner's works as constituting a vast ocean. Its immense variety of applications is such that I could only focus on the parts that seemed most biblically related. In general, those are what he gave in the first fourteen years of the twentieth century, up till the commencement of the war in 1914. In those fourteen years he gave the "core" of Anthroposophy, all of which was relevant for deeper comprehension of the biblical message, but major parts of which were explicitly on books or segments of books in the canon. When hostilities commenced that fully embroiled Germany, not only had he earlier found it necessary to move to Switzerland, but he also said that conditions were not right during those times for his investigations into the spiritual realms to further expound upon these biblically-related areas. From that time on he began to devote himself to the many "applications" of Anthroposophy in various walks of life, such as education, various avenues of healing, agriculture, and many others. Nevertheless, there were still works of his from these later years that were helpful to me in my biblical application and beyond.

Some idea of the immensity of the "ocean" is indicated by the number of titles of his work in the bibliography in *BB*. By my count, there are 903 listed. Of course, a lot of Steiner's work had not yet been translated and published in English, and these 903 are only those that I was able to acquire in some manner. The list of books I read, starting with *Holy Blood*... and ending with the last Steiner book I read before starting to write *BB* was lengthy, and purported to be in the order in which read. By coincidence, it included exactly 100 Steiner titles (not counting his analysis of Goethe's *Fairy Tale* of the Green Snake and the Beautiful Lily, which I read just before his *Four Mystery Dramas*). I had come across the name of Steiner in reading Schuré's *The Great Initiates* in 1988, but I remember delaying a good while before checking him out with the Tech bookstore librarian, and my reading list indicates I read 32 other books after Schuré's before reading my first book by Steiner. That first one was his autobiography, then called *The Course of My Life*, the one the Tech Bookstore librarian ordered for me. According to my "Introduction" in the current edition of Steiner's *Turning Points in Spiritual History*, I received this autobiography in February 1989, but my note in the first of the autobiography says that I finished reading it in May or early June 1989. I have prepared and attached to the end of this section a list of the 100 Steiner books. Where the date of reading could be known from my notes, it is included on the list. The last indicated date was October 1991 for the 78th book. I did not start writing *BB* until 1994 while in Colorado. Between reading the autobiography and the last of the 100 Steiner titles, I read some 61 relevant books by other authors, 34 of which were after the 78th of Steiner's books, which was read in October 1991. While I read an additional 22 Steiner titles between October 1991 and the start of *BB* in 1994, an appreciable amount of my time between those dates can be attributed to the events surrounding the sale of Resthaven.

Steiner's autobiography is not of like character with any other I have ever read. It gave few, if any, dates, and "dropped names" only if they related intensely to the course of development of his spiritual path in life. It was written to show what was of greatest importance to him, that spiritual path. Others have assembled accounts of what was happening in his life year by year. Such a compilation, and one of great value, can be found at the back of every volume of *CW*, at least all those published to date, and I presume also all that will follow. But these events, typical of a history or normal biography, simply were not his focus if they did not bear importantly on the path to the spiritual mission he was to give his life for.

The Threefold Denouement: The Appearance of Destiny

Steiner's *The Course of My Life* comprised seventy installments appearing in the weekly anthroposophic newsletter. The first was written by him on December 2, 1923, and appeared on December 9 in the newsletter. The last, probably dictated, appeared in the April 5, 1925 issue. He had died on March 30. By the last issue he had gotten only into the year 1906, his 45th. A sentence from the back cover of the 1999 edition says it well, "This is no ordinary narrative of life's successes and failures—it is the autobiography of a soul, and we are witnesses to the evolving consciousness of a modern spiritual master."

I came away from that autobiography convinced that here was a man quite different from any other, one who stood on a higher plane of spiritual perception than any I have otherwise encountered, save for such as Jesus of Nazareth, Lazarus/John, and Paul, but of such as these Steiner seeded humanity with greatly elevated levels of understanding, available to all who seek, and essential on its long journey toward perfection.

Prior to my start into Steiner's works, I had already begun to write on the indications of reincarnation in the Bible, at least in the New Testament. I had started at the first of the New Testament and gone through Matthew and Mark and was into Luke. At that point I had three hundred pages of typed manuscript. That got put on hold, and in no time it was clear to me that none of it would serve any purpose. What I was reading in Steiner was plowing a deep trench in my psyche. It was of such overwhelming power that everything I had written went quickly into the recycle bin.

Assuming that "my reading list," the list of readings that I had started after reading Weatherhead's *The Christian Agnostic*, is to be relied upon, as I generally feel is the case, between the autobiography and the book of lectures on Luke's Gospel, I read a Steiner two-lecture booklet called *The Ten Commandments and The Sermon on the Mount*.

Here there is a discrepancy between my reading list and my memory. Clearly, my next readings were of the five books specifically on the Gospels, as they were in printed book form. My list, however, puts them in this order: *John, Luke, Matthew, Mark*, and *John and its Relation to the Other Gospels*. That said, the most searing memory I have from my impressions back then, is that Luke was next because of its surprising content. Inasmuch as I was at that point, in my previous writing project, into Luke's Gospel, and had not yet reached John, the next book that sticks in my mind after the autobiography was Steiner's ten-lecture cycle on Luke (September 1909). It was here, in Basle, that Steiner first disclosed the account of the two Jesus children. This cold-cocked me. I shook it off, cleared my head, got up from the floor, dusted myself off, and came charging back in again. There was too much substance, from the Bible, in it to walk away in defeat. This account, essential, in my estimate, to comprehending the Incarnation, became central to my work from then on. Its substance is incorporated into the opening essay of *BB*, "The Nativity" and is elaborated in a more popular style in *IBJ*.

Interspersed between Steiner's works on my reading list were quite a few other books that I read before beginning to write *BB*. Starting with my 58th Steiner book, I began giving the month and year in which it was read. That first date was April 1991. This form of dating was continued through the reading of my 78th Steiner book, but none thereafter. The Steiner book, *The Principle of Spiritual Economy* was the basis for the first essay in *BB* after "The Nativity," and in that essay I state (*BB*, 87), "How the existence of this cycle and its importance escaped my attention until the research phase of this project was nearly complete, and writing begun, is simply beyond my imagination. Remembering the difficulty this deferment presented to me undoubtedly influences my introducing it early in this work." This spiritual economy book was the 93rd Steiner book on the list, and the list ended, soon thereafter, at 100 of his works. It was not that I read none after that, but that I had moved beyond those halcyon days where one luxuriated in the exciting discovery process and into the demanding realm of bringing it all together meaningfully in book form.

The Threefold Denouement: The Appearance of Destiny

What I had done, up through those one hundred Steiner titles, is read virtually everything that I had been able to purchase in bound and printed form that constituted his core anthroposophic writings or lectures and everything that related in some meaningful way to the Bible. Essentially, both came to an end on July 28, 1914, with the commencement of World War I. He clearly indicated that the conditions were not right in the spiritual world after that to continue with his research in those directions. The last book that fit the biblical mold before the war was his *Christ and the Human Soul*, comprising four lectures, July 12, 14–16, 1914.

From that point on, he began to lay the foundation for the various anthroposophic initiatives, such as Waldorf education, biodynamic farming, anthroposophic medicine, economic principles, and many others. Probably far more people are involved today in these activities than in the study and promotion of core Anthroposophy and biblical understanding. While I am in full sympathy with all these ancillary activities, I mourn that more focus is not given to the basics that Steiner laid prior to the war. It is in his pre-war works that I have been primarily engaged. However, his important works did not come to an end then, and I have read much of his work between the start of the war and his death in 1925.

Much important Steiner work was not in print in book form as I was assembling my library. There is much in the machine reproduced copies from the RS Library that was essential reading for me also. An example of a critically important one is a series of lectures published in 1934, but out of print at least from 1988 until 2007. The publication bore the title *Turning Points in Spiritual History* and comprised six lectures in Berlin from January 19, 1911 to January 25, 1912, successively on Zarathustra, Hermes, Buddha, Moses, Elijah, and Christ. Since Steiner only gave two lectures that meaningfully touched upon Elijah, by far the more important being in this series, I set up a hue and cry to put that cycle back in print. Finally, proposing to finance it myself, the Press published it, but asked me to write the Introduction, which I was pleased to do. In it, I cite the only other place Steiner speaks to any extent about Elijah, namely, in lecture 3 in the cycle on Mark's Gospel. Of course, Elijah appears in manifold places in Steiner's works, but not in the definitive way of these two, particularly the one in *Turning Points*. My recent book, *The Temple Sleep of the Rich Young Ruler*, has a short section entitled "A Giant in Human Evolution" (111–114) that brings together a lot about who Elijah was as an individuality and how much of a "giant" he was. In *The Temple Sleep*, as in my keynote speech to the 2012 SteinerBooks Seminar, I mention that scripture only tells us of two persons who were initiated by Christ himself to the highest level, namely Lazarus/John and Saul/Paul, the first shortly before his crucifixion and the second after his resurrection and ascent, and I elaborate how almost all of the New Testament came directly or indirectly from these two personalities/individualities. They are the two witnesses who appeared to Peter, James and John with Christ at his Transfiguration, and they seem clearly to also be the "two witnesses" in the eleventh chapter of Revelation. They were Elijah and Moses, respectively. The Elijah spirit indwelt Lazarus/John, and Paul embodied the Moses being.[1]

All one hundred of those Steiner titles that are on the list I read before starting to write *BB* were important, some extremely important, and many of them figured directly into what went into that first book and all the rest I wrote. But one stands out that I often said, for me, was the most important book ever written outside of the Bible itself. It was the 8th Steiner book in my reading list, the first one after the five Gospel books. On the title page, in my handwriting is the notation, "Completed reading 9-12-89." The version that was in print when I read it was published by the Anthroposophic Press in 1972 and was entitled, *An Outline of Occult Science*. Because of the atrocities of several infamous cults in later years, anything identified as "cultic" or "occult" got a lot of bad press. A new and greatly

---

1 On Lazarus/John as Elijah, see *The Temple Sleep...(TSRYR)*, 60, 111–114. On Paul as Moses, consider the "Pillars on the Journey" essay in *BB*, esp. pages 543–544 and n. 5. On both, see *David's Question...(TQWIM)*, 67–68.

The Threefold Denouement: The Appearance of Destiny

improved edition of it was published by the Press in 1997, when it was renamed, *An Outline of Esoteric Science*. Its first four chapters do more to express what I call core Anthroposophy than any other single volume of Steiner's works. Steiner began to write it in 1906. It appeared in 1909. The Press's 1997 edition is far easier to study than the 1972 version that I read. The later edition has headings that help to avoid the immense confusion that I had in keeping straight where we were in the long, long stretches that involved our descent through various conditions of consciousness prior to Earth evolution, and then prior to our post-Atlantean epoch.

At an early point in my Steiner readings, my best guess, based on the weather, is that it was in the spring of 1990, though possibly in the fall after reading *An Outline of Occult Science*, I became immensely curious about where these wonderful books were coming from. The Anthroposophic Press was located at that time in Hudson, New York, a town on the east bank of the Hudson River. Jo Anne and I drove up there from Lubbock. A Texas relative of Jo Anne's had worked in Rochester and a California relative of mine had gone to school at Syracuse. We drove through Michigan to New York, passing through these two cities, then to the state capitol in Albany before taking the interstate south and crossing the river into the town of Hudson. We may have come back through New York City, and almost certainly stopped in Flora, Illinois either going up or coming back. Desirable lodging was hard for us to find in Hudson, and we did not have a very definitive address for the Press's location. Whatever we had, it seems we drove forever before we located it. The day was blustery, chilly, typical of early spring. The Press's premises consisted of a modest one-story metal warehouse structure with a front door. The setting overall was rural and plain. The building was simple, functional, and economical. There was only one person in the building, a lady, whom I have later characterized as an angel in human garb, named Mary Giddens. Mary has been not only a dear friend, but she was very helpful in my early reading days to guide me in certain directions to find what would be the most helpful to me. Mary is still a critical cog around which the offices of the Anthroposophical Press, now d/b/a/ SteinerBooks, operate. Jo Anne and I will always hold her close to our hearts.

As I worked my way through all those first one hundred books, while also reading many others that were related to my subject matter and are generally included in the larger bibliography in *BB*, it seemed to me that every Steiner book opened another wonderful panorama of insight, either new or significantly incremental. Certainly it is beyond the scope of this present endeavor to elaborate on more than these few. But by the time I was nearing the end, it was obvious to me that the time for me to begin writing was quickly approaching.

That time arrived in the summer of 1994, while I was in our Lake City house. It had been ritual on our annual migrations up there from Lubbock that I load the back end of our roomy SUV (sports utility vehicle), back seats laid flat, with my complete Steiner library and many other related books, Bible versions, and leading commentaries; also all the necessary word processing, printing, and copying equipment and paper. Soon I acquired a separate set of this equipment and these supplies to leave in my office there. A bedroom with windows on two sides, with a closet for supplies, became my office.

Such was the situation when I took the original steps to write.

How well I remember how I started. Having struggled mightily to remember schemes and sequences in the enormous scope of all that I had come through in Steiner's work, I desired to try to pave an easier path for those who came after me. Many who had been studying Steiner for years still had difficulty developing a meaningful path through the maze for themselves. I set out to construct and assemble a significant structure of what I called "Charts and Tabulations." There are 89 of these, occupying 133 pages (545–677, both inclusive) following the last essay in *BB*. They are designated, sequentially, I-1, I-2, I-3..., the Roman numeral indicating the volume and the arabic numeral indicating the chart. Certain of these

The Threefold Denouement: The Appearance of Destiny

are, in my judgment, essential. All of the really important ones are found among the first 33 items, and at a minimum the information in ten of these (I-1, I-6, I-9, I-11, I-19, I-22, I-24, I-27, I-32, and I-33) needs to be assimilated by any serious student. Over the years I have found myself referring back to these continually.

The main charts had been prime targets of mine from the beginning, but wanting to bring in all of Steiner's works, I laboriously scanned every one of the 903 titles that had not been a part of the more significant charts, looking for what seemed to me to be other "chartable" facts. I spent a lot of time on the floor of the Colorado office going through all of the titles.

Then a critical demand faced me. It was so important that only very important terms and phrases be embodied in this first volume, and their arrangement had to constitute a line of development of the main theme of the book. It had to pull away the blinders of conventional theology and doctrine that blocked comprehension of the "burning bush," the "I Am" in its Christ aspect and in the aspect of every human being. To the extent of my capability, the essays were arranged in the order that seemed most nearly fashioned to accomplish that goal. The content of each essay had, to the best of my ability, to carry out the heavy burden imposed upon it, and yet to do so in a way that the serious student could absorb the depth of its meaning. A lot of me went into the book. I had no "credentials" within the world of Anthroposophy, other than that it had burned its way deeply into my soul, and I wanted desperately to make it available to others.

The size of the book is itself daunting, and the original print was made even more so by the fact that the printer used a heavy grade of paper that added an extra half inch or so in the thickness of the book. Largely unspoken, but surely there, is the question of why I made the book so long. My reason was clear. To have picked small parts of it to present, one at a time, would expose it to an easier attack by those who might choose to controvert it. My answer was that before I would expose any of these precious contents to these attacks I wanted "a barn full of ammunition" of such connected nature that the walls of what surrounded any part that someone might choose to attack would come cascading down on the attacker like the waters of the Red Sea on the Egyptian chariots coming after Moses and his band of fleeing Israelites.

What I expected was for Bible students who read it, including my friends, to immediately recognize its merits that seemed so obvious to me. In this, I was more than a bit naive. Most professed not to understand it, and only a small number who did understand it could give it the attention that I felt it deserved. The first printing was of two thousand copies. These sold out rather quickly and another two thousand were printed. Not all of these have yet been sold, but the sales continue each and every year, and while never on the New York Best Seller list, it has been received otherwise in a way that has been gratifying. It does seem to be filling a need.

Times in the publishing business, like in almost all of life's varied activities, have changed dramatically since *BB* was first published. Large printings have given way to the more feasible on-demand printing. Today, many read my books on my bibleandanthroposophy.com website. Others get the free or e-Book version, so that the inventory of hard print is for those, like myself, dinosaurs perhaps, who want a printed book in their hands. Ultimately, many who are sufficiently serious in their study, may come eventually to the point of acquiring a hard copy of their own.

Of course, by now, my writings have included other books that help to flesh out the foundation laid in and by *BB*. By no means did the publication of *BB* put an end to my spine-tingling inner experiences. And neither in *BB* nor in my studies and writings since do I give anything but illustrative examples. These are far from being an exhaustive listing of the constant experiences of peering into new and rich depths of awareness and understanding. But to proceed onward from *BB*, I give three examples from works that were to follow.

The first such experience arose in working on Volume 2, *David's Question "What Is Man?" (DQWIM)*. That book, after a series of

The Threefold Denouement: The Appearance of Destiny

important but shorter essays, takes up sequentially three terms of major biblical significance, "Fire," "Light," and "Blood." Because of length, each gives its own table of contents at the outset; "Fire" comprises 89 pages, "Light" 96, and "Blood" 89. This triptych is followed by the concluding 30-page title essay "What Is Man?"

Probably my most intense inner experience arose when I realized that I had intuited the meaning of the mysterious and problematical 144,000. It is the 144 that is important, the thousand was simply a term of magnification of importance, and perhaps was added because of the way the multiple of twelve seems to reverberate into even more distant stages of the long human journey, as suggested in what follows. The number 144,000 appears in an anticipatory way in Revelation 7:4, but it culminates in 14:1, 3 after the blowing of the "last trumpet," the seventh, in 11:15. Paul's letters were written before Lazarus/John's apocalyptic vision and account. Revelation's passages put flesh on the flashes of Paul's own intuition that seem, ever and again, in the letters to his churches, simply to emerge without elaboration, but are nevertheless sufficient to evidence the depth of his insight as it was more fully revealed in his "letter" to the Hebrews. Paul speaks of the "last trumpet" in 1 Corinthians 15:52 when we shall "be changed" from perishable to imperishable, and again he speaks of this "trumpet" in 1 Thessalonians 4:16–17 when "we...shall...meet the Lord in the air," an appropriate way of suggesting a change in the nature of our existence after the sound of that last trumpet.

The significance of the last trumpet is described in the "Trumpet(s)" essay in *BB*. It is in the "Fire" essay in *DQWIM*, in the segment entitled "Fire, the Spiral, and the One Hundred Forty-Four Thousand," 166–204, and particularly in the sub-segment "The One Hundred Forty-Four Thousand," that we see that this number is not a numerical limitation but a descriptive one. It is describing all those who will by then have reached the point, under the guidance of Christ as the Lord of Karma, when their physical (mineral or solid) and etheric (life) bodies have dissolved away through, in effect, a slow crucifixion of the lower bodies toward a Christ-like perfection over the ages, to the point where they are able to live in the astral world for the continuation of their long journey, including through ever higher realms in subsequent conditions of consciousness. The transition is at the point where earthly fire is transformed into matter-free spiritual fire—what Christ came to cast upon the earth (Luke 12:49). It happens immediately after the blowing of the last trumpet, when, as Revelation shows, we move from the sevens (letters, seals, and trumpets), into the twelves that take us through the end of Revelation and the condition of consciousness that follows the entirety of the Earth condition of consciousness—which is known in Anthroposophy as the Jupiter condition. Steiner calls this the Holy City of Revelation 21. Only those subjected to the "bowls of wrath" (Rev 16) remain in the realm of seven, those whose existence in future conditions of consciousness is in a lower, still to be perfected, realm, prior to the final union of all (Eph 1:9–10), unimaginably far into the evolving stages of consciousness. Only a small portion of humanity will be unable to eventually attain such union. A characteristic of these retched souls is that their joy comes from inflicting great pain upon other creatures, such as vivisection and other torture, a practice that Steiner labeled as "black magic," in contrast to the "white magic" that helped raise other creatures.

But what was the path to my intuition of this meaning? Strangely enough, as seems the case with most of those events of destiny whose significance can only be seen in retrospect, it probably started with my investment activities during the Resthaven years. It was Robert Prechter's Elliott Wave theories that introduced me to the Golden Mean, or more precisely its famous Fibonacci ratio (1.618/1.00). That ratio is reflected not only in the creative spiral of our galaxies but manifests pervasively throughout the physical world's phenomena. I call it the spiral of creation. The number of creation is seven, as suggested in Proverbs 9:1. There are four series of seven in Revelation up through the seven trumpets and bowls of

The Threefold Denouement: The Appearance of Destiny

wrath. From there it moves into the realm of twelves all the way to the end of Revelation.

It was Prechter's expositions on the Fibonacci ratio where its progressive numbers are charted on a Cartesian graph into the creative spiral that instilled its significance in me for the rest of my life. Thus, the first step in the road to intuition started with one of life's practical observations of phenomena.

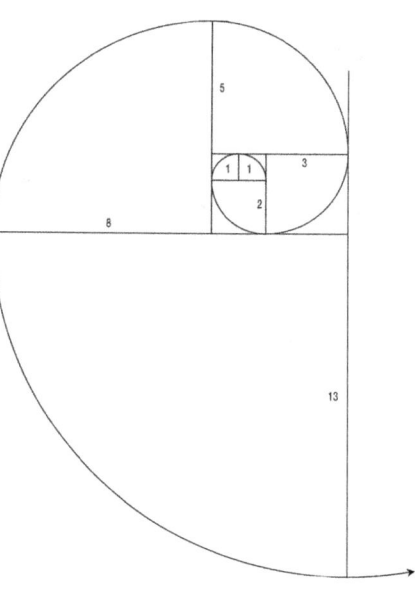

But what was it that brought the connection of this spiral to the 144,000? I take it to have been the planting by my guardian angel of the suggestion in my mind, as I was going out for a jog in one of those last years in the 20th century, that I should check out whether there was a relationship of seven, the significant creative biblical number seven, to the number twelve that was the square root of 144. In the first book of the Bible, there are seven creative periods, "days," in Genesis and there are twelve zodiacal stars implicit in Yahweh's instruction to Abraham in Genesis 15:5 played out collaterally in the twelve sons of Abraham's son Ishmael, but then directly and primarily in the twelve sons of Abraham's grandson Jacob, for it was "through Isaac [that Abraham's] descendants [were to be] named" (Gen 21:12). Christ later called "twelve" disciples, and after the four realms of seven in Lazarus/John's apocalyptic vision, the pathway forward becomes twelvefold to the end, where we experience in many ways the number 144. Out of the twelvefold zodiacal realm of our galaxy, descent became subject to the creative laws of seven, but even in the depths of the valley the twelves appeared and then again as we journey from the material world upward in the far reaches of Revelation.

What about that spiral? I remember exactly where I was when the suggestion came into my mind to check out how the Fibonacci spiral might relate to the number 144. I was jogging westward, not far from our house at 3519 57th Street, and turning northward where 57th Street "T's" into Nashville Avenue, near the southeast corner of the Christ the King Catholic School and Church property. It was as I was stepping from Nashville onto the sidewalk that bordered that church property that this idea came into my mind. It gripped me till I had completed my jog. Back home I began entering the Fibonacci numbers as follows:[1]

1.	1		=	1
2.	0	+ 1	=	1
3.	1	+ 1	=	2
4.	1	+ 2	=	3
5.	2	+ 3	=	5
6.	3	+ 5	=	8
7.	5	+ 8	=	13
8.	8	+ 13	=	21
9.	13	+ 21	=	34
10.	21	+ 34	=	55
11.	34	+ 55	=	89
12.	55	+ 89	=	144

Voila! The spiral downward from the spiritual realm into the materialization of our galaxy and then our own Earth and Solar Mass would be the same spiral in reverse (the picture of the Zodiacal Cancer of intertwining spirals [creating the crab image], a sign signifying transition). An exciting sequel to the 144 (expressed in thousands) that characterizes the passage out of the mineral and etheric Earth into the Jupiter condition is that the intersection of the twelve multiple and the Fibonacci series reoccurs only on each subsequent

---

[1] These, with their description, can also be found at *TSRYR*, 62, in the Apocalypse portion of the "Creation and Apocalypse" essay.

twelfth Fibonacci number—this would seem to indicate passage upward through the subsequent major conditions of consciousness until complete union of all (see endnote for subsequent intersections).

When Will Marsh, my editor on the first two volumes, saw this illustration in the draft of my manuscript, he said, "Ed, I think you have something here." I have pondered this intuition with gratitude over the years.

The second of my three examples is fleshed out in the essay "Karma as the Law Christ Came to Fulfill" appearing early in my third volume, *The Soul's Long Journey/How the Bible Reveals Reincarnation* (*SLJ*). That essay is readily available to any who desire to read it for themselves. For those desiring to do so online, it is accessible on my *bibleandanthroposophy.com* website. In his excellent commentary on Matthew in *The New Interpreter's Bible* (1995), volume 8, cited in footnote 3 of my essay, M. Eugene Boring, of the Brite Divinity School, Texas Christian University, expresses what I take to be the more common modern academic view. That view identifies the "instructional core" of the Sermon on the Mount as beginning at 5:17 and ending at 7:12, and it clearly indicates that the Golden Rule ("Whatever you wish that men would do to you, do so to them") "is the law and the prophets" referred to in 5:17–18, as stated in 7:12, and that it is of equal dignity, and is essentially synonymous with, the "great commandment" (Matt 22:37–40), on which "all the law and the prophets depend." What academic writers have thus written is, to this extent, in accord with my essay, but they do not go on to recognize that it is virtually impossible for any person in our age to comply with the Golden Rule, and thus the Great Commandment, throughout life in all situations, and thus the necessity of the wonderful grace of karma and reincarnation. Based on Steiner's insights, I spell out this necessity in the essay. The essay imports by reference certain other parts of *SLJ* and *BB* that help to solidify the proposal that karma is the law that Christ came to fulfill.[2]

---

[2] Footnote 12 in *SLJ* refers to the Epilogue in *DWJL*. There is no Epilogue in *DWJL*; the reference is in error and should have been to *IBJ*.

The third of my three examples was something I had written about many years before that returned to me powerfully as I prepared for an event. As a result of the speech I gave at the SteinerBooks Seminar on my new book *TSRYR* in March 2012, I was invited to conduct a St. John's Day weekend seminar for the Southeast Region of the Anthroposophic Society in Cartersville, Georgia, on June 22–24 of that year. *TSRYR* had been about Lazarus/John, or Evangelist John, who also gave us his Apocalypse. St. John's Day is at the summer solstice, and the John then honored is John the Baptist. However, (as related in *TSRYR*) inasmuch as the spirit of the Baptist, after his death and the "raising" of Lazarus/John, entered and indwelt the being of the latter down through his consciousness soul, it is appropriate to expand the festival to include Lazarus/John. The invitation to present the seminar included the suggestion that they were interested in the book of Revelation. In preparation, I did once more an advanced study of the book, perhaps penetrating more deeply than I had ever done before, but building upon what had gone before. If I am granted the time and energy to do so, I hope to write a book embodying the fruits of that latter effort. It had to do with the scriptural use of the "rainbow" and the depth of its meaning.

The most important of all of the Charts and Tabulations, in my judgment, is the first one, identified as I-1. It appears at the back of volumes 1, 2, and 3 (*BB*, *DQWIM*, and *SLJ*) and at p. 187 of *TSRYR*. There is a full-page description preceding it in those first three volumes. What needs to be said here is that Steiner drew the chart below for his hearers as he gave the 10th lecture in the 12-lecture cycle in June 1908 at Nuremberg:

This chart is a schematic that helps to stretch the imagination of the length of the journey we are all making as human beings. It is easy to look around us and think that all we see and observe as we travel around our planet is everything there is. But when we lift our eyes toward the sun and, more appropriately toward the stars in the heavens at night and begin to contemplate the universe, we have to stretch our minds to their limit. The two, our human journey and

The Threefold Denouement: The Appearance of Destiny

the reaches of the stars above us, at least as to they encompass our own galaxy and its "animal circle" (zodiac), are corollaries.

Much is encompassed in this chart that is far beyond what can be said here. The aspect of it that was so inspiring to me, returning to me as I prepared for the St. John's Day seminar in Cartersville, was that the *rainbow* appears three, and only three, times in our canon, and each appearance relates to the three major epochal transitions that encompass our present existence. I awoke shortly after midnight, at 12:33 a.m., Memorial Day (2012) with the three rainbow passages in my mind. The fact that they appeared at both the beginning and end of our post-Atlantean Epoch and at the end of the last Evolutionary Epoch of the Mineral-Physical Condition (of Form and Life) of the Earth Condition of Consciousness seemed deeply and powerfully significant, demanding contemplation. After that seventh and last Epoch, time will be no more, though based on Chart I-1, 171 conditions will remain in the long human journey through the higher realms to the end of Vulcan (each condition subdivided 7 x 7, or 49, times as with our own Epoch). We are staggered as we ponder the journey's immensity in our parabolic return, though without the weight of time, and with the acceleration of ascent, comparison with what we know in the mineral-physical state is inappropriate.

The three appearances of the rainbow in the canon are as follows:

1. The first rainbow is in Genesis 9:13–16 in the account of the Noah voyage. That voyage was related to the final submergence of the ancient continent of Atlantis that sank into the sea over a period of time as the last great ice age was ending, ten to twelve thousand years ago. Noah was called Manu in its more ancient accounts. This rainbow occurred when the Atlantean Epoch ended and the present post-Atlantean period began. See it on the chart.

2. The second rainbow appears in Revelation 4:3, which is at the end of our post-Atlantean Epoch. We shall presently consider how this appearance is shown to be at the end of our present Fifth Evolutionary Epoch and before the Sixth.

The Threefold Denouement: The Appearance of Destiny

3. The third rainbow appears in Revelation 10:1, at the end of the Seventh Evolutionary Epoch, just before the last trumpet is blown. The process is begun for humanity to leave the world of matter as it ascends into the astral realm, called the "More Perfect Astral" on Steiner's schematic. All who, through the long process of perfection, have become Christlike to the point that their physical (mineral) and etheric (life) bodies have dissolved and fallen away, on the path prepared by the risen Christ, will make this transition and be able to live in the astral realm. They, not measured in numbers but in Christlikeness, are the 144,000, moving away from the world of matter and time. Those not sufficiently perfected will feel the "second death," and fall onto a lower pathway to await perfection in far later stages of human evolution in the higher realms.

The seven "churches" in Revelation 2 and 3 are not to be understood as local churches of John's time frame, but as the seven Cultural Ages, each of 2,160 years. The solar year of 25,920 regular years comprises twelve zodiacal ages, each of which is 2,160 years. The post-Atlantean Epoch thus runs for some 15,120 years, from 7227 B.C.E. to 7894 C.E., one year being lost in the transition from B.C.E. to C.E. (Chart I-19 at *BB*, 573).

The seven churches are followed by the seven seals, when what was "sealed" in each Cultural Age of the post-Atlantean Epoch is "unsealed" in the Sixth Evolutionary Epoch. The process of dissolution of matter runs it course as the trumpets are blown in the Seventh and last Evolutionary Epoch.

For reasons set out in the "Fire" essay in *DQWIM*, in its section "Christ, the J-Curve and the Right Time" (pp. 175–181), it seems clear that the Fifth Epoch, our post-Atlantean, is the slowest developing in our long journey from, and then back to, the spiritual realm, and that these time periods, such as the 2,160 years, cannot be projected back prior to, or forward beyond, our own post-Atlantean Epoch (see the Gospel scriptures cited in the last paragraph of the section just cited). Time as we know it, seems to be a phenomenon affected by our descent into and then out of the realm of matter, for time can exist only in a realm of matter, where density is not a constant in our long journey.

So, returning to the second rainbow, clearly it appears after the letters to the seven churches (Cultural Ages) of our Fifth Epoch and prior to the seven seals of the Sixth Epoch.

Are we not compelled to infer some great depth of meaning in the word *rainbow*? For now, and unless and until I am able to write more fully on Lazarus/John's Apocalypse, I give in the next few paragraphs a segment from my notes prepared for the Cartersville St. John's Day seminar:

> What may we infer as the meaning of the rainbow at the end of the last Epoch? Let us first consider that sound relates to the trumpets, the last of which ends the Seventh Epoch, and that light relates to the colors of the rainbow. Let us then consider how both sound and light reflect both seven and twelve. There is much of vibrational physics in sound, but simply stated, the normal scale of seven notes is reflected by the seven white keys on the piano, while adding the black keys brings the total to twelve. The chromatic scale includes all twelve keys. But what is the significance of the word "chromatic"? The Greek "chroma" means "color." Modern theory is that the word chromatic came from the fact that both white and black colored keys were played in the scale. But this assumes that such keys were in existence at its origin—not likely! We are told that "The chromatic scale…was…ancient. Aristoxenus' view is that its origins "go back into the night of time."[1] "Aristoxenus [a student of Aristotle, was a] 4th century B.C.E. Greek peripatetic philosopher, the first authority for musical theory in the classical world."[2] So somehow it seems that the origin of the twelve key scale had to do with color. But the connection to color is still mysterious as it pertains to the sound ether.
>
> When we move to the light ether with its colorful rainbow the meaning becomes clearer in the light of what Steiner, with his Goethean Science, demonstrates. I discuss this in the

---

1 See http://www.dolmetsch.com/musictheory25.htm.
2 See http://www.britannica.com/EBchecked/topic/34721/Aristoxenus.

The Threefold Denouement: The Appearance of Destiny

"Fire" essay in *DQWIM* in the section subtitled "Heat and the Other Ethers," pp. 145–166, immediately preceding the section subtitled "Fire, the Spiral and the One Hundred Forty-Four Thousand." When we look at the rainbow we only see seven colors, but the two colors at the extreme are only there in part, and above the rainbow is a second rainbow where the colors appear in exactly the reverse order of the first. The implication of these phenomena is that there are twelve colors that encircle a sphere, implying a continuation on the opposite side. The peach color of human skin is in the center of the back.[3] In short, the light ether in its twelvefold aspect more clearly points us toward the human being.[4]

So in the last three Epochs we move in reverse of what we did in the first three Epochs, from life ether to sound ether to light ether, and then through the fire ether at the "last trumpet" to the point where it touches the twelvefold nature reflected at the end of the book of Revelation when we reach the Jupiter Condition of Consciousness. The point at which the spiral and the number twelve intersect, which is at every twelfth (Fibonacci) number (the first "twelfth number" being 144), points to and suggests the meaning of the three dimensional cube in Revelation—the measurement of the Holy City Rev 21:15–17 (twelve by twelve by twelve).

May we contemplate that there is a foreshadowing of this reality at the conclusion of each of the three indicated Evolutionary Epochs of the Mineral-Physical Conditions (of Form and Life) of the Earth Condition of Consciousness, each pointing humanity to Jupiter and perhaps to each succeeding Condition of Consciousness by virtue of the relationship between the graphic spiral of the Fibonacci numbers and the fact that every twelfth Fibonacci number intersects such spiral?

3　No idea of race superiority should be gathered from this, but rather that peach-blossom was the archetypal color of human skin before differentiation brought about genetically due to geographical and cultural differences in tribal exposure to the Sun.

4　For the three ether levels, namely, life, sound, and light, see chart I-22 at *BB*, page 585.

With these three illustrations of my inner experiences in continuing to write beyond the publication of *BB*, all that remains is to describe how I came to see my writings on Steiner's work as being my primary destiny in this life.

Endnote

The first three subsequent intersections of the twelve multiple and the Fibonacci series (at 24, 36 and 48) are shown below:

13. 89 + 144= 233   233/12=   19.4167
14. 144 + 233= 377   377/12=   31.4167
15. 233 + 377= 610   610/12=   50.8333
16. 377 + 610= 987   987/12=   82.2500
17. 610 + 987= 1,597   1,597/12= 133.0833
18. 987 + 1,597= 2,584   2,584/12= 215.3333
19. 1,597 + 2,584= 4,181   4,181/12= 348.4167
20. 2584 + 4,181= 6,765   6,765/12= 563.7500
21. 4,181 + 6,765= 10,946   10,946/12= 912.1667
22. 6,765 + 10,946= 17,711   17,711/12= 1,475.9167
23. 10,946 + 17,711= 28,657   28,657/12= 2,388.0833
24. 17,711 + 28,657= 46,368   46,368/12= 3,864.0000
25. 28,657 + 46,368 = 75,025   75,025/12 = 6,252.0833
26. 46,368 + 75,025 = 121,393   121,393/12 = 10,116.0833
27. 75,025 + 121,393 = 196,418   196,418/12 = 16,368.1667
28. 121,393 + 196,418 = 317,811   317,811/12 = 26,484.2500
29. 196,418 + 317,811 = 514,229   514,119/12 = 42,843.2500
30. 317,811 + 514,229 = 832,040   832,040/12 = 69,336.6667
31. 514,229 + 832,040 = 1,346,269   1,346,269/12 = 112,189.0833
32. 832,040 + 1,346,269 = 2,178,309
    2,178,309/12 = 181,525.7500
33. 1,346,269 + 2,178,309 = 3,524,578
    3,524,578/12 = 293,714.8333
34. 2,178,309 + 3,524,578 = 5,702,887
    5,702,887/12 = 475,240.5833
35. 3,524,578 + 5,702,887 = 9,227,465
    9,227,465/12 = 768,955,4167

The Threefold Denouement: The Appearance of Destiny

36. 5,702,887 + 9,227,465 = 14,930,352
    14,930,352/12 = 1,244,196.0000
37. 9,227,465 + 14,930,352 = 24,157,817
    24,157,817/12 = 2,013,151.4167
38. 14,930,352 + 24,157,817 = 39,088,169
    39,088,169/12 = 3,257,347.2167
39. 24,157,817 + 39,088,169 = 63,245,986
    63,245,986/12 = 5,270,498.8333
40. 39,088,169 + 63,245,986 = 102,334,155
    102,334,155/12 = 8,527,846.2500
41. 63,245,986 + 102,334,155 = 165,580,141
    165,580,141/12 = 13,798,345.0833
42. 102,334,155 + 165,580,141 = 267,914,296
    267,914,296/12 = 22,326,191.3333
43. 165,580,141 + 267,914,296 = 433,494,437
    433,494,437/12 = 36,124,536.4166
44. 267,914,296 + 433,494,437 = 701,408,733
    701,408,733/12 = 58,450,727.7500
45. 433,494,437 + 701,408,733 = 1,134,903,170
    1,134,903,170/12 = 94,575,264.1666
46. 701,408,733 + 1,134,903,170 = 1,836,311,903
    1,836,311,903/12 = 153,025,991.916
47. 1,134,903,170 + 1,836,311,903 = 2,971,215,073
    2,971,215,073/12 = 247,601,256.083
48. 1,836,311,903 + 2,971,215,073 = 4,807,526.976
    4,807,526.976/12 = 400,627,248.000

Steiner Books I Read before Writing **The Burning Bush**

1. *The Course of My Life* (read May 1989)
2. *The Ten Commandments and The Sermon on the Mount*
3. *The Gospel of John*
4. *The Gospel of Luke*
5. *The Gospel of Matthew*
6. *The Gospel of Mark*
7. *The Gospel of John and Its Relation to the Other Gospels*
8. *An Outline of Occult Science* (completed reading September 12, 1989)
9. *Deeper Secrets of Human History in the Light of the Gospel of St. Matthew*
10. *Background to the Gospel of St. Mark*
11. *The Spiritual Guidance of Man*
12. *From Jesus to Christ*
13. *The Fifth Gospel*
14. *Christ and the Human Soul*
15. *Christianity as Mystical Fact*
16. *The Apocalypse of St. John*
17. *Genesis*
18. *Practical Training in Thought*
19. *Occult History*
20. *Knowledge of the Higher Worlds and Its Attainment*
21. *Reincarnation and Karma: Their Significance in Modern Culture*
22. *The Philosophy of Spiritual Activity*
23. *Man and the World of Stars*
24. *Karmic Relationships*, Vol. 1
25. *Lucifer and Ahriman*
26. *Theosophy*
27. *Rosicrucian Esotericism*
28. *Building Stones for an Understanding of the Mystery of Golgotha*
29. *Karmic Relationships*, Vol. 2
30. *Life Between Death & Rebirth*
31. *The Lord's Prayer*
32. *Christianity in Human Evolution*
33. *The Inner Development of Man*

The Threefold Denouement: The Appearance of Destiny

34. *The Significance of Spiritual Research for Moral Action*
35. *The Four Sacrifices of Christ*
36. *Preparing for the Sixth Epoch*
37. *Social Understanding Through Spiritual Scientific Knowledge*
38. *Anthroposophy and Christianity*
39. *Universe, Earth & Man*
40. *Karmic Relationships*, Vol. 3
41. *Karmic Relationships*, Vol. 4
42. *True and False Paths in Spiritual Investigation*
43. *Wonders of the World*
44. *How Can Mankind Find the Christ Again?*
45. *Prayer*
46. *Philosophy, Cosmology & Religion*
47. *The Cycle of the Year*
48. *Michaelmas and the Soul Forces of Man*
49. *The Redemption of Thinking*
50. *Correspondence and Documents*
51. *Gospel of St. John* (RS Lecture on June 26, 1905)
52. *Turning Points in Spiritual History*
53. *The Bhagavad Gita and the Epistles of Paul*
54. *The Wisdom Contained in Ancient Documents and in the Gospel: The Event of Christ*
55. *The Gospels* (Lecture November 14, 1909)
56. *The Gospel of St. Matthew and the Christ-Problem*
57. *Jesus and Christ* (Lecture November 15, 1913)
58. *From Jesus to Christ* (Lecture October 4, 1911)
59. *The East in the Light of the West* (read April 1991)
60. *Christianity Began as a Religion But is Greater Than All Religions* (read April 1991)
61. *The Mysteries of the East and of Christianity* (read April/May 1991)
62. *Egyptian Myths & Mysteries* (read May 1991)
63. *The Christ Impulse and the Development of Ego Consciousness* (read May 1991)
64. *I Am The Way, The Truth and the Life* (read May 1991)
65. *On the "Fifth Gospel"* (read May 1991)
66. *The Sermon on the Mount and the Return of Christ* (read May 1991)

67. *The Spiritual Hierarchies* (read May 1991)
68. *The Temple Legend* (read June 1991)
69. *Christ and the Spiritual World—The Search for the Holy Grail* (read July 1991)
70. *Theosophy of the Rosicrucian* (read July 1991)
71. *World History in the Light of Anthroposophy* (read July 1991)
72. *The Child's Changing Consciousness and Waldorf Education* (read August 1991)
73. *The Kingdom of Childhood* (read August 1991)
74. *Cosmic Memory* (read September 1991)
75. *The Stages of Higher Knowledge* (read September 1991)
76. *Karmic Relationships*, Vol. 5
77. *Karmic Relationships*, Vol. 6 (read October 1991)
78. *Karmic Relationships*, Vol. 7 (read October 1991)
79. *Karmic Relationships*, Vol. 8
80. *Four Mystery Dramas*
81. *Occult Signs and Symbols*
82. *The Easter Festival in the Evolution of the Mysteries*
83. *Faith, Hope, Love*
84. *The Threefold Social Order*
85. *Foundations of Esotericism*
86. *The Influence of Spiritual Beings Upon Man*
87. *The Bible and Wisdom*
88. *Problems of Nutrition*
89. *Isis & Madonna*
90. *The Etherization of the Blood*
91. *Reading the Pictures of the Apocalypse*
92. *The Reappearance of Christ in the Etheric*
93. *The Principle of Spiritual Economy*
94. *The Being and Essence of Anthroposophy*
95. *Et Incarnatus Est*
96. *The Evolution of the Earth and Man*
97. *The Karma of Materialism*
98. *Manifestations of Karma*
99. *The Search for the New Isis, the Divine Sophia*
100. *The Occult Significance of the Bhagavad Gita*

The Threefold Denouement: The Appearance of Destiny

RECOGNITION OF MY PRIMARY DESTINY

Jo Anne said to me, as I was about to start this final part of this final section, "You are most fortunate to have recognized your primary destiny in life. Very few people ever do." I suspect that if the question were posed, on the spot, to any array of persons, only a very small portion of them would be able to give a meaningful, or even a proximate, answer. Given more time, still likely few could do so. I myself could not have done so until recent times. The mere requirement of attempting an in-depth autobiography demands not only a lot of resurrecting of memories of things long past, but also a lot of soul searching as to what all these things seem to be saying on this deep question. Many will doubt that the question is even a proper one. A certain kind of philosophy, and much contemplation, seems necessary to the process.

The third and last question, as originally posed, is: What has led me to recognize my involvement with Steiner as being my primary destiny in life? This recognition seems to me to come whether I approach the question deductively or inductively. What seems clear to me is that, in light of what has been set out in this writing, I could not have recognized my primary destiny until my life had essentially run its course. It is hard for me to imagine, in my eighty-third year, that any significant new initiatives, either spiritual or worldly, can arise that could greatly change my existing retrospection. Of course, life is precious and one must look forward to positive involvement with it to the end. But general human experience suggests to me that one's primary destiny in any life is either fulfilled or is still in process at this age and, in any event, is not something that will make its first appearance at a more advanced age. It is thus, only in looking back that I have been able to make what I deem to be a sound judgment on this question. Of course, one's karmic path, insofar as it addresses past lives or ages, is completed by age sixty-three, according to my earlier postulate on the matter. Clearly, however, one's full life from beginning to end will have effects that reach into the individuality's future lives and ages. But what goes into the make-up of any future personality has nothing to do with what one's primary destiny is coming into the present life. That is what I now judge. What is probably the most significant factor for any valid judgment on this issue for most people, and certainly for me, is simply having reached a time in life when looking back offers the greatest possible perspective.

There is no need to reiterate what I have already extensively written. Probably no one thing is more persuasive to me than the circumstances that brought me into my lifelong relationship with Jo Anne. The starkness with which that impresses the setting is, for me, overwhelming.

That "setting" is tied tightly to what was to come of it, namely, a life purpose closely aligned with what Steiner himself declared his principal task in this incarnation to be, namely, bringing into Western consciousness the reality of reincarnation and karma.[1]

That setting would be sufficient standing alone. Of course, it does not. Another circumstance that is convincing for me is the answer to the question, "What will I leave behind, at death's gate, that will be meaningful to humanity as time moves on?" Of course, Jo Anne and I leave descendants who will make their own mark. But that is the common requisite of all who are able and willing. An individuality of great significance for humanity needs parents who are able and willing to provide the heredity and childhood nurture that will best assist this great individuality in the fulfillment of mission. One

---

1 See *SLJ*, "Preliminary Remarks," 2, fn. 5. Steiner's specific response to that particular question put to him by Walter J. Stein in April 1922 in The Hague was "Reincarnation and Karma," according to Sergei O. Prokofieff, in *The Encounter With Evil*, 8. Also cited in the *SLJ* footnote is Robert McDermott's "Foreword" to René Querido's anthology, *A Western Approach to Reincarnation and Karma* (abbreviated in the footnote as WARK, from the bibliography in *BB*). McDermott said that with only one exception, all that Steiner gave us was responsive to requests from others; "the one work that Steiner took upon himself on his own initiative...is...the double concept of karma and reincarnation."

can imagine the ancestry, for instance, of the two Jesus children, or of John the Baptist, or of other persons who have been critical for the advancing evolution of humanity and God's other creatures. Probably parenting for some few who are privileged to produce such illustrious offspring is a primary destiny in a given life. Jo Anne and I are proud of our children and their issue, but I do not judge that producing them was my primary purpose in life, as wonderful as having done so has been for us, and as grateful as we have been for them. It is a common destiny of most human beings in our age to do this, hence it would seem to seldom be a "primary" destiny.

Descendants aside, I ask myself what of my involvements or accomplishments will survive me in a way that benefits the march of human evolution. Life is complex, and every thought and deed carries forward and affects the future of human evolution in some way or ways and to some extent. Of these things, karma, both favorable and unfavorable, takes account. But in things that I can make a more tangible assessment of, what can I see surviving me that I have accomplished, with purpose, in this life? On this question, the answer is clear to me.

When I was working with Chris Bamford, chief editor at the Anthroposophic Press, on the draft of *BB*, he made a comment that surprised me at the time, though now it does not. He said that what I was writing was "for the next one hundred years." I believe that is true. It has made an impact already for many, though not in a way that is contemporaneously popular as so many books or works of art are. It is my deep conviction that the contents of the books I've written, based upon insights made possible by the works of Rudolf Steiner, have great value for humanity in the days and ages ahead. My subject matter has not been based on what is popular at the moment, but upon the deepest aspects of our existence, at least as I have perceived them.

This judgment is not mine alone, but, most importantly, it is mine, and it serves up the answer for me as to what my primary destiny in life was, is, and will continue to be—though my capabilities are not now what they were in the prime period when these existing writings were produced.

That I did not come to Steiner's works until I was fifty-six years old is not a negative consideration for this issue. That I was fifty-six and entering the last of my karmic septenaries makes this one more factor that convinces me that presenting biblical understanding in the light of his works has been my primary destiny. The capability of writing these things did not just happen. Fifty-six years of diversified experience took place. I came into life blessed with circumstances that were conducive to the development, over that considerable period of time, of a variety of involvements, each of which added to my capability of rising to the immense challenge these writings presented.

There is an ancient saying, generally considered Buddhist, but I believe it is a spiritual reality, "When the student is ready, the master appears." I think it applied in the life of my dad's employer, J. J. Lynn, when he met the Paramahansa Yogananda. Lynn, born May 5, 1892, was 39 years old when, in January 1932, he met that master, and his life of massive worldly accomplishment was changed. It is my belief that Rudolf Steiner came into life as an exalted individuality rich beyond imagination from prior incarnations.[1] His was a destiny of immense proportion. Yet, he had his master, humble by worldly standards, mentioned but never named. It was in the winter when Steiner turned twenty-one that he met this master.[2] It was in 1988 that I met my master, Rudolf Steiner, and my own life changed.

The use of the term *master* should be understood as subordinate, of course, to the Christ Spirit, the master of all the masters—and of all else.

---

1 See *BB*, "Pillars on the Journey," 543–544.

2 Christoph Lindenberg, *Rudolf Steiner: A Biography*, 42–46, esp. 46; Steiner, *Self-Education/Autobiographical Reflections, 1861–1893*, 23–25, esp. 25 (a lecture in Berlin, February 4, 1913).

Timeline of Significant Events in the Life of Edward Reaugh Smith

1905   Father (dad), Frank Edward Smith, birth in Clay City, Illinois June 4, 1905.

1906   Mother, Frances Elizabeth Reaugh, birth in Flora, Illinois, October 14, 1906.

1922   Dad plays end on Flora's undefeated and unscored-on football team, receiving "mention" for All-Southern Illinois Team.

1927   Parents married in Flora August 21, 1927.

1932   Birth in Flora on autumnal equinox, 1:15 a.m. central time, September 23, 1932.

1936   Death of grandfather, Hiram Savage Smith (birth 1865), September 4, 1936; remember his corpse on catafalque, but do not attend funeral.

1938   Enter first grade at Flora Grade School, but like outdoors better. First awareness of wars in Europe and Asia. Experience a primitive television at Ford Garage.

1939   Birth of only sibling, sister Mary Anne, January 22, 1939.

1940   Death of grandfather, Richard Sprigg Canby Reaugh (birth November 23, 1870), January 26, 1940; have only vague memories of him while alive; remember seeing his corpse in his reading chair; attend his funeral. Begin piano lessons, but still like outdoors better. Enter third grade in fall; laugh a lot in class; get poor grade in deportment. Wrestle victoriously on school grounds, till decisively beaten. Love to fish with dad. Experience first memorable headache.

1941   Change to piano teacher, Miss Ellis, in spring; start fourth grade in fall. Japanese bomb Pearl Harbor and U. S. declares war on Axis Powers. Miss Ellis has me play piano solo for my 4th grade class in spring, which triggers positive change of attitude about practicing piano.

1941–1945   December 7, 1941, to September 2, 1945, nation at war; make wooden war toys to fight Germany and Japan in backyard; shortages of all things for war effort; earn money carrying coal, picking blackberries, and mowing yards to buy savings stamps and war bonds; life centers around the war; but shoot baskets, play school ground football and go from fourth grade through seventh grade. Begin playing intramural basketball in fifth grade. Play Paderewski's Minuet piano solo at grade school band concert in spring of 1945 to rousing applause. Grandma Smith dies July 23, 1945. Start eighth grade in fall of 1945, Am captain of grade school basketball team.

1946   Dad tries unsuccessfully to buy, and then resigns from, F. H. Simpson Fruit Brokerage. In spring, win first in district piano solo competition, and then win First Superior rating at state meet at Illinois Normal campus playing Christian Sinding's "March Grotesque." Also play that solo at the annual grade school band concert to much ovation, and play it second time for encore. Graduate from grade school; receive American Legion award during graduation ceremony. J. J. Lynn Oil Division employs Dad as land man. Begin high school in fall and play football and then basketball with freshman-sophomore team. Attic of home converted to bedroom with dormers, the south one for study loft.

1948   Family drives employer's Chevrolet to San Fernando Valley to visit mother's sister Ruth and family. Meet J. J. Lynn in his office in Kansas City.

1946–1950   Enter high school in fall of 1946; graduate in spring of 1950. Vertical nature of life activities; religious (biblical), athletic, musical, and academic, takes definite shape. Play football, basketball, and tennis all four years. Captain of undefeated freshman-sophomore football team, at fullback and line backer positions in 1947; starter on football team last two years, including 1948 conference championship team. Interscholastic piano competitions in spring of first three years. Present own piano recital on grand piano at First Methodist Church April 5, 1949, the day of the tragic Effingham hospital fire. Win interscholastic essay contests junior and senior years. Deliver Easter Sunrise Service

Timeline of Significant Events in the Life of Edward Reaugh Smith

sermon in spring of 1950. Valedictorian of 125-student class of 1950. Date Sara my senior year.

1950   Dad has first seizure from brain tumor while riding to out-of-town basketball game. Family visits Washington D. C. and Gettysburg in spring; then leaves Flora for Wichita Falls, Texas; Korean War starts while driving there. Register for draft in Wichita County on eighteenth birthday. Make high score on four-year draft deferment test. Rankins bring Sara to Wichita Falls in July. Family joins First Methodist Church, where meet Jo Anne and have first date with her on September 9, 1950. Receive academic scholarship at Midwestern University and play football as a freshman walk-on in the fall. Sara writes that she is seriously dating another, whom she soon marries. Dad has brain surgery at Barnes Hospital in St. Louis in November and convalesces in Flora.

1951   Parents return to Wichita Falls and move from rent house on Tenth Street to rent house on Hayes Street. Lynn Oil Division moves dad to Abilene, where he and mother rent apartment; sister Mary Anne returns to Flora to stay with Grandma Reaugh. Dad not well enough to work; parents return from Abilene to Flora. Family gives up rent house on Hayes Street. Move into neighbors Walter and Maisy Bachman's upstairs apartment on Hayes Street. Buy a motor bike. Start working as life guard at YMCA.

1950–1953   Win essay contest awards in creative writing; participate in intercollegiate debate tournaments. Major in accounting; in spring of 1953 pass the three parts of CPA exam that can be taken before experience requirement met for practice part. Awarded bachelor of science degree at Midwestern University graduation. Receive notice that regional scholarship to the SMU Law School has been awarded for the 1953 fall term. Spend summer of 1953 in Flora with dad. Take up residence in Lawyers Inn at SMU for fall term.

1954   Dad dies February 1, 1954. In August, awarded watch by Dallas law firm as highest standing first-year law student. Marry Jo Anne Myers September 10, 1954 and move into apartment on Potomac Street near campus. Four-year draft deferment expires in September; drafted, leave from Dallas day before Thanksgiving flying to El Paso; report to Fort Bliss for eight-week infantry basic training. Receive credit for all courses taking in fall term. Jo Anne joins in El Paso for three-day leave at Christmas.

1955   Finish basic training, and Jo Anne completes degree in elementary education at SMU, in late January. Ordered to report in February to Army Audit Agency (AAA) office on Montgomery Street in San Francisco. In early March, receive orders to report to the AAA office at 1201 Santee Street, in Los Angeles. Jo Anne receives teaching contract; teaches second grade at El Sereno School in East Los Angeles. Rent garage apartment on Eagle Rock Drive near Hill Drive in Eagle Rock. Sit for practice part of CPA exam on U. S. C. campus and receive notice in summer that passed it. Navajo Ordnance Depot (NOD) audit assignment in August/September where enjoy northern Arizona sites with Jo Anne. Enter night school at Loyola Law School downtown L.A. for fall semester. Chum there in evenings with fellow outlander Bill (William P.) Clark, who would eventually become President Reagan's closest adviser. Spend times with California family.

1956   Spring semester at Loyola Law School. NOD audit assignment August/September. Jo Anne gets contract with Dallas Independent School District for fall semester to teach fourth grade at Rufus C. Burleson Elementary School in southeast Dallas and leaves for Dallas. Leave for Flagstaff on final AAA audit assignment at NOD. She finds and rents apartment on Normandy Street near SMU campus. Climb Humphreys Peak north of Flagstaff; hike into Grand Canyon. Meet other Ed Smith at restaurants and hike with him into Havasupai Indian Reservation on Labor Day weekend. Receive early release from two-year enlistment to return to SMU Law School for late registration in fall. Receive army discharge September 17 at Fort MacArthur in San Pedro. Drive to Dallas for fall semester.

1957   Take and pass Texas Bar exam. Graduate cum laude from SMU Law School standing third in class of 1957. Start law practice with VEWS in Houston in July. Buy house in Bellaire.

Timeline of Significant Events in the Life of Edward Reaugh Smith

1957–1984   Active law practice in 1960s and 1970s; less so as involvement with other activities grows in 1978–1984.

1958   Mark and Michael born New Year's morning—first babies of 1958 in Bellaire. Strained working relationship with immediate superior leads late in year to plan to practice in Lubbock.

1959   Start law practice with NMH in Lubbock on February 1.

1960   Discover and make first visit to Lake City, Colorado; visit every year but one 1960 through 2012. Admitted to blue lodge as Master Mason, but never thereafter active. Late in year begin first running activity to relieve stress for partnership negotiations at NMH. Grandma Reaugh dies December 31.

1961   Leave NMH to open own law office March 1. Daughter Jill (later Jillian) born June 14.

1962   Smith & Baker law partnership starts in August. Lubbock County chairman for Robert Morris's unsuccessful Republican candidacy for Texas governor. With others, start Briercroft Savings & Loan Association (BS&L). Buy first shares in American Founders Life Insurance Company (AFLIC). Rushing and Tidmore engage to handle what becomes the famous "Rushing tax case." Borrow money to give, at Christmas, funds for European trip to our parents.

1963   Sunday after Easter, begin twenty-five years of biblically-related teaching Cornerstone Sunday School class. Run three miles a day. First climb of Uncompahgre Peak in Colorado in July. Near death experience night of August 19–20. Select and start paying $5.00 per month for two burial spaces in Resthaven Memorial Park (RMP). Offer to purchase such cemetery rejected.

1963–1966   Serve three years on Lubbock Planning & Zoning Commission; chairman of it the third year.

1964   Climb Uncompahgre Peak again in July; lightning in cloud knocks all three of us to ground on peak. Purchase RMP in October, with others.

1965   Form Resthaven Mortuary, Inc. (RMI), taking 52½ percent of its stock and R. P. Brown 47½ percent. RMI starts construction of funeral home on southwest corner of cemetery.

1966 Survive 1966 credit crunch. Make money on RMP (cemetery) operation, lose money in RMI (funeral home). Operations at BS&L very successful, including for several more years. Lubbock County Chairman for Republican Bill Hayes' unsuccessful candidacy for Lieutenant Governor. Buy tent-top camper for eight or nine years of family trips.

1967 Start first record keeping on running. Sell American Founders Life Insurance Company stock. RMI losing money; RMP making money. Make camper trailer trip to Glacier National Park and Canadian Rockies.

1968—1975 Dates approximate; serve on executive committee of Texas Tech University Foundation, first as secretary, then as chairman; also serve as member and chairman of Texas Tech University Medical School Foundation.

1968 RMI losing money, RMP making money. Chairman for Republican Eddie Paxton's unsuccessful candidacy for state representative. Purchase E-Systems bonds and associate Dean Carlton as co-counsel to file class action suit against the company for failure to disclose material facts in promotional flier.

1969 Anticipate 1969 credit squeeze; along with Bob Brown, sell RMI to Singleton group with right of first refusal upon any later sale by that group; keep RMP. Make first cruise in winter to Caribbean.

1970 Returning from legal hearing in Colorado City, Texas, go to sleep driving alone at 75 mph and total new Buick LaSabre insured only for liability. Serve as Lubbock County chairman for George H. W. Bush 1970 Republican candidacy for U. S. Senate against incumbent Lloyd Bentsen; carry Lubbock County but lose statewide. Buy new Buick Electra in time to pick up Bush for scheduled campaign appearances in Lubbock; bring him to home on 57th Street between appearances. Publish two articles in "The Journal of Taxation" on issues in the Rushing case, and turn down Prentice-Hall invitation to write a book on taxation.

Timeline of Significant Events in the Life of Edward Reaugh Smith

1971   Law firm incorporated as Smith & Baker, Inc., ownership equal. Serve as assistant leader of "mountain man" Boy Scout troop backpacking trip to Tres Ritos, New Mexico.

1972   Cruise Norway for two weeks. Lead "mountain man" Boy Scout backpacking trip to San Juan Mountain Range in Colorado. Smith & Baker, Inc. hires Mike Field as attorney in August.

1973   Law firm hires top three 1973 graduates from Texas Tech Law School. Lead "mountain man" backpacking trip to Colorado. Tax problems for both RMP and S&B stockholders, by mutual agreement, prompt purchase of Norton's stock becoming sole stockholder of RMP. Terminate Subchapter S election for RMP whereby it becomes taxed as regular corporation. Increase daily running distance to six miles.

1973–1974   Arab oil embargo in 1973 causes sharp jump in interest rates to 9 or 10%; Brown, dissatisfied with 4% interest rate on RMP's note to him, requests raise in rate; rate increased from 4% to 6%, for which Brown makes concessions on note terms and agrees to security modifications that become very profitable for RMP and also work out well for Brown.

1973–1978   Very busy with law practice, RMP management and investment, running, and resumption of purposeful piano practice.

1974   Buy half interest in section of irrigated grain farmland in Ochiltree County in NE Texas panhandle, near Perryton; Don Cooper, John Deere dealer in Perryton, buys other half. Family makes spring break trip to Washington, D. C.

1975   Family makes spring break trip to Mexico: Mexico City, Cuernavaca, and Acapulco. Under leadership of Tom Weaver, president of RMP, the praying Christ in Gethsemane feature completed at RMP. Buy from Bill Hall half of his 558 acres of Fourth of July Creek property in Colorado.

1976   Family makes spring break trip to Hawaiian Islands of Oahu, Hawaii, and Maui.

1977   Corporate "head hunter" lures RMP manager Tom Weaver to major cemetery in Denver; Weaver takes RMP sales manager with him.

1977–1978   To retain top management employees, RMP buys cemetery/funeral home operation in Longview, Texas; a costly diversion. Sell 25% of RMP stock to top four management employees on favorable terms and with protective buy-back option. Active in West Texas Running Club; run in many distance races.

1978   Run first marathon, in Palo Duro Canyon in January, in qualifying time for Boston but do not apply for Boston. Attend international cemetery convention in Vienna, Austria; locked in Bosendorfer Piano factory in Vienna for two hours during company's holiday weekend, playing on its display pianos. Late in year, ask Dr. Harold Luce, head of Texas Tech's Music Department, if "out of mind" to think of playing one of the great piano concertos with an orchestra; Luce's reply evasively ambiguous, but advises music theory essential first, which he agrees to give in his office in 1979. Sell Smith & Baker, Inc. stock to younger lawyers in firm, Karl Clifford and Mike Field. Name of firm changed to Smith, Baker, Field, and Clifford (SBFC). Continue to practice on same compensation terms as before. Train for December qualifying race for 1979 Boston Marathon.

1979   Begin taking music theory from Dr. Luce continuing till fall. Run Boston Marathon April 16. Form Resthaven of Lubbock, Inc. (ROL); it reacquires funeral home from the Singleton group. All cemetery and funeral operations begin to function under one ownership. Make two-week dream cruise from Amsterdam to Athens with the Miles in September to celebrate both silver wedding anniversaries. Begin study of piano performance with Dr. William Westney in November.

1980   Continue some running, but heavy commitment to piano practice squeezes time from law practice. Active in Resthaven management and investments.

1981   Intense piano practice many hours each day. Sell Fourth of July Creek property in Colorado in July. Sell BS&L on note September 1. Give four piano recitals in November for friends in our living room to prepare for public performance in 1982. Record my 1981 piano recital on reel to reel tape. Hemmle Recital Hall reserved for March 23, 1982 for Steinway Dedication Concert.

1981–1985 Years of agony in BS&L work out before final settlement with Krupps in 1985 shortly before BS&L is shut down.

1982 Intense piano practice for hours each day; perform Beethoven's 3rd Piano Concerto with encore, followed by festive reception, March 23; start work on additional piano numbers for 1983 recital series; perform locally as invited; record my 1983 piano recital. Heavy management and investment activity at ROL.

1983 Take Caribbean cruise with the Miles. Continue piano performance and record 1983 recital program. Continue heavy management and investment activity at ROL. Corporation reacquires the RMP stock previously sold to four management employees. Terminate Ward as ROL president, replace with Phillip Welch; terminate McWhorter as park superintendent, replace with Ron Hillis. Cemetery irrigation system located and totally replaced by Hillis. Numerous complaints on park appearance turn to compliments about beautification. Visit Toronto friends and see Niagara Falls in October.

1983–1997 Vacation for one to two weeks each winter in Puerto Vallarta.

1984 Continue piano performance, and record 1984 recital program on April 24, ending serious piano study and performance, having accomplished those goals, all a life-enriching experience in music. Later, when CDs developed, technician at Texas Tech converts reel to reel recordings to CDs. Reproduce them commercially in lots of one hundred. Give hundreds to others over the years. Son Mark returns from Denver to become president of ROL upon Welch's return to similar family business in Big Spring. Retire from law practice August 31. Take office space upstairs at Resthaven Funeral Home. Begin attending Elliott Wave lectures and ISI (Investment Seminars, Inc.) seminars traveling to distant places including Europe and Asia.

1984–1988   Intense, extensive, and highly profitable investment activity with rapidly increasing funds from ROL interests.

1984–1990   Working together with son Mark on ROL affairs is wonderful personal experience and profitable for ROL. Mark begins night school MBA program at Texas Tech University Business School in 1987. Has four-point grade average and serves as business school graduation speaker in 1990. His two children born in Lubbock in 1984 and 1986. Mark leaves ROL in 1990 for position in public corporation; before his departure, consult together with Stewart Enterprises in New Orleans about possible sale of ROL; Stewart offer inadequate.

1986   *The Christian Agnostic,* prominent Methodist clergyman Leslie Weatherhead's 1965 book, recommends taking a fresh look at reincarnation; accept it provisionally and begin intense study of reincarnation; attend meetings of Edgar Cayce related A. R. E. (Association for Research and Enlightenment), and, along with many other sources, read its complete recommended reading list. ROL sells Longview operations to Gibraltar Mausoleum Corporation, of Indianapolis. Make gifts of 39% of ROL stock to three children in May and December (and again in January, 1987) Accurately call top in stock market and go heavily short S&P contracts making large profit on the October 19 stock market crash; offset by trading losses by Geneva, Switzerland manager of some ROL funds. Take bearish position, based upon analysis by previously successful Robert Prechter Elliott Wave advisory, and miss both the technology boom of the 1990s and the dot.com bust in 2000. Reduce investment activity after the crash. Focus then upon reincarnation studies. Attend ISI investment seminar in Hong Kong, with pre-conference week in Singapore and post-conference 10-day tour of China.

1987   In fall, Mark begins study on MBA program. Purchase second home in San Juan Ranch Estates Addition near Lake City, Colorado.

Timeline of Significant Events in the Life of Edward Reaugh Smith

1988   First learn of Rudolf Steiner in Introduction to Edouard Schuré's *The Great Initiates*, from the A. R. E. recommended reading list.

1989   Order first Steiner books and begin period of intensive study of his vast oeuvre and its esoteric Christianity and deep biblical insights. Develop system of collating to biblical passages, a system that becomes invaluable in later writing.

1990   Mark leaves ROL; Katy Pendergrass, CPA and comptroller of ROL, promoted to president.

1988–1994   Heavily devoted to Steiner studies.

1992   Needing meaningful valuation of ROL in relation to estate planning, establish relationship with Thomas, Pierce & Co. (TPC), of Tallahassee, through its representative Larry Garrigan. TPC hired to appraise ROL; based on appraisal, give TPC contract to sell ROL.

1993   Contract to sell to SCI (Service Corporation International) closed in February 1993.

1994   Celebrate 40th wedding anniversary with tour of Alaska and cruise inland waterway to Seattle.

1994–1997   Write *The Burning Bush*, published in 1997.

1997–2009   Serve two six-year stints on Lubbock Symphony Orchestra board of directors. Join Maestro Circle of financial supporters.

1998   Seven-day Christmas cruise: Panama Canal, Costa Rica, Ochoa Rio (Jamaica).

1998–2011   Member of SBL (Society of Biblical Literature) 1998–2011. Attend its annual national conventions in November, successively in Orlando (1998), Boston (1999), Nashville (2000), Denver (2001), Toronto (2002), Atlanta (2003), San Antonio (2004), Philadelphia (2005), Washington DC (2006), San Diego (2007), Boston (2008), New Orleans (2009), Atlanta (2010), and San Francisco (2011).

1998–2001   Write, and publish *The Incredible Births of Jesus* (in 1998), *The Disciple Whom Jesus Loved* (in 2000), and *David's Question, "What Is Man?"* (in 2001).

2000 In January cruise Australia, Tasmania, and New Zealand for fourteen days, plus 3-day pre-cruise tour of Cairns and Sydney. Three-week May–June Sophia Tour of Chartres Cathedral (first week) and spiritual sites in England, Wales, and Scotland.

2001 Three-week trip in June with Bakers and Mitchells retracing England, Wales, and Scotland tour of 2000. Christmas in Sierra Vista, Arizona.

2002 Car trip to Florida, Key West, North Carolina, and Georgia in April.

2003 Publish *The Soul's Long Journey/How the Bible Reveals Reincarnation.* Car trip to Texas valley for Christmas.

2004 Travel with Bakers and Mitchells to Chicago, Detroit, and Mackinac Island in May and June.

2003–2005 Prepare manuscript for book, *The I AM and the Blood*, never published due to delays and errors in editing process; abandon effort after Carlson book, *The Gospel Hoax,* is introduced at November 2005 SBL convention, prompting work on new writing project.

2005 Globus tour of Germany with Bakers in July, ending with only visit to Goetheanum in Dornach. Personal visit and tour with Sergei Prokofieff. Hike to and through the ancient caves of the Hermitage. While not mentioned in the text, begin study and work with Scott Brown and others responding to attacks by Carlson and others on Morton Smith's claimed discovery at Mar Saba Monastery of what he termed "The Secret Gospel of Mark."

2005–2011 Work on response to Carlson and others; publish *The Temple Sleep of the Rich Young Ruler* in November, 2011.

2007 Transfer Lake City, Colorado home by gift to three children and spouses.

2012 Deliver keynote address in March at ninth annual SteinerBooks Seminar in NYC. Begin in mid-year working on autobiography. Honored at August gathering in Colleyville by Jo Anne and all our descendants and their spouses, where daughter Jillian, with Jo Anne's assistance, presented a picture book of the first eighty years of my life. Make family portrait.

Bibliography

Baigent, Michael, et al. *Holy Blood, Holy Grail*. New York: Dell, 1982.

Brokaw, Tom. *The Greatest Generation Speaks: Letters and Reflections*. New York, Random House, 1999.

Hedrick, Charles W. *When Faith Meets Reason*. Santa Rosa, CA: Polebridge Press, 2008.

Hirst, Stephen. *I Am the Grand Canyon: The Story of the Havasupai People*. Grand Canyon, AZ: Grand Canyon Association, 2000.

Kengor, Paul, and Patricia Clark Doerner. *The Judge: William P. Clark, Ronald Reagan's Top Hand*. San Francisco: Ignatius Press, 2007.

Lindenberg, Christoph. *Rudolf Steiner: A Biography*. Great Barrington, MA: SteinerBooks, 2012.

Mata, Sri Durga. *A Paramahansa Yogananda Trilogy of Divine Love*. Beverly Hills, CA: Joan Wight Publications, 1992.

Prokofieff, Sergei O. *The Encounter With Evil and Its Overcoming through Spiritual Science*. London: Temple Lodge, 1999.

Self-Realization Fellowship. *Rajarsi Janakandanda: A Great Western Yogi: The Life of Paramahansa Yogananda's First Spiritual Successor*. Los Angeles, CA: Self-Realization Fellowship, 1996.

Smith, Edward R. *The Burning Bush: Rudolf Steiner, Anthroposophy, and the Holy Scriptures: Terms & Phrases*. Hudson, NY: Anthroposophic Press, 1997.

———. *David's Question: What Is Man? (Psalm 8:4)—Rudolf Steiner, Anthroposophy, and the Holy Scriptures: An Anthroposophical Commentary on the Bible*. Hudson, NY: Anthroposophic Press, 2001.

———. *The Disciple Whom Jesus Loved: Unveiling the Author of John's Gospel*. Hudson, NY: Anthroposophic Press, 2000.

———. *The Incredible Births of Jesus*. Hudson, NY: Anthroposophic Press, 1998.

———. *The Soul's Long Journey: How the Bible Reveals Reincarnation*. Great Barrington, MA: SteinerBooks, 2003.

———. *The Temple Sleep of the Rich Young Ruler: How Lazarus Became the Evangelist John*. Great Barrington, MA: SteinerBooks, 2011.

Steiner, Rudolf. *Christianity as Mystical Fact: And the Mysteries of Antiquity*. Great Barrington, MA: SteinerBooks, 2006.

———. *How to Know Higher Worlds: A Modern Path of Initiation.* Hudson, NY: Anthroposophic Press, 1994.

———. *Intuitive Thinking as a Spiritual Path: A Philosophy of Freedom.* Hudson, NY: Anthroposophic Press, 1995.

———. *An Outline of Esoteric Science.* Hudson, NY: Anthroposophic Press, 1997.

———. *Self-Education: Autobiographical Reflections, 1861–1893.* Spring Valley, NY: Mercury Press, 1985.

———. *Theosophy: An Introduction to the Spiritual Processes in Human Life and in the Cosmos.* Hudson, NY: Anthroposophic Press, 1997.

———. *Turning Points in Spiritual History: Zarathustra, Hermes, Moses, Elijah, Buddha, Christ.* Great Barrington, MA: SteinerBooks, 2007.

———. *A Western Approach to Reincarnation and Karma: Selected Lectures & Writings* (R. Querido, ed.). Hudson, NY: Anthroposophic Press, 1997.

Tikalsky, Frank, Catherine A. Euler, and John Nagel. *The Sacred Oral Tradition of the Havasupai: As Retold by Elders and Headmen Manakaja and Sinyella 1918–1921.* Albuquerque: University of New Mexico Press, 2010.

Weatherhead, Leslie D. *The Christian Agnostic.* Nashville: Abingdon Press, 1965.

Westerlund, John S. *Arizona's War Town: Flagstaff, Navajo Ordnance Depot, and World War II.* Tucson: Arizona University Press, 2004.

Yogananda, Paramahansa. *Autobiography of a Yogi.* Los Angeles: Self-Realization Fellowship, 1972.